LOCKHEED HUDSON
IN WORLD WAR II

LOCKHEED HUDSON
IN WORLD WAR II

ANDREW HENDRIE

Airlife

England

By the same author

Seek and Strike; Lockheed Hudson Aircraft in World War II (1983)
Flying Cats; Consolidated Catalina Aircraft in World War II
  (1988)
Short Sunderland Aircraft in World War II (1994)
Canadian Squadrons in Coastal Command (1997)

British Library Cataloguing-in-Publication Data
  A catalogue record for this book
  is available from the British Library

ISBN 1 84037 0939

Typeset by Servis Filmsetting Limited, Manchester
Printed in England by Bath Press Ltd, Bath.

Airlife Publishing Ltd
101 Longden Road, Shrewsbury, SY3 9EB, England
E-mail: airlife@airlifebooks.com
Website: www.airlifebooks.com

Acknowledgements

In preparing this work a number of official bodies readily helped me; they included the Research Center at Wright-Patterson Air Force Base, Ohio; the Research Division at Maxwell AFB, Alabama; Dept of the Navy, Washington, (Dr Bernard F. Cavalcante); the Public Relations Officer, (Air), Defence HQ, Wellington, New Zealand; RAAF Archives, Air Force HQ, Canberra, (Mrs Mollie Angel); the National Archives of Canada and the Directorate of History, Dept of National Defence, Ottawa, and Canada readily provided copies of microfilm records of the RCAF on loan; the British Public Record Office supplied copies of RAF records; the Brazilian Embassy in London gave details concerning the Brazilian Air Force. Editors of publications including *RAF News, RAAF News, Air Force, Air Mail, Intercom* published requests on my behalf. I also wish to thank *The Canberra Times*, *The Sydney Herald* and *RAAF News*. Staff of the Lockheed Corporation who were directly involved with the Hudson corresponded with me including notably, the late Clarence 'Kelly' Johnson, MSc, FRAeS, who prepared the drawings of the Hudson and flew in its first test flights.

Many former 'Hudson' personnel, both aircrew and ground staff representing the various air forces wrote to me. They included my former Flight Commander on 224 Squadron W/Cmdr Geoffrey Bartlett, AFC; my CO at No.6 COTU, the late Air Vice-Marshal, C.D. Candy, RAAF, my Flight Commander at the OTU, Marshal of the Royal Air Force, Sir Denis Spotswood, and my CO on No.48 Squadron, W/Cmdr A. de V. Leach, DFC. Three friends have corresponded with me throughout my writings; Geoffrey Bartlett, the late F/Lt Bill Cleaver of 53 Squadron, and F/Lt Ray Kelly, BEM, RAAF (retd) of No.6 Squadron RAAF.

May I now record my thanks to all those listed hereunder for their kind help:

F/Lt Terry Andrew (500 Sqdn); F/Lt Don Baird (459 RAAF Sqdn); W/Cmdr G.C.C. Bartlett AFC (224 & 59 Sqdns); G/Capt. Baudoux (233 Sqdn/6 COTU); F/Lt Don Bray (161 Sqdn); Cmdr Jack D. Bruce USN; Capt. Denis Busbridge (233/224 Sqdns); AVM C.D. Candy RAAF (206 Sqdn RAF/No.6 COTU); G/Capt. DFC Carr AFC (220 Sqdn); Dr Bernard F. Cavalcante Naval Historical Center, Washington DC; Keith Chew RAAF(SU); F/Lt W.C. Cleaver (53 Sqdn); AM Sir Robert Craven KBE, CB, OBE, DFC, (No.6 COTU); Lt M.J.C. De Liefde (320 Sqdn); Barry East RNZAF (MOTAT); Robert C. Ferguson, Lockheed Corporation; S/Ldr M. Gardner (206 Sqdn); F/Lt Geof Goad (59 Sqdn); F/Lt Frank Goff (279 Sqdn); W/Cmdr John Graham DFC (269 Sqdn); James V. Guthrie Lockheed Corporation; Lt/Cmdr Hale RN (53 Sqdn); F/Lt Ken Harper (233 Sqdn); F/Lt Fred Harrison (24 Sqdn); ACM Sir Derek Hodgkinson KCB, CBE, CB, DFC, AFC, RAF (220/1COTU); Ken. Ingram (407 RCAF Sqdn); F/Lt Bill James RAAF (608 Sqdn); Wilf Jones (233/269 Sqdns); F/Lt Ray Kelly BEM, RAAF, (No.6 RAAF Sqdn); Lt/Col P.J. Kendell CAF (407 RCAF Sqdn); F/O Murray Kidman RAAF (48 Sqdn RAF/2 RAAF Sqdn); Capt. Mark Labreque CAF (407 RCAF Sqdn); F/Lt John Lake RAuxAF (retd) (608 Sqdn); Murry Lawson RAAF (2 RAAF Sqdn); W/Cmdr A. de V. Leach DFC, (224/48 Sqdns); F/Lt Stan Lee DFC (24 Sqdn); G/Capt. J. Leggate DSO (53 Sqdn); G/Capt. Paul Lynham DSO (279 Sqdn); F/Lt John McKenzie RAAF (459 RAAF Sqdn); G/Capt. McMurtrie DSO, DFC, (269 Sqdn); F/O A. Majoram (220 Sqdn); Capt. Jock Manson (53 Sqdn); S/Ldr John Maylam MBE, DFC(224 Sqdn); F/Lt Ian Moyes (2 RAAF Sqdn); E.H. Nelson (206 Sqdn); Dr Axel Niestlé; John Noble (220 Sqdn); G/Capt. H. O'Neill DFC (224 Sqdn); F/Lt Bill Pacey (6 RAAF Sqdn); James Parkinson RNZAF; G/Capt. H. Plenty DFC (8 RAAF Sqdn); F/O Vic Pounder (200 & 206 Sqdns); F/Lt Eric Robinson (608 Sqdn); W/Cmdr Romanes DFC (206 Sqdn); Gilbert Rothery Esq., MRAeS; G. Shead (13 RAAF Sqdn); Robert Shimmell (233 Sqdn); Per Skaugstad (Norway); S/Ldr Alan Smith (206 Sqdn); MRAF Sir Denis Spotswood GCB, CBE, DSO, DFC, FRAeS (500 Sqdn); A/Cmdre Spurgeon DFC (8 RAAF Sqdn); Sgt N. Swannick (206 Sqdn); S/Ldr Cameron Taylor DFC (407 RCAF Sqdn); John Tubb (62 Sqdn); W/Cmdr RGM Walker, DFC (224 Sqdn); Lt/Col. R. Wardner DFC, USAF (ret); Dr F.J. Waterer (2 RAAF Sqdn); F/O Don Wells (413/422 RCAF Sqdns); F/Lt Doug Whittaker (279 Sqdn); Gilbert F. Whittamore (206/608 Sqdns); F/Lt Doug. Williams (194 Sqdn); Ernest Winfield (1404 Met. Flt); F/Lt David Withey (269 Sqdn); W/Cmdr L. Womersley DFC (224 Sqdn); F/Lt Ian Virgo (233 Sqdn); Mrs Mary Wells; Ministério Da Aeronáutica, Brazil; Ron. C. Ziesing (2/13 RAAF Sqdns).

Introduction

The Lockheed Hudson was a military version of the Lockheed 14 airliner which began service in Coastal Command, RAF, initially for reconnaissance covering the exit to the North Atlantic from Britain to Norway. Its duties were then extended with anti-submarine and convoy escorts over the Atlantic and reconnaissance over the Bay of Biscay.

Further duties within Coastal Command were shipping strikes off the Norwegian and Dutch coasts, meteorological flights, photo-reconnaissance, air-sea rescue, and some bombing raids on Norway, Germany and The Netherlands.

The Hudson operated along the eastern seaboard of the Americas from Canada down to Brazil; from Iceland, Gibraltar, North Africa and West Africa. It served in the front line from Malaya down to Australia and operated from India, Burma, Papua, Guadalcanal and other islands in the South Pacific.

In addition to sinking U boats and enemy-controlled ships, it acted on occasions as a long-range fighter such as at Dunkirk in protecting Allied troops. It not infrequently was in aerial combat with Fw Kondors, Me 109s, Me 110s and other German aircraft and in the Far East and South Pacific had frequent encounters with Japanese Zero fighters.

Apparently 'peaceful' missions of transport trips from Britain to Malta or over Burma in support of General Wingate's Chindits were hazardous as were others on an aggressive role.

The Hudson served with Australia's RAAF, America's USN and AAC, the Brazilian Air Force, the RCAF and the RNZAF. Although some Hudsons went to China I was unable to obtain copies of such records.

The Hudson achieved a number of 'firsts'. The first enemy aircraft shot down in World War II by an RAF aircraft was claimed by a 224 Squadron Hudson in October 1939. The Hudson opened the 'Atlantic Bridge' with Capt Don Bennett (the late Air Vice-Marshal Bennett), flying a Hudson across the North Atlantic to the United Kingdom in 1940. The first airborne lifeboat was designed for the Hudson and used with success initially with 279 Squadron RAF. An RAAF Hudson sank the first Japanese ship of any type in World War II. In the RAF it was the first type of aircraft to sink a U boat using rocket projectiles. It made history being the only aircraft to 'capture' a U boat. It was the first aircraft manufactured in USA to operate in World War II.

Although it was not the only type of aircraft to be used on 'special ops', i.e. dropping or picking up agents in enemy occupied territory, it was probably unique in using a 'Royal' aircraft from His Late Majesty's Flight for that purpose in such 'cloak and dagger' work over France, and, it is believed at King George VI's suggestion. Some of the first RAF pilots to be inspected by the King in World War II were Hudson pilots of Coastal Command.

In the text I have endeavoured to cover all recorded anti U boat successes achieved by Hudsons but am aware that some data may still be controversial. Most anti-shipping successes have been included together with some representative air-to-air combats.

Andrew Hendrie
Storrington, 1999

Contents

Chapter 1 The Lockheed Hudson Aircraft   8
Chapter 2 North Sea Patrols   21
Chapter 3 Shipping Strikes   39
Chapter 4 Anti-submarine Operations – Atlantic Ocean   48
Chapter 5 Gibraltar and the Mediterranean   64
Chapter 6 Other Operations   80
Chapter 7 The Far East   92
Chapter 8 The South Pacific   109
Maps   116

Appendices
A   U boats Sunk or Damaged in Attacks by Hudson Aircraft   120
B   Ships Sunk or Damaged by Hudson Aircraft   121
C   Royal Air Force Serial Numbers   123
D   Royal Australian Air Force Hudsons   169
E   Royal New Zealand Air Force Hudsons   176
F   Lockheed Hudsons with American Designations   179
G   Technical Data   180

Glossary and Abbreviations   182
Bibliography   183
Index   184

Chapter 1

The Lockheed Hudson Aircraft

Early History

The brothers Allan and Malcolm Loughhead (pronounced 'Lock-heed'), began building their three-seater floatplane, Model G hydroaeroplane in San Francisco in 1912. That aircraft flew in 1913.

Near Santa Barbara, California, the brothers established the Loughhead Aircraft Manufacturing Company in 1916. The company failed in 1921 but after a total of four aircraft had been built.

In 1926 Allan Loughhead founded a new Lockheed (so spelt for the first time) company with the production of Vega aircraft. The company flourished and a move was made to new facilities at Burbank, California in 1928. Lockheeds was purchased by the Detroit Aircraft Company for $1,000,000 in 1929 but with the crash in the stockmarket, the company was made bankrupt taking with it the solvent Lockheed in 1931.

By 1932 Lockheed's production line comprised one Vega aircraft and with the prospect of no further orders. Carl B. Squier, the General Plant Manager, looked for investors, and

Below: A Lockheed 14 at Heston, England; the civil precursor of the Hudson military aircraft.

Below: The Hudson cockpit with approximately one hundred instruments and controls.

Below: A Hudson pilot's instrument panel.

1. Left Engine Tachometer
2. Gun Charging Handle
3. Right Engine Tachometer
4. Gun Charging Handle
5. Left Manifold Pressure Gauge
6. Right Manifold Pressure Gauge
7. Aero-Mixture Indicator
8. Air-Temperature Indicator
9. Fuel Gauge Front Tanks
10. Knob for Opening Bad Weather Panel
11. Pull Handle of Bad Weather Panel
12. Knob for Opening Bad Weather Panel
13. Directional Gyro (Automatic Pilot)
14. Caging Knob (Automatic Pilot)
15. Rudder Knob (Automatic Pilot)
16. Aileron Knob (Automatic Pilot)
17. Bank and Climb Gyro (Automatic Pilot)
18. Elevator Knob (Automatic Pilot)
19. Level Flight Knob (Automatic Pilot)
20. Oil Pressure Gauge
21. Vacuum Gauge (Automatic Pilot)
22. Left Cylinder Head Temperature
23. Right Cylinder Head Temperature
24. Fuel Gauge Rear Tanks
25. Release Handles for Flotation Equipment (Nose Compartment)
26. De-Icer Gauge

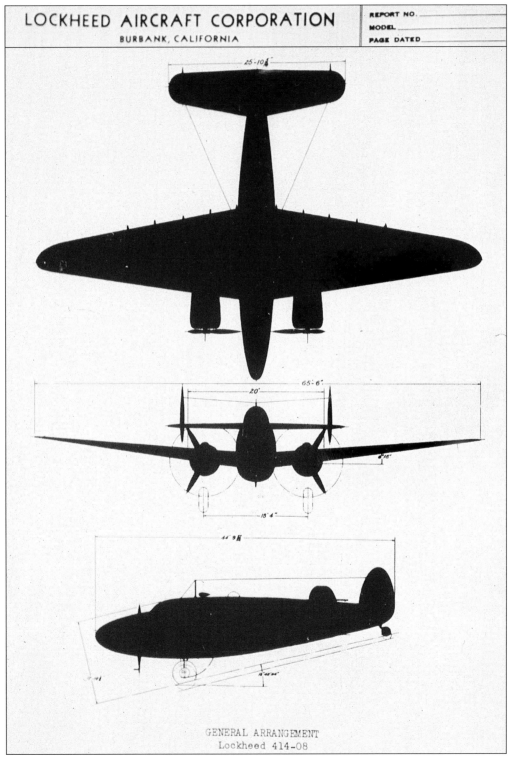

Above: Silhouettes of the Lockheed Hudson.

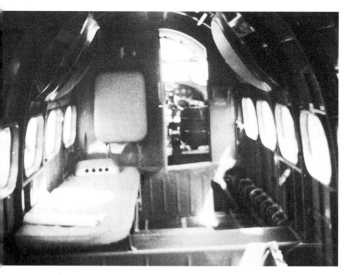

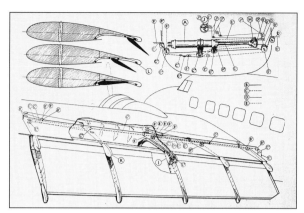

Above: A diagram of the Lockheed/Fowler flaps as fitted to Hudsons; they could reduce stalling speed by seventeen knots, and fully extended, would have a strong braking effect.

Above: A Hudson cabin looking forward. Covers for the astro-hatch are visible in the roof; the bed was not typical and located in that area would be the IFF and (for those with British radio) a TR9 transmitter/receiver for R/T.

Below: The British 1082/1083 radio transmitter/receiver which, in the author's experience, was still in use in 1942.

one, Robert Gross, successfully bid $4,000 for the company.

In 1934, the Model 10 Electra became the first American all-metal production passenger transport and two years later, the first Model 12 Electra junior was the fastest of its size and type ever built. The Model 14 Super Electra followed in July 1937. This aircraft was a fourteen-seater midwing monoplane powered by two Wright Cyclone 840hp engines which achieved 257mph on its maiden flight. Its crew included Lockheed's chief test pilot, Marshall Headle and their research engineer, C.L. 'Kelly' Johnson. The aircraft's sixty-five feet single-spar wings pioneered the use of integral fuel tanks and were fitted with the newly-developed Lockheed-Fowler flaps. They increased the effective lifting surface, acted as a brake to provide slower, safer landings, but when retracted, reduced the wing area to permit higher performance in the air.

In the following eight years over 3000 Model 14s in various military and civil versions were produced with sales of $263,000,000.

The British Minister for Air, Lord Swinton, suggested to Air Chief Marshal Sir Edward Ellington of the Air Staff in September 1936 that orders be placed in America for both fighter and bomber aircraft.[1] At a critical time in British history, 12 May 1938, Lord Swinton was dismissed by the Prime Minister, Neville Chamberlain.[2]

However, in April 1938, the British sent a Purchasing Commission to the USA with $25,000,000 to spend. The Commission included one who in 1933 had commanded No.210 Squadron as W/Cmdr A.T. Harris; he was later to be C-in-C Bomber Command as Sir Arthur Harris.[3]

According to one of Lockheed's staff, Mr Chappellet, they knew nothing of the visit until five days prior to arrival, when a telegam came from the British Air Attaché in Washington. The telegram advised that the Commission would visit California's aircraft factories within a week. Kenneth Smith of Lockheed's sales, studied newspaper photographs of the

References
1. JT p.38; RAF I/p.16 2. WSC I/p.208 3. RAF II/p.118

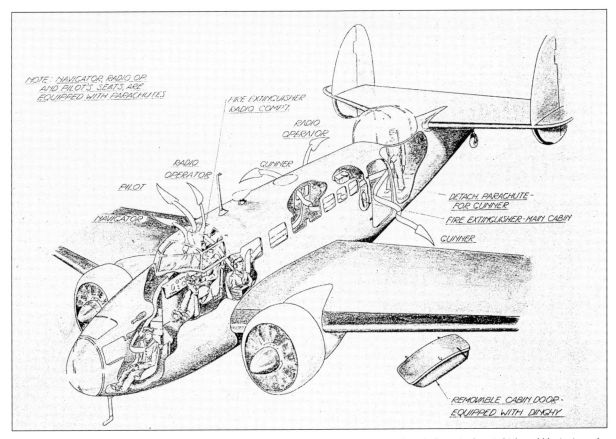

Above: The Hudson had five possible exits; one over the cockpit, hatches to both port and starboard; the main door (which could be jettisoned with the dinghy), and the astro hatch; the latter however, had four bolts to loosen.

Commission, memorised names, and was at Glendale Airport when the British Commission arrived and was able to greet each member by name.

Lockheed had only Model 14s to show, ironically, due to an order from Japan. In five days and five nights, the engineering department and shop designed and constructed a

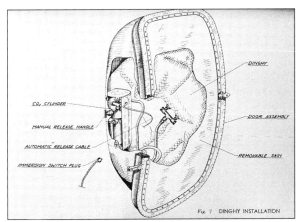

Above: The main Hudson aircraft dinghy contained within the door. It would release automatically on impact or immersion. Crews additionally had individual K-type dinghies.

Above: The late Clarence 'Kelly' Johnson, the Lockheed engineer who worked in London, England preparing drawings for the Hudson.

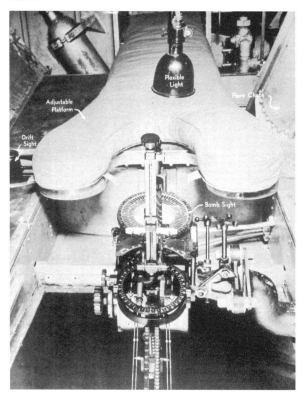

British Air Ministry pass Johnson used in summer of 1938 while transforming Model 14 into bomber.

Above: 'Kelly' Johnson's British Air Ministry pass; he was one of the first to fly over Britain as a passenger, albeit an active one, in a Hudson.

Above: The bomb-aimer's position within the navigator's compartment in the nose of the Hudson.

full-scale wooden mock-up of a Model 14 converted to a medium reconnaissance bomber, a task which normally took three months.

The Commission suggested a number of major and minor changes. 'We promised them the modifications would be designed and installed by the next afternoon,' said Chappellet; 'Much to their amazement, such was the case.'[4]

Lockheed's engineer at that time, the late C.L. 'Kelly'

Johnson, writing to the author in 1982 stated:

. . . of the engineers at Lockheed who worked on the development of the Hudson bomber, Mr Hall Hibberd was my boss and Chief Engineer at the time. Mr Jim Gerschler ran our research lab and did work on the basic structure.

The Hudson was actually redesigned in England from the initial proposal that was shown to your purchasing group who came to Burbank. They turned down our proposal design the first day it was shown to your technical people in England. It was necessary for me to hire drafting equipment and a drafting board and install the equipment in our apartment in Mayfair Court just off Piccadilly.

In a period of eighty hours, working alone, I was required to revise our proposal to incorporate English armament such as turrets, torpedoes, mines, bombs and forward-firing guns. This proposal turned out to be acceptable for your Government.

Data on your military equipment was sent to Burbank in a diplomatic pouch so that when I returned we had proper data to carry on the production engineering. When the first three airplanes were delivered to Martlesham Heath, our test pilot, Milo Bursham and I spent a number of months checking out your pilots and crew particularly squadron leader Red Collins.

When it came to prove our guaranteed range and dive speed I was given an RAF uniform so that I could be considered an official member of the crew during our long flights over England, Scotland and Wales.

You asked me what was my particular speciality. I would have to say that as Chief Research Engineer with a Bachelor's and Master's degree in Aeronautical Engineering, I was well trained in aerodynamics, structural design and flight testing. I was in charge of these activities on all our airplanes about that time. The Hudson program was one of the most successful for us here at Lockheed for a long, long time, and one from which I derived substantial pleasure of accomplishment.

I am enclosing a photo which you requested with some later airplane designs which are considerably beyond the performance obtainable of the good old Hudson.

Sincerely,
(Signed) Clarence L. Johnson

In addition to Kelly Johnson, others working on the project were Courtland Gross, Sales Manager Carl Squier, while R.A. Von Hake was the Manufacturing Manager. Concerned with the contracts for Lockheed was Bob Proctor. Shortly after the proceedings at Burbank, a group of Lockheed officials was invited to London by the director of contracts for the Air Ministry, Sir Henry Self. The contract, which was signed on 23 June 1938, was for Lockheeds to supply 175 Hudsons plus as many more as could be delivered up to 250 by December 1939. Lockheeds completed the order in November 1939, seven weeks ahead of schedule.

The *London Evening News* reported on 10 June 1938 that the Hudsons cost £17,000 (or $90,000) each. Of the 2941 Hudsons built, one was given free to the RAF; the materials by the company, and the labour by their workforce. It was dubbed *Spirit of Lockheed-Vega Employees* and saw service with No.269 Squadron in Iceland coded UA-N and with the RAF serial No.T9465. As the aircraft was intended by the RAF to serve largely in a maritime role with Coastal

Above: The Lockheed Hudson assembly lines at Burbank, California.

Above: Fitting the port wing of a Hudson at Lockheed, Burbank, California.

Command, it was named after the sixteenth century navigator, Henry Hudson.

The Machine

The Hudson was a military version of the twin-engined, mid-wing, all-metal monoplane, of stressed skin construction, the Lockheed Model 14 Super Electra airliner.

Notable features of both the Lockheed 14 and the Hudson were integral fuel tanks, the Lockheed-Fowler flaps, and slots just aft of the leading edge of the wing tips. The flaps enabled stalling speeds to be reduced by as much as seventeen knots but fully extended would have a strong braking effect. For take-off on short runways some pilots would deploy fifteen per cent flap; typically on landing, thirty per cent was used. The slots were intended to centralise any stall and apparently were installed following tests on the Lockheed 14 by Z. Lewis Leigh.[5]

Incorporated in the tail-wheel assembly was a dog clutch which could be locked in to avoid castoring after line-up of the aircraft for take-off. *Pilot's Notes* for the Mark VI Hudson refers to the reversed aileron effect when the aircraft was near stalling speed; the author was made aware of this, occurring only once in his experience.

Although RAF pilots were trained to make three-point landings, the Lockheed handbook for the Marks I and II recommended 'wheelers' and as Z. Lewis Leigh states (albeit for the Lockheed 14): 'we found that unless this machine was landed on its main wheels with its tail near the flying position, it became very troublesome'.[6]

Military variations were a bomb bay and bomb distributor gear, a compartment in the nose for the navigator, and a dorsal turret aft of the main door. In the roof of the main cabin was an astro hatch, serving also as an emergency exit in ditching. There were removable hatches to both port and starboard of the main cabin. Few aircraft could compare with such escape facilities for typically a crew of four; a hatch over the cockpit, and from the main cabin, the astro hatch, the two side hatches and the main door. The latter contained the main aircraft dinghy which would automatically inflate on impact or immersion, or if the door was jettisoned.

Hudson Marks I, II and III were fitted with Wright 'Cyclone' engines. The Mark II differed from the Mark I by having Hamilton constant speed hydromatic propellers rather than those with coarse and fine, two-speed positions. With the Mark IIIs came a retractable ventral gun position in addition to the dorsal turret. In the Mark III also, more powerful engines of 1200hp were installed.

The final three marks – IV, V, and VI – were all powered by Pratt & Whitney twin 'Wasp' engines which were apparent because of gills on the nacelles. Traces of the civil lineage were green curtains to all windows and flooring which, on at least one squadron was actually polished by ground crew!

Armament

Initially there were two fixed forward guns to be fired by the pilot and a Boulton & Paul turret with two belt-fed .303 Brownings. Subsequently, single .303 Vickers Gas Operated (VGOs) were available at both of the side hatches, plus a single .303 Browning in the ventral position. The record number of guns carried on a Hudson however, is 11, possibly 12, and with an RAAF squadron.

Bomb loads varied up to 1200lb. Typically on anti-submarine operations, four 250lb depth charges were carried with possibly the addition of two 100lb bombs. The flying detail for No.59 Squadron on the 1000 bomber Bremen raid shows some Hudsons taking four 250lb bombs, and others with ten 100lb bombs.

A Gunner's Point of View

The rear gunner on an aircraft was in uncomfortable isolation from the rest of the crew. This was most obvious on the Hudson

References
4. LH July 1957; JTp.39   5. ZLL p.111   6. ZLL p.1056. ZLL p.105

Above: Hudsons lined up at Burbank for delivery and without turrets.

where the other three in the crew were together forward of the one interior door. With the Boulton & Paul turret in Hudsons, there were no long vulnerable hydraulic leads as prevailed for the rear turret of a Sunderland; there were no turret doors to contend with as on a Wellington for example.

Below: A Lockheed magazine extract with the London Evening News *account dated 10 June 1938 of the purchase of Hudsons at £17,000 each [or $90,000].*

Entrance was past the main door, and with the later marks, past also the ventral position. One then stepped up over the Elsan. It would have been difficult for the average man to sit in the turret with an Irvin jacket, a Mae West and parachute harness, if not impossible. Most would have opted for just the Mae West and even that presented a hazard. When the 'table' was lowered, or following any undue movement, there was the real risk of activating the CO_2 bottle, thus inflating the Mae West; it would then be difficult indeed to exit.

There was a gun interrupter gear and, assuming it functioned properly, one would not have expected to shoot off either the twin rudders, the elevator or tail plane. From the author's limited experience and those of others, it was apparent that some *Luftwaffe* and some Japanese pilots were unaware of the ventral gun, which would not always be deployed as it would reduce the speed of the aircraft, as for the deployment of the two side guns.

Perhaps the need to be ever vigilant but with nothing to do otherwise but watch both sea and sky, was the main problem.

The Wireless Operator

The radio was located on a bulkhead immediately behind the pilot and the wireless operator's position was just forward of the main spar; he was thus on a mini-flight deck and able to operate not only the radio but view if necessary the ASV fitted on the starboard side behind him. From that position it was possible to see many of the cockpit instruments and assist the pilot in that respect for checking such as the cylinder head temperatures and if necessary to operate the manual hydraulic pump for the undercarriage.

The early Hudsons were equipped with the out-dated 1082/1083 radio, while located in the cabin was the TR9 which was intended for R/T transmissions. The 1082/1083 was powered by accumulators and a dry battery. For changing frequencies it was necesary to exchange coils for at least the receiver. Later marks had the American Bendix radio which was powered by motor/generators off the main aircraft batteries. The transmitter had eight fixed crystal controlled frequencies, and frequency changes were made simply by switching which operated a motor. The receiver was very easy to tune and proved stable. The power of the equipment was such that one could operate, ground to air, from Liverpool to Gibraltar, and from ground to ground, from Oran to Gibraltar. In addition to the main Bendix transmitter and receiver, there was a Bendix 'radio compass' which proved simple to operate and obtain a series of radio bearings very rapidly indeed.

With usually only one pilot, aircrew were expected to have some knowledge of the work of others in the crew. According to the area of operations, wireless operators might take over controls in the left-hand seat to give the pilot a rest; a diversion also for the wireless ops.

When signalling by Aldis lamp to the SNO in the escort ship of a convoy, there was always the aspect of: 'Which window to use?' Circling a convoy, relative positions changed rapidly and no one window was ideal. The pleasures of the wireless op's station were its location and feeling more part of a close-knit crew; having plenty to occupy one, and

Bombers for Britain

Aboard ship in Long Beach harbor, first Hudsons began ferry trip to England. Deliveries started early in 1939.

Over Dunkirk, waves of Hudsons bombed German boats, strafed Nazi soldiers, helped bring off evacuation.

Hudson bombers were shipped from both coasts. This one was loaded on lighter in New York, then on boat.

By sea and air they came. In 1941 Hudsons crossed the Atlantic on their own power to speed deliveries.

Ability to come back earned name of "Old Boomerang" for Hudsons. This one returned despite gaping hole.

Wartime cartoon captured crew's appreciation of "Old Boomerang's" ability to take it and come back again.

George VI of England climbed out after ride in Hudson. Versatile airplane performed variety of wartime jobs.

Hudsons at Lockheed Air Terminal awaited delivery to the British. Lockheed built a total of 2941 of them.

Front to rear, Hudson, Douglas Havoc, Vega Ventura started journey overseas by Long Beach Ferry Command.

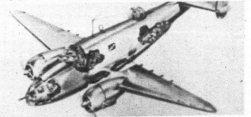

Pleased with the Hudson, the British placed orders for the newer Ventura, a conversion of the Lodestar.

Above: Bombers for Britain; *from a Lockheed Corporation house magazine of July 1957.*

Above: Hudson N7216 airborne at Leuchars on 30 July 1939 with 224 Sqdn. Slots at the wing tips and extended flaps are visible.

having faith through knowledge of both the aircraft and equipment.

The Navigator

David Whithey who served as a navigator with No.269 Squadron based in Iceland found that the navigator's position in the nose of the Hudson was too cramped for two people. Entry was by stepping down past what could serve as a seat for a second pilot. For his dead reckoning (DR) navigation, Whithey used a Distant Reading Compass and for taking drifts he used a Course Setting Bombsight (CSBS), although he adds that 'an assessment of windspeed and direction could

also be made with fair accuracy by observing the *wind lanes* on the surface of the sea.' He found, as did others, that the magnetic compass did not perform well in northern latitudes. Of astronavigation he adds that it was 'little used'.

F/Lt Fred Harrison flew on night trips with No.24 Squadron to Malta from the United Kingdom. He had the usual equipment available at that time for navigation, parallel rule and dividers, an air almanac and a Mark 9 sextant. He found the Hudson fitted with a flare chute and a drift sight behind and to starboard of the navigator. An astro compass was positioned in the astro hatch in the cabin of the Hudson which he used to obtain bearings from flashing beacons on the Portuguese coast. As he adds: 'Navigation was mainly by

Below: Hudson N7212 at Leuchars, Scotland in May 1939 when it had apparently just been delivered.

astro, but using loop bearings on the last few miles to Malta or Gibraltar.' It appears that although some Hudson navigation compartments were equipped with an airspeed indicator and altimeter, Fred Harrison referred to those in the pilot's cockpit.

The Pilot

Geoffrey Bartlett in addition to being an instructor, served on two Hudson squadrons – as a Flight Commander on 224 Squadron and he later commanded No.59 Squadron. He gives this account:

Recollected in tranquillity after a lapse of four decades, the Hudson was a pretty smooth and comfortable flying machine as compared with most of its military contemporaries. Considering its size and weight it was very manoeuvrable, and the flying controls were light and effective. The view from the cockpit was good and the general layout convenient. The interior finish in light green upholstery to match, was much less stark and utilitarian than was customary, but as the record shows, it was no aerial boudoir but a highly successful warplane.

When the Mark I started arriving in Coastal Command of the RAF in mid-1939, it was a much more sophisticated aircraft than the average squadron pilot had yet laid hands on, and it needed a correspondingly elevated degree of care and skill. Anyone inadequately briefed on its peculiarities would undoubtedly find himself in difficulties or real danger – the

Below: No.224's CO, W/Cmdr Hodgson, checking the bombing up of Hudsons at Leuchars on 3 September 1939.

'Hudswine' as it was affectionately called was never in the 'foolproof' category.

Entry through the door at the rear was pleasantly easy – no metal ladder to climb. On arrival at the cockpit through the well-filled radio compartment, the incomer was faced with many levers, switches and dials unfamiliar to British eyes. One particular instance was the dial of the Cambridge gas analyser, which was required for setting up in flight the correct fuel/air ratio for each engine, since the Holley carburettors on the Mark I did not have automatic mixture control. The pilot had to keep an eye on the settings throughout the flight and adjust the mixture strength when required by means of a pair of levers beside the throttles.

The panel carrying the Sperry Gyropilot was also a novelty to most. 'George' as it was inaccurately nicknamed (the real 'George' was the current British autopilot), needed its own special routines for checking while warming the engines before flight.

Propeller and wing de-icers were new to most people, likewise the system of fuel jettisoning. In the phrase of the time, most of the gubbins was within easy reach of the pilot, and the Hudson could be flown completely solo if necessary, although some emergency systems required another person to help.

Help too, was useful when starting the engines from the cockpit; it required dexterity single-handed. What with working the hand-pump (the 'wobble' pump), priming via an electric push-button, pushing the separate starter and booster buttons simultaneously, and turning on the ignition switch after one full revolution of the propeller. Co-pilots assisted when the crews included two pilots; later when observers and navigators came into Coastal Command and only one pilot was carried, they usually helped with 'pressing the tits' and sat beside the pilot during take-off.

When opening up for take-off, there was a slight initial swing to port as the two thirty-litre radials accelerated towards their take-off power of 1100hp each. The pilot would have locked the Hudson's tail-wheel in the straight-ahead position to help prevent such deviations, and if he used his throttles judiciously he would have no difficulty in remaining straight and getting airborne quite rapidly.

The performance figures issued for the Mark I claimed that it would clear a twenty-four metre (80ft) obstacle in 600 metres – presumably using some flap, which was not always the case in normal take-offs over smooth surfaces. The take-off distance with full war-load was a different matter, but the Hudson never used miles of runway like the 'heavies'.

A poor pilot could let the Hudson bounce off the ground before adequate flying speed had been reached. This could lead to really nasty scenes. The proper drill was to keep the control column forward to get the tail up as soon as possible and to hold the main wheels quite firmly onto the ground surface until speed had been built up sufficiently.

Safely airborne, a short upward movement to the undercart lever was quickly followed by a satisfying 'clunk . . . clunk' as each main wheel in turn locked up; they moved independently of each other by hydraulic rams. After acceleration through the safety speed of 110 knots, the pilot could ease into the climb and relax a bit, knowing that after that moment, even if one engine failed completely, he could get back round the circuit and land again with only one engine giving power.

The initial deliveries of the Mark I had ordinary Hamilton Standard constant speed propellers. These were recognisable by the short black spinners fitted over the hubs. Single-

Above: The first enemy aircraft shot down by the RAF in WWII; a Dornier 18 in the North Sea claimed by F/Lt Womersley of 224 Sqdn on 8.10.39.

Above: The Dornier 18 crew about to be rescued by the Danish fishing vessel Teddy *on 8.10.39.*

engined performance became even safer when the Series II (and all future marks), arrived fitted with the Hamilton Hydromatic airscrews which could be fully-feathered in flight to reduce drag.

The bright metal hubs of the Hydromatics were a conspicuous feature. For the pilot, the sight of the pair of red feathering buttons mounted above the top edge of the centre panel was very comforting, even if he never had to press one in genuine emergency. All pilots were trained to cope with a practice 'engine out' when airborne, and found the Hudson flew quite comfortably with one engine feathered and the other humming away at rated power, all flying controls balanced out with the trimmers.

Although not of course stressed for violent manoeuvres, the Hudson could nevertheless be thrown about in a spectacular manner when not heavily loaded. The rate of roll was modest by fighter standards, but very good for a reconnaissance bomber of the day. In the dive, officially limited to an indicated 290 knots, the elevator trim had to be used as the aircraft became increasingly tail heavy as the speed built up, and untrimmed during the recovery. Many a squadron Hudson came back to base with sprung rivets and rippled wings after brushes with the enemy had led to an over-enthusiastic race for the deck, but they were sturdily built by Lockheed and did not fall to pieces easily.

Some of the battle damage they sustained without

breaking up had to be seen to be believed. They were often flown unmercifully low, and came home sprouting branches torn from trees, or with the prop tips bent back after hitting the sea.

Hudsons were not easy to ditch in the sea successfully but it was done many times, and they floated if the fuel tanks were empty and intact. They could be force-landed with the wheels up on dry land with little drama if the run was reasonably unobstructed.

Landing the Hudson had a few snags for the unwary. The Fowler flaps had a long range of movement and had an extremely powerful effect if run all the way out at 100 per cent. With the 100 per cent flap setting it was difficult to make a fully tail-down, three-point landing, but the slowest possible touchdown could be achieved. It was dangerous to be in a position of having to apply full engine power when 100 per cent flap was down owing to the change of trim caused by the slipstream acting on the flaps. On the other hand, at intermediate flap settings the handling was perfectly straightforward.

The Hudson Circus

On 25 November 1938 Geoffrey Bartlett then a Flying Officer with No.224 Squadron based at Leuchars, was informed by his CO 'Colonel' Waite that he had been selected to attend a course on the Lockheed 14 at British Airways training school, Heston, Middlesex. Thereafter he and others would be required to take part in the conversion of several Coastal Command squadrons from Ansons to Hudsons. This was part of the urgent re-armament following the tense political situation. No.224 Squadron was due to be the first to receive Hudsons as they became available, it was hoped, in the new year.

In February 1939 Bartlett met several other Anson squadron pilots at Heston where they had a fortnight's ground instruction, learning about the vital systems of the aircraft and also gaining some air experience.

F/O Bartlett had his first Hudson flight in a Mark I, N7208 at RAF Martlesham Heath in April 1939. This was under S/Ldr R.W.P. Collings, OC of 'B' Performance Testing Flight. Martlesham Heath was then base for the Aeroplane and Armament Experimental Establishment (A&AEE), which eventually moved to Boscombe Down.

Above: HM King George VI inspecting the Hudson Circus – *pilots involved in converting Coastal Command Anson squadrons to Hudsons.*

Above: HM King George VI leaving a Hudson of No.220 Sqdn at Thornaby in November 1939.

The Hudson, amongst other new military aircraft, was there to be test-flown and generally evaluated for Service use prior to issue to squadrons.

Before being passed fit for solo, every pilot had to demonstrate his ability to make a safe circuit and landing after the instructor had cut one engine without prior warning while still at full power climb after take-off. Probably the 'Single-engined Circuit' and 'Emergency Lowering of the Undercarriage', were the most important parts of the flying programme, after the pupil pilot but experienced on Ansons, had shown his ability to control an incipient swing on take-off, dangerous bounces on landing, engine failure and so forth.

At Leuchars in the first week of May 1939, Hudsons N7210 and N7212 fitted with dual controls became available for flying, and the Hudson Training Flight got underway with S/Ldr W.E. Rankin, who was detached from No.269 Squadron, in charge. The instructors with him were S/Ldr D.Y. Feeny (233), F/Lt G.T. Gilbert (220), F/O W.D. Hodgkinson (220), and F/Sgt C. Holdway, the latter a very experienced pilot and a qualified flying instructor.

Lockheed representatives visited Leuchars and the two best remembered by Geoffrey Bartlett were Al Doe and Jim Guthrie. Al Doe went out with the photo-reconnaissance unit to the Middle East in N7364 and was killed in an accident there. Jim Guthrie wrote to the author in 1982: 'I have warm memories of my visit to Leuchars with Al Doe to present the model of the Hudson. It was a pleasure for me to meet and talk with members of 224 Squadron.' The Lockheed Hudson bronze casting referred to by Jim Guthrie is in the RAF Officers' Mess, Gibraltar, and is put on display during dining-in nights.

At Leuchars a syllabus of ground and flying instruction was organised as more and more flyable Hudsons appeared at the base and conversion flying gained momentum. The pilots sat through a syllabus of nine hours of lectures on the Wright Cyclone engines and 21 hours of airframe lectures to ensure they understood the main systems and operating characteristics of the Hudson and how to cope with emergencies in the air.

These could range from a minor fault in the electrical systems to a full loss of hydraulic fluid after battle damage.

There was an urgent need to get 224 Squadron operational and the whole station under Gp/Capt. Brian E. Baker, DSO, MC, AFC worked to that end. The engineering side of the Hudson effort was given expert assistance by Lockheed's and Wright's representatives, Bill Bailey and Al Doe, who worked in the hangars with maintenance crews all hours of the day and night.

By 23 August 1939 enough 224 Squadron crews qualified for W/Cmdr E.A. Hodgson to have 224 on a war footing and by 3 September many North Sea patrols had been flown although the Hudsons still lacked turrets and with the two fixed forward guns as the main armament. By then, the Training Flight known as the *Hudson Circus* moved on after 224 to its sister squadron 233 which was also at Leuchars. Sgt Pilots W.R. Acott, Harry Arden and Vic Morrison, all 224 and all shortly to be commissioned, were brought in as extra instructors during 233's training.

The Circus left S/Ldr Feeny with 233 Squadron and moved down to Thornaby to convert Anson squadrons Nos 220 and 206. Here instructors were reinforced by F/Lt Bill Coulson, a Trans-Canada Lockheed 14 pilot. Ross Marshal appeared as the manufacturer's representative and moved with the Circus to RAF Silloth. Derek Hodgkinson stayed with No.220 Squadron.

Silloth was still being built and was muddy when the Hudsons arrived. The Circus became No.1 (Coastal) OTU.

The success of the Circus had much to do (in the opinion of W/Cmdr Geoffrey Bartlett on whose notes this account is based), with two Australians, S/Ldr Rankin and his second-in-command, Gradon Gilbert.

No.6 (Coastal) Operational Training Unit

On 11 November 1941 I was posted to No.6 (Coastal) Operational Training Unit at RAF Thornaby near Stockton-on-Tees. RAF Thornaby was the home base of the Auxiliary squadron No.608 which was operating Hudsons from there in 1941. Earlier in the war, No.220 Squadron had been flying Hudsons from there on North Sea patrols and Battle Flights, and much of the spirit of 220 and 608 pervaded the station. Unlike many Coastal Command bases, Thornaby was in a built-up, and heavily industrialised area with fumes from a chemical works and a gantry bridge at Middlesbrough providing useful navigational aids.

For the OTU's formation early in July 1941, S/Ldr R.E. Craven, DFC who had earlier served on flying-boats with 201, 210 and 228 Squadrons, took about half the instructors from No.2 Army Co-operation School, Andover up to Thornaby. W/Cmdr C.D. Candy, the new unit's Australian CO was ill and S/Ldr Craven became acting CO; as he says:

There was little time for a measured bureaucratic approach to the formation. Within days, a special train delivered NCOs and airmen of the technical grades. We lined them up on the tarmac, split all trades and ranks into three and hey presto, we had A, B and C Flights. Much the same rough and ready methods were used for splitting up the instructors and over a week-end some twenty-five Hudsons were delivered; these again were split up into three flights and within hours we were in business.

Unquestionably there was a great spirit in the unit. I put this down to the fact that most of the staff were only lately off operations and to the leadership of Doug Candy whose energy, good nature and dedication were outstanding,

For the author, then very inexperienced aircrew, it was truly so; we respected the instructors, not because of their rank, but for their experience and attitude. A South African, S/Ldr A. de V. Leach, DFC from 224 Squadron, commanded 'A' Flight; from 209 Squadron came S/Ldr D. Spotswood to command 'B' Flight, while a New Zealander, F/Lt Pedersen who had served with 220 Squadron, took over an Anson/Lysander Flight. Canada was represented by S/Ldr Baudoux from 233 Squadron.

There was some truth in the adage: 'Survive OTU and you'll survive the war.' One night while in Stockton, I saw an aircraft burning in the sky; it was an OTU Hudson which crashed at Eaglescliffe. I later saw three empty bed spaces in my billet. My turn came later but with a happier ending. On 22 December we were airborne in Hudson N7243 at 1420hrs for a flying exercise but one-and-a-half hours later when about to land, the pilot, Sgt Dunnett, reported that the elevator had jammed. There was not enough height for us to bale out and we crash-landed on Brambles Farm, Middlesbrough. The Hudson ploughed through a hedge of brambles and one engine was torn right off. Three of us had sat with our backs to the bulkhead and immediately on crashing, exited through the two side hatches. The door had automatically jettisoned the dinghy it contained and it had inflated the right way up. Dunnett suffered a cut to his head as he had been thrown forward onto the windscreen. Seeing petrol pouring from a severed fuel pipe, the navigator calmly went back to the aircraft and stemmed the flow with a handkerchief; remarkably it didn't catch fire. We all four walked to the farmhouse where Dunnett 'phoned base and the farmer's wife insisted on giving us a glass of rum. An officer came with the RAF ambulance to collect us and found that the elevator was then quite free. When questioned by F/Lt Pedersen about the crash at the time, it was suggested that the pilot might have put in the auto-pilot control, but three of us pulling on the control column together had been unable to overcome any resistance.

Post-war, our former CO, by then AVM Candy, suggested in a letter to me that there was a special type of Gremlin at Thornaby as no fault had been found in the Hudson.

For pilots who had trained on such as Ansons, it was a task to convert to Hudsons; even to start the engines was an achievement, but to attempt three-point landings with a lightly-loaded Hudson was too much for some and ballooning and

'frog-hopping' was not uncommon. One pilot was scrubbed for apparently either attempting to land fifty feet up in the air or fifty feet below ground. The winter of 1941–1942 brought ice and snow to Thornaby which limited flying training and S/Ldr Craven organised visits for pupil aircrew to a munitions factory producing bombs for the RAF and one to Dorman & Long's steelworks at Middlesbrough. At Middlesbrough I saw for the first time a ship which had been torpedoed and was able to talk with the engineer through a gaping hole in the side of the ship. The engineer commented on the engines of the vessel having the same power as those of the Hudson – 2000hp.

In February 1942, aircrew who had passed No.5 course were posted to various Coastal Command squadrons, numbers 48, 220, 224, 233, 500 etc. My posting was to 224 Squadron then at St Eval. It coincided with the immediate aftermath of 'Channel Dash'. Post-war, I met only one other from the OTU course, John Chapman who was then a medical student at Jesus College, Cambridge. Of the instructors, apparently only F/Lt Pedersen failed to survive; it was said that he undertook operations instead of going on leave.

The instructors, like the pupils, experienced the hazards of OTU flying. The Canadian, S/Ldr Baudoux, on one occasion found the undercarriage unserviceable on coming into land. Using little flap to avoid damaging them, he was able to bring the Hudson safely down with damage to only propellers and the pitot head and the aircraft was put back into service. On another occasion, a Canadian crew on returning from a North Sea exercise, found that fog had rolled in and they were unable to see the coastline. They landed on sands at West Hartlepool and heard from the Army that they were in a minefield. Fifty gallons of fuel were taken to the scene; the aircraft was lifted by crane, new propellers were fitted and S/Ldr Baudoux took-off the aircraft before the tide returned. While at Thornaby, between his tours of operations, S/Ldr Baudoux satisfied himself that Hudsons could be safely recovered from a spin and could be rolled. He returned to his former squadron No.233 and during the *Torch* operations was acting CO of 233 at Gibraltar. S/Ldr Leach was posted to No.48 Squadron as CO when the unit was on Norge patrols from Wick; S/Ldr Spotswood took command of No.500 Squadron then at Stornoway but later to serve over the Mediterranean in one of the most successful periods for the unit. S/Ldr Craven, DFC went to the RAF Staff College, and W/Cmdr Candy returned to Australia to command No.1 OTU, RAAF.

On Anzac Day 1983 AVM Candy wrote to me mentioning his team at Thornaby – 'The Regiment' as he knew them – and his former RAF squadron No.206. I believe it was one of his last letters.

After completing a tour of operations on Hudsons, I returned to Thornaby; it appeared dead; the spirit to which Sir Robert Craven referred was gone. It lacked a certain group of men.

Chapter 2
North Sea Patrols

Coastal Command

In 1936 the area structure of the RAF was changed to that of *function* of fighter, bomber or coastal reconnaissance aircraft and thus did Coastal Command come into being under Air Marshal Sir Arthur Longmore.[1]

On 1 December 1937 the Air Ministry issued a directive that the primary role of Coastal Command in time of war would be trade protection, reconnaissance and co-operation with the Royal Navy.[2] The Admiralty considered that surface raiders would be the most serious threat to our sea communications and despite the lessons learned in 1917, felt that actions by U boats were 'unlikely to be serious'. In the event of war with Germany, Coastal Command aircraft would thus be required to cover the North Sea exits to the North Atlantic. The numbers of aircraft specified as being required for maritime duties in home waters were: 165 for convoy escorts, reconnaissance over the North Sea eighty-four, over the northern area of the North Sea twenty-four, plus eighteen for northern patrols covering passages to the Atlantic between Scotland and Greenland. Forty-eight aircraft were estimated as being required to cover Atlantic convoy assembly points. By 1 April 1939 only 194 aircraft out of the required total of 339 were available.[3]

Priority in aircraft was being given to fighter aircraft to defend cities, and bombers to raid Germany; thus Coastal

Below: An account in the Daily Telegraph *dated 27.1.40 of F/Lt Womersley's photo-recce of Heligoland.*

References
1. RAF I/26; CCWRp.1 2. SWR I/30 3. SWR I/35

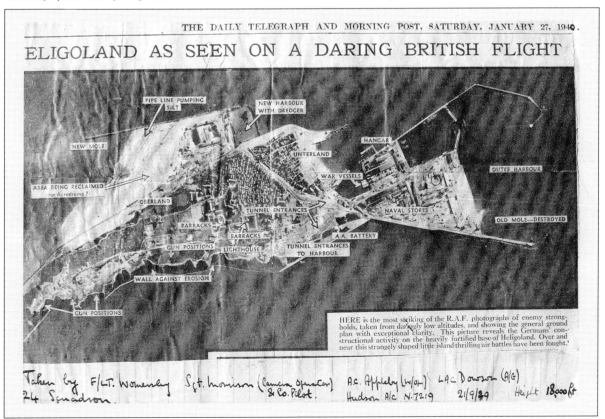

THE DAILY TELEGRAPH AND MORNING POST, SATURDAY, JANUARY 27, 1940.

ELIGOLAND AS SEEN ON A DARING BRITISH FLIGHT

HERE is the most striking of the R.A.F. photographs of enemy strongholds, taken from daringly low altitudes, and showing the general ground plan with exceptional clarity. This picture reveals the Germans' constructional activity on the heavily fortified base of Heligoland. Over and near this strangely shaped little island thrilling air battles have been fought.

Taken by F/Lt. Womersley Sgt. Morrison (Camera Operator) A.C. Appleby (W/Op) L.A.C. Dowson (A/G)
24 Squadron. & Co. Pilot. Hudson A/c N.7219 21/9/39 Height 18,000ft

Above: A Battle Flight *of 224 Sqdn Hudsons over Romsdal fjord on 23 April 1940. The two sister squadrons, 206 and 220, flew battle flights at the time of Dunkirk evacuation of troops effectively acting as fighters.*

Above: N7266 at Sumburgh 21.6.40 after bombing the battle-cruiser Scharnhorst *off Norway.*

Command rated third – the 'Cinderella' service. The general reconnaissance squadrons of Coastal Command equipped with Ansons had insufficient range to reach the Norwegian coast and thus cover the North Sea exits; duties for the Coastal squadrons were however promulgated on 31 March 1939. No.233 was to provide an 'endless change patrol' in daylight between Montrose, Scotland and Obrestadt, Norway. Nos 224 and 269 were to search from Flamborough Head south of the Montrose – Obrestadt line. Of second priority were the anti-submarine operations of 224 and 217 covering the Thames Estuary and the English Channel. The available flying-boat squadrons were to be deployed for areas requiring their greater range. The final version of these plans was issued in June 1939 but with no provision to escort east coast shipping for which Fighter Command subsequently received Blenheim fighters.[4]

When war was declared on Germany on 3 September 1939, of Coastal Command's eleven reconnaissance squadrons, only No.224 was fully equipped with Hudsons. They were Mark Is coded QX and initially armed with only the two fixed forward-firing Brownings. The Boulton & Paul turrets had not arrived. On that same day however, 224's Hudsons were bombed up and parallel track searches were

flown by F/Lt J.L. Atkinson with Sgt Everest and P/O R.A. Barker with Sgt A.L.T. Cargill in Hudsons N7218 and N7252.

The following day there were North Sea patrols by F/Lt Womersley, Sgt Illingsworth and F/O Green. Green had a brief engagement with a Dornier 18 with one of his fuel tanks damaged and he returned to base. One of 224's first losses was on 7 September when four of the Hudsons were on a parallel track patrol. Only three returned; another aircraft, N7247 captained by F/O Green, had been seen diving into the sea.

From 18 to 27 September No.224 Squadron had a detachment at Thornaby as W/Cmdr Womersley adds:

> . . . to carry out reconnaissance on German ports around the Elbe Estuary. We were known as the 'Death or Glory Boys'. My co-pilot Sgt Morrison took photos of Sylt and Heligoland etc. and on one occasion went over Cuxhaven at 100ft below fog. These trips were most hazardous and on 27 September I had to return to Leuchars as my aircraft was due for a major overhaul. However I permitted two crews to carry out *one* more mission from which they didn't return although one crew were taken prisoners. On returning to Leuchars I urgently advised the CO to have collected the other crews as they were nervous wrecks. This he did that day.[5]

On 30 September P/O Heaton-Nicholls was lost on a recce in Hudson N7219 to Sylt but taken prisoner, while P/O John Hollington failed to return from a flight over Wilhelmshaven. By the end of the month 224 Squadron had undertaken 114 sorties with durations up to seven hours and had lost three crews

In October 1939 *Battle Flights* of three aircraft became a feature of the Hudson squadrons. No.224 had detachments at Wick, Thornaby and Bircham Newton. While RAF aircraft headed eastwards, German aircraft were on westward recces and there were many encounters with largely B&V 138s and Do 18s.

The First Enemy Aircraft Claimed by the RAF in WWII

On 8 October F/Lt Womersley of 224 Squadron led such a flight to the Skaggerak. He was airborne in N7217 at 0705hrs followed by F/O Burton and Sgt Cargill. W/Cmdr Womersley continues:

> Some 110 miles out Sgt Morison who was in the nose taking a drift reported we had just gone over a Do 18 which was close to the sea. I alerted Sgt Cargill (F/O Burton had diverted to investigate a suspected U boat), to prepare to attack. I opened fire with my front guns in a dive at the Dornier who retaliated with his rear gunner who scored a hit on my aircraft. The Dornier then landed on the sea and the five crew took to a dinghy. I then went to a nearby Danish vessel *Teddy* and signalled to them to pick up the crew which they did. Then the three of us fired on the abandoned aircraft and virtually sank her. Then out of ammo we returned to base.[6]

This proved to be the first German aircraft claimed by the RAF in World War II.

Towards the end of 1939 various pieces of equipment in Hudsons gain a mention in 224 Squadron's records; thus on

Above: A Wop/AG of 220 Sqdn at Thornaby with another airman. Both are equipped with the early type of flying helmet; the Wop/AG wears a 'sparks' badge and the early air-gunner's badge, the 'flying bullet'. In the background a Hudson is coded 'NR' for 220 Sqdn.

31 October N7250 captained by P/O Barkley force-landed at Montrose with generator trouble putting out of action both the radio and gun turret. In November automatic bomb distributors were being fitted as also were remote controls to cameras. In December two of 224's Hudsons were sent to St Athans to be fitted with the new IFF (Identification Friend or Foe) and the Mark I ASV (Aircraft to Surface Vessel). On 6 December the Boulton & Paul turret in the Hudson is mentioned being in action against a Dornier 18. It was to be 10 January 1940 before the first use of ASV is recorded by 224 Sqdn. This was by a Battle Flight led by F/Lt Clifford Wright airborne from Wick which located a convoy at twenty-five miles range.

No.220 Squadron operating from Thornaby encountered a number of enemy aircraft resulting in combats. On 7 November a battle flight of three Hudsons led by F/Lt Sheahan attacked a Heinkel 115 and three days later F/Lt Sheahan's flight again attacked enemy aircraft, destroying one and badly damaging a second. Sgt Culver in A/220 on 6 December was less successful in a series of attacks on a Dornier 26 which appeared to be hit but the Hudson suffered considerable damage.

F/Lt Sheahan was again in action on 27 December when he made two attacks on a Dornier with his front guns. The Dornier in making a series of tight turns gave Sheahan's rear gunner a chance to fire his guns. A second Dornier then joined the affray but several bursts were seen to enter the Dornier's fuselage. That same day F/O Selley sighted two enemy destroyers with four minesweepers and seven patrol vessels. Signals were exchanged to confirm the ships as enemies before Selley made two dive-bombing attacks despite heavy AA fire throughout. One bomb exploded on the stern of a minesweeper.

While still at Thornaby on 1 January 1940 three of 220's Hudsons were apparently in combat with enemy aircraft. A/F/Lt Clarke attacked a Heinkel 111 and was last seen giving way. He had transmitted an SOS giving his position twenty miles east of St Abb's Head. P/O Carey had been in

company with Clarke and reported sighting two Heinkel 111s. Carey's second pilot, P/O McNeil, saw his first attack register and one of the Heinkels crash into the sea in flames. He then turned his attention to the second Heinkel and after using all the ammunition for the two fixed front guns, turned for his rear gunner, LAC Crompton, to bear on the enemy which then entered cloud. The Hudson pilot then saw a cloud of smoke over the sea and as many bursts of machine-gun fire had been seen to have found their mark, it was considered that the second Heinkel was probably destroyed also.

Sgt Culver was airborne from Thornaby for a patrol on 29 January and at 1407hrs was attacked by an Me 110 which approached at about 250 knots on the starboard quarter and opening fire at 400 yards' range. Culver climbed to 2500ft and his rear gunner Creegan opened return fire at 300 yards. Bursts entered the enemy's port engine and it dived towards the sea with smoke emitted. At the same time Culver put the Hudson's nose down and fired a burst with the front guns. The Me 110 pulled out at 500ft but the Hudson had also been hit and entered cloud. It had suffered damage to flaps, fuselage, port propeller and one tyre was burst.

The Prison Ship *Altmark*

Following the sinking of the pocket battleship the *Admiral Graf Spee* in December 1939, its supply ship the 12,000-ton *Altmark* remained in the South Atlantic until 22 January before attempting to return to Germany. The *Altmark* arrived off Trondheim on 14 February and was reported passing Bergen on the 15th. The Royal Navy undertook a search as did Coastal Command and from No.220 Squadron three Hudsons, K, M, and V were airborne at 0825hrs on 16 February. They were captained by P/O O'Neil, F/Lt Downton and F/O Fleetwood, detailed for a search round the Norwegian coast in a sortie of almost eight hours. The first

References
4. SWR I/36–38 5. Letter to author 6. Letter to author

Above: The 'prison ship' Altmark *in Jøsing fjord February 1940 after it was sighted by a 220 Sqdn Hudson. It had been a consort to the* Admiral Graf Spee. *The Allied prisoners were rescued by HMS Cossack.*

report was from O'Neil's Hudson at 1255hrs which had sighted *Altmark* apparently in Jøsing fjord south of Egersund. Although the British cruiser *Aresthusa* had sighted the *Altmark* under steam the Navy had been thwarted by the Norwegians' apparent 'neutrality' exemplified by their supposed search of *Altmark* and their gunboat *Kjell*. Ultimately Winston Churchill intervened ordering Captain Vian on the destroyer HMS *Cossack* to enter Jøsing fjord, capture *Altmark* and release the 300 prisoners it was holding. At night HMS *Cossack* entered the fjord; *Altmark* attempted to ram the destroyer but ran aground. The Navy sent a boarding party and in a skirmish, four Germans were killed and five wounded, some of the crew escaped, others surrendered, but 300 Allied prisoners were taken aboard the Navy's destroyers. The rescue of those prisoners for Churchill was 'a dominating fact'.[7]

Air to Air Combat

Three Hudsons from 220 Squadron were detailed for a special recce on 13 April including F/Lt Sheahan who was to fly between Oberstad and Kristiansund. At 1016hrs he signalled that he was being attacked by Me 110s when over Stavanger aerodrome. In a second attack the enemy damaged the rear turret and in a fourth attack his rear gunner, P/O Nicholas, suffered a bullet in his arm. An Me 110 was however seen with black smoke from an engine and it later dived into the sea in flames. P/O Petrie was also attacked by an Me 110 but after 400 rounds had been fired by the Hudson the enemy broke off the action.

Two days later P/O Lingwood in U/220 while on a patrol to Lillesand was attacked by two Me 110s but he was able to take avoiding action and escape into cloud. He then sighted two enemy destroyers and despite intense AA fire made repeated attacks on the vessels but was thwarted also by low cloud.

A battle flight of three 220 Squadron Hudsons was airborne from Leuchars at 0430hrs to escort three destroyers which they left at 0746hrs. Two Me 109 fighters were then seen and in their first attack the port engine of L/220 flown by Sgt Peachey burst into flames. Peachey attempted to ditch near a destroyer but lost control and crashed with his rear gunner LAC Dobson firing until the end. One of the crew attempted parachuting but the chute caught alight. P/O Petrie's aircraft was also attacked and last seen diving into the sea. Sgt Arnott flying N/220 apparently returned safely.

Roles were reversed on 9 May when P/O Carey of No.220 Squadron attacked a Dornier 18 and saw a number of bursts of machine-gun fire achieving hits. Its rear gunner didn't respond and was assumed to have been killed. The Dornier was last seen with smoke pouring from its engines. Three more of 220's Hudsons on escort to three destroyers shot down a Dornier 18 and then saw the enemy crew on the Dornier's float platform with their hands raised. When F/Lt Sheahan went down to investigate he was fired at by the Dornier's front gun and his Hudson was hit by an explosive bullet.

S/Ldr T.H. Carr was posted from 206 to No.220 Squadron on 15 May 1940 and on the 22nd succeeded W/Cmdr A.H. Paull, AFC to command the unit.

As Gp Capt. T.H. Carr, DFC, AFC writing in retrospect states:

> I was sent to 220 with a definite brief from Coastal Command to pull it together . . . it was a difficult job . . . we were very short of first pilots and in fact of all flying crews doing a very boring job of Anti-Invasion patrols and had twelve crews altogether for eight sorties to do daily morning and afternoon. They were from Thornaby to the Danish coast and then from Horns Reef to Lister Light in Norway and then home. The sorties took seven hours which left little for combat, or more likely evasion and the Mark I Hudsons were then operating with no self-sealing tanks . . . altogether morale was very low.[8]

A Wop/AG, John Noble who joined 220 Squadron in August 1940 recalls also the patrols to the Danish and Norwegian coasts and adds: '. . . seek and strike against enemy shipping, sometimes in "Battle Flights" of three aircraft against E boats, U boats and aircraft.' He confirms Gp Capt. Carr's reference to shortage of aircraft and crews adding:

> . . . so it had to be a case of strike only if conditions were favourable to us and adverse for the *Luftwaffe*, i.e. cloud cover or fog. In the event of a strong enemy attack on one of our convoys we were not expected to engage but warn the standby fighter aircraft. Usually we placed ourselves between the convoy and the enemy coast . . . The *Luftwaffe* on their part sent over reconnaisance aircraft to locate our convoys using He 115, Do 18, Ju 88, He 111 and Do 215s and we had several brushes with them with some success. On 25 September in Hudson T7310 L/220 we drove off two He115s. On 24 February 1941 A/220 P5158 drove off a Do 215. On 11 March 1941 Jack Hall's crew in V/220 R5059 shot down a Do 18.

Of the Hudson patrols over the North Sea John Noble gives 206 Squadron operating from Bircham Newton, 220 from Thornaby, 269 from Wick and 224 with 233 operating from Leuchars, adding that: 'The patrols overlapped so that if one squadron couldn't cover, it was taken over by adjacent units. The object was to locate enemy shipping, and if the conditions were right, to strike.'

On 21 May 1941, Noble's crew was on a strike against the battleship *Bismarck*.

> Cloud from 0–6000ft made an attack impossible so we went for the secondary target, the aluminium works at Bergen. This was our first encounter with a night-fighter. Twenty miles off the coast we experienced heavy flak which made the navigator think that his DR was incorrect. In fact it was almost certainly the *Bismarck* on her way out of Bergen.[9]

Norway

Both Britain and Germany were conscious of the importance of Norway primarily because it served as a route for Swedish iron ore via the port of Narvik and then by sea through the naturally protected 'leads' southwards; the alternative Swedish port of Lulea being ice-bound from mid-December to mid-May. Early in October 1939 Admiral Raeder had drawn Hitler's attention to the advantages of having bases in Norway. Winston Churchill's memorandum dated 16 December 1939 which advocated interrupting the supplies by mining the Norwegian leads was

| 1941 | 220 (G.R.) SQUADRON. WICK. | | | | Time carried forward :— | 341·05 | 76·15 |
Date	Hour	Aircraft Type and No.	Pilot	Duty	REMARKS (including results of bombing, gunnery, exercises, etc.)	Day	Night
Oct. 1st	0615	L/220 HUDSON Ù	SGT TRAVELL	W/OP	FIGHTER ESCORT TO CONVOY 84 W.N	4·00	
			SGT CARPENTER	A.G-SGT DAVISON			
Oct. 9th	1120	D/220 HUDSON Ù	F/O JACKSON	W/OP	FIGHTER ESCORT TO CONVOY "PATTERN"	5·00	
			P/O CROKER	A.G-SGT DAVISON			
Oct. 9th	1850	W/220 HUDSON Ù	F/SGT SMITH	W/OP	STRIKE: AALESUND (N.W. NORWAY).		6·20
			SGT JONES	A.G-SGT DIPLOCK	ATTACKED FIVE PATROL BOATS SINKING TWO. ATTACKED RADIO STATION WITH INCENDIARIES SETTING IT ON FIRE. ATTACKED FLAK POSITIONS WITH MACHINE GUNS SILENCING FOUR. ALL ATTACKS MADE FROM 20 FEET. M/G BARRACKS.		
Oct. 14th	1550	F/220 HUDSON Ù	F/SGT TRAVELL	W/OP	PATROL: RECCE STAB (STAVANGER-BERGEN)	3·00	2·00
			SGT CARPENTER	A.G-SGT DAVISON	NEGATIVE REPORT.		
Oct. 16th	1450	F/220 HUDSON Ù	F/SGT TRAVELL	W/OP	FIGHTER ESCORT TO CONVOY "MUSTER"	4·00	0·40
			SGT CARPENTER	A.G-SGT DAVISON			
Oct. 18th	0640	F/220 HUDSON Ù	F/SGT TRAVELL	W/OP	FIGHTER ESCORT TO CONVOY "CHITTY"	4·35	0·30
			SGT CARPENTER	A.G-SGT DAVISON			
Oct. 20th	1055	F/220 HUDSON Ù	F/SGT TRAVELL	W/OP	FIGHTER ESCORT TO CONVOY "RUSTY"	4·20	
			SGT CARPENTER	A.G-SGT DAVISON	AIRCRAFT CARRIER H.M.S. VICTORIOUS + 2 DR.		

Above: The page from John Noble's log. A Wop/AG with 220 Sqdn dated 9.10.41 giving details of a raid on Ålesund. A subsequent raid by 220 Sqdn was given coverage in the Illustrated London News *and was the subject for a wartime national poster.*

considered by the Cabinet on 22 December.[10] While the Allies were inhibited by Norway's neutrality, Hitler, on 12 December decided to take Norway.[11]

In addition to ensuring Germany's supplies of Swedish iron ore its ports would provide natural defences for both surface craft and U boats and with additional defences by adjacent airfields. Coastal Command's aircrews were to become acutely aware of this right up until April 1945. With control of Norway and its 1000-mile coastline, a northerly exit to the Atlantic could be covered and with the later ability to attack Russian convoys.

On 21 February 1940 Hitler ordered General Falkenhorst to plan the invasion of Norway; on 26 March *Weserubung* – the occupation of Denmark and Norway – was approved, and on 2 April orders were given for attacks on the ninth.[12]

Churchill's wish to mine the Norwegian leads was to be carried out on 5 April under operation *Wilfred* and with the prospect of opposition, if necessary, to undertake 'plan R4' the occupation of Narvik, Trondheim, Bergen and Stavanger. The operation was postponed until 8 April and on that date Oslo received reports of a German troopship *Rio de Janeiro* bound for Bergen torpedoed by the Polish submarine *Orzel*. Within forty-eight hours all Norway's major ports were taken by the Germans.[13] Figures quoted vary for the German forces employed in the invasion of Norway but they include at least six army divisions and over 1000 aircraft which included at least 200 transport aircraft. Naval forces included the two battlecruisers *Scarnhorst* and *Gneisenau*, a pocket battleship, five cruisers, 14 destroyers and twenty-eight U boats.

The German heavy cruiser *Admiral Hipper* had sailed with four destroyers at 2200hrs on 6 April to be joined on the seventh by the battlecruisers *Scharnhorst* and *Gneisenau* with ten more destroyers. One of the first encounters with the Royal Navy was the destroyer HMS *Glowworm*. *Admiral Hipper* opened fire with four eight-inch guns; *Glowworm* rammed the 10,000-ton cruiser, withdrew and blew up. Peter Cremer on one of the German destroyers comments: 'For the first time I had learnt what bravery meant.' The captain of HMS *Glowworm*, Lt/Cmdr P.G. Roope, was awarded a posthumous VC.[14]

The Allied forces made landings at Narvik, Åndalsnes,

References
7. Public Record Office A27-1365; RAF I/57; SWR I/151–2; WSC I/505–8
8. Letter to author   9. Letter to author
10. WSC I/478, 479, 483   11. RAF I/77   12. RAF I/78; JKp.40; SWR I/163
13. SWR I/157; WSC I/532   14. PC p.13

Namsos and Trondheim but by 8 June all were evacuated. King Haakon who had hoped for continued resistance by Norwegian troops in the North, was picked up by the cruiser HMS *Devonshire* from Tromsø on 7 June.

For the RAF's historian, Denis Richards, the Norwegian campaign demonstrated the over-riding importance of air power.[15] The Naval historian, Capt Roskill, said that the campaign safeguarded Germany's iron ore supplies, gained it bases for U boats, increased its control of sea passages across the Baltic Sea but had no major unit fit for sea.[16]

Peter Cremer, an officer in *Weserubung* gives his summary with the Allies landing at three places only to withdraw; the battle for Narvik decided in Germany's favour and Norwegian forces had capitulated at Trondheim. The *Kriegsmarine* however had lost three cruisers and ten destroyers, the latter to HMS *Warspite*, and *Admiral Hipper* was out of action for a month.[17]

Winston Churchill gives the Allied losses at sea as one aircraft carrier, two cruisers, one sloop and nine destroyers, but with the Germans left with an effective fleet at the end of June with one heavy cruiser, two light cruisers and four destroyers; thus the *Kriegsmarine* ceased to be a major factor in the intended invasion of Britain.[18]

Hudsons Attack German Naval Task Force

At 0700hrs on 4 June 1940 the battlecruisers *Scharnhorst* and

Above: N7266 with two of the crew, P/O Lynn and Sgt Cliff of 224 Sqdn after bombing the battle cruiser Scharnhorst *off Norway. They were in a flight led by S/Ldr D. Feeny of 233 Sqdn who was shot down.*

Gneisenau together with the heavy cruiser *Admiral Hipper* and four destroyers sailed from Kiel to attack British naval units at Harstad which were involved with our forces at Narvik. On the eighth the carrier HMS *Glorious* with its

Below: 'Old Boomerang', a Hudson cartoon fully justified by the number of Hudsons returning to base with serious damage.

OLD BOOMERANG—Cartoonist Dick Shaw captured the spirit of the Hudson which led pilots and crews to boast of the converted model 14's ability to "take it" and come back—most desired quality of a warplane from crew's point of view. Hudson performed variety of war functions.

Above: No.224 Sqdn officers at Limavady, Northern Ireland with their Australian CO, W/Cmdr Curnow.

Above: A squadron inspection of 224.

destroyer escort was engaged and *Glorious* was sunk together with two of the destroyers, HMS *Acasta* and HMS *Ardent*, but not before *Scharnhorst* was torpedoed by *Acasta*. The battlecruisers sailed to Trondheim joining the cruiser and destroyers which had been detached.[19]

At 1600hrs on 10 June twelve Hudsons of No.269 Squadron flew from Wick to Sumburgh to prepare for an attack on the damaged *Scharnhorst* then at Trondheim. The weather for the eleventh was reported as mainly fair with a few scattered showers with cloud 2/10ths to 7/10ths above 1500ft and visibility twenty to thirty miles with a south-westerly wind of fifteen to twenty knots. At 1130hrs 269's twelve Hudsons were airborne from Sumburgh led by W/Cmdr Pearce and at 1437hrs were over Trondheim harbour where they subsequently reported *Scharnhorst* with two cruisers, three destroyers and two supply ships.

The Hudsons attacked from 15,000ft in four flights of three aircraft in line astern and hits were claimed on two cruisers with one seen to be on fire. Smoke was also seen from one of the supply ships. Anchored in the harbour were eighteen to twenty flying boats.

AA fire was heavy and accurate and Hudson P5131 with Sgts Robson, Sherwood, Craig and Napier was shot down into Buvik harbour. Five Me 109 fighters were encountered and Hudson N7361 was shot down in Gulosen fjord. Three of its crew became PoWs – W/Os E.B. Lascelles, A.M.S. Brodie and J.C. Hepburn. The fourth man, Sgt E.T.D. Machell, died of wounds the following day. Remarkably, the other ten Hudsons returned to Sumburgh at 1735hrs before continuing to Wick three hours later.

Of the crew from Hudson P5131, Sgt Robson was presumed lost with the aircraft, Sgt Sherwood escaped to Sweden, Napier became a PoW, while Craig was shot by an Me 109 when parachuting down. The two bodies were never found. Ten days later there was to be a further attack on the *Scharnhorst* by Hudson aircraft but when it was at sea.

No.206 Squadron based at Bircham Newton was no less active. On 13 June F/Lt Jim Romanes led two flights of Hudsons in an attack on motor torpedo boats in Boulogne harbour with their aircraft releasing a total of twenty-four 250lb bombs. It was about this time that two of 206 Squadron's Wop/AGs, LACs K.S. Freeman and W.D. Caulfield, were awarded DFMs for their successful combats with enemy aircraft over Dunkirk while in F/Lt Biddell's flight. At 1110hrs on the fourteenth 206 Squadron aircraft were on recces off the Dutch coast for enemy invading forces.

F/O Bullock while flying at 8,000ft altitude off the Frisian Islands on the seventeenth attacked a German destroyer and claimed a direct hit with a 250lb SAP bomb. The following day F/Lt Romanes was detailed to lead a flight against MTBs reported off IJmuiden but on not sighting the vessels a shallow diving attack was made on Norderney aerodrome claiming many possible hits. A further attack on an enemy-occupied aerodrome was made on 19 June by P/O Henderson with 206's CO W/Cmdr Constable-Roberts.

This was on Borkum and direct hits were claimed on hangars. Two days later, W/Cmdr Constable-Roberts and F/Lt Biddell led nine Hudsons for an intended attack on five merchant vessels and two destroyers off Texel. On failing to sight the ships, a harbour on Den Helder was bombed. W/Cmdr J. Romanes writing to the author remarks:

Whilst most of the trips that we did in June 1940 were fairly hairy, one trip stands out in my memory. It was a daylight job on 18 June in Hudson P5143. Our briefing stated that a returning night bomber had reported a cruiser at anchor in the mouth of the Elbe. I was to lead a flight of three Hudsons to carry out a high-level bombing attack on this vessel. It was a most beautiful day without a cloud in the sky and we were a bit distressed to find that we couldn't get more than 10,000ft high with our bomb load. As we were flying in full view of the Frisian Islands, we were surprised that nothing took any notice of us although we could see lots of aircraft on Norderney.

References
15. RAF I/105   16. SWR I/201   17. PC p.14   18. WSC I/592
19. SWR I/158

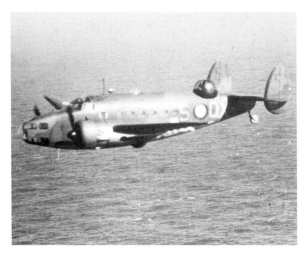

Above: S-QX of 224 Sqdn over the North Sea possibly flown by F/Lt Womersley.

Above: Limavady airfield with a 224 Sqdn Hudson on fire in December 1941.

When south of Heligoland we turned SE into the Elbe only to find that there was no cruiser in sight. Just to show that we were not friendly we did a dive bombing attack on Norderney and made for home at the more usual height of 20ft off the sea. All we came across on the way home was a string of six German mine-sweepers who we gave a burst of machine-gun fire which was not returned.[20]

The area covered by Romanes' flight remained extremely hazardous throughout the war even for the well-armed Beaufighters and for a daylight raid without cloud cover many would say was suicidal. In 1942 W/Cmdr J. Romanes took command of 206 Squadron but when they were no longer equipped with Hudsons.

The Battlecruiser *Scharnhorst* Attacked by Hudsons

Hudson N7251 captained by P/O Baudoux of No.233 Squadron was airborne from Leuchars at 0735hrs on 21 June for a recce off the Norwegian coast. Landfall was made at Bremanger at 1025hrs when Baudoux headed south. He was chased by two enemy aircraft but escaped into cloud. On emerging from cloud at 1500ft *Scharnhorst* was sighted with five screening destroyers and another astern. He reported to base and shadowed the force for an hour before being recalled

References
20. Letter to author

Below: N7210 at Leuchars, Scotland April 1939. It was first flown by 224 Sqdn from Leuchars on 4.5.39.

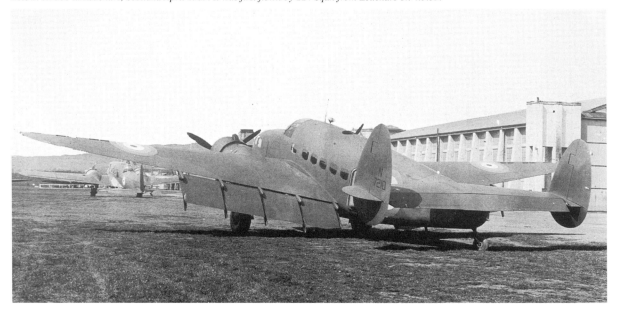

Above: Hudson N7264 at Wick on 23.4.40 after being shot up when over Romsdal fjord by the cruiser HMS Curacoa *which had been landing troops.* Curacoa *was itself damaged by the enemy the following day.*

Above: The Lockheed representative Mr Guthrie presenting a bronze Hudson casting to W/Cmdr Hodgson of 224 after the squadron had completed a million Hudson flying miles.

Above: A convoy escort by 233 Sqdn Hudsons. Convoy escorts were a routine task for Coastal Command up to June 1945.

and landing at Wick.

Between 1230 and 1245hrs three of 233's Hudsons flown by S/Ldr Feeny, Sgt Bailey and P/O Piejus were airborne as part of a strike force but Bailey and Piejus failed to locate the enemy ships and returned to base. S/Ldr Feeny in Hudson N7246 led two from No.224 Squadron including the deputy leader, F/Lt Womersley in N7305. W/Cmdr Womersley writing to the author in retrospect states:

Before leaving Leuchars at 1315hrs we were told the *Scharnhorst* and *Prinz Eugen* plus destroyers had been sighted off Norway and we were to attack en route to Sumburgh. Flying at 10,000ft we sighted the enemy some five miles away. We were challenged, but not knowing the answer were immediately met with terrific AA fire. Our height was a give away for we were close to cloud base. As we neared the target the AA was fierce and S/Ldr Feeny, only some feet away from me got a direct hit and his aircraft disintegrated. Below on my right I could see some thirty German fighter aircraft rapidly climbing in our direction. Meanwhile my bomb aimer/co-pilot/navigator kept giving me instructions. The fighters were getting very close. 'For Christ's sake let the bloody things go.' 'Bombs gone and plotted, Sir.'

I made for cloud cover only to see an Me 109 miss my tail by a matter of feet. The bombs had straddled the bows of *Scharnhorst*.

Also on the strike from 224 was P/O H. O'Neill and as G/Capt. O'Neill he writes:

I flew in number four position as co-pilot to P/O R.G. Lynn, did the navigation and fired the window Lewis gun at Me 109s. Feeny was shot down by AA and Me 109s just above us. I crashed-landed at Sumburgh with most of the starboard aileron shot away. I don't suppose anyone has heard of Dunstan Feeny. He was a southern Irishman like Lt/Cmdr Esmonde but unlike Esmonde who got the VC attacking *Scharnhorst* in the Channel, Feeny got nothing.

The battlecruiser *Scharnhorst* returned to Kiel; it was later to survive in 'The Channel Dash' [*Ibid*] but to be sunk by the Royal Navy during the Battle of North Cape in 1943.

A Raid on Hamburg

On 18 May 1940 No.233 Squadron operating from North Coates detailed seven Hudsons for a bombing raid on

Three Nazi War Ships Bombed

A GERMAN destroyer at Brest and two German supply ships off the Norwegian coast were bombed and probably sunk by aircraft of the Coastal Command during a series of night attacks on enemy territory.

The destroyer was hit three times by one Blenheim, and the bomb bursts were followed by explosions. In a later attack, at least one bomb exploded on the stern.

The destroyer had been using its full anti-aircraft armament against the bombers, but before the raid ended the warship was shrouded in smoke and its guns were silent.

The enemy used a force of fighters in an unsuccessful attempt to resist the attack on the port of Brest. One of our aircraft was confronted by 12 Messerschmitt 109's, but it evaded them and went on to its target.

After two Messerschmitt 109's had repeatedly tried to drive off another aircraft one of the enemy broke up in the air from the counter-fire.

Conditions and visibility were extremely poor, but several sticks of bombs fell directly on the target areas.

One of our Blenheims is missing.

Hudsons of the Coastal Command patrolling the Norwegian coast successfully attacked two German supply ships.

Six bombs burst on the deck of the larger ship, and at least three, and probably five, on the smaller. Both pilots approached at very low altitude, and then climbed steeply to make dives.

A wide tower of dense smoke rose 200 feet high after heavy explosions from the larger ship.

There were also several explosions in the other vessel, and debris from this ship came up to what the crew described as "four times the height of a house."

Both supply vessels were found close inshore at Lister and Obrestad—so near the land that the German coastal batteries were firing at the low-flying Hudsons from less than 400 yards. Neither aircraft was damaged.

Targets in Hamburg were also attacked during the night, and several fires were seen to be raging. Our bombers were again hampered by weather conditions.

Blenheims is missing.

BOMBS ON SUPPLY SHIPS

Hudsons of the Coastal Command patrolling the Norwegian coast (says the Air Ministry) successfully attacked two German supply ships. Six bombs burst on the deck of the larger ship, and at least three, and probably five, on the smaller.

Both pilots approached at very low altitude, and then climbed steeply to make dives.

A wide tower of dense smoke rose 200ft. high after heavy explosions from the larger ship.

There were also several explosions in the other vessel and debris from this ship came up to what the crew described as "four times the height of a house."

Both supply vessels were found close inshore at Lister and Obrestad—so near the land that the German coastal batteries were firing at the low-flying Hudsons from less than 400 yards.

Neither aircraft was damaged.

Daily Mail   News Chronicle

5th Jan. 1941

Larger vessel M.V.Snyg off Egersund, Norway.

Attacked by Hudson I   N7298 "O" - Oboe
A Flight 224 Squadron, Leuchars - F/Lt Davies.

Above: Reports in the Daily Mail *and* News Chronicle *of shipping strikes by Blenheims and Hudsons. Shipping strikes remained one of the most dangerous tasks for any type of aircraft throughout the war.*

Hamburg. N7255 captained by F/O Coventry was airborne at 2100hrs armed with 250lb bombs. F/O Edwards in N7340 followed five minutes later and all were airborne by 2235hrs.

F/O Coventry was over the target area at 0030hrs and released three bombs from 16,500ft despite very heavy AA fire and searchlights which were on both north and south banks of the River Elbe. There was also AA fire from Wangerooge Island and searchlights from all the Frisian Islands.

F/O Edwards was blinded by searchlights for half-an-hour and picked up by five of them at Cuxhaven. He dived to 200ft altitude and flew up the River Elbe. At Brunsbuttel there was very heavy AA fire and eleven searchlights, at Gluksted further AA fire.

Edwards was forced to keep low in the banks of the river and used his bombs to attack an aerodrome two miles south of Stade although only one exploded due to his electrical circuits being hit by AA fire as also was his radio which became u/s.

F/O Butler in N7251 was also deflected by the searchlights which he estimated as fifty over Hamburg. He found searchlights from north of the River Elbe and along its banks. The AA fire was accurate at 1500ft but he remained in the area for thirty minutes and on returning released four 250lb bombs on an AA battery at Stade. Sgt Price captained N7243 from 2235 until 0415hrs having remained in the target area for one-and-a-half hours and due to the searchlights didn't release his bombs. Sgt Muir in N7207 was unable to open his bomb

Above: A hand-held camera being used by a 206 Sqdn Wop/AG through the port hatch of a Hudson.

doors and had spent an hour in the effort, returning to base at 0415hrs.

Sgt Ather was at Cuxhaven when daylight was breaking but flew down the River Elbe at 15,000ft. He saw enemy aircraft take off from Midlum aerodrome and due to lack of cover abandoned the sortie.

F/O Dunn was over the target at 0015hrs in N7324 at 15,000ft suffering heavy and accurate AA described as 'black and grey with flaming onions'. His second pilot was seriously wounded and his wireless operator was also wounded. His bombs failed to release. S/Ldr Feeny (who was later to be lost attacking the *Scharnhorst*), was off Cuxhaven at 0100hrs in heavy and accurate AA fire from flak ships off the mouth of the Elbe which persisted right up to Hamburg and in constant glare of searchlights. He selected a very active AA battery and released three 250lb bombs causing a fire.

That same night seven of No.220 Squadron's Hudsons were each given separate objectives in Germany their targets including Wilhelmshaven, Cuxhaven, Hamburg and Bremen.

Dunkirk

By 24 February 1940 Germany had formed a plan for operation *Schikelschnitt* in which the French Maginot Line would be by-passed with a break through in the Ardennes and in so doing encircle the British Expeditionary Force (BEF)

together with a French Army and drive them to the sea.[21]

The German attack began on 10 May; the Dutch surrendered on the fourteenth and Belgium capitulated on the twenty-eighth. There was a brief respite on the twenty-third when General von Runstedt halted his advance on the BEF. Field Marshal Viscount Gort advised the withdrawal of the BEF and it was approved by the Cabinet on 26 May. At 1857hrs that day operation *Dynamo*, the evacuation of troops from the Dunkirk area, was initiated.[22] All types of vessel were used, Churchill giving the total as 861 including 39 destroyers and with two-thirds of the men embarking from Dunkirk harbour. Both ships and men were subjected to German bombing. Both Fighter and Coastal Command gave cover and Coastal's contribution included 'Battle Flights', typically of three Hudsons from squadrons such as Nos 206 and 220. Although some of their records are undated, they were very active at the end of May. Thus from Bircham Newton No.220 operated fourteen Hudsons with some flying to IJmuiden harbour to give warning of any enemy vessels such as MTBs while others were on Battle Flights from North Foreland to Calais and Dunkirk beach. They reported the area 'absolutely thick with craft of all kinds, destroyers, trawlers, tugs and barges, minesweepers, pleasure cruisers, week-end motor launches and rowing boats, going to and fro taking troops of the BEF back to England.'

No.220 Squadron proceeded by air on detachment to Bircham Newton on 28 May for operational duties. One of their Hudsons, N7314, was airborne from Thornaby at 0520hrs captained by P/O Dalcombe. From Bircham Newton it was airborne again at 1230hrs in a Battle Flight then captained by P/O Humphreys for a four-and-a-half hour flight along the French coast. The wireless operator in both crews was Anthony Majoram who on 31 May flew again but with S/Ldr Carr. This was again in a Battle Flight lasting five hours along the French coast and when they were attacked by seven Me 109 fighters. The Hudsons flew low towards the British coast only to suffer AA fire from their own coast batteries.

After a number of such patrols, Majoram returned to Thornaby on 4 June. Writing to the author he remarked: 'It was only then when we got back that we realised the full import of the evacuation of Dunkirk especially when we were asked to hand in our second pair of boots for the evacuated troops.'

While at Bircham Newton, No.220 Squadron had maintained two patrols; one, a cross-over patrol by single Hudsons between IJmuiden and Texel to look for enemy warships and MTBs heading south towards Dunkirk. The other patrol was by a Battle Flight of three Hudsons between North Foreland, Calais and Dunkirk protecting troops on the beach and ships of all types evacuating the troops across the Channel from Dunkirk. These were maintained throughout the hours of daylight.

The Hudson crews reported Hurricanes and Spitfires 'continuously on patrol' in the area but themselves were expected to protect the troops from Junkers 87s and Heinkel 115s. F/O Wright captain of Hudson U/220 on a cross-over

References
21. JK 42–3 22. RAF I/30; SWR I/227

patrol reported enemy warships in IJmuiden harbour on 29 May and P/O Scotney in Z/220 sighted enemy warships before being pursued by two enemy aircraft. S/Ldr Carr on a 'Sands Patrol' reported heavy bombing at Dunkirk which included the bombing of a hospital ship. Another in his battle flight – P/O Lingwood – saw a large merchant vessel on fire at the stern. Another flight from 220 Squadron led by P/O Dacombe directed HMS *Killarney* to a raft carrying three wounded soldiers.

No.206 Squadron had been converting from Ansons to Hudsons in March but while at Bircham Newton on 4 April received its eighth Hudson. Its aircraft were deployed on reconnaissance along the coasts of Germany and The Netherlands but at the time of Dunkirk Battle Flights were formed with such as Hudsons N7333, N7343 and N7351 flown by P/O Curtis, P/O Gilbert and F/Lt Biddell respectively on 28 May from 0935 to 1335hrs. On the thirtieth F/O Marvin in N7396 led a flight of three Hudsons from 1730 to 2145hrs. The following day further flights were led by F/Lt Romanes and F/Lt Biddell.

On 2 June 206 Squadron sent six Hudsons in two flights to cover the evacuation of the British Expeditionary Force (BEF) and one of these flights encountered heavy AA fire. 206's operational record for 3 June shows that a flight of three Hudsons was deployed from Detling, Kent and at 2015hrs during what is given as an 'enemy patrol' they encountered nine Me 109 fighters which were attacking Fleet Air Arm Skuas. The Hudsons joined the affray, attacked the German fighters destroying two and damaging others before the enemy withdrew. The Hudsons were led by F/Lt Biddell who subsequently was awarded the DFC. Two of the Hudsons' Wop/AGs, LAC K.S. Freeman and LAC W.D. Caulfield, were awarded DFMs. On 19 May Field Marshal Lord Gort in command of the BEF had considered the possible withdrawal of his forces to Dunkirk. [23]

Operation *Dynamo*. The evacuation of troops by small ships was decided on 22 May and authorised by the British Cabinet on 26th with the order to proceed given by the Admiralty at 1857hrs. The operation was officially concluded at 1423hrs on 4 June. Out of 848 ships used in the evacuation, seventy-two were lost by enemy action, 163 by other causes. A total of 338,226 troops were recovered according to the Admiralty and of those over 100,000 were taken by destroyers and torpedo boats. Out of those fifty-six ships, nine were lost. [24]

The RAF official history gives for sorties in support of operation *Dynamo,* 2,739 by fighters, 651 by bombers and 171 recces. It is not clear in which category the Coastal Command Hudsons were placed but the one illustration given in the RAF's official history to represent Dunkirk (and so titled) shows a lone Hudson over the small ships! [25]

In an address to Parliament on 4 June, Churchill referring to the evacuation of the troops stated that it was a deliverance and a victory gained by the RAF and he added, 'I will pay my tribute to these young airmen.' [26]

No.233 Squadron

In October 1940 No.233 Squadron Hudsons were based at Leuchars near Dundee and engaged on patrols to Norway. On the twenty-third Sgt Bailey was airborne at 1236hrs for a coastal recce from 20°E off Lister to 59°30′N. At 1515hrs landfall was made at Lister for the recce to be made northwards along the coast at 2000ft altitude. Three ships were sighted at various times including one painted white and sailing south. Five minutes after sighting Obrestadt and at 1540hrs the Hudson T9377 was attacked by three Me 109 fighters which came from the south-east and 200ft below. Bailey took evasive action and returned fire, escaping into clouds at 1600hrs. Ten minutes later on emerging from cloud, the Hudson was again attacked by one of the Me 109s. Bailey was fortunate to be flying a Hudson then equipped with a ventral gun covering the very vulnerable underside of the aircraft and as he reported, it was continually in use.

Although not given in 233's record this sortie was probably the one in which a journalist, Godfrey Winn, was taken. Certainly Godfrey Winn gives an account of his trip with 'Ginger' Bailey and mentioned him in the magazine *Woman*! 'Ginger' Bailey subsequently flew with No.48 Squadron as a Flying Officer, was twice decorated (DFC and DFM) and with the final rank of squadron leader.

S/Ldr Bill Kearney led a flight to Bergen in Hudson T9284 on 14 October. Three quarters of an hour after taking off the flight was shadowed by an enemy aircraft to the Norwegian coast. As Kearney was unable to lose the shadower, he turned his formation towards Haugesund and made another change of course at 1010hrs. The recce was continued to Utsire before returning to base at 1230hrs. P/O Weaber was airborne the same day at 1332hrs in N7257. On sighting an He 115 Weaber attacked from up sun but without result. He continued his patrol and at 1530hrs attacked another He 115. His rear gunner was killed but it was thought that the enemy gunner was also killed.

The first recorded successful attack on a German U boat by an aircraft of No.18 Group was on 25 October 1940. Three Hudsons of 233 Squadron were credited – P5156, T9365 and T9284 captained by P/O Maudsley, P/O Winnicott and P/O Walsh respectively. They were airborne at 0915hrs

Above: A 206 Sqdn crew at Benbecula in the Hebrides with T-VX in the background.

and the formation was 10 miles from Stavanger at 1125hrs flying at 6000ft in good visibility They flew southward and at 1131hrs set course for base. Four minutes later a surfaced U boat was sighted and they attacked separately with Maudsley, diving down to 500ft, releasing ten 100lb bombs. One direct hit was claimed in a straddle. The U boat opened fire with cannon and machine-guns and P5156 had two petrol tanks holed and its elevator made u/s, for Maudsley to return to base using trimming tabs. Winnicott then attacked from 500ft, straddling the vessel. The bombs in the third Hudson T9284 failed to release.

The U boat was U-46 captained by KL E. Endrass and was only damaged. It was subsequently realised that the 100lb bombs were not lethal to U boats.

W/Cmdr E.C. Kidd assumed command of No.233 Squadron in May 1941 and on the twenty-eighth flew a notable sortie with S/Ldr Devey in N7218. They were airborne at 1455hrs to escort two destroyers at Slyne Point and at 1610hrs sighted one destroyer and then AA fire from a destroyer against an He 111 approaching from 6000ft. The Hudson climbed to attack and opened fire at 500 yards with full deflection and no hits seen. The He 111 turned and dived taking evasive action. The enemy rear gunner opened accurate fire at 1000 yards and a dogfight ensued until 1620hrs. During the affray the Hudson had scored many hits with its front guns at 400 yards range. The enemy climbed into cloud cover four minutes later and then a second He 111 was seen ahead at about 7000ft with the Hudson then at 6000ft. As ammunition in the front guns was exhausted the Hudson climbed to engage with the rear guns and closed to 200 yards for an attack. The enemy took evasive action with short plunging dives but the Hudson maintained contact and opened fire at fifty yards. The He 111 burst into flames and crashed into the sea at 1630hrs. Two of the enemy crew had managed to bale out and the Hudson set course for base with ammunition exhausted.

The Channel Dash

Hitler expected the British to invade Norway and wished also to avoid the risk of his warships *Scharnhorst, Gneisenau* and *Prinz Eugen* from being attacked while in Brest, At a meeting with Admiral Raeder on 29 December 1941, Hitler demanded that the ships should sail to Germany from Brest at night under Operation *Cerberus*. The sailing was planned for 1930hrs on 11 February 1942.[27]

The British Admiralty issued an appreciation which anticipated with remarkable accuracy Hitler's intention with the three major warships sailing up the English Channel screened by ten destroyers and covered by twenty fighters. The Admiralty was wrong in expecting the ships to negotiate the Dover Straits during darkness and to counter the move Operation *Fuller* was planned which involved Bomber, Coastal and Fighter Commands of the RAF in addition to the Royal Navy. Air Chief Marshal Sir Philip Joubert of Coastal Command anticipated the breakout from Brest to be between 10 and 15 February and Hudsons were detailed for patrols off Brest. The Navy provided a lone submarine HMS *Sealion* for a similar mission.[28]

No.224 Squadron was based at St Eval with Hudsons in February and on the eleventh P/O H. Jenkins captained QX-G AM781 on a patrol from 0351 to 0804hrs. He made one radar contact but presumed it to be from British forces. F/Sgt Bennett followed in the same Hudson from 1845 to 2251hrs. At 2000hrs in position 48°55′N 03°40′W he suffered flak apparently from a ship a mile away. His radar became u/s at 2055hrs and the Hudson was recalled.

F/Lt Wilson was on patrol from 1827 to 2030hrs in QX-W AM565. A Ju 88 was intercepted at 0200hrs in position 48°14′N 05°46′W, Wilson took evasive action and his radar became u/s at 1920hrs. Although the early marks of radar or ASV as they were known, were used by aircrews with reserve, it appears possible that radar in the aircraft might well have suffered jamming as occurred for the ground stations. The last patrol on the eleventh by 224 Squadron was flown by S/Ldr Bartlett in V9092. He was aware of an orange light astern of his Hudson in position 48°25′N 05°25′W and took evasive action.

The German naval forces sailed from Brest at 2245hrs commanded by Admiral Ciliax but it was 1042hrs before they were sighted by Spitfires. Six destroyers off Harwich were at 1156hrs ordered to attack. Lt/Cmdr Esmonde of No.625 Squadron FAA led six Swordfish armed with torpedoes and escorted by ten Spitfires. All the Swordfish were lost and there were just five survivors. Esmonde was posthumously awarded the VC.

The main effort by Coastal Command was intended to be by torpedo-bombers but with Hudsons from 500 and 407 Squadrons attracting the flak with diversionary bombing. No.500 Squadron had five Hudsons captained by F/Lt Mackenzie, P/O Ensor, F/Lt Ensor, Sgt Frewen and S/Ldr Paterson airborne at 1335hrs on 12 February for an attack on the *Scharnhorst* and *Gneisenau*. On arriving at Manston they circled but as no fighter escort appeared they returned to Bircham Newton arriving at 1645hrs.[29]

No.407(RCAF) Squadron had received reports of twenty-five to thirty ships with five escorts of large sloops or destroyers and with the force including three battleships (*sic*). Their Hudsons flew down to Manston from North Coates; two flights were formed, one led by S/Ldr Anderson, the other by F/O Cowperthwaite whose flight included one from No.59 Squadron. All were airborne by 1330hrs on the twelfth. P/O Race in RR-S reported weather conditions as very bad but he thought the formation had flown over the main target where bombs were released from 900 to 1000ft. There appears little doubt that Hudsons from 407 broke through the screen of E-boats, R-boats and destroyers, itself no mean achievement and from a 407 Squadron pilot, Kim Abbott's account, Anderson and Cowperthwaite may have attacked the heavy cruiser *Prinz Eugen*. After studying the records of many squadrons, for this author, two names stand out – Anderson and Cowperthwaite of 407 Squadron. In this their final sortie, their courage and determination was no less

References
23. WSC II/52 24. SWR I/219–227, 603; RAF I/130; WSC II/52, 83, 83-103
25. RAF I/156. 26. WSC II/103 27. SWR II/149; WSC IV/98
28. RAF I/363 29. ORB Air-27-1942

NO, 224 SQUADRON, "MAYFLY" as from 0001hrs to 2359 hrs, WEDNESDAY 11.2.42.

A/C LETER ORER & NUMBER.	OFF.	CAPTAIN.	NAVIGATOR.	WOP/AG.	WOP/AG.	4 DCs, 2,4,6,10. 3 Flares,1,3, 5.
			EFFECTIVE CREWS.			
J AM641 X	1.S.	P/O Jenkins	P/O Phillipps *Harriott*	F/O Quas	Sgt Bell	Sgt Morriss
G AM781 ≠ 2.		S/L Lynn	Sgt White (O)	Sgt Blackwell	Sgt Woods	
W AE643	3.	Sgt Harvey	Sgt Potter	Sgt Rose	Sgt Went	Sgt Briggs
X AM686 X	4.	F/S Bennett *Hago Palink*	Sgt Wilson	Sgt Cornfield	Sgt Barham	
F AM625	5.	P/O M-Smith	Sgt Simpson (O)	Sgt Clent	Sgt Flavell	Sgt Derks
E AM631 X	6.	F/O Arden	F/S Bent	F/S Purcell	Sgt Clifford	Sgt Steen
M AM667 Q AE	7.	F/O Maylam *1st Stopper*	Sgt Ballard	Sgt Cooke C	Sgt Foster	Sgt Cliffe
Q AE639 X	8.S.	F/L Wilson	Sgt Thomas G (O)	F/S Eden	Sgt Francis	
X	9.S.	F/L Carmichael *3rd stopper*	P/O Gibb	Sgt Toone	Sgt Feast	Sgt Bramwell
S/B Till 1300 hrs U AM729		P/O Carswell	Sgt Willis (O)	Sgt Bristow	Sgt Wright	Sgt Cordes
S/B 1200-0100 hrs D AM827 X		F/S James	Sgt Sayer	Sgt Clafton	Sgt Woode	F/S Johnston

X *2nd Stopper 2220 - 0425*

TRAINING & SPARE :-	S/L Bartlett	Sgt McAvoy (O)	Sgt West	Sgt Thomas W
DESPATCHING CREW;;-	P/O Manley	F/S Moore	Sgt Alderton	Sgt Chapman

NON-EFFECTIVE CREWS.

DAY OFF ;-	F/O Beckingham	F/S Busbridge	Sgt Dunnett	F/S Edgar	Sgt Hendrie
	P/O Knowles	P/O Graham	Sgt Page	Sgt Hunter	Sgt Bell G
DETACHED :-	P/O Graham	F/S Marriott	Sgt Cooke R	Sgt Thompson	

LEAVE TILL 23.2.;-	P/O Stewart	P/O Sleep	Sgt McIntosh	Sgt Baker	Sgt Smith F
	F/S Crowe	Sgt Antoncich	Sgt Martin	Sgt Hickman	Sgt Douglas
	F/O Everest	P/O Garland	Sgt Morley	Sgt Fisher	Sgt Bayley
	F/O Pearl	P/O Seal	F/S Liley	Sgt Cole	
	F/O Prime	F/S Liddington	Sgt Taylor	Sgt Cross	Sgt Wallis
	Sgt Willerton	Sgt Stow	Sgt Goadby	Sgt Scott	Sgt Horsey

NOT AVAILABLE;- Sgt Williams Sgt Perry Sgt Mattison Sgt Cooper (Sick) P/O Fisher (S/O

(a) Other S Op A/C ;- A MKIII LR K awaiting air test (N O MKIII LR) (S Detached Non-Dp)
(b) Other U/S Op A/C with reason ;- X Z 60 hr)
SQUADRON DUTY OFFICER ;- P/O Manley (Phone 59)
"A" FLIGHT STAND CREWS N/S PHONE 70 ;- Sgt Bussey Kelly Cook Holloway Dickie Haddon
Attenbrough Ewan Boys.
"B" FLIGHT STAND CREWS N/S PHONE 88 ;- Sgt Syme Bloomfield Anderson Plews Arthur Grayson
Dalzell Lodge Edgar Alexander

DUTY DRIVERS AS DETAILED BY M.T. NCO.

A.C.P.;- F/S Moore

DUTY ARMOURERS ;- Sgt Brierley Barr Back
                   Pearson, Wright
DUTY SGT "BOMA" (TIELINE) Sgt Hustler

DUTY DEFENCE SECTIONS, "A" & "B" FLIGHTS AS ABOVE FOR STAND CREWS N/S.

[signature] P/c

Wing Commander, Commanding.
No, 224 Squadron, R.A.F.

Above: 224 Squadron's flying detail dated 11 February 1942 which coincided with the 'Channel Dash' of the battle-cruisers Scharnhorst *and* Gneisenau *with the cruiser* Prinz Eugen.

than that of the VC – Lt/Cmdr Esmonde.[30]

At 1431 hrs the *Scharnhorst* struck a mine but was able to continue at 25 knots; at 1955hrs *Gneisenau* was mined and at 2134hrs *Scharnhorst* struck another mine but reached Wilhelmshaven on the thirteenth; *Gneisenau* and *Prinz Eugen* were at Brunsbuttel on the thirteenth.

The Royal Navy's Home Fleet was at Scapa Flow and it had no intention of risking major units in the confines of the Channel. The many aircraft deployed by the RAF had been ill-prepared and briefed and the weather was not conducive to bombing heavily escorted ships.

The summing-up for the German Naval Staff was 'a tactical victory but a strategic defeat'. For Winston Churchill, the North Atlantic naval problem had been simplified.[31]

Thousand Bomber Raid on Bremen

On the night of 25/26 June 1942 a raid was laid on by Bomber Command to Bremen. Included in the operation *Millennium II* were twenty Wellingtons and eighty-two Hudsons from Coastal Command. The latter were intended to make diversionary attacks on the Deschimag yards involved with the production of U boats. Hudson squadrons included Nos 59, 206, 224, 407 and some from the Hudson OTUs.

The CO of 59 Squadron at that time, W/Cmdr Geoffrey Bartlett records:

Last week of June unusual number of Hudsons appeared at North Coates, when No.206 from RAF Aldergrove and No.224 arrived from Tiree. Ops room crammed when secret briefings for aircrew . . . temporarily under Bomber Command . . . Coastal Command produced ops squadrons of Hudsons and Wellingtons but also crews from OTU captained by experienced instructors. Bomber Command 960 aircraft; Coastal 102; Army Co-op five; total 1067.

At 2300hrs on 25 June I had the doubtful privilege of leading 12 of No.59's Hudsons off into the dark sky towards the city of Bremen. Our target was the Deschimag U boat building yards, upon which each of us hoped to drop a load of 1000lb of bombs. Twelve aircraft of No.206 followed us into the air, and 224's twelve were timed to take off at 2310hrs.

However, all of No.59's aircraft got home unharmed. No.206 were not so lucky, losing two aircraft, one in which the CO, W/Cmdr Cooke, was flying as passenger. Some of 224 were battle-damaged, and my friend Derek Hodgkinson, DFC, ex-220, was captain of a Silloth crew which took off with others from RAF Thornaby . . . shot down on return trip by a night-fighter.

The Canadian squadron, No.407, appear to have had their account of the raid written by the adjutant F/Lt Whalley who flew as a passenger with P/O O'Connell. Eleven crews were detailed and '. . . with disappointment seen on the faces of those . . . to stay at home.' On being told the target was Bremen there were 'shouts of glee'. Six of 407's Hudsons reached Bremen but it was impossible to see what damage was caused due to cloud, apart from one crew which lost height through a break in the cloud. Some were unable to reach the target due to lack of fuel; two were attacked by fighters, and one of these believed one fighter was damaged by the Hudson's fire. One of 407's captains, Cameron Taylor, recorded:

. . . helluva flap – oxygen equipment to be placed in service – most a/c it is u/s as it is never used on our low level operations. At 1845hrs all crews briefed in station cinema – target BREMEN in conjunction with Bomber Command – our specific target is to be the large naval shipyards. Further briefing at 2215hrs. Airborne 2320 – oxygen on at 8000ft doesn't work – climbed to 13,000ft. S/c Bremen – dodging heavy flak round Wilhelmshaven – over Bremen at 0151hrs dropped bombs – three immense fires burning – sky full of flak – can't get over it so must dodge round it – returned to base *very* short of fuel – landed at 0500/June 26. All our a/c returned but five or six did not reach the target because of shortage of fuel. Most a/c including 'R' had some flak damage.

No.407 were 'elated' and 'hoped that further opportunities to bomb Germany will occur.'

The two Hudson Coastal OTUs Nos 1 and 6 provided aircraft and crews and Terry Andrew from No.6 at Thornaby gives this account:

I flew on Hudson T9407 with P/O H.B. Hunt, DFC as captain and in company over the North Sea with a Halifax at our bombing height of 12,000ft. Shortly after crossing the enemy coast near Emden two Me 110 night-fighters were seen and soon our friendly Halifax was seen to explode in mid-air; as the fighters were still around Hunt took evasive action and we saw them no more. Over Bremen heavy flak was encountered but having dropped our bombs we had a fairly uneventful flight home descending out of Germany to a height more suited to Coastal Command crews. We had a one-sided skirmish with a flakship off the Frisian Islands and then saw flares from a dinghy which could have been the survivors of the aircraft flown by the Flight Commander of No.1 C OTU [F/Lt D. Hodgkinson], the only aircraft missing from the combined force of sixty from Thornaby. My friend F/Sgt Wally Cavett flew with F/O Blakeley and they were alarmed to find themselves coned by searchlights and the target of heavy flak over a very large city; they had bombed Hamburg alone by mistake and surprisingly got away with it.[32]

No.224 Squadron, then based on Tiree in the Inner Hebrides, detached eleven of their Hudsons to North Coates and they were all airborne from there between 2310hrs and 2330hrs on 25 June with Bremen as the target. They were led by W/Cmdr W.H. 'Bill' Kearney in QX-O V9090. He plotted his position by flak from Cuxhaven and Wilhelmshaven to release bombs from 10,000ft on Bremen. He saw clearly the decoys and reported a heavy AA barrage.

F/O David Sleep flying at 8000ft was attacked by two Me 110s with cannon fire and dived to cloud cover at 6000ft. On sighting another fighter over Borkum he again dived for cloud cover. His two 250lb and seven 100lb bombs were released through a gap in the clouds.

Hudson AM677 flown by F/O Mervyn-Smith was picked up by searchlight and a night-fighter but he saw no gunfire. Shrapnel from a heavy shell passed right through the nose of S/Ldr Mirylees' Hudson but with no casualties. F/O Jenkins in AM827 saw an aircraft shot down over Bremerhaven and suffered AA from four flak ships off the Frisian Islands.

References
30. KA p.130   31. SWR II/159; WSC IV/100   32. Letter to author

Above: Reports in the Daily Mail *and* Sunday Times *of the 1000 bomber raid on Bremen in June 1942 in which the Coastal Command Hudson squadrons took part.*

AE643's captain, F/Lt Everest, after releasing his bombs saw three other aircraft shot down.

F/Sgt Williams had engine trouble with AM700 when over Wesermunde but returned safely at 0432hrs. A heavy AA burst below AM779 flown by F/Sgt Willerton blew one side gun into the aircraft and the other side gun out. The bombs released by P/O Dennis Busbridge in AM714 were seen to burst among warehouses causing fires although he suffered some AA. Busbridge in AM714 was the last of 224's captains to return, landing at Thornaby after a trip of almost six-and-a-half hours. Post-war the author was able to meet again four of 224's captains who had been in this Bremen raid: S/Ldr Sleep, W/Cmdr Kearney, Capt. Dennis Busbridge and W/Cmdr Geoffrey Bartlett who had led No.59 Squadron.

Appendix

1,000 Bomber Raid (Millenium II)   BREMEN 26th. June, 1942.

59 SQUADRON FLYING PROGRAMME.

PERIOD: FROM 12.00 HOURS ON 25.6.42 UNTIL 12.00 HOURS ON 26.6.42.

AVAILABLE AIRCRAFT AND CREWS.

A/C.	CREW.		FLT.	LOAD.	DUTY.
B.	S/LDR.EVANS.(DFC)	P/O.SMITH.	"A"	4 x 250 LB. A.S. 3 SECS. DELAY. CAMERAS.	AVAILABLE OPS.
	P/O.FOX.	SGT.GOAD.			
A.	F/O.OSBORN.	P/O.LAFORME.	"A"	10 x 100 LB. A.S. 3 SECS. DELAY. CAMERAS.	AVAILABLE OPS.
	SGT.GOODMAN.	SGT.MYERS.			
F.	P/O.WRIGHT.	SGT.MCCARTNEY.	"A"	DITTO.	AVAILABLE OPS.
	SGT.LIVINGSTON.	SGT.SPRIGGS.			
D.	F/SGT.DUPLOOY.	SGT.BLACK.	"A"	DITTO.	AVAILABLE OPS.
	SGT.COATES.	F/SGT.MACDONALD R.V.			
C.	F/SGT.N.NIERVIS.	F/SGT.BLAKEY.	"A"	DITTO.	AVAILABLE OPS.
	SGT.MCEWEN.	SGT.BARRY.			
H.	W/CDR.BARTLETT.	P/O.COLE.	"B".	DITTO.	AVAILABLE OPS.
	P/O.EVANS.	SGT.CLARKE.			
X.	S/LDR.DUNKERLEY.	P/O.LONGMUIR.	"B"	4 x 250 LB. A.S. 3 SECS. DELAY. CAMERAS.	AVAILABLE OPS.
	P/O.PENNYCUICK.	F/SGT.DRABBLE.			
P.	P/O.LUCKWELL.	P/O.WECKER.	"B"	10 x 100 LB. A.S. 3 SECS. DELAY. CAMERAS.	AVAILABLE OPS.
	SGT.GAMBLE.	SGT.GRAYSON.			
Y.	P/O.MORAN.	P/O.STEVENSON.	"B"	DITTO.	AVAILABLE OPS.
	SGT.PEEK.	F/SGT.STEPHENS.			
T.	P/O.NEILSON.	SGT.MENZIES.	"B"	DITTO.	AVAILABLE OPS.
	SGT.WHITNEY.	SGT.TUCKWOOD.			
R.	P/O.MOODY.	SGT.SPELLING.	"B"	DITTO.	AVAILABLE OPS.
	F/SGT.BRADLEY.	F/SGT.BRUNDELL.			
V.	SGT.HALL.	SGT.JOHNS.	"A"	4 x 250 LB. A.S. 3 SECS. DELAY. CAMERAS.	AVAILABLE OPS.
	SGT.STALKER.	SGT.LUDLAM.			

CREWS NOT DETAILED FOR OPERATIONS.

"A" FLIGHT.	"B" FLIGHT.
P/O.FORSWICK AND CREW.	P/O.WEBB AND CREW. (TRAINING)
SGT.SOAME AND CREW (LESS OBSERVER) (TRAINING)	P/O.HOPWOOD AND CREW. (TRAINING)

CREWS ON LEAVE AND PASS.

"A" FLIGHT.	"B" FLIGHT.
PASS :-	LEAVE:-
F/LT.TILLER AND CREW.	P/O.YOUNG AND CREW.
P/O.KELVIN AND CREW.	PASS:-
P/O.ALLEN AND CREW.	F/LT.COLLIE AND CREW.
F/SGT.LYNCH AND CREW.	P/O.BARSON AND CREW.
	P/O.CHARLTON AND CREW.
	SICK :- SGT.TOMPSON.

AIRCRAFT STATE.

SERVICEABLE.		UNSERVICEABLE.	
"A" FLIGHT.	"B" FLIGHT.	"A" FLIGHT.	"B" FLIGHT.
A. B. C. D.	P. R. T. V.	E.	NIL.
F. H.	X. Y.		

SQUADRON DUTY OFFICER AND DESPATCHING OFFICER.......................... P/O. WEBB.
OFFICER I/C NIGHT FLYING.. 415 SQUADRON.
AERODROME CONTROL PILOT, NORTH COATES..................................... P/O. LIPMAN.
AERODROME CONTROL PILOT, DONNA NOOK....................................... 415 SQUADRON.
SQUADRON AIRCREW DUTY N.C.O... SGT. BAMBRIDGE.

(SIGNED) G.C.C.BARTLETT,

Above: No.59 Squadron's flying detail for the Bremen raid dated 25/26 June 1942. They were led by their CO W/Cmdr Geoffrey Bartlett.

Above: A composite illustration of a 206 Sqdn Hudson B-VX at Bircham Newton.

No.206 Squadron based at Aldergrove detached twelve Hudsons to North Coates only to be ordered to Donna Nook in preparation for the raid. They were airborne from 2310hrs on the twenty-fifth in four formations of three led by S/Ldr C.N. Crook, S/Ldr R.C. Patrick, DFC, F/Lt W. Roxburgh and F/O F.S. Wills.

Due to cloud they reported it impossible to locate the Deschimag U boat yards and dropped their bombs in the vicinity of large fires. None were engaged with night-fighters although several were seen. However, No.206 Squadron lost two Hudsons captained by A/S/Ldr Crook and Sgt Wright. On or about 3 July the bodies of A/S/Ldr Crook and his gunner F/Sgt Hubbard were taken from the North Sea by the Germans.

Published reports differ concerning the total number of aircraft on this raid but forty-eight appears as the number of aircraft lost, including four Hudsons from Coastal Command.

The naval historian, Capt. Roskill, states heavy bombing attacks on German naval yards had little effect and that it was not until April 1944 that a completed U boat was destroyed in one of the yards.[33] Winston Churchill states that while in 1942 night bombing was becoming more accurate, war production in Germany was not reduced.[34] The overall losses of approx five per cent including some inexperienced crews with probably aircraft of debatable serviceability, may be compared with Coastal Command's losses on shipping strikes which ranged up to fifty-four per cent for numbers 407 and 404 Squadrons (the latter with heavily armed Beaufighters).

References
33. SWR II/353
34. WSC V/457; JT 490; MM 280; RAF II/138; RCAF III597; RAAF III/315

Chapter 3
Shipping Strikes

In 1939 the prime duty of Coastal Command over the North Sea was reconnaissance to cover the possible breakout of German warships and the Command's aircraft were restricted in what they might attack. By October 1940, and following the German occupation of Norway, Denmark and The Netherlands, the RAF was permitted to sink on sight shipping in certain areas.[1] Prior to that time however, Hudsons of Nos 233, 220, 224 and 206 Squadrons had sunk or damaged merchant ships from Norway to the Dutch coast.

By mid-1941 restrictions on bombing enemy-controlled merchant shipping were virtually removed and from July to September No.2 Group Bomber Command aircraft were used. Their high losses resulted in them being withdrawn in November although Hudsons of Nos 16 and 18 Groups Coastal Command continued.[2]

Following the German invasion of Russia and as part of the effort to relieve pressure on that new ally, Coastal Command developed an anti-shipping offensive at the end of June.[3] To monitor results, the Air Ministry set up an Anti-Shipping Operations Assessment Committee in July. No.18 Group aircraft became responsible for strikes in the northern North Sea, No.16 Group the southern North Sea to the Norwegian coast, and No.19 Group the Bay of Biscay.[4] In practice two main areas applied; one off the south Norwegian coast, the other off The Netherlands. Both Germany and Britain were ever mindful of the prime traffic from Norway to Germany and Rotterdam of high grade Swedish ore via Narvik. Attacks by Hudsons on enemy shipping had begun with success in April 1940 and continued until 1943, although other types of aircraft such as Beaufighters carried on until the end of the war.

The Hudsons employed in shipping strikes were typically armed with two fixed .303 Brownings operated by the pilot, two Brownings in the turret, and in later marks, a ventral gun position. Possibly also, two VGOs with pans for ammunition available for port and starboard hatches. Bomb loads were typically four 250lb or ten 100lb bombs. To obtain any degree of accuracy many flew at literally mast height and with high casualty rates as a result with as much as fifty-four per cent losses in a strike by 407 Squadron. The risk of air attacks on their shipping resulted in Germany diverting much effort to protect them and in addition to heavily armed escorts, the merchant ships were armed.

In July 1942 losses of RAF aircraft attributed to mast height bombing attacks resulted in Air Chief Marshal Sir Philip Joubert ordering attacks to be made from medium height; this resulted in fewer sinkings.[5]

Norge Strikes

The first success recorded by Coastal Command was damaging *Theodor* a merchant vessel of 1939 tons in Grimstad fjord on 29 April 1940 by 233 Squadron. On that date three Hudsons from 233 were airborne captained by F/Lt Butler, F/O Edwards and F/Lt Cooper but it is not clear who bombed the ship. This was followed by 220 Squadron with P/O Joualt in NR-D sinking a fishing vessel the *Kristine* off the Danish coast on 8 July.

No.233 gained another success on 25 July by Hudson N7326 captained by F/O Fuller. While on a coastal recce from Utsire to Lister at 1620hrs, Fuller sighted a merchant vessel heading north. He attacked by diving from 1400ft to 800ft releasing five 100lb GP bombs which fell five yards from the vessel. He made no claim but a 3604-ton ship, *William Blumer*, is given as damaged.[6]

No.233's sister squadron, No.224 was also on Norge recces and on 30 July F/O R.G. Lynn was airborne from Leuchars at 1120hrs and two-and-a-half-hours later attacked a merchantman in Bommel fjord with seven 100lb bombs apparently damaging *Anna Sofie* of 3100 tons.[7]

F/Lt A. 'Bertie' Leach of 224 Squadron was airborne in N7252 at 1430hrs on 27 December and on crossing the Norge coast at 1648hrs sighted a merchant vessel in Egersund fjord. In a diving attack he released four 100lb bombs which overshot but in a second run scored three bomb hits and the ship was seen to rock from an explosion. Credited as sunk was *Arfinn Jarl* of 1159 tons.[8]

I'd been sent on a *Stand* (Stavanger to Kristiansand) patrol, which was one of three simultaneous patrols covering the Norwegian coast from Ålesund in the north to Kristiansand in the south-east, designed to get information on all shipping, particularly iron ore ships, moving around the Norwegian coast to the Baltic ports via the Skagerrak and Kattegat.

Our briefing was to report all shipping and to attack where possible. We left Leuchars at 0935hrs for the 360-mile crossing to Stavanger, making our landfall about two-and-a-quarter hours later. It was a bright clear day.

Turning to starboard to begin our patrol at 4000ft, we spotted a large ship with several flak ships and went into a diving-bombing attack releasing four 250lb bombs from 800ft. The flak was intense but the ship was straddled with a near miss.

Back on patrol, I spotted two small dots, enemy aircraft

References
1. RAF I/352   2. SWR I/506   3. RAF I/354   4. SWR I/503   5. RAF II/95
6. CCWR p.24   7. CCWR p.24   8. CCWR p.24

approaching from Sola aerodrome, near Stavanger. Our defensive armament was a pair of .303 Brownings in front, and a pair of .303 Brownings in the turret. The turret guns had a wide arc of fire but cut out automatically as they swung towards the two rudders. The Germans knew this, and when attacking tried to keep the tailplane between themselves and the turret.

I felt we would be safer near the water, to avoid being attacked from below where the Hudson was very vulnerable. I opened the throttles wide, locked them there, and with props in fully fine pitch, dived for the sea.

On flattening out, I looked around; there were the two Me 110s, one on the starboard quarter, one on the port quarter and looking very business-like. The one on the left attacked first, and as he came in, I threw the Hudson into a very tight turn to the left towards the 110, at the same time lifting the aircraft up a few feet. The sea beneath absolutely boiled with shells and bullet strikes. The Me 110's front armament was two 20mm cannon and six machine-guns! As we swung in towards him he did a very tight left-hand turn away, and then the other 110 came in to attack from the starboard quarter, and trying to keep the Hudson's tailplane between himself and the rear turret. My response was to throw the Hudson into a vertical bank and turn to the right to get in towards his attack.

Again the sea boiled with shells and bullet strikes, and the Me 110 broke away to the right. The whole sequence was then repeated. On the second attack from the right rear Me 110, an armour-piercing bullet came up through the aircraft and hit me in the shoulder, knocking me against the windscreen. Had I not been leaning over the the left trying to keep an eye on the left-hand Me 110, the bullet would almost certainly have gone through my spine.

The action seemed to last half-an-hour but was probably less. The Me 110s got numerous strikes on the Hudson. About two square feet of the turret was blown off. The noise of cannon shells exploding in the aircraft was terrific. I always recall looking back into the smoke-filled Hudson and seeing the two homing pigeons crowding in the bottom of their baskets and looking browned-off!

After several attacks, my rear gunner, Sgt Eardley, who was miraculously uninjured, set the starboard engine of one of the fighters on fire, and he high-tailed it back to Norway. It was just about this time that the other 110 must have run out of front gun ammunition, for he decided to have a go with one free-firing gun which the Me 110 carried at the back of the crew's conservatory. He came across very close to port and I could see the gunner's face very clearly, as he fired at us from very close range. It didn't need much manoeuvering to get him in the front gun sights and one short burst with the two front Brownings got him in the face. The burst must have blown his head off. It certainly smashed the end of the conservatory and put the gun completely out of action.

All this time the engines had been going flat out. We must have been doing about 250mph and were now approaching some cloud. I pulled the aircraft up into a steep climb, and at 2000ft we were enveloped in the comforting folds of the cloud. We set course for Leuchars and checked on damage sustained. Our engines and fuel tanks appeared undamaged. When we settled down I felt inside my tunic with my left hand; all appeared well until I withdrew it to find it red with blood up to the wrist. F/O Flowers, the second pilot who navigated for this trip was on his first operational sortie. He took over the controls; I went back and the rear gunner gave me a shot of morphine from our first-aid kit.

Back at Leuchars, snow was piled high on each side of the

Above: Hudson FH426 with three of its crew captained by S/Ldr Phil Evans of 59 Sqdn on 6.8.42, after suffering AA fire off the Dutch coast.

Above: V-TR of 59 Sqdn was one of a number of Hudson units engaged o shipping strikes off the Dutch coast.

Below: Three Canadians with a 407 (RCAF) Hudson. This illustrates the on the arc of fire from the turret guns due to the tail assembly of the Hud

runway but Flowers made a good belly-landing as the hydraulics had been shot up. We skidded along the icy runway into thick snow.[9]

'Bertie' Leach became CFI at No.6 COTU and later commanded No.48 and also No.206 Squadrons, retiring to South Africa as W/Cmdr A. de V. Leach, DFC.

One of the most successful squadrons was No.220 operating around the Norwegian coast. On 5 July 1941 four of their Hudsons were airborne including N7281 captained by P/O Basil Ainsworth who flew north from Stavanger along the coast. At 1625hrs he attacked a ship from astern with two 250lb bombs diving from 2000ft to 800ft. They undershot but in a second attack scored a direct hit. Clouds of steam, smoke and debris arose and the vessel appeared to be settling by the stern. It appears that Ainsworth could claim sinking the *Advance* of 881 tons.[10]

Airborne from Sumburgh at 1310hrs on that day was P/O Jameson detailed for a 'Trost' patrol. After flying for three hours he saw several merchant vessels. At 1715hrs he attacked a merchantman by diving from cloud at 2000ft to 200ft releasing three 250lb bombs with eleven seconds delay. Two burst on the stern of the ship and it was seen to be badly damaged.

P/O Tarrant, while on a patrol from Stavanger to Bergen on 24 September, attacked a tanker sailing in convoy with two merchantmen and three escort vessels together with a flak ship. He estimated two bomb hits and from Coastal Command's record he sank *Tiger* of 3941 tons.[11]

A strike by 220 Squadron was led by the CO, W/Cmdr Wright, against Ålesund on on 9 October with nine Hudsons airborne from Wick at 1853hrs.

S/Ldr Barron and P/O Hunt bombed the herring oil factory on the quayside, P/O Tate bombed a large warehouse, Sgt Heppell and W/Cmdr Wright attacked merchant ships in the harbour despite heavy flak. F/Sgt Smith bombed an escort vessel in a harbour south of Kristiansund before dropping incendiaries on a W/T station south of the town.

These captains were uncertain of their results but Sgt Ramsey claimed a hit on a 2000-ton merchant vessel first after releasing four 250lb bombs followed by incendiaries. This raid was a precursor of one of the most successful strikes to be achieved and by 220 Squadron. [*Ibid*]

P/O Holland was airborne from Wick in Hudson P/220 on 11 October 1941 to patrol the Stavanger-Bergen coastline. His report was brief: 'Two direct hits on M.V. 4000-ton in Sogne fjord.'

P/O Tate in A/220 on the thirteenth attacked a naval vessel with bombs and machine-guns in Hjelte fjord. Two violent explosions were seen amidships and all the vessel's guns were silenced. Credited to 220 Squadron on the thirteenth was the 480-ton MV *Brategg*.[12]

Hudson B/220 captained by F/Lt Simpson who was on a similar patrol shortly after Tate, failed to return.

Ålesund Strike by No.220 Squadron

On the night of 29 October 1941 No.220 Squadron made one of the most successful shipping strikes by Hudson aircraft. It was led by the CO W/Cmdr Wright who, quite exceptionally

had the AOC, Air Vice-Marshal Marix as passenger. Their nine aircraft were all airborne just after 1600hrs. W/Cmdr Wright attacked a 2000-ton MV in Ålesund harbour despite intensive flak. There was smoke and fire and the ship was reported as sinking. Sgt Houghton attacked another MV in Nord fjord and there were violent explosions with sections of deck and superstructure thrown into the air. Two ships moored along the shore were attacked by F/O Holland, while F/O Tarrant scored a hit on a 2000-ton MV before attacking transport and shore installations. Two other captains who attacked shore installations were P/O Tate and Sgt Heppell.

F/O Birchall silenced the guns of an escort vessel north of Ålesund, while S/Ldr Barron saw a ship in Ålesund harbour sink following his attack. Sgt Hall bombed two MVs one of which was already on fire and saw it sink. All the Hudsons returned to base with Sgt Hall, the last, arriving at 2300hrs.

There were two wartime posters of Coastal Command Hudsons; one of those depicted this raid. Credited as sunk by 220 in this operation were *Barcelona* 3101 tons; as damaged, *Vesla* 1108 tons and *Swanefjell* 1371 tons although a Norwegian account gives only *Barcelona* and *Vesla*.[13] Additionally it is understood another ship *Archimede* was sunk.

Four of 220's Hudsons were detailed to patrol the Stavanger-Bergen coast on 2 November with all airborne by 1625hrs. Sgt Heppell bombed a radio or power station and a small fire was seen. Sgt Ramsey and Sgt Gamble bombed a fish oil factory on Florø island; while Sgt Hall made a low level attack on a merchant vessel in a fjord with 250lb SAP bombs and incendiaries. Credited to 220 Squadron as damaged was *Hornelen* of 257 tons.[14]

On 28 November F/Sgt Ramsey was airborne at 1322hrs detailed for a strike. His report is brief: 'MV sunk near Stavanger – ablaze from stem to stern as though filled with oil and then sunk within 2 mins.'

He was the only one from 220 on a strike that day and credited with the 142-ton *Vindafjord* as sunk. V/220 captained by F/O Tate failed to return from a patrol.[15]

Two from 220 Squadron claimed hits on merchant ships on 4 December; they were F/Sgt Sanderson on a 'S. Bert' patrol and F/O Tarrant on a shipping strike. Sanderson claimed a hit on a 2500-ton vessel and F/O Tarrant claimed setting a ship on fire near Ålesund. Tarrant was wounded by flak, the port engine was damaged but the second pilot, P/O Haggas brought the Hudson back to Sumburgh on one engine. Credited as sunk was the 499-ton *Vestri*.[16]

On 9 December 220 undertook just one sortie; F/Sgt Stone was airborne at 1220hrs for a 'Vaaro' patrol. He sighted a merchant vessel with four escorts but attacked and estimated three, if not four hits on the merchantman. From the Command's record the ship was *Bjonn* of 5509 tons and sunk on that date.[17]

The same record gives another ship – the *Karmsund* of 287 tons – being damaged on 21 December by 220 Squadron. On

References
9. Letter to author 10. CCWR p.24 11. CCWR p.24 12. CCWR p.24
13. CCWR p.24; JOF & HG 14. CCWR p.24 15. CCWR p.24
16. CCWR p.24 17. CCWR p.24

Above: S/Ldr Cam. Taylor, DFC of 407(RCAF) Sqdn with two of his crew before Hudson E-RR FH361. Taylor was on the Bremen raid, on many shipping strikes, and later (when on Wellingtons) sank a U boat.

Above: P/O Larry O'Connell of 407(RCAF) Sqdn with his Hudson lacking a bomb door which he left on the mast of the ship he attacked.

the 22nd however, attacks were made on ships off Norway by Sgt Clark who claimed two hits on a vessel and resulting in a red glow forward of the ship's funnel. F/Sgt Carpenter bombed a ship which was followed by an explosion seen amidships. He had flown so low that the Hudson fouled the ship's mast.[18]

No.608 Squadron RAuxAF

No.608 Squadron based at Thornaby had detachments in Scotland before being posted to Wick in January 1942 with, as one of its Wop/AGs, Eric Robinson states: '. . . B flight going to Wick in December and A flight to Skitten . . . and joined up in early January and operated with 48 Squadron to Norway carrying out patrols down the Norwegian coasts on anti-shipping reconnaisance.'

On 15 October 1941 F/Lt Disney led a raid on Esbjerg docks in AM610 with P/O Hunter in AM642 and Sgt Kirwan in AE642. They were all airborne just before midnight and as Eric Robinson who flew with P/O Hunter recalls:

We approached the Danish coast at about 30ft slightly south of Esbjerg, turned north and came over the docks aiming for a troopship on which troops were lined . . . we were under orders not to machine-gun civilians and we could see the faces of civilians looking up at us as we went down the street adjacent to the docks, and windows of shops disappearing as our bullets ricocheted into the shop fronts. The bombs went, people were scattering and looking up. Some were in grey uniforms, obviously Germans and we turned west across the beach and headed for home. Guns opened up behind us and one could see the shells being lobbed seawards but falling

Below: A flight of Hudsons coded RR for 407(RCAF) Sqdn. No.407 was one of the most successful units on shipping strikes but suffered serious losses.

Above: No.407(RCAF) Sqdn on parade with their Hudsons in the background.

short. In the distance to the east one could see fighters climbing but we were down on the sea and going west . . . We landed and later heard that the attack had damaged the German troopship and several Germans were killed.[19]

From 608's records it can be seen that four 250lb bombs with eleven seconds delay had exploded on warehouses on the southern end of the docks and P/O Hunter's crew which had been unable to release bombs, had fired on searchlights and on a sound locator on Fanó Island. Sgt Kirwan's were released on the quayside causing two explosions.

In May 1942 No.608 Squadron was based at Wick and in addition to providing escorts to convoys was very active in strikes to Norway. On 2 May V/608 claimed a hit on a tanker in Ålesund harbour on releasing six 100lb bombs and Q/608 sighted three bombs bursting on the tanker. Hudson V/608 was shaken by the violent explosion which had resulted from its attack. H/608 attacked a merchant vessel north of Ålesund with two 250lb bombs and saw a fire on the target.

E/608 AM644 attacked two merchant vessels at the entrance to Nord fjord with ten 100lb bombs and saw smoke belching from the ships. This was on 4 May and on that same date Q/608 attacked two other merchantmen in Kristiansund harbour and estimated that both were hit. AM644 captained by F/O Tony Scholefield had as one of its Wop/AGs, Eric Robinson who gives this account:

We were turning on one leg when we saw flak and an aircraft caught in the searchlight. Tony said: 'There must be a ship there'. We turned north and saw two ships side by side in a fjord. We came down to fifty feet. The flak started, searchlights caught us and, firing from the beam gun, one could fire upwards at these guns which were firing down on us. It was like flying into a dark tunnel. We dropped our bombs and there was an explosion. There was a crash on our starboard bomb door right under my feet and we knew we'd been hit. Tony called for the searchlights to be put out as he was blinded and finding it difficult to find his way up the fjord. I fired my machine-gun at the searchlight as we moved towards it. We made our way up the fjord to make for the open sea and when clear heading westward examined the damage. We had a large hole in our starboard bomb door which was hanging down but Tony eventually landed at Wick safely. We didn't know at the time but since learned that one of the ships *Klaud Fritzen* of 2936 tons was sunk. Tony can justify claiming that.[20]

On 13 May F/Sgt Livingstone was airborne at 1933hrs in AE642 for a strike on Ålesund and attacked two merchant vessels outside the harbour. His bombs were seen to explode on the stern and amidships of a vessel with debris flying in all directions and with the ship left listing and smoke pouring from it. 2nd Lt Callaghan, an American serving with 608 Squadron bombed a 6000-ton ship which was aground off Vaagso island that same night scoring two hits and leaving the ship in flames. It appears likely that F/Sgt Livingstone could claim *Tampa* of 4694 tons listed by the Command as damaged by 608 Squadron.[21]

References
18. CCWR p.24   19. Letter to author   20. Letter to author
21. CCWR p.24

Three of 608's Hudsons were airborne at 1800hrs on 17 May and when off the Naze in southern Norway sighted an enemy cruiser with four or more destroyers. P/O Keeble in AM802 attacked the cruiser but saw two aircraft crash into the sea. P/O Scholefield flying AE642 was about to attack the ships when two Me 109 fighters appeared and in the combat which followed his aircraft was slightly damaged but several hits were claimed on one of the fighters.

For the following month of June 1942 No.608 was credited with damaging two ships on the second and third. P/O Thompson captained V9108 and was airborne at 0847hrs on the second. A merchant vessel with two escorts was sighted off Obrestad and Thompson attacked with nine 100lb bombs and believed that he had obtained eight hits. Black smoke was seen rising from the bridge structure amidships of the vessel. The *Dietrich Oldendorff* of 1876 tons is recorded as having been damaged.[22]

P/O Keeble was on a Vaaro patrol in AE642 the following morning and located a tanker with an escort north of Ålesund. There was flak from both ships and the Hudson's rudder and brakes were damaged but the ship was believed to have been hit and damage to *Worth* of 6256 tons is recorded for that date.[23]

No.608 Squadron remained operating from Wick on the Scottish mainland and Sumburgh in the Shetlands until August when it became one of the Hudson squadrons deployed from Gibraltar and North Africa in support of Operation *Torch*. [*Ibid*]

From 2 September 1941 when a crew of four was lost in Flekkefjord and where they were buried, to 22 April 1942, No.608 lost nineteen aircrew over Norway with four buried at Trondheim, six at Stavne and others commemorated at Runnymede.[24]

Strikes off The Netherlands

Although a number of types of aircraft were used in shipping strikes, during 1941 and 1942 much of the work was covered by the Hudsons. For operations off The Netherlands, aircraft of numbers 53, 59, 320 (Dutch) and 407 (Canadian) Squadrons, on occasions, in co-operation with Hampdens. No.59 Squadron commanded by W/Cmdr C.M.M. Grece, DFC was posted to North Coates on 17 January 1942 and its sister squadron No.53 was to follow in February with their CO, W/Cmdr J.R. Leggate, arriving on the twenty-third.

One of the first losses was AM563 PZ-X of No.53 Squadron captained by P/O D.A. Ray which failed to return from a Rover patrol on 24 February. An Australian, Sgt Ralph C. Guthrie with 53 Squadron, made an attack on a convoy of seven merchantmen with four escort vessels off Horns Reef two days later releasing four 250lb bombs on a 7000-ton ship. His Hudson AM584 was so badly damaged that he crash-landed on the satellite field, Donna Nook. One of his Wop/AGs, Sgt. R. Rayner, was badly wounded by shrapnel.[25]

Sgt R. Thornhill in AM549 of No.53 Squadron attacked a convoy off the Frisian Islands on 8 April but the Hudson was hit by AA fire and the petrol tanks were holed. Further heavy fire from Sylt was suffered and AM549 was ditched. The crew made for the shore and became PoWs.

AM560 L-PZ captained by F/O A.N. McLintock was lost with its crew on 11 April and F/Sgt D.G.S. Corden and crew failed to return from a sortie in AM803 PZ-V on the night of 16 April. No.53 Squadron lost another Hudson, AM542 on 22 April off Texel.

No.59 Squadron was no less active. On 26 March four of their Hudsons – captained by S/Ldr Evans, F/O Boggon, P/O Charlton and P/O Moss – were airborne. Phil Evans, one of their Flight Commanders, attacked the second in line of four ships each estimated as being between 2000 and 3000 tons. This was twenty miles north-west of Norderney He released four 250lb bombs from mast height and his gunner saw smoke and steam amidships as seemingly the result of a direct hit by one of the bombs.

One of a number of Australians with 59 Squadron, F/O N. Barson, RAAF, made an attack on 15 April against a well-defended tanker which was beached. His Hudson was hit but he was able to return on one engine.

Two Hudsons were lost by 59 Squadron on 16 April; one flown by Mike Boggon was believed to have been shot down by Ju 88s while the second, captained by P/O Thesiger, hit the sea in a low level practice run with all the crew killed.

A Canadian, W/Cmdr R.H. Niven, DFC, succeeded W/Cmdr Grece as CO on 21 April but his time was to be short indeed. [*Ibid*]

Sgt Hastie was on a Rover patrol for 53 Squadron northwards off the Danish coast on the night of 26/27 April when three merchantmen were sighted just after midnight. Hastie released four 250lb bombs against the third vessel and two hits were scored followed by black smoke and with the ship on fire. Another 53 Squadron Hudson captained by Sgt Guthrie located the ship off Horns Reef and attacked also with four 250lb bombs scoring a direct hit on its stern. There was return gunfire and one of the Hudson's Wop/AGs, Sgt Rayner, was wounded by shrapnel. The ship *Inga* of 1,494 tons was sunk and credited to 53 Squadron.[26]

On 4 May the sister squadrons numbers 53 and 59 had Hudsons airborne on a strike. P/O Puckridge of 53 took off at 1029hrs and flew in formation with five others. At 1144hrs he sighted eighteen miles ahead an enemy convoy of seven ships. Six minutes later he attacked the second largest vessel and smoke and steam was seen to belch from the base of its funnel. P/O M.G. Gummer in AM565 PZ-W was seen to press home an attack despite having his starboard engine smoking and had to ditch. Hudson TR-M of 59 Squadron photographed the 53 Squadron crew on the wing of AM565. Puckridge had encountered much AA fire and on sighting an enemy aircraft, turned to attack but was unable to close the range. His port engine was smoking due to shrapnel which also entered his navigator's compartment. The port propeller was hit by a shell and he jettisoned his ammunition and sent an SOS but managed to return at 1328hrs on one engine. No.53 Squadron, in addition to losing AM565 with P/O Gummer, lost also AM530 captained by Sgt Nichols who had with his crew an American, 2nd Lt Summers. From Jock Manson's account, P/O Gummer and one of his Wop/AGs, Sgt T. McDamm, became PoWs but his navigator and the other Wop/AGs were lost. Credited as damaged by 53 Squadron was *Taarnholm* of 1420 tons, and to 59 Squadron,

Above: V9122 dubbed Vageningen *by 320 Sqdn. It was lost on operations 30.5.42.*

Jantje Fritzen of 6582 tons and *Troma* of 5029 tons, all off IJmuiden.[27]

On 8 May No.53 Squadron lost another aircraft, AM683 PZ-Y, while on an attack against a convoy off Terschelling. All the crew were killed when the Hudson crashed near Den Helder. They were F/Sgts C.J. Wyllie, A.T. Thompson and Sgts W.J. Rowe and W.R. McLeod.

AM540 PZ-C captained by the Australian P/O J.P. Rickards was attacked by Me 110s on the same day and three of the crew including Rickards were wounded but Rickards was able to crash-land at Langham in Norfolk. Rickards was later to attack a U boat when the squadron was operating off the American coast and was awarded the DFC.[28]

Three of No.59's aircraft captained by P/O Neilson, Sgt Scoulter and P/O Moss sighted an enemy convoy of eight ships twenty miles off Borkum Riff on 11 May and with the escort including two destroyers. Neilson attacked a destroyer by diving from 300ft to 50ft and releasing two 250lb and six 100lb bombs. The Hudson's hydraulics failed affecting both the bomb doors and the undercarriage but Neilson was able to return and made a belly-landing at North Coates. The two other Hudsons failed to return. On the night of 29 May seven crews from No.59 attacked ships off Borkum.

For W/Cmdr Niven, DFC, the new CO, it was his first operational trip and he made up a crew with P/O D.J. Richards, F/O J.J. Reilly and Sgt Howarth. They failed to return. Another captained by F/Lt Collie was badly shot up and he jettisoned his bombs. One of 59's Wop/AGs, Geoffrey Goad, who flew with S/Ldr Evans in AM857 recalls: '. . . we picked our target, it was a moonlight night, went in below mast height, lobbed our delayed action bombs on the superstructure, pulled up over the masts and from the gunner's turret there was this almighty red hot flame. Afterwards we got the hell out of it despite the efforts of the flak ships.' Credited to 59 Squadron was the auxiliary *Nordcap* VP1103 of 385 tons.

On 30 July S/Ldr Evans captained FH426 from 59 Squadron on a sortie to the Frisian Islands. It was a pitch black night and on sighting a light, Evans headed for it.

Suddenly they were hit and the Hudson flipped over on its back. A great hole had been blown in the wing. Evans managed to right the aircraft and as one of his crew, Geoffrey Goad, recalls: 'We then flew towards the Dutch coast as the aircraft was staggering a bit. We did wonder if we should bale out over the land or have a bash at getting home, the trouble was I could see the bits of wing flapping about and the others couldn't.'[29] Evans' crew opted to attempt the return flight and made a successful landing on one wheel.

Goad attended an interview for commissioning the next day and was asked by the AOC, 'When was your last ops trip?' 'Last night, Sir.'

No.59 Squadron remained based at North Coates until August but 53 Squadron moved down to St Eval on 16 May 1942 and it effectively became a prelude to a further move to the USA. [*Ibid*]

No.320 (Dutch) Squadron

Following the invasion of The Netherlands in May 1940 eighty aircrew of the Royal Netherlands Air Service (MLD) escaped via France to Britain bringing twenty-four seaplanes although eleven of the latter were subsequently sent to Surabaya in the Netherlands East Indies.

The aircrew formed a nucleus for No.320 (Dutch) Squadron formed at Pembroke Dock on 1 June 1940 within the RAF's Coastal Command. In October 320 Squadron became based at Leuchars equipped with Hudsons but in April 1942 was deployed at Bircham Newton. One of 320's pilots, Lt Thijis de Liefde, writing to the author recalls:

Here we started almost immediately flying operationally, making low level strikes (mast height) at German shipping off the Dutch coast, mostly between Flushing and Den Helder. These strikes were usually at night after a reconnaissance aircraft had reported a convoy.

In the meantime crews of 320 and 407 – mostly six crews of each squadron – were standby and took off at once after the report. One Hudson went ahead to drop flares, one picked a ship, went down to almost sea level and at mast height one had to fly over the convoy, not being able to do any evasive action.

During the last stage of the attack run, the observer or second pilot sat next to the pilot flying the aircraft, calling out speed, height and looking after the bomb doors. The pilot in command dropped the bombs a split second before the attacked ship disappeared under the nose of the aircraft.

After the attack we kept flying as low as possible, while the air gunner enjoyed himself shooting away like hell and the Wop stood in the dome to warn for other aircraft or surprise attacks by fighters.

We flew practically every other day and the losses of crews from both squadrons [320 and 407] in the period April till July 1942 were very high.

The Germans split up convoys in two and increased their flak ships. Coastal Command changed tactics and after July we attacked shipping more individually at a height of at least

References
22. CCWR p.24   23. CCWR p.24   24. Letter to author
25. RAAF III/272; JM p.42   26. CCWR p.20; RAAF III/278   27. CCWR p.20
28. RAAF III/287   29. Letter to author

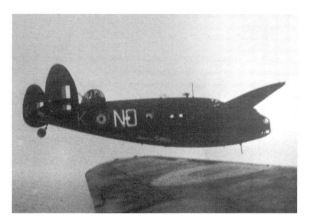

Above: Hudson K-NO T9381 with No.320 (Dutch) Sqdn. No.320 operated with 407 off the Dutch coast on shipping strikes.

4000ft depending on weather, making a proper bombing run and using a bomb-sight. Now the Germans didn't use big convoys any more but sent ships in threes or fours, bigger and faster enabling them to use the facilities of IJmuiden or Den Helder to make harbour.[30]

On 8 May 1942 No.320 Squadron had six Hudsons on 'Nomad patrol' with all airborne by 0150hrs. At 0350hrs Hudson V9041 captained by Otten sighted a ship in position 53°55′N 06°25′E. Otten attacked two minutes later and saw a bomb explode ahead and three bombs aft of the vessel.

Bruens in AE525 sighted two ships of about 3500 tons in position 53°36′N 05°30′E and five minutes later five more enemy merchantmen. He selected one ship, attacking from starboard at mast height releasing ten bombs. One bomb was seen to explode in the water starboard of the ship but he believed that six of his bombs had scored hits.

De Groot flying V8952 at 0400hrs while in position 53°30′N 05°00′E sighted a 2000-ton ship. In his attack two direct hits were seen and it appears very likely that it was the *Burgundia* of 1668 tons and credited to 320 as damaged off Emden. That same night Jansen who was airborne at 0135hrs in V8981 failed to return. The other five Hudsons returned safely.

Five of 320's Hudsons were airborne for a strike on 29 May. Otten in V9058 lost contact with the formation and in position 53°25′N 04°50′E sighted an enemy fighter; he took evasive action and returned to Docking.

Van de Meer, captain of V9122, after turning south along the reported track of a convoy sighted several ships in position 53°33′N 05°47′E. He attacked a heavily laden vessel of 3000 tons in the centre of the scattered convoy. There was light AA fire from a number of ships but Van de Meer claimed a direct hit and there was dense smoke followed by a fire breaking out amidships from the target. He reported seeing three ships on fire but also what was thought to be an aircraft in the water also burning, between his target and Ameland. This may well have been the Hudson from 407 flown by F/O Race but with F/Sgt Clark's crew.

Leading 320's formation was the CO, Lt/Cmdr Van Olm in T9396. He saw at least twelve merchantmen in convoy at position 53°33′N 05°23′E heading north-east. He attacked a 3500-ton ship in the centre of the convoy despite seeing a balloon at 300ft and escort on either side and he was aware of both heavy and light AA fire. Ten bombs were released from mast height and five direct hits on the ship aft were claimed and confirmed by the rear gunner.

De Groot in Hudson T9435 released his ten bombs but made no claim due to dense smoke but saw a ship on fire from a previous attack. Credited to 320 Squadron was a *sperrbrecher* of 750 tons, the *Veriato* which was sunk.[31]

Six Hudsons from 320 were again airborne by 2300 hrs on 30 May and led by S/L (*Sic*) Schaper in AM939. After following the enemy convoy's route, Daniels in Hudson T9396 sighted seven merchant ships with eight escorts in position 53°28′N 05°13′E. He selected a ship of 6000 to 8000 tons, climbed to 2500ft and then dive-bombed from 800ft. His rear gunner saw two flashes and the pilot saw two explosions on the ship. Schröder in V9058 saw flak from the convoy at five miles but closed to attack and at position 53°30′N 05°25′E selected a 7000-tonner but in three attempts at bombing was followed by a Ju 88 which closed to 200 yards and the bombs were jettisoned.

Lt De Liefde captained V9033 and attacked a ship of 800 to 1000 tons from mast height releasing ten bombs and his gunner saw an explosion on its deck followed by the vessel bursting into flames. De Liefde experienced AA from shore batteries and from the convoy and had to take evasive action from enemy aircraft. De Groot selected a merchant vessel of 6000 tons; attacked from mast height releasing ten bombs and estimated four hits followed by heavy explosions. Debris flew into the air, there was accurate heavy and light flak and the Hudson T9435 was damaged in the turret. On his return flight to Docking, two occupied lifeboats were sighted heading west. From this strike two of 320's Hudsons, V9122 flown by Buynink and AM939 with Schaper, failed to return. Schaper had ditched and became a prisoner-of-war. Four of 320 Squadron's Hudsons were airborne just before 1800hrs on 18 January 1943 detailed for a strike. Bevelander sighted a convoy in position 53°38′N 04°35′E and attacked a ship, scoring a hit behind its funnel. Laamens claimed one hit on a ship as also Sillevis who captained EW924. Credited as sunk by 320 Squadron was *Algeria* of 1619 tons off Terschelling but shared with No.407 Squadron.

Although Coastal Command continued with shipping strikes up to the end of the war, this sinking appears as the last successful attack recorded for Hudson aircraft.

While on shipping strikes 320 Squadron had lost twenty-one Hudsons but in March 1943 transferred to No.2 Group, Bomber Command and was equipped with Mitchell bomber aircraft.

The Canadian 'Demon' Squadron

No.407 (RCAF) Squadron had become operational on 1 September 1941 at North Coates and worked in co-operation with 320. Two of its Hudsons attacked a ship in the Borkum-Terschelling area on the sixth No.407's first recorded success was on 13 October when a dredger, *Hamm-19*, was sunk off Terschelling in a strike led by S/Ldr V.H.P. Lynham in

Hudson RR-Q. He made a bow attack from 100ft on a 2000 to 3000-ton vessel with four 250lb bombs but didn't see the results.[32]

On 1 November a number of 407 Squadron Hudsons attacked ships off the Dutch coast including those flown by F/Sgt Ross, F/O Cowperthwaite, P/O McCulloch, F/O Codville, P/O Shankland, P/O Cooper, Sgt Moss, and S/Ldr Lewis. All claimed hits and credited as damaged by 407 was the *Braheholm* of 5676 tons.

Trevor Hawkins, a Wop/AG with 407 gives this account of that night:

Four crews including Monty Styles were out in our respective sectors of the Dutch coast from IJmuiden to the Heligoland Bight. The other three crews saw nothing, but I had the good fortune to find on ASV a stationary convoy just off Borkum. We attacked what we estimated to be a 6000-tonner from below mast height. There was a lot of flak, principally light stuff; we had caught them sleeping. We cleared the convoy, climbed to about 2000 to 3000ft to send a sighting report then back to deck to return to Donna Nook our satellite airfield to be transported back to North Coates. Meanwhile, Peter Lewis acting squadron CO in place of Monty who was still out, called his own and seven other crews and said: 'You know what to do, do it.' Don Moss was the first at the convoy attacking a 7000-ton tanker but had to belly-land at base but without casualties. Peter Lewis attacked a 4000-tonner a few minutes later but by this time the convoy had woken up and the flak was getting thick. Jimmy Codville was next into a 800-tonner followed by Dale Cowperthwaite taking on a 5000-ton merchantman. Lucky Cooper followed with a 3000-tonner and last came Bill Shankland who took on a 6500-ton merchantman. All the ships were seen to have suffered hits; Bill lost his port engine through cannon fire and although unable to feather the prop was able to fly back to Donna Nook.[33]

Another ship the *Vios IV* of 190 tons was credited as sunk by 407 on 11 November off IJmuiden but it is not clear which captain could claim it.[34]

A Rover patrol from Borkum to Den Helder was flown on 5 January 1942 by 407 led by S/Ldr Anderson. P/O Cowperthwaite sighted three or four merchantmen in IJmuiden harbour while Anderson saw a convoy leaving the harbour. A leading ship was attacked with two direct hits scored on its aft hatch. That night 407 operated again but with 217 Squadron. Credited as sunk by 407 was the merchantman *Cornelia Maersk* of 1892 tons off IJmuiden.[35]

The squadron's English CO, W/Cmdr Styles, DSO was succeeded by the Canadian, W/Cmdr Alan Brown, DFC on 7 January 1942. W/Cmdr Styles was later lost on a flight to Gibraltar.[36]

On the night of 3 May five crews from 407 Squadron were operating from North Coates but there was only one attack; that by F/Sgt Howey who left a merchantman burning. Credited to the unit was *Sizilien* of 4647 tons sunk off Terschelling.[37]

By 7 May 407 Squadron was considered 'on the mark' with twelve serviceable aircraft and a strike was laid on for off the Dutch coast. W/Cmdr Brown led a strike against twelve ships near Texel and all picked their targets. One ship

of 3726 tons was sunk *Ruth,* and *Namdo* of 2860 tons was damaged.[38] F/Lt Christie led twelve of 407's Hudsons while 320 Squadron provided eight aircraft for a strike off the Dutch coast on 15 May. Three aircraft led by F/O Kay of 407 made first contact and his Hudson was seriously damaged and he wounded. It was against a strong, heavily armed convoy and one of 407's Hudsons was seen to explode in mid-air while others were shot down. One aircraft from 320 was lost and four from 407 failed to return. P/O Creedon crashed-landed at Coningsby and he with his crew were killed. Others crash-landed at Docking. Two ships were recorded as sunk, *Selje* of 6698 tons and *Madeleine Louise* an auxiliary of 464 tons.[39] No.407 Squadron was on a strike on the night of 29 May led by F/Lt Christie. The Canadian squadron claimed three ships seriously damaged. P/O O'Connell of 407 flew so low that one of his bomb doors was left on the mast of a ship. F/O Race of 407 was last seen attacking through intense flak; he failed to return. Coastal Command's record gives *Niels R. Finsen, Veriato,* a *sperrbrecher,* and *Nordcap,* an auxiliary as being sunk by 407, 320 and 59 Squadrons respectively on the 29th off Ameland; *Varmdo* of 2956 tons was sunk off Terschelling by 407.[40]

Four Hudsons were on a recce off the Dutch coast on 12 June. P/O Taylor attacked a ship in position 57°55′N 07° 34′E. His gunner saw at least three direct hits followed by an orange glow and debris thrown into the air. The merchantman *Senta* of 1497 tons was credited as sunk off Borkum.[41]

In October 1942 No.407 Squadron moved down to St Eval to undertake A/S patrols but were able to attack shipping and on the 25th and 27th damaged the fishing vessels *Emma* and *La Mouette* of 150 and 303 tons respectively in the Bay of Biscay.[42]

Coastal Command continued to deploy aircraft on shipping strikes from Norway to France right up to the end of the war in Europe but with the squadrons such as No.404 (RCAF) operating aircraft more suited to the task including Beaufighters and Mosquitoes but still with serious losses.[43]

The official Coastal Command record gives a total of 366 sunk by aircraft under its control and with damage to 134 ships. These were for a loss of 876 aircraft. From the total of 500 ships sunk or damaged, Hudsons may be credited with 56 between 29 April 1940 and 18 January 1943.

The official RAF historian Denis Richards states for mid-1941 that 'As a healthy occupation for aircrew bombing ships by day had much less to commend it than bombing German towns by night.' For the last quarter of 1941 he gives Coastal Command losing forty-six aircraft for fifteen ships sunk; for the period January-April 1942, fifty-five aircraft lost for six ships sunk and with much of the work going to Hudsons.[44] Against these figures are those for minelaying where 369 ships were sunk for the loss of 329 aircraft.[45]

References

30. Letter to author 31. CCWR p.20 32. CCWR p.20 33. Letter to author
34. CCWR p.20 35. CCWR p.20 36. KA p.199 37. CCWR p.20
38. CCWR p.20 39. CCWR p.20 40. CCWR p.20 41. CCWR p.20
42. CCWR p.28 43. AH CSCC pp 175–182
44. RAF I/354; RAF II/pp.94–99 45. RAF II/99

Chapter 4
Anti-submarine Operations –
Atlantic Ocean

Canada

Following the Munich crisis in 1938 Canada turned its attention from the Pacific to the Atlantic. It declared war on Germany on 10 September 1939 and the first Atlantic convoy sailed from Halifax, Nova Scotia on 16 September.

The prime task of Canada's Eastern Air Command was in the maritime role and in co-operation with the British and Canadian navies.[1] Although at least eight squadrons of the RCAF came to deploying Lockheed Hudsons, maritime operations forming part of the Battle of the Atlantic were given largely to squadrons numbered 11, 113, and 145.

No.11 RCAF was formed as a Bomber-Reconnaissance squadron at Rockcliffe, Ottawa where ten Hudsons were delivered by pilots of the Lockheed Corporation but on 3 November 1939 was deployed at Dartmouth, Nova Scotia with S/Ldr A. Lewis as Commanding Officer. S/Ldr Lewis

Above: F/Lt 'Jimmy' Leggate with his two brothers at St Eval in 1941. He commanded No.53 Sqdn when they flew to USA and operated off the American eastern seaboard in 1942.

Below: No.11 Sqdn RCAF Hudsons, coded OY and one without a turret. They operated over the vital St Lawrence estuary and Halifax, NS areas.

undertook the first operational sortie on the 10th from 0855hrs to 1035hrs with Hudson BW761 in co-operation with HMS *Repulse* and HMS *Furious*.

On 10 December the first Canadian troop convoy sailed from Halifax which included the *Aquitania, Empress of Britain, Duchess of Bedford, Monarch of Bermuda,* and *Empress of Australia* together with twelve escorts. By the end of 1939 of the fourteen Canadian squadrons on active service only two were considered adequately equipped including No.11 with ten Hudsons; it was Eastern Air Command's first modern maritime patrol aircraft.[2]

No.11 Squadron's duties were to escort convoys, make sweeps ahead of convoys and searches following the reported sighting of such as a possible U boat. Such occurred on 1 June 1940 when F/O Michalski was on a patrol. Near the entrance to Halifax harbour he sighted what appeared to be a U boat crash-diving. He directed a destroyer to the position and four Hudsons were airborne on a search. Convoy HX47 postponed sailing for twenty-four hours.

By 20 February 1941, No.11 Squadron had three Hudsons equipped with gun turrets and three days later Hudson BW764 was test flown with the armament officer to evaluate the turret but to have it jammed for two hours. By 2 March

six Hudsons were so equipped and an establishment of twelve Hudsons with three in reserve was achieved by 30 April. No.11 Squadron provided flights of aircraft for the films *49th Parallel* on 30 September 1940, and on 18 September 1941 for *Captain of the Clouds*. More seriously was a sighting of a U boat on 18 June 1941; five aircraft were sent from Dartmouth but had to return due to very bad weather. A representative of the United States Navy, Lt/Cmdr M.B. Gurney visted 11 Squadron at the end of October to gain information regarding the maintenance of aircraft.

In World War II Halifax, Nova Scotia was one of the major Atlantic ports for convoys which were coded 'HX', and following America's entry into the war after Pearl Harbor, Admiral Dönitz ordered U boats westwards. This was under operation *Paukenschlag* and included the *Seydlitz* group to the Newfoundland Bank while others were diverted to Trinidad and Aruba. Seven medium U boats arrived off Newfoundland between 7 and 9 January 1942 independent of *Paukenschlag* and in February the sea area south of Halifax became a 'battle ground'.[3]

In March 1942 No.11 Squadron began to be equipped with Mark III Hudsons and by 31 July had fourteen on the strength. Although no successful attacks on U boats are

Below: A No.11 Sqdn RCAF Hudson on convoy escort duty.

References

1. RCAF II/pp.377–8   2. RCAF II/p.345   3. GüH paras.169, 170, 171

recorded in the unit's records, from the German U boat diaries it is apparent that patrols flown by such as No.11 seriously thwarted operations by the enemy in the Halifax and St Lawrence areas – '. . . persistent air patrols had forced U boats to remain submerged during daylight'.[4]

By July 1943 the squadron was beginning to convert to Liberators but continued to operate Hudsons. The Auxiliary squadron No.113 was re-formed at Yarmouth, Nova Scotia on 15 February 1942 and its commanding officer, S/Ldr A.G. Kenyon, ferried from Debert Hudson BW623 that day. Over the next few weeks sixteen more Hudsons were received.

On 25 March F/Lt Michalski undertook a special search in Hudson BW620 and on 22 April S/Ldr Kenyon in BW617 flew the first patrol. By the beginning of June there were fifteen officers and 183 airmen on the strength; on that day Hudson BW631 failed to return from a flight over the Bay of Fundy. In the crew were Sgts McPherson, Scheley and McDonald

S/Ldr N.E. Small succeeded S/Ldr Kenyon as CO of No.113 Squadron on 26 June; Coastal Command's tactics of flying at higher altitudes were adopted and with aircraft in white camouflage; while under his command the unit achieved a remarkable record.

About this time German U boats were operating from off Brazil up to Newfoundland and the Gulf of St Lawrence and in January 1942 seven U boats were off Newfoundland but moved down to the Halifax area at the end of the month.[5]

The Sinking of U-754

One of the squadron's first sightings was by S/Ldr Small on 31 July. The day was clear apart from high scattered cloud with visibility six to ten miles and with a north-westerly wind of six to twelve knots. Three convoy patrols were laid on for position 42°30′N 65°00′W at 0900hrs and S/Ldr Small was airborne at 1700hrs in BW617 on a sweep.

About position 42°30′N 65°00′W he sighted a U boat three miles ahead. It was still on the surface when he attacked with depth charges and some of the boat's crew were seen scrambling towards a hatch. The U boat submerged for a few minutes and when the conning tower emerged again it was machine-gunned. The enemy again submerged and large air bubbles appeared. About 55 minutes later there was a large underwater explosion. U-754 had sailed from Germany on 19 June captained by Kl Hans Oerstermann; it was sunk in this attack position 43°02′N 64°52′W. Kl Oerstermann had claimed a total of fourteen ships from 21 January to 28 July.[6]

Later when P/O G.T. Sayre was on a search in position 42°30′N 66°00′W, he attacked U-132 but apparently without causing damage. U-132 had sailed from France on 10 June and returned there on 16 August completing its second voyage. It had sunk three ships all at position 49°30′N 66°30′W and all on 6 July.[7]

While on a sweep about the area of 43°30′N 63°50′W on 2 August, S/Ldr Small in Hudson BW625 attacked U-458 but with doubtful results. U-458 sank its second ship the *Arletta* on 5 August in position 44°44′N 55°22′W before returning to France on 26 August.[8]

Three days later, No.113 Squadron had eight Hudsons on

Above: The Hudson T9465 Spirit of Lockheed-Vega Employees *which was presented to the RAF by Lockheeds. Here coded UA-N for 269 Sqdn and with their CO, W/Cmdr McMurtrie.*

sweeps over the Gulf of Maine and Bay of Fundy. S/Ldr Small after being airborne at 1050hrs in BW620 attacked another U boat; first by machine-gunning and then releasing depth charges which straddled the vessel. This was on U-89 which survived the attack returning to France on 21 August. Captained by Kk D. Lohmann it had sunk *Lucille M* in position 42°02′N 65°38′W on 25 July.[9]

By 23 August three large U boats occupied both sides of the Strait of Belle Isle before sailing to the Gulf of St Lawrence. While U-165 went to the area 100 miles south-west of Anticosti, U-517 positioned between Anticosti and the New Brunswick coast. Seven ships were sunk and two others torpedoed. However, the U boat diary shows that air patrols over the Gulf of St Lawrence forced the U boats to remain submerged during daylight and during September 1942, U-517 was attacked six times by the Hudsons albeit to survive.[10]

No.113 Squadron had a detachment at Chatham on 9 September with three Hudsons on patrol and two on searches. Weather conditions were given with both ceiling and visibility unlimited and with an easterly wind of 10 to 20 knots. P/O R.S. Keetley while flying at 4000ft in BW403 20 miles south of Anticosti saw in position 48°44′N 62°59′W what at first was thought to be a sailing boat but was in fact U-165. He made a diving attack but by then the U boat had submerged. Subsequently two corvettes and a minesweeper made a search. U-517 which was to survive a number of attacks was depth-charged by Keetley on 16 September; the vessel was straddled but the charges were apparently too widely spaced and were the earlier type, Amatol-filled.[11]

While escorting convoy QS37 on 24 September F/Sgt A.S. White sighted U-517 in position 49°35′N 65°35′W. He dropped sea markers, warned the convoy and then attacked but only one depth charge was released due to a blown fuse. The following night F/O Belanger was airborne in Hudson BW624 from Yarmouth and in position 49°45′N 65°48′W saw a U boat cruising a mile away in moonlight. It was attacked and later when it surfaced in position 47°32′N 62°37′W, a second attack was made which resulted in an extensive oil patch covering ten square miles. From the official Canadian history 113 Squadron made seven sightings and three attacks in twenty-four hours.[12]

U-517 which had suffered no serious damage attacked another ship on 29 September before returning to France on 19 October.[13]

One of the last attacks on U boats by 113 Squadron was made by S/Ldr Small on 24 November in position 49°35′N 65°35′W but apparently without success. He had earlier gained the AFC for his service and on 2 January 1943 was awarded the DFC. He had been credited with one kill, one possible, and one U boat damaged. S/Ldr Small, DFC, AFC was killed in a flying accident on 7 January and was succeeded as CO of 113 by W/Cmdr A. Laut.

By 9 March crews were being sent to San Pedro, California by train to ferry back Ventura aircraft to replace 113's Hudsons and on 4 April three crews returned with Venturas (PV-1s). It was 14 April before the more efficient depth charges filled with Torpex arrived.

The Sinking of U-658

No.145 Squadron RCAF was formed as a Bomber/Reconnaissance unit at Torbay, Newfoundland on 18 May 1942. S/Ldr R.H. Batty assumed command on 30 May 1942 but by 1 June had on strength only six officers and forty-six airmen. By the end of July 145's strength had doubled to ten officers and ninety-two airmen when, by that date, general reconnaissance, anti-submarine patrols and special searches for July totalled 332 hours. Its first operational sortie however, was by F/Sgt James in Hudson BW771 for a patrol on 2 June. The first notable success for the squadron was achieved by F/O E.L. Robinson on 30 October. About that time sixteen U boats were operating off the Newfoundland and Canadian coasts and they were aware of convoy SC107.[14]

F/O Robinson was flying Hudson 784, on a sweep ahead of the convoy when a conning tower was seen breaking the surface two miles ahead. He lost height from 2000ft and released four 250lb depth charges set for twenty-five feet depth from port astern to starboard bow, and as the U boat was almost fully surfaced, the vessel was straddled with one of the charges falling on the deck before rolling off. The explosions raised the stern about sixty feet. After settling, oil and air bubbles were seen despite a rough sea.

U-658 had sailed from a French port on 6 October captained by Kl Hans Senkel; during its first voyage it had attacked seven ships, sinking three. On this second voyage it was sunk on 30 October as a result of this attack at position 50°32′N 46°32′W about 290 miles north-east of Torbay. That night F/Lt Robinson with his crew, Sgts K.U. Lunny, P.A. Corbett and E.F. Williams were received by the Governor of the island and complimented.[15]

From the German U boat diary the *Veilchen* group made their first contact with an ON convoy on 29 October but no attacks were made and they moved south-west. Three U boats were heading for Halifax and the Gulf of St Lawrence when one of the three, U-522 sighted convoy SC107 which was eastbound. On 31 October Hudsons from No.145 Squadron were on a sweep ahead of SC107 when a radar contact was obtained eleven miles to port of SC107's track. P/O L.T. Ross located a fully-surfaced U boat then 120 miles east of St John's. During his attack the U boat took evasive action and his four DCs were released at 90° to the vessel. It was U-521 which attacked the convoy on 2 November sinking *Hartington* in position 52°30′N 45°30′W and on the third sinking *Hahira* in position 54°15′N 41°57′W. It attacked three ships in ONS 144 on 18 November, returning to France on 8 December.[16]

By May 1943, No.145 Squadron had received thirteen Lockheed Venturas but must have been flying Hudsons as late as 9 July 1943 when F/Lt J.R. Hastie was killed at Charlottetown due to engine failure in Hudson 762.

The First German U boat to be Sunk by American Forces in WWII

Germany declared war on the USA on 11 December 1941 and on the 12th decided to send U boats to the American coast under Operation *Paukenschlag*. Initially five U boats were to operate between the St Lawrence and Cape Hatteras but to be free to move southwards. Additionally seven medium-size boats operated independently of *Paukenschlag*.[17]

A Lockheed Hudson (PBO) 82-P-8 from VP-82 of the United States Navy commanded by Ensign William Tepuni, USNR was airborne from Base Roger, Argentia at 1100hrs on 1 March 1942. This was for an anti-submarine patrol between Latitude 45°N to 47°N and Longitude 50°W to 54°W. While flying on a northerly course at 600ft Tepuni sighted a surfaced U boat fifteen miles ahead in position 46°22′N 53°10′W off Cape Race. There was less than five-tenths cloud at 700ft with a fifteen knot north-west wind.

Tepuni prepared to attack from down sun while the U boat was heading eastwards; two Mark 17 depth charges were set to detonate at fifty feet. They were released from fifty feet altitude while the U boat was still surfaced. All the Hudson crew including Ensign A.P. Spenser, mechanic T.S. Hawley and radioman L.E. Griffin saw the vessel straddled by the two depth charge detonations. The U boat crash-dived thirty seconds after the attack and within five minutes oil was rising to the surface. Tepuni in 82-P-8 left the scene at 1440hrs for base. His squadron, VP82, sent three more aircraft, 82-P-10, 82-P-5 and Tepuni again with 82-P-8 at 1530hrs and each released a further depth charge on the area of the oil slick, resulting in air bubbles and more oil surfacing.

The following day two destroyers, USS *Gleaves* and USS *Bernadou* dropped more depth charges. This marked the sinking of U-656 then on its second voyage from a French port which it left on 4 February captained by OL Ernst

References
4. GüH para.226 5. GüH para 175 6. GüH p.126; USSL p.161; JRpp 75–111
7. JR p.107; GüH p.120; RCAF II p.120 8. JR p.113; RCAF II/520; C12243
9. JR p.111; RCAF II/520 10. GüH para.26 & p.124
11. RCAF II/503; C12243 12. RCAF II/505 USSL p.176; JH p.35; JR 293
13. JR p.126; GüH p.124; RCAF II/503 14. RCAF II/527
15. JR pp.115–116; USSL p.161; GüH p.126; C12256
16. RCAF II/529; JR pp.132–3, 137; GüH para.261
17. SWR II/94; GüH paras 169, 170

to 200ft. Mason left the scene at 1455hrs because of fuel shortage and to re-arm.

Two more aircraft were sent to the area at 1550hrs but with a distance of 285 miles, a furthur search was abandoned.

Mason's attack marked the demise of U-503 captained by Kk Otto Gerhicke which had sailed on its second voyage from a French port on 28 February only to be lost on 15 March in position 45°50′N 48°50′W.[19]

Squadron VP-82 of the United States Navy could claim at least two 'firsts' in respect of their Hudsons; the unit had received the first of its Hudsons (PBO-1s) at Naval Air Station (NAS) Norfolk on 29 October 1941; Hudsons initially intended for the RAF and with British markings. As is stated in the official *United States Naval Aviation* it was '. . . the beginning of what became an extensive use of land planes . . .' eventually displacing flying boats for the Navy's reconnaissance sorties.[20]

The Caribbean

The first operational group of U boats for the Caribbean under Operation *Westindien* commenced on 16 February with the *Neuland* group deployed in the areas about Aruba, Curaçao and Trinidad. The intention was to attack ships of 10,000 tons or more and disrupt supplies of oil and bauxite but concentrating on tankers. Between February and July 1942 114 ships were sunk. Professor Morison gives the problem for America with a strategic area from Labrador to the Brazilian bulge to cover requiring many bases and machines.[21]

Above: An investiture by HM King George VI with W/Cmdr McMurtrie, CO of 269 Sqdn being awarded the DSO or DFC.

Kröning. Both *United States Naval Aviation* and the American historian Professor Morison give Tepuni's attack on 1 March 1942 as resulting in the first sinking of a German U boat by American forces in WWII. [18]

On 15 March, Hudson (PBO) 82-P-9 was airborne at 1155hrs from Base Roger, Argentina piloted by Chief Aviation Machinist's Mate Donald Mason, USN to escort convoy ON72. At 1400hrs Mason reached the convoy's estimated position and then commenced a search for it down its track southwards. Eleven minutes later a submarine was sighted at one mile on the port bow with its decks awash in position 43°50′N 48°45′W. Mason was then flying at 800ft with broken cloud at 1500ft, a twenty knot north-west wind and visibility one mile and a rough sea. The bridge with two periscopes of the U boat were seen but none of its crew.

Armed with four Mark 17 depth charges set to detonate at fifty feet depth, Mason dived down to attack at 185 knots and fifteen feet altitude and at fifteen degrees to the vessel's starboard quarter. It was the first time apparently that the bomb distributor on the Hudson had been used by the unit and giving a spacing of sixty feet at 180 knots. Analysis from photographs taken during the attack indicated that one depth charge had dropped safe but that at least one other had detonated within ten feet of the U boat, thus well within lethal range. Mason's co-pilot, Albert Jurca, saw a large air bubble with oil and debris followed by the oil slick spreading

An American Army Air Force Squadron

The 6th Reconnaissance squadron of the USAAF was organised on 15 January 1941 at March Field, California under the command of Captain D.O. Monteith. On 16 May it was deployed at Davis-Monthan Field, Tucson, Arizona with five officers and sixty-eight men but by July 1941 numbers of personnel had increased to eleven officers and 218 men.

No.6 Reconnaissance Squadron was ordered to Muroc Bombing and Gunnery Range, Muroc, California to be given coastal patrol duties and with its Type LB-30 aircraft being replaced by A-29 Lockheed Hudsons. There was further training at Sacramento, California with coastal patrols and on 8 April 1942 twenty-five officers and 153 men moved to the Naval Air Station, Alameda, California for training with a Fleet Air Arm detachment.

From 10 April to 9 May 1942 coastal patrols were flown from Alameda. The squadron was re-designated the 296th Bombardment Squadron (M) on 21 April. The 396th's Air Echelon of thirty-five officers and fifty-five men was deployed at Cherry Point, North Carolina on 12 June 1942. Under the command of Lt/Col D.O. Monteith they undertook coastal patrols.

The Sinking of U-701

On 7 July 1942 Hudson 9-29-322 A-29 #41-23392 was airborne crewed by 2nd Lt Harry J. Kane, 2nd Lt L.A. Murray and corporals G.E. Bellamy, L.P. Flowers, and P.C.

Above: The American crew of A29-41-23392 commanded by 2nd/Lt H.J. Kane of the 396th Bomber Sqdn which sank U-701 in position 35°13′N 74°46′W on 7.7.42.

Brousard. At 1412hrs while heading north-east, Lt Kane sighted through a break in the cloud, a surfaced U boat steering north-west seven miles to port.

At five miles the U boat's crew had not seen the aircraft and Kane prepared to attack but at two miles distance the vessel started to dive and was submerged in fifteen seconds. Three Mark 17 depth charges set for twenty-five feet depth detonation were released from fifty feet altitude at 220 mph, with two charges possibly striking the vessel and then sliding off. A bubble appeared with a man in its centre and he was followed until there was a group of about fifteen survivors. Kane circled at 300ft and saw another group of survivors to which he dropped a rubber dinghy and lifebelts before locating a coastguard vessel which was directed to the scene. Due to fuel shortage, Kane left at 1630hrs. A Panamanian freighter was also signalled but didn't alter course.

Lt Kane's attack thirty-six miles south-east of Cape Hatteras in position 35°13′N 74°46′W had sunk U-701 captained by Kl Hörst Degen on the U boat's third voyage having left Brest on 19 May but refuelling at Lorient and armed with fourteen torpedoes. On 12 June it had been attacked by another Hudson but only slight damage was caused and U-701, on that date, attacked five ships, *Robert C. Tuttle*, *Esso Augusta*, *Kingston Ceylonite*, *Bainbridge* and *Santore*. On the nineteenth U-701 sank the cutter YP389; on twenty-sixth *Tamesis*; *British Freedom* on twenty-seventh and on twenty-eighth *William Rockefeller.*

From 6 January 1942 fourteen ships are recorded against U-701, eight sunk and six damaged with as captain, Kl Degen.[22] Lt Kane's depth charges had ruptured the pressure hull of U-701 but at least eighteen men escaped through the conning tower hatch. Not all had lifejackets and Degen was supported in the sea part of the time by his quartermaster – Kunert.

On 9 July a Naval blimp commanded by Ensign G.S. Middleton A-V(N) USNR located survivors in position 36°18′N 73°31′W where men were in the water. A life raft was dropped together with food, water, first aid kit and a blanket. A coastguard aircraft touched down at 1425hrs and the blimp directed it to the survivors. Seven men with a raft were picked up at 1525hrs. Another official account gives the

pick up as being at 1605hrs in position 36°18′N 73°32′W, 65 miles from the sinking of U-701.[23]

A Coastal Command Squadron Moves to America

No.53 Squadron RAF had by the summer of 1942 gained experience of anti-shipping and anti-U boat operations over the Bay of Biscay and the North Sea. It was warned on 26 June that it was to proceed to USA and the first three Hudsons left St Eval, Cornwall on 5 July; while their CO, W/Cmdr J. Leggate, arrived at Quonset Point, Rhode Island on 9 July in Hudson FH421 /PZ-S. The United States Navy with which the unit was to co-operate, provided a Liaison Officer, Lt/Cmdr Sutherland. Of this, Gp/Capt J. Leggate, DSO writes in retrospect:

The move of the squadron of comparatively short-range aircraft from Cornwall to Trinidad was more than just interesting for all the pilots and aircrew, both in mid-summer and midwinter on the return. Prestwick–Reykjavik–Bluie West One – Goose Bay, Montreal–Quonset Point, Rhode Island – New York – Jacksonville–Miami–Guantanamo Bay, Cuba, San Juan-Puerto Rico – and so on to Port of Spain in Trinidad.

The effort in moving a squadron over such a distance was in no way connected with teamwork, but was the effort of each individual in his own sphere. The teamwork was required and was there, amongst the crew of each aircraft.

After a few days in the Caribbean it was agreed with our Engineer Officer that he would be able to remove the turrets from all the marks of Hudsons in the squadron. The absence of the turret made a considerable difference – not only to the handling qualities of the aircraft, but also its speed and range. As we were operating outside the range of enemy aircraft, these improvements were vital to the efficiency of anti-submarine work.

By 31 July fifteen of 53's Hudsons had arrived with three others en route and due to move to AAF station, Waller Field, Trinidad in early August. On 22 August a further move was made to Edinburgh Field, Trinidad, B.W.I. and in September, there was a detachment to Atkinson Field, British Guiana. During the following three months No.53 Squadron achieved a number of attacks on U boats; beginning with S/Ldr Hilditch attacking U-108 on 15 August and F/Sgt Henderson causing slight damage to U-217 the same day.

On 27 August F/Sgt Sillcock in Hudson AM797 caught U-173 surfacing in position 09°21′N 53°25′W and released four depth charges. U-173 had sailed from Germany on 15 June but was so damaged that it returned to port arriving in France on 20 September.[24]

Hudson AM727 was lost on 15 September with all on board when it struck a tree while attempting to land on

References
18. SEM I/154; USNA p.110; GüH II/126; USSL p.160
19. GüH p.123; USSL p.160; SEM I/pp.154–5
20. USNA p.108; GüH II/123; USSL p.160; SEM I/154–5
21. GüH para.174; SEM I/144–237 22. JRpp.73–106
23. JR p.104; reports from Wright-Patterson AFB & Maxwell AFB
24. GüH p.120

Above: Hudson UA-K flown by F/Lt Bowen of 269 Sqdn operating from Iceland.

Edinburgh Field during a storm. The crew included two Australians, P/O G.T. Risbey and P/O J.W.P. Walker, Sgts A.M. Parkin, N.F. Brassington, and from the USN, AMM3C W.M. Boots.

As already mentioned, U-217 had first been attacked by F/Sgt Henderson on 15 August north of Puerto Rico. On 20 September F/Sgt Jesty located it on the surface in position 11°02′N 57°05′W and released four DCs at 1210hrs but caused no damage. At 1629hrs it was attacked by F/O Puckridge in V9096 causing damage to hydroplanes, rudder and an electric motor. It returned to base in France on 16 October.[25]

An Australian with No.53, F/O J.P. Rickards, captained FH433 on 22 September and attacked a surfaced U boat at the mouth of the Orinoco river. The U boat, U-512 commanded by Kl W. Schultz, was damaged but later on 2 October was sunk by the US 99th Bomber squadron in position 06°50′N 52°25′W.[26] A week later, 53's CO – W/Cmdr Leggate – captained FH421 and while off Paramaribo attacked U-332 but only slight damage was caused and it returned to France on 6 December. W/Cmdr Leggate's crew included Capt. Philippe Livry-Level, a navigator who later flew on special operations with W/Cmdr Leggate's brother David on No.161 Squadron.[27]

The Australian, F/Sgt R.R. Sillcock was killed with all his crew including a US Navy man, H.L. Drew, on 10 November. Sillcock had attacked U-505 in position 10°10′N 59°04′W but one of the depth charges struck the deck of the U boat exploding and shrapnel from the blast damaged the Hudson fatally. U-505 returned to France on 12 December.[28]

There were to be other attacks by No.53 Squadron before they left America for the United Kingdom. On 19 November the squadron was informed of the intended return home via Quonset Point, and on the twenty-third the Hudsons left for US Naval Air station, Norfolk, Virginia. Those returning home by sea left the same day but for New York and embarking on 8 December.

The American naval historian, Professor Morison sums up the four-month period when No.53 Squadron was operating along the Americas' Atlantic coast referring to the success of the RAF's white-camouflaged Hudsons making some comparison with the slower PBYs of the USN and also the US B-18As, rating those Hudsons the best planes for anti-submarine patrols in the Trinidad area. Professor Morison gives for that same period, 1360 ships arriving and 1462 departing from ports in Trinidad or the Gulf of Pria but with total losses of fifty-three ships of 270,000 tons due to enemy action. Of the fifty-three ships lost, eleven were in convoys.[29]

Brazil

In July 1941 it was decided to form an air link with North Africa from the USA via north and north-east Brazil and major bases were constructed at Belém, São Luis, Fortaleza, Natal, Recife, Maçeio, Salvador and Caravelas. Brazil broke off diplomatic relations with the Axis powers on 28 January 1942 and a Brazilian ship *Cabedello* was sunk by U-156 on 14 February. This was one of nineteen Brazilian ships attacked by German U boats up to19 August.[30]

On 15 June Hitler decided to attack shipping off the Brazilian coast and eight 500-ton and two 700-ton U boats were deployed together with a 'milch cow', U-460 for refuelling.

Between 15 and 17 August five Brazilian ships were sunk including *Baependi* by U-507 on 16 August off the Rio Real estuary in position 11°50′S 37°00′W. Lost with the ship were fifty-five crew and 215 passengers including 124 soldiers. There was a public outcry and Brazil declared war on Germany and Italy on 22 August.

With a coastline from 5°N to 32°S and a limited internal transport system, Brazil depended much on coastal shipping. For the Allies however, Brazil's entry into the war ensured control of shipping being extended down to the River Plate; availability of Brazilian bases and closer control of the South Atlantic route to African ports such as Freetown due to the Brazilian bulge providing a nearer point.

The US Navy had co-operation with Brazil and had deployed VP52 there on 11 December 1941 followed by VP83 on 13 June 1942.[31]

In April and May 1943 the Brazilian Air Force made two attacks on U boats but without achieving a kill; but in July it

Above: A painting of a Brazilian Air Force Hudson. A Brazilian Air Force Hudson was involved in attacks on U-199 which ultimately sank in position 23°54′S 42°54′W off Rio de Janeiro.

was rather different. U-199 captained by Kl Hans Werner had sailed from Germany on 13 May and on 27 June attacked an unescorted Liberty ship about fifty miles off Rio de Janeiro. It shot down a PBM Mariner of the US Navy on 3 July and on 24 July sank *Henzada* a British ship.

On the thirty-first in an attack by Lt W.F. Smith flying a PBM, U-199 suffered damage which precluded it submerging. Convoy JT3 was due to sail from Rio de Janeiro and two Brazilian aircraft forming part of its cover now entered the fray; a PBY commanded by *Capitao Aviador* Jose Maria Mendes Coutinho Marques and a Hudson piloted by *Tenente Aviador* Sergio C. Schnoor from Galeao air base. They were able to co-ordinate their attacks and between the first and second runs made by the PBY, Werner ordered his crew to abandon ship and it sank three seconds after the PBY's second run. The Hudson had claimed no hits with depth charges but its machine-gun fire must have countered the U boat's AA for the PBY to attack. U-199 sank in position 23°54′S 42°54′W and there were twelve survivors including its captain. The PBY dropped some dinghies and remained in the area until the US tender *Barnegat* arrived.

For the two months 20 June to 20 August the U boat diary gives seven U boats operating off the Brazilian coast as far as Rio de Janeiro and sinking fourteen ships for the loss of five U boats. From Trinidad to the Amazon three U boats were lost out of eight; in the Caribbean area four U boats out of nine were lost against the sinking of three ships.[32]

Italian submarines also operated off the Brazilian coast with five of them detailed for the early part of 1943. *Capellini* sailed from La Pallice on 26 December 1942 and by 21 January was in the area of Fortaleza. After reaching Marinique in February, it was short of fuel and returned to Bordeaux on 4 March. *Barbarigo* and *Bagnolini* followed from La Pallice in January and February respectively. All three submarines were subjected to attacks by aircraft but suffered no serious damage and *Barbarigo* returned to Le Verdon on 3 April followed by *Bagnolini* on the thirteenth.

Torelli left Le Verdon on 21 February captained by Lt/Cmdr Antonia de Giacomo on 11 March. He received twenty-five tons of oil from *Barbarigo*, but later when about 270 miles from Fernando de Nironha Island, *Torelli* was

located by a reconnaissance aircraft and suffered a series of aerial attacks in which much oil was lost and the radio damaged. De Giacomo decided to return to port. The final foray was by *Archimede* commanded by Lt Guido Sacardo who sailed from Le Verdon on 26 February to operate in the Pernambuco or Recife area. On reaching position 16°45′S 37°30′W Sacardo was short of fuel and contemplated returning to port although there was the possibility of a rendezvous with a German supply submarine. The official Italian history records that *Archimede* was attacked on 15 April and sunk. This was by Ensign Robertson and Lt Bradford of the US Navy flying PBYs.[33]

The British naval historian, Capt. Roskill gives the greatest advantage to the Allies of Brazil's entry into the war as the whole of the South Atlantic coming under greater control from the use of Brazilian bases at Natal and Recife, this in addition to the Allied shipping organisation extending to the River Plate.[34]

Iceland

Iceland lying on the great circle route from Canada to the United Kingdom was of obvious interest to both Hitler and Winston Churchill. Churchill on 28 April 1940 addressed a directive to the First Sea Lord proposing that a base be set up in Iceland for flying-boats and for refuelling ships.

The first RAF Catalina P9630 a PBY-4 was flown by W/Cmdr L.K. Barnes on 25 September 1939 from Pembroke Dock via Invergordon to Iceland to undertake a

References
25. GüH p.121   26. RAAF III/297; USSL p.161
27. HV p.80; GüH p.122   28. RAAF III/287; GüH p.123
29. SEM I/259   30. BAF p.4; JR p.81
31. BAF pp.3–5; SWR II/203; SEM pp.376, 378, 281
32. GüH para365; App. p.109; SEM I/214; AH 'FC' pp.14 &18
33. AH 'FC' pp.16–17; UB Vol. XII pp.255–173 & Grafico 28
34. SWR II/203

Below: A parade of 269 Sqdn personnel in Iceland. Nissen huts used as billets were well-earthed up against gales and served for additional insulation. Walls of their billets were hung with blankets for further warmth and sleeping bags were issued.

Above: No.269 Sqdn at Kaldadarnes, Iceland on 27.4.41. When the River Olfusa flooded its base, No.269 moved to Reykjavik.

reconnaissance of the Icelandic fjords seeking any German ships.[35]

Following the occupation of Norway and Denmark, the British sent an advance party of Royal Marines in the cruisers HMS *Glasgow* and *Berwick* to arrive at Reykjavik on 10 May 1940. This was to forestall any move by the Germans in that direction.[36] They were followed by Canadian troops from Halifax, Nova Scotia in June and July. No.98 Squadron RAF, equipped with Fairey Battles was sent to Iceland in August but they were considered unsuitable for the task and in January 1941 the decisision to send a Hudson squadron and one equipped with Sunderlands was made.

No.269 Squadron, then at Wick, sent a detachment of Hudsons to Iceland in March 1941 and by 26 June were based at Kaldadarnes. The Norwegian squadron No.330, equipped with Northrop float-planes, was also deployed from Iceland. The units came under No.15 Group, Coastal Command control but an area headquarters was set up in Iceland. Subsequently, other squadrons such as Nos 162 RCAF, VP63, and VP84 of the USN also operated from Iceland and with success. Liberators from such as No.120 Squadron later helped to close the Mid-Atlantic gap.

In March 1941 Hitler specified Icelandic waters as a war zone and President Roosevelt ordered a reconnaissance of the area. This was undertaken by the USS *Niblack* in April. On 16 June 1941 Roosevelt directed US forces to relieve British Garrison units in Iceland for which an invitation was received from Iceland's Prime Minister, Herman Jonasson. The American task Force No.19 led by the battleship USS *New York* reached Reykjavik on 7 July 1941. The defence of Iceland became America's responsibility.[37] A Wop/AG with No.269 at that time was Wilf Jones who describes their living conditions at Kaldadarnes thus:

We were accommodated in Nissen huts which were anchored down with hawsers and banked halfway up with earth to resist the strong winds which could reach 120mph. The heating was the usual RAF stove and coal being rationed and insufficient, some American Army friends supplied us with a 'pot belly' stove and a lorry load of fuel for which we were very thankful. We bartered spirits for bacon, butter, cigars etc. There were no laundry facilities, so we had to wash our own

clothes in water which was always brown. For entertainment there was a small cinema which had been a barn, with no heating; Irvin jackets and flying boots being worn to keep out the cold. The films were right up to date as they came direct from the USA for the American troops who lent them to us. We had problems with wings icing on early take-offs and had to use heaters to de-ice the mainplane. I had difficulty with 'dead spaces' for radio communications and we had to use gyro compasses as others were unsatisfactory. The three things I remember most about Iceland are Northern Lights, most spectacular, never to be forgotten; always windy; very cold in winter and very little daylight.

The Capture of a U boat

On 27 August 1941 No.269 had nine serviceable Hudsons and they were deployed on an A/S sweep. At 0640hrs Sgt Mitchell was flying at 1000ft when he sighted a swirl and a wake at 800 yards distance. At 0730hrs after a search a U boat was sighted on the surface in position 62°43'N 18°55'W and at one mile distance. Mitchell dived from 800ft down to attack at 100ft but the DCs failed to release. A square search was continued until 1220hrs.

S/Ldr Thompson captained one of three Hudsons intended for a strike and was airborne at 0845hrs. He sighted a fully surfaced U boat in position 62°13'N 18°35'W and attacked first with four DCs from 100ft and released from fifty feet. The operational record states that they 'hit' the U boat which was straddled. A minute after the disturbance from the explosions ceased, the U boat began diving but re-surfaced with its bow down and ten to twelve crew appeared on deck. It was attacked with machine-gun fire until a white flag was waved and more of the crew appeared displaying a large white board. The Hudson requested assistance and was relieved by a Catalina from 209 Squadron at 1345hrs when S/Ldr Thompson returned to base. It was effectively the 'capture' of U-570 commanded by Kk Hans Rahmlow by the Hudson and was later illustrated in one of two wartime posters depicting Hudsons. U-570 later served with the Royal Navy as HMS *Graph*.

On the same day, Sgt Jones who was en route from Wick

Above: A landing strip at Höfn, Iceland which was used by 269 and very briefly by 48 Sqdn. Here with Hudson UA-Z of 269 is F/Lt C. Bardswell.

to Iceland made two attacks on a U boat at 1135hrs in position 62°00'N 17°40'W. He was aware of two explosions but claimed only a near miss. The American destroyer, USS *Greer* was attacked by U-652 at 0840hrs on 4 September 1941 in position 62°45'N 27°37'W and as Professor Morison states, '*De facto* war began' between USA and Germany. On that date five of No.269 Squadron's Hudsons were on an anti-submarine sweep and one of their captains, F/Sgt Reen, DFM, reported attacking a U boat with the help of an American destroyer. Reen had sighted a U boat in position 62°55'N 28°00'W at 1030hrs. From Reen's report it was located by the destroyer and the Hudson attacked the U boat two hours later releasing four 250lb DCs set at fifty feet depth. That afternoon 269 Squadron sent out three more Hudsons on a search from between 1325 and 2300hrs.[38]

On 5 October 1942 No.269 Squadron had eight Hudsons airborne including one captained by F/O J. Markham to cover convoy ONS136. The weather was becoming fair as Markham commenced a creeping-line-ahead (CLA) in position 59°50'N 23°30'W. At 1151hrs he sighted a fully-surfaced U boat at five miles heading west at six knots. Markham dived from 4000ft down to twenty feet releasing four Torpex DCs set at twenty-five feet depth. A patch of oil appeared and air bubbles and oil with wreckage surfaced ten minutes later. These marked the demise of what is now recorded as U-619 in position 58°41'N 22°58'W captained by Ol Kurt Makowski. He had sailed from Germany on 10 September although the U boat diary gives the 15 October for the sinking.[39]

The writer had formed part of a detachment from No.48 Squadron to Iceland in September 1942 flying initially to Höfn in the south-east. He was airborne in Hudson FH361 captained by F/O Beck at 0800hrs from Sumburgh on the twenty-fourth for a flight of four-and-a-quarter hours. Höfn appeared like a scene from *Mash*, the only indication of it being a flying field was a windsock. There was no runway and the thick volcanic ash was deeply rutted. One of the Hudsons captained by P/O R.A. Massey failed to get

airborne and went straight into the sea. Lost with Massey were the gunner P/O A.R. Glennie and the Wop/AG, Sgt R.S. Darke; only the Canadian navigator managed to climb into the dinghy and was rescued. At that time the base was occupied by American forces who told the author that although they had seven radios, not one of them functioned due to lack of spare parts. Refuelling would have meant using petrol tins and with the real risk of volcanic ash getting into the fuel systems; the 48 Squadron detachment elected to fly on to Kaldadarnes and share accommodation with 269 Squadron personnel.

Kaldadarnes had runways but conditions were still grim. Nissen huts were well earthed up, no doubt serving a double function of helping to anchor them against gales and providing additional insulation. In those used as billets, stoves were in full operation and the walls were hung with blankets. Personnel were issued with sleeping bags and uniforms were supplemented with special greatcoats and boots. A notable feature in the messes were dishes of vitamin C tablets due to lack of fresh fruit and vegetables. The 269 Squadron aircrew appeared remarkably cheerful considering the rather bleak landscape with the 'buildings' either Nissen huts or structures made of petrol tins filled with earth projecting from a very grey background.

No.269 Squadron detailed two aircraft to escort convoy UR44 and one Hudson to escort convoy RU43 on 10 October 1942 while T/269 was to patrol off Budereyri to cover minesweepers. 'T' was captained by F/Sgt W.S. Bowen and while in position 65°20'N 13°20'W at 1242hrs and in sight of two minesweepers had a Northrop float plane come up from astern to fly alongside for a minute. Bowen gave the letter of the day and the Northrop pilot waved and left. At 1255hrs six minesweepers emerged from a fjord; the Hudson signalled but received no reply. It was later challenged by the ships and responded. At 1301hrs Bowen was leaving the area in good visibility, below cloud at 1500ft when his second pilot said he'd seen a red rocket, later thought to be tracer. P/O Walthinshaw came from the Hudson's turret stating that a Northrop aircraft had attacked something astern and apparently used DCs. There was then a loud explosion and P/O Walthinshaw collapsed killed by a bullet which had entered the dome from behind and above. It also wounded Bowen in the head who was near Walthinshaw and splinters wounded the second pilot. Base was signalled and Bowen landed at 1450hrs. It appears likely that that the lethal bullet came from an over-zealous or careless Northrop crew from No.330 (Norge) Squadron.

Despite bad weather, No.269 had eight aircraft airborne on 6 February including F/S Bowen, captain of 'D' and P/O A.L. Greenacre flying 'T'. Bowen was airborne from Kaldadarnes at 0919hrs and as he recalls:

Cloud base was almost nil and I decided to climb out of it. The severe icing became apparent immediately and we did not get out of cloud until about 5500ft. We had the pulsating

References
35. AH 'FC' p.34   36. SWR I/245; SEM I/57
37. RAF I/222; SWR I/345; SEM I/74,77
38. SEM I/79; SWR I/472; Air 27-1565   39. GüH p.125; HH 290

leading edges in operation the whole time; there was St Elmo's fire with both props complete circles of vivid flames and they were throwing off ice particles which were hitting the fuselage like machine-gun fire. The building up of ice on the nose occurred three times.

We were helplessly watching the ice appearing on the nose and getting bigger and bigger until there was a loud explosion as it disappeared. Then it immediately started building up again. We had full power on both engines as we entered clear air and the aircraft was obviously within seconds of stalling and falling out of the sky like a brick of ice!

P/O Greenacre was airborne at 0924 for an ice recce and set course from Bjargtanger on a 330° track. In position 66°46'N 26°20'W he was over 1/10th brash ice and at position 66°51'N 27°27'W he reached drift ice. Ultimately Greenacre reached position 70°03'N 11°40'W from which he was able to sight Jan Mayen island. It was a feature of those serving in northern latitudes that on crossing the Arctic circle they became eligible for a 'Blue Nose' certificate. P/O Greenacre's was well-deserved. He landed at base at 1827hrs

after a flight of nine hours four minutes; no mean achievement for a Hudson under such hostile conditions.

Kaldadarnes is Flooded

On 6 March 1943 the River Olfusa burst its banks and the RAF station at Kaldadarnes was flooded; Wilf Jones serving there with No.269 Squadron gives this account:

I got back from UK leave. It was Saturday and we were spending the evening in the Mess, being entertained by the resident band which included Sam Costa, Denny Dennis and the late Cyril Stapleton. About 2200hrs the orderly sergeant came in to say that a flood warning was in force and the River Olfusa which ran past the camp was overflowing. Half-an-hour later someone looked outside and there was about two feet of water. We left the Mess immediately and returned to the billet through freezing cold water in order to collect our kit and stack it on shelves, hopefully out of reach of the flood water. We decided to spend the night in the Officers' Mess which was originally a farmhouse, as this was on the highest ground of the camp.

Below: An American Hudson without turret. They were operated by both the USN and AAC on anti-submarine sorties.

Next morning we could see the aircraft were up to the mainplanes in water and by this time it was decided to evacuate the camp. The American Army had a depot about six miles away and they brought boats to ferry us to waiting lorries which took us to Reykjavik. It was about two weeks later that the water receded sufficiently for us to fly the aircraft out. Kaldadarnes was never used again.

At Reykjavik 269 Squadron was accommodated in Camp Corbett.

No.269 Squadron at Reykjavik

The first operational sortie by 269 after the move to Reykjavik was appropriately one of their 'ice patrols'. This was on 15 March captained by P/O Coles who was airborne at 0903hrs with course set from Bjargtanger. In position 66°33'N 25°45'W dense cumulus cloud prevailed from the surface to 8000ft. The edge of brash ice was encountered. At position 66°33'N 26°00'W thick cloud again obscured the ice edge and P/O Coles returned to base.

No.269 Squadron had five aircraft flying on 17 May for an anti-submarine sweep from Reykjanes and then south-east to 60°30'N 20°00'W returning via Portland light.

F/O H.A. Henderson was airborne at 1402hrs. In position 62°04'N 13°54'W he sighted a fully surfaced U boat from 2000ft and ten miles away. The vessel disappeared three seconds before DCs were released 100ft ahead of the swirl which was straddled by two of the four charges which had been set for twenty-five feet depth and spaced at 100ft. F/Sgt J.M. Turnbull was airborne five minutes after Henderson and while flying at 3200ft sighted the wake of a U boat in position 60°55'N 17°30'W five miles away. An attack was made five seconds after the U boat had crash-dived. This was seen by F/O J. Coles in Hudson R/269 and an oil patch formed half-a-mile long by about forty-five yards wide.

J/269 captained by Sgt F.H.W. James was airborne at 1907hrs and undertook a creeping-line-ahead (CLA) search up and down the U boat's track. It was sighted fully-surfaced in position 62°07'N 14°48'W. James approached keeping as close to the water as possible and pulled up to fifty feet to release DCs spaced at 100ft set for twenty-five feet depth. The attack was at fifteen degrees bow to stern with the U boat completely surprised. All the charges exploded close to the vessel and photographs were taken to confirm the results.

James circled and saw large columns of smoke and an oil patch 150 yards diameter with debris including narrow reddish coloured objects about six feet in length. It was the demise of U-646 in position 62°10'N 14°30'W captained by Ol H. Wulff which had sailed from Norway on 12 May.[40]

Two days later No.269 Squadron claimed another victory. On the nineteenth F/O J.N.P. Bell sighted a U boat on the surface through gaps in the cloud but eight miles away when in position 58°38'N 25°48'W. The vessel dived before any attack could be made and Bell adopted baiting tactics. He flew ahead of the U boat's postion and on sighting the vessel again, used cloud cover, lost height to 600ft when the U boat was six miles ahead and dived on its port quarter releasing DCs. Five seamen were seen on the conning tower and one man attempted to use AA guns but he was machine-gunned

and panic ensued. The U boat circled to starboard losing oil before disappearing. U-273 which had sailed from Germany on the eighth was lost in this attack.[41]

No.269 Squadron flew nine sorties on 8 June 1943 including one by Sgt R. Couchman who was airborne at 1040hrs. He was in five-tenths cloud at 1200ft when a U boat was sighted six miles away heading west at fourteen knots. Using cloud cover, Couchman lost height to 700ft when the vessel was three quarters of a mile away. He attacked from eighty feet with Torpex DCs spaced at 100ft. They straddled the U boat, two falling either side aft of the conning tower. The vessel went round in circles losing oil and was down at the stern. There was an exchange of gunfire before the U boat went down after eighteen minutes. An oil patch two-and-a-half miles by 300 yards was left. U-535 had sailed from a home port on 25 May and was only damaged in this attack but was sunk by 53 Squadron on 5 July in position 43°38'N 09°13'W.[42]

F/Sgt E.L.J. Brame was airborne at 0439hrs on 3 August for a 'Moorings' patrol and in position 62°03'N 12°52'W sighted a fully-surfaced U boat. He attacked from 3500ft with two A/S bombs but in a second attempt was unable to achieve a bow-on attack due to heavy AA fire and the U boat's avoiding action. Although only a near miss was claimed, U-489 captained by Ol A. Schmandt was damaged by the Hudson only to be sunk the following day by a Sunderland of 423 Squadron in position 61°11'N 14°38'W.[43] No.269 Squadron achieved two more successes in October. P/O H.B. Smith was airborne in V9047 for an A/S sweep at 0730hrs on the fourth and at 0910 hrs sighted a surfaced U boat six miles away in position 62°02'N 28°27'W. Smith attacked immediately with guns and DCs. From the Command's record this was U-731 which was damaged in this attack. It had sailed from France on 29 August and returned there on 1 November.[44]

The following day F/Sgt G.C. Allsop was airborne in FK764 and after just over an hour was in position 62°43'N 27°17'W where a U boat was sighted. Allsop attacked with Rocket Projectiles (RPs) and the forepart of the vessel was covered in smoke. It rose at an angle of forty-five degrees out of the water before sliding down. An oil patch appeared with about fifteen bodies. It was the demise of U-336 commanded by Kl Hans Hunger. From the U boat diary, U-336 was one of three U boats of the *Rossbach* group sunk while attempting to attack convoys ONS 19 and ON 204 during the first week of October.[45] This sinking by F/Sgt Allsop of No.269 Squadron proved to be the last sinking by a Lockheed Hudson. The turning point in the Battle of the Atlantic had been 24 May 1943 when Admiral Dönitz ordered the withdrawal from the North Atlantic of U boats which had suffered severe losses.[46]

No.269 Squadron remained based in Iceland with Hudsons until January 1944 and was equipped with Hudsons until July

References
40. USSL p.163; GüH p.126   41. USSL p.163; GüH p.122
42. USSL p.164; CCWR p.18; GüH p.113
43. AH 'SS'p.92; GüH p.112; USSL p.164   44. CCWR p.18; GüH p.114
45. HH p.285; USSL p.163, GüH para.381   46. SWR II/377

1945. It was one of the longest serving and most successful of the Hudson squadrons. The RAF shared the honours and the discomforts with units from USA and Canada and ultimately, what had long been required for anti-U boat warfare, long-range Liberators to complete the closure of the 'Mid-Atlantic Gap'.[47]

Atlantic Patrols from the United Kingdom

From the outbreak of war in September 1939 until 17 March 1941 most of the sinkings of Allied merchant ships by U boats occurred close to the United Kingdom's western coast. By December 1941 sinkings of ships were thinning out but extended from Cape Farewell, Greenland down to Freetown, West Africa.[48] Bases had been contructed in Northern Ireland, The Shetlands, Scotland, and the Inner and Outer Hebrides. More squadrons had been formed in Coastal Command and what came to be the main anti-submarine device for their aircraft, the 250lb depth charge was developed and was coming into service in 1940 initially filled with Amatol and subsequently Torpex. An improved pistol for detonation for depths of thirty-two feet and later of twenty-five feet was also produced.[49]

Coastal Command crews became more fully trained and experienced in anti-submarine warfare. While U boats were limited in the routes taken from French bases, there was more latitude for them in the northern routes. The aircrews experienced more severe weather to the north although in summer months there were very long days with the midnight sun, thus limiting the time for U boats to charge their batteries. Hudson squadrons came to use St Eval, Cornwall; Nutt's Corner, Ballykelly, Aldergrove and Limavady in Northern Ireland; Tiree in the Inner Hebrides, Stornoway, Outer Hebrides; Wick in Scotland, and Sumburgh in the Shetlands. Their prime duty became the protection of the North Atlantic convoys which could be by actually circling the convoy; by undertaking sweeps with perhaps three or more Hudsons flying parallel tracks ahead of a convoy, or possibly a search ahead of the ships.

Below: FH237 Q-OY of No.48 Sqdn at Sumburgh, Shetlands on 22.10.42. No.48 Sqdn operated from both Sumburgh and Wick for Norge sorties and suffered losses accordingly.

Above: The operations room at Derby House, Liverpool; the nerve centre in WWII for the Battle of the Atlantic.

The relatively few attacks by Hudsons operating from bases in the United Kingdom over the Atlantic may be attributed partly to the success of aircraft in driving U boats away from the north-western approaches, and the limited range of Hudsons compared with such as Catalinas, Sunderlands and Liberators. No.269 Squadron by operating from bases much further westwards in Iceland and also with a detachment at Bluie West One (BW1) in Greenland, were well placed to encounter U boats which expected to locate convoys from North America rather than aircraft from the east.

No.53 Squadron was based at St Eval in October 1941 and their first anti-U boat success was on 30 October. P/O Henry captained PZ-H which was airborne at 1140hrs. His radar operator obtained a blip and a surfaced U boat was seen in position 48°00'N 09°10'W. Henry dived from 600ft and at 300ft released three DCs. Catalina AH545 captained by F/O D.M. Ryan of 209 Squadron appeared and released two more DCs. These attacks on U-81 damaged it requiring it to return to base.[50]

From January 1942 No.48 Squadron was operating from Wick and undertook many Norge patrols suffering appreciable losses as a result. In September it moved up to Sumburgh in the Shetlands undertaking not only patrols to Norway but a number of sorties covering the north-western approaches.

On 26 September P/O E. Thammes was airborne in OY-A

at 0839hrs and two hours later sighted a surfaced U boat four miles away. He attacked with four DCs released from fifty feet when the U boat was still visible. P/O R. Hornby was airborne at 1230hrs in OY-Z on a similar patrol near the Faeroes and he located the U boat eight miles away. He dived to attack releasing four DCs from fifty feet which fell thirty yards ahead of the U boat swirl it having submerged just twelve seconds earlier. Hornby remained for eighteen minutes before undertaking a square search and returning to the scene. Both attacks were on U-262 captained by Kl H. Franke and which was damaged.[51]

Hudson Versus Kondor (Fw 200)

In addition to U boats Germany used aircraft to attack shipping. These included the Fw 200 Kondor which was able to fly a long circuit from France to Norway and return. They were able, in addition to bombing ships, to report the positions of convoys to U boats. During the months of June, July and August 1941 enemy aircraft in all waters destroyed forty-four ships totalling 94,551 tons and damaged others.[52]

The Fw 200s were particularly dangerous for the Gibraltar convoys as their routes were under observation for much of the time. In July the threat was so serious that Gibraltar convoys were routed further west.[53] In that month No.233 Squadron was based at Aldergrove in Northern Ireland and on the seventeenth F/Lt Winnicott captained Hudson T9430 to escort convoy OB346. On sighting a Kondor he tried to close the range but the enemy made off. A signal from a destroyer 147 gave: 'Q/502 shot down by Kondor crew safe on *Wescott*.'

On 23 July P/O Ron Down captained AM536 ZS-J on an escort to a Gibraltar convoy OG69. He was airborne at 0316hrs and met the convoy at 0707hrs in position 54°08′N 13°28′W then on course 205° at six to eight knots. At

Below: A Focke-Wulf 200 Kondor shot down by a 233 Sqdn Hudson crew captained by F/O R. Down in position 54°08′N 13°28′W on 23 July 1941.

0801hrs as the Hudson was about to leave the convoy having reached PLE, a corvette flashed the message: 'suspicious aircraft on starboard'. It was a Fw 200 which P/O Down closed to within 400 yards on its port quarter at 180 to 200 knots having dived down to 100ft during a four-mile approach. Down opened fire with his two fixed .303 Brownings and the enemy responded with his top and rear guns. Ken Harper then in the Hudson's turret continues:

A turn was made which brought our Hudson alongside and a bit lower than the enemy at a range of about 200 yards and I was able to open fire over our starboard propeller . . . I could see tracer hitting the Kondor's port inner engine and the port side of the fuselage aft of the cockpit. At the same time the second pilot P/O Corken was shooting the Vickers gun from our starboard cabin window. The Kondor was using all the guns he could bring to bear but missing his target.

From 233's records it can be seen that the Hudson became as close as twenty to thirty feet to port and beneath the Kondor enabling point blank range for both side and rear guns.

Firing continued until the range was down to about thirty feet off the Kondor's port wing tip when a face appeared at one of his windows but disappeared when the window shattered . . . both the Kondor's port engines were seen to be on fire and trailing smoke . . . it turned away and I was able to shoot at his underside. We turned and had to pull up over the enemy as we were dangerously low over the sea. This gave Hugh Fisher a chance to have a go with our ventral gun. The Kondor continued to fly away but was shortly seen to land on the water. Its dinghy opened and five crew members were seen in the water with one walking along the top of the fuselage. We made a few circuits of the sinking aircraft to see the crew climb into the dinghy and a Naval corvette heading away from the convoy to pick them up. Our relief aircraft, a Wellington, arrived and we left after seeing the ships' crews on the decks waving to us. We landed at Aldergrove after a flight of six-and-a-half hours. The only damage to our aircraft was a small bullet hole in the starboard rudder hinge. We learned later after the German airmen had been landed at Liverpool that the crew consisted of six *Luftwaffe* airmen on their third war flight and one, a civilian meteorological observer, was shot and killed. Our first burst hit one of their cannon shell magazines and started a fire and the pilot, a warrant officer had been badly burned when he tried to open an escape hatch.

No.233 Squadron moved down from Aldergrove, Northern Ireland to St Eval, Cornwall in August 1941. It had a detachment at Gibraltar where in June 1942 it became based.

The Loss of Hudson AE613

P/O T. Kennan of 206 Squadron was airborne from St Eval at 0400hrs on 7 July 1941 in Hudson AE613 for a cross-over patrol off the French coast This was intended to cover the

References
47. See also AH 'FC' pp.34–43; AH 'SS' pp.50–55
48. WSC III/135–137   49. RAF II/100–101; SWR I/135–136
50. CCWR p.17   51. CCWR p.16   52. SWR I/456
53. SR I/468

Above: An A-29 of the USAAC complete with turret and two fixed forward-firing guns.

possible escape of the battle-cruisers *Scharnhorst* and *Gneisnenau* from Brest. Two-and-a-half hours later while flying at 500ft altitude and about 100 miles off Ushant, his starboard engine caught fire; the fire was extinguished but the engine was u/s. Kennan attempted to return to base but the port engine also failed and at 0630hrs the Hudson was ditched. An SOS had been received by base and Hudsons, a Blenheim and a Wellington were alerted. At 1220hrs P/O Wills in M/206 sighted the dinghy with all of Kennan's crew on board and it was circled until Wills reached PLE.

Sunderland RB-L T9047 from No.10 Squadron RAAF captained by F/Lt G. Thurston was en route for a cross-over patrol and twice received diversion signals, the second requiring him to search for the dinghy. He made a square search of the position given and was then directed by a Hudson (probably P/O Wills') at 1600hrs.

Although calm, there was a heavy swell on the sea and during what proved a hard landing the port outer engine of the Sunderland was torn off and cables to the float were broken and some of the Sunderland crew went on to the starboard wing to maintain an even keel.

The Hudson dinghy was about 300 yards away and Cpl Asker of the Sunderland crew launched a dinghy, rowed out to the Hudson crew and towed them back to the flying boat. With now both crews aboard, F/Lt Thurston began taxying towards the Scilly Isles and was sighted by two other Hudsons. Hudson E/206 saw also two destroyers at 2200hrs and (from 206's records) one was alongside the Sunderland at 0100hrs with the second destroyer circling. The one alongside, HMS *Brocklesby* lowered a boat and both Hudson and Sunderland crews were rescued. The destroyers withdrew to about 2000 yards for them to sink the Sunderland by gunfire.

Postwar, the writer was speaking to an ex-Secretary General of the RAF Association, Frank Neale. On finding that Frank served in the Navy he asked: 'Which ship?' – HMS *Brocklesby*! Frank Neale was one of the crew at the time of the rescue which took place on 10 July 1941.[54]

West Africa

In early 1941 U boats in the South Atlantic were able to refuel in the Canary Islands with the connivance of the Spaniards and in May 1941 thirty ships of 176,168 tons were sunk within 600 miles of Freetown and Bathurst.[55]

No.95 Squadron had Sunderlands based at Freetown under W/Cmdr Fergus Pearce in March 1941 but they were to be reinforced by Hudsons of No.200 Squadron. This Unit was re-formed at Bircham Newton in May with the Australian W/Cmdr C.D. Candy as Commanding Officer. Seven Hudsons left on 12 June flying via Gibraltar and on 18 June five Hudsons arrived at Jeswang near Bathurst. A Wop/AG, Vic Pounder who served with both 206 and 200 Squadrons, gives this account:

> As the Hudsons were fitted with long range tanks only three of the crew flew and the rest went by sea. We still used the code letters VX [those of No.206 Sqdn]. We were used mostly on convoy duties over the South Atlantic from off Dakar to south of Bathurst. We also flew photo-recces over the Cape Verde Islands because they were used for refuelling U boats and German aircraft; also over Dakar where a French battleship *Richeleau* was berthed. I was with 200 Squadron until June 1942 and most of the replacement crews were from the South African Air Force.

Vic Pounder had an eventful trip in October when one of the crew in Hudson AE622. It was airborne from Jeswang at 0715hrs on the tenth for a recce of the Cape Verde Islands and equipped with long range tanks. Three hours later the Hudson was over St Vincent. A signal to abandon the recce and to escort convoy 05S/7/34 was received and course was set for Bonvista and thence to the convoy. While on a square search for the convoy at 1215hrs the oil pressure in the port engine dropped and the pilot endeavoured to maintain height on one engine at 2600rpm. Excess equipment was jettisoned and an SOS transmitted. At 1415hrs the Hudson was ditched 136 miles from land and along the swell. The door failed to jettison and the dinghy which remained uninflated was flung fifty yards ahead of the aircraft. It remained waterborne for twenty seconds and the crew of four were able to exit and swim to the dinghy which was inverted. Two sharks appeared and in driving them off the dinghy pump was lost.

They clung to the dinghy so positioned that each could cover his opposite number against sharks which were driven off by splashing. After about two hours a Hudson was sighted four miles away; the distress signal was u/s however due to sea water and emergency rations were lost in an attempt to attract attention. The air valve on the dinghy was located and the dinghy was inflated by mouth. A second Hudson was seen six miles away; by then the crew had entered the dinghy and baled out water and blocked two holes in the bottom with epaulettes from shirts. Their stock was now one dinghy, four Mae Wests, one u/s signal rocket, one drogue used for baling, an empty ration tin and a small flask of brandy. At dusk a Sunderland was seen heading west. During the night two stayed on watch while the other two attempted to sleep. The dinghy required baling out every half hour. After moonrise two searchlights were seen over the horizon and two to three hours after sunrise on 11 October, a Hudson was sighted on a square search. At about 1130hrs a Hudson passed within 200 to 400 yards at 500ft. An hour later another appeared about 800 yards away. A third one at two or three miles was followed shortly after by a fourth and attention was gained. Its crew dropped a smoke float and released a canvas bag with the message 'Help coming, Navy on the job.' This with three partly filled bottles of lime juice.

This was Hudson E/200 captained by F/O Donalds who circled for about an hour before dropping two sea markers and a marine distress signal before returning to base. A violent storm broke out during the night with heavy seas and rain; the dinghy shipped water but rode the sea well but constant baling was necessary because of holes in the bottom. It lasted for about three hours. A yellow rocket had been seen and the survivors fired theirs but without response.

An hour after sunrise on 12 October a Hudson was sighted making a search eastwards and ninety minutes later a ship's mast was seen and then the approach of a destroyer. A boat was lowered and the crew of four, F/Lt Webster, P/O Henry. F/Sgt Foy and Sgt Pounder were taken aboard HMS *Vimy*. The Navy had been alerted by some paper on the water which was investigated but had seen the dinghy from two miles in fine weather but with a heavy swell.

Following the withdrawal of U boats from the North Atlantic on 24 May 1943, groups such as *Monsun* of eleven U boats headed for the Indian Ocean but in July were refuelling between the Azores and the Cape Verde Islands.[56]

Between 20 June and 20 August fifteen U boats were operating off the West African coast from Dakar to the Gulf of Guinea. They claimed nine Allied ships but sank five totalling 30,453 tons and damaged two totalling 10,644 tons for the loss of two U boats.[57]

In August No.200 Squadron Hudsons were operating from Yundum and during this period eleven U boats were short of fuel and seeking supplies west of the Azores.[58] The Hudsons were deployed in escorting convoy SL135 and the Corbrae group comprising a merchant ship with four escort vessels. Additionally a Hudson was used to ferry personnel of *L'Armee de l'Air* who had been on detachment at Yundum for training.

On 17 August F/O P.R. Horbat with his crew of F/O C.J. Whiles and Sgts G. Berry and J.L.A. Cote were detailed to escort convoy SL135 in Hudson O/200. They were airborne at 0617hrs and met the convoy at 0640hrs. They first sighted a 'suspicious object' at 0725hrs and again at 0929hrs when it was confirmed as being a U boat. F/O Horbat attacked from fifty feet releasing four DCs four seconds after the U boat had submerged. The convoy was notified giving the position; an oil patch appeared together with some debris. The Hudson was relieved by a Sunderland and Horbat returned to base landing at 1326hrs.

On the 18th an attack was made by Wellington HZ697 then with No.344 Squadron flown by the Free French but under RAF control. Both No.200 Squadron and Wellington HZ697 were credited with sinking U-403 captained by Kk Rolf-Heinrich Heine which went down in position 14°11'N 17°40'W. U-403 had sunk three Allied ships but when commanded by Kl Clausen.[59]

No.200 Squadron had been receiving Liberator aircraft in July and on 11 August P/O L.A. Trigg, a New Zealander, captained BZ832 D/200 which attacked U-468. Trigg was shot down in the action and U-468 was sunk. Some of the U boat's survivors were able to use the aircraft's dinghy and it was due to their testimony that Trigg was awarded a posthumous VC.[60]

Indian Ocean Interlude

No.8 Squadron RAF based at Khormaksar began receiving Hudsons in February 1943 and was operating them in March. After the capture of Italian East African colonies, No.8 Squadron had detachments in Somaliland and undertook A/S patrols over the Indian Ocean. In July 1943 they made three attacks on submarines the last of these being on the fourteenth.

The Japanese submarine I-29 captained by Izu had, between 10 September and 23 November 1942, sunk five ships in the Indian Ocean and on 12 July 1943 sank the *Rahmani* of 5463 tons in position 14°52'N 52°06'E at 0922hrs.

Hudson FK628 captained by F/Sgt N. Miller was airborne at 0956hrs on the fourteenth and at 1210hrs sighted a submarine in position 12°13'N 51°13'E. Miller attacked releasing three depth charges which straddled the vessel before it submerged. An oil patch appeared followed by a long trail of oil. Some reports gave this as a 'kill' but it is now believed that the submarine was the Japanese I-29 which was only damaged. From official lists, I-29 captained by Kinashi was sunk off Luzon in position 20°10'N 121°50'E by USS *Sawfish* (SS-276) on 26 July 1944.[61]

References
54. Air 27-1223; KB pp.157–163
55. SWR I/470; GüH para.158 56. GüH plan 62 57. GüH para 365
58. SWR III/I p.31 59. JR. p.304 60. CBp.333; SWR III/I p.32
61. SAAF VII/275; NF 259; SWR III/2/p.470; USSL p.176; JH p.35; JR p.293

Chapter 5

Gibraltar and the Mediterranean

Gibraltar has been British since 1704; in World War II it served as a base for the Royal Navy and the RAF and circa 1942 to 1943, was garrisoned by the Devon Regiment.

British strategy had been based on having France as an ally rather than as an enemy and with France responsible for protecting the western Mediterranean and the British, the eastern basin. With the fall of France in 1940, there remained a powerful French fleet which could be hostile. Entry of Italy into the war at the same time resulted in a further powerful hostile fleet including about 100 submarines. Thus was the route to the Far East closed via the Mediterranean.

'Force H' was based by the Navy at Gibraltar and for the RAF, the harbour provided a base for flying boats and what had been a racecourse served as an airfield for other aircraft. Additionally, Gibraltar became an important staging post for aircraft moving in all directions. The British were determined to maintain Malta and it was supplied via Gibraltar. The Army's engineers were circa 1943 extending the runway into the harbour, i.e. westwards using rock blasted from the north face of what had originally been spoil from tunnelling within the rock.

One of the vital roles for Gibraltar in World War II was to serve as the hub for Operation *Torch*, the invasion of former French bases in North Africa. Hudson-equipped squadrons played an important part in that operation. From Gibraltar, Hudsons undertook patrols round the Portuguese coast, southwards around the north-west African coast, and eastwards typically to seven degrees east. The Australian squadron, No.459, operated over the eastern Mediterranean assisting in covering Allied convoys and attacking enemy shipping and submarines. No.233 Squadron was one of the first Hudson units to operate from North Front, Gibraltar and one of their wireless operators, Wilfred Jones states: 'Three aircraft were detached to Gibraltar in September 1941; we all returned to St Eval with ground crews on 2 October. The landing strip in September 1941 was still fairly rough and they had squads of men working on it while we were there.'

Jones had flown in T9430 with S/Ldr Devey who was to see if Hudsons could operate from Gibraltar and had taken their ground crews with them. They found the landing strip to be about 900 yards long and initially had no radio facilities but were able to use Spanish beacons to obtain bearings with the Bendix radio compass. The Royal Navy set up a transmitter for them on one of the Hudson's frequencies. While there, Jones' crew flew five sorties including a Malta convoy escort on 27 September which comprised nine merchant vessels with HMS *Nelson, Rodney, Prince of Wales, Ark Royal,* five cruisers and eighteen destroyers.

On 29 September HMS *Nelson* was escorted back to Gibraltar having been damaged by a torpedo. Lack of a suitable flarepath resulted in the Hudson making seven attempts in a night landing before touching down. The following year No.233 became based at Gibraltar and although we were at war with Germany and Italy, the serious enemy for the Hudsons were the Vichy French who, during one operation, shot down four out of five of 233's aircraft. When No.48 Squadron arrived at Gibraltar in December 1942 their aircrew were warned to beware of French aircraft.[1]

No.233's first anti-submarine success from Gibraltar was on 1 May 1942. P/O Camacho in T9387 attacked a U boat at 1305hrs apparently without success. At 1456hrs Sgt Brent in AM735 sighted a U boat heading east at eight knots. He made a diving attack from 1700ft releasing three DCs from thirty feet set at twenty-five feet depth and spaced at sixty feet. Two DCs exploded to starboard abaft the conning tower and the vessel submerged. A minute later ten feet of its bows appeared perpendicular to the surface before sliding down and settling on an even keel. About 100 to 120 of its crew appeared with hands raised until Brent left at 1520hrs.

Some lists give U-573 as being sunk in this attack at position 37°00′N 01°00′E, another as being damaged.[2]

Operation *Torch*

In 1942 Churchill gained the support from President Roosevelt for a second front with landings against the French in Morocco, Algeria and Tunisia.[3]

The date of 8 November was fixed to invade French bases in North Africa; Admiral Andrew Cunningham arrived at Gibraltar in HMS *Scylla* on 1 November to be responsible for all Naval operations; General Eisenhower flew in on 5 November as Allied Commander-in-Chief. RAF Gibraltar came officially under Eisenhower's command before reverting to Coastal Command control in October 1943.

Operation *Torch* for the Navy meant about 340 ships passing Gibraltar between 1930hrs on the fifth and 0400hrs on the seventh in a definite sequence.[4] For the Army, about 70,000 troops were to be deployed in attacks against the areas of Casablanca, Oran and Algiers on 8 November. Air Forces at Gibraltar were to include fourteen squadrons of fighters in addition to 233 and others such as 500 Squadron with Hudsons.

General Eisenhower refers to Gibraltar making possible the invasion of North Africa, Churchill states that the greatest contribution to the war from Gibraltar was its airfield, and Capt. Roskill refers to Gibraltar as the 'hub' of Operation

Above: The author's billet at North Front, Gibraltar in 1943 after it was hit by rock, intended for extending the runway westwards and blasted from the north face.

Torch.[5]

There were twenty-five U boats in the Mediterranean about the time of *Torch* and the Italians deployed thirty-four submarines between 02°E and 11°E off the North African coast in November.[6]

Operation *Torch* took the German High Command by surprise thinking that a second front was impossible and the French were expected to resist resulting in a final break of the French from the Allies. On 8 November the German U boat group *Streitaxt* was shadowing convoy SL125 and five from the *Delfin* group were entering the Straits of Gibraltar with the other two from *Delfin* off the coast of Portugal. Three others were outward bound from Biscay ports and twenty-one other U boats were in the North Atlantic 23°West or more.[7]

For the Italians: '*Il mese di novembre 1942 rappresento il "turning point" della 2 guerre mondiale nel Mediterraneo.*'[8]

The Two Auxiliary Squadrons

No.500 Squadron moved down from the UK in November and began operating from both North Front, Gibraltar, Tafaraouri, a former French station near Oran, and Blida. Some of the ground staff had been landed from invasion barges in Operation *Torch* on the beach north of Oran on the night of 8 and 9 November and when the French were still hostile. They camped that night on a breakwater and in the morning obtained food and water from an English ship. The US Army transported them to Tafaraouri on the eleventh. Tafaraouri aerodrome was considered 'well constructed' with two runways each of about 1200 yards. That same day F/O Green operating from Gibraltar on convoy escort witnessed the sinking of *Viceroy of India* which had been torpedoed by U-407.

On 7 November a 202 Squadron Catalina met a submarine and picked up General Giraud to fly him to Gibraltar. F/O Blakeley of 500 Squadron was briefed on the eighth for a flight in Hudson AM828 B/500 which had been painted in Vichy French markings, livery which for Nos 233 and 48 Squadrons were to be considered hostile. Terry Andrew in

Blakeley's crew gives this account:

At 0945hrs on 9 November we took off in AM828 from Gibraltar with the General and a small staff for Blida twenty-five miles SW of Algiers, escorted by six Spitfires. The flight of three-and-a-half hours was uneventful; the Hudson and its escort skirted around Oran where fighting was still going on and landed at Blida. The situation there was confused, some British commandos had occupied the airfield and they said that there was still sporadic fighting going on, in particular from a French fort just outside the town of Blida. General Giraud was driven away in a car to Algiers and the Hudson and crew were left not really knowing what the next move was; our six Spitfires were out of fuel and the Army was worried about our safety. F/O Blakeley decided to fly to Maison Blanche airfield, Algiers, which was known to have been secured and at 1400hrs we took-off, landing there after thirty minutes. Maison Blanche was receiving the first flights of Hurricanes from Gibraltar and the RAF servicing commandos who had just reached the airfield were awaiting the first cans of aviation fuel which came just as we landed. We loaded the cabin of the Hudson with five gallon tins of fuel and flew back to Blida where we gave our six Spitfires ten gallons each. We then took off with four of our Spitfires for Maison Blanche collecting a few bullet holes from whom we never found out.

Our arrival at Maison Blanche was dramatic; a raid by ten Ju 88s was in progress, bombing from about 8000ft; the newly arrived Hurricanes were taking off to engage them and we with our Vichy French markings were a target for all and sundry so we went straight in and landed followed by our Spitfire escort.

We spent the rest of the day at Maison Blanche dodging bombs and refuelling and arming the Spitfires to which we had got quite attached and which, once they were fuelled, got into the action just in time for the next and subsequent raids and they had a hand in knocking down several Ju 88s.

We had a supply of compo rations and lived and had our food in or near our Hudson. The next day our captain managed to get into Algiers to find out what our next move was to be and on 13 November 1942 we returned to Gibraltar landing first at La Senia near Oran which was very dodgy as the airfield had been badly bombed and shelled. Our aircraft was restored to its RAF livery and on 15 November we were in action against a U boat.

Under No.608 Squadron's adjutant, F/Lt Crump, 400 other ranks and eight officers sailed in HMT *Strathmore* from Gourock on 4 November. This was in support of the North African landings on the eighth but these personnel were due to arrive four days later. The unit's twenty-three Hudsons were at Exeter between 7 and 9 November and by the tenth P/O Penn and F/O Calvesbe were flying C/608 and D/608 on escort to a convoy which included HMT *Strathmore*.

From Gibraltar No.608 flew five A/S patrols including B/608 which attacked a U boat in position 36°00'N 01°30'W. Another Hudson which was airborne at 0816hrs failed to return.

References
1. RAAF III/p.412
2. USSL p.160; HH p.289; SWR II/p.467; CCWR p.14; NF p.142
3. WSC III/p.585; WSC IV/ pp 288, 289, 398 4. SWR II/pp.312–3, 320
5. SWR II/p.315; WSC IV/p.546 6. SWR II/p.333; MB Chart 11; AH 'SS' p.63
7. GüH para.269 & plan 25 8. MB p.99

No. 48 Squadron - Roster of aircraft and crews - 1200 hrs 4.2.43 to 1200 hrs 5.2.43.

Flight.	Aircraft.	Load.	Pilot.	Navigator.	W.Op./A.G.	W.Op./A.G.	Remarks.	CALL	MEAL	OPS	TAKE OFF
A.	H.	4 D.C's & 2 ASB.	Sgt. Davenport.	F/Sgt. Pearson.	Sgt. Mortenson.	Sgt. Hill.		0440	0500	0515	0640
B.	W.	Ditto.	P/O. Reid.	F/Sgt. McDonald.	Sgt. Revell.	Sgt. Best.			1130	1200	1330
A.	G.	Ditto.	P/O. Barrett.	P/O. Bonney.	Sgt. Passmore.	Sgt. Smiley.		0440	0500	0515	0640
B.	Q.	Ditto.	P/O. Mayhew.	P/O. Stewart.	Sgt. Matheson.	Sgt. Sargent.			1130	1200	1330
A.	J.	Ditto.	X P/O. Rollowfield.	F/Sgt. Sanders. X	Sgt. Coulson. X	P/O. Day. X		0550	0620	0620	0750 (St
B.	X.	Ditto.	P/O. Lawson.	F/Sgt. Bowen.	Sgt. Catterall.	Sgt. Stopford.					STRIKE
A.	B.	Ditto.	Sgt. Clarke.	F/Sgt. Oakley.	Sgt. Fisher.	Sgt. Pearson.					
B.	Q.	Ditto.	P/O. Fogal.	F/Sgt. Crick.	Sgt. Tyers.	Sgt. Haygens.					
A.	G.	Ditto.	P/O. Beck.	F/Sgt. Butcher.	Sgt. Hendrie.	P/O. Richmond.	Late trip.				

Aircraft available	-	Q, B, W, X, Z. Y(?). B, E, F, G, H - K (Non-ops).	
" detached	-	S.	
" U/S	-	J, D, U & T (Minor). V (Spares).	
Available	-	S/L. Disney & Crew. P/O. Turner & Crew. F/Lt. Howard & Crew. F/Sgt. MacDonald & Crew.	
		Sgt. Reynolds & Crew. P/O. Harrop. Sgt. Touhey.	
Detached	-	S/L. Fuller & Crew. F/Lt. Ainsworth & Crew.	
H.Qtrs Flight	-	W/Cdr. Devitt. F/Lt. Cansdale. P/O. Dawson.	
Day off	-	P/O. Bailey & Crew. Sgt. Friend & Crew.	
Training	-	P/O. Tunes & Crew. P/O. Mulheron.	
Sick	-	Sgt. Tunes. P/O. Chattaway. Sgt. Chapman.	
D.C.O.	-	W/Cdr. D.J. Devitt.	
S.D.O.	-	P/O. Richmond (1200 hrs 4.2.43 to 1200 hrs 5.2.43). P/O. Parsons (1200 hrs 5.2.43 to 1200 hrs 5.2.43.)	
S.D.S.	-	Sgt. Hendrie	Ditto	Sgt. Touhey	Ditto.

Above: No.48's flying detail for 4/5 February 1943 when based at Gibraltar.

Hudson AM629 was flown to Tafaraouri with personnel to set up a radio station at Oran and make a recce of Oran with naval personnel. P/O Livingstone brought the first despatch from General Eisenhower, the C-in-C, *Torch* landings.[9]

From Gibraltar on the thirteenth D/608 attacked a U boat in position 37°20′N 00°11′E and on that day the squadron personnel disembarked from HMT *Strathmore* at Algiers and marched to Jardin d'Essai to spend the night there. The following day they marched to the railway station and entrained for Blida where the aerodrome was to become RAF Blida. The squadron record stated: '. . . everywhere was quiet and the population both French and Arab seemed pleased to welcome the troops both at Algiers and Blida.' British destroyers however were attacked by the French at Algiers which was then controlled by the anti-British, Admiral Darlan.[10]

Below: A composite illustration of a 233 Sqdn Hudson coded O-ZS. While at Gibraltar 233 lost a number of aircraft; not to the Luftwaffe *but to the Vichy French.*

Above: The Governor of Gibraltar, General McFarlane, with W/Cmdr Gilbert and S/Ldr E.L. Baudoux of 233 Sqdn. Baudoux made one of the first successful attacks on a U boat when operating from Britain with 233 Sqdn.

No.608 Squadron at Blida

Eric Robinson Wop/AG who served with 608 gives this account:

The squadron arrived at Gibraltar on the morning of the invasion of North Africa Operation *Torch* and proceeded a couple of days later to Maison Blanche in a formation of three Hudsons navigating for and being escorted by nine Spitfires. As soon as we sighted Maison Blanche the Spitfires peeled off and landed, and without the pilots getting out of their cockpits they refuelled and took off straight away to do battle with Ju 88s driving them off.

On 12 November my crew was ordered to Blida arriving there in Hudson AM739 with Tony Hunter in command. It was a thirty minute flight from Maison Blanche. The French Commander saluted Tony and said: 'The airfield is yours'. We approached the Mess and some French officers invited us to join them in a drink. They told us they were flying Bostons

and had been under the orders of the Vichy French. I became friendly with a French airman who told me they had attempted to bomb Gibraltar on three occasions but found the flak very daunting.

Blida was a new airfield, there was no accommodation but I found a partially completed bungalow on the fringe of the airfield and made one room habitable. We had to service our own aircraft until the ground staff arrived by sea . . . food was sparse and we lived on what we could scrounge from the Arabs who were only too anxious to exchange anything including their daughters for food.

Our flying from Blida was in all directions, east, north, south and west but largely along the coast eastwards towards where the Africa Korps were doing battle with the 1st and 5th Armies. Our job was reconnaissance, anti-U boat and anything that commanders could dig up as a useful job for a Hudson.

Blida was a pleasant change from the winters of England. It had fruit in abundance, and of course there were the advantages of duty free at Gibraltar.

There were now to follow a whole series of successful attacks on U boats by Hudsons under the control of Headquarters at Gibraltar and with Coastal Command's record listing seven within eleven days, 14 to 24 November 1942.

S/Ldr J.B. Ensor of No.500 Squadron was airborne at 1150hrs on 13 November from North Front for an A/S sweep. On sighting a U boat five miles away he made a diving attack down to fifty feet releasing four DCs 150 yards ahead of the swirl forty seconds after the U boat had submerged.

Ensor made no claim for either a kill or damaging the vessel but it is given as U-511 sunk in this attack although the U boat diary gives U-511 sailing from France on 10.5.43.[11]

The other Ensor on 500 Squadron, F/O M. Ensor, DFC was airborne from Tafaraouri at 0927hrs on the thirteenth to

References
9. WSC IV/p.472
10. WSC IV/pp.550–1   11. GüH p.124; NF p.144 (now assessed 'sunk')

Below: Aircrew of No.500 Sqdn. This unit was posted to the Mediterranean area and was directly involved with Operation Torch *serving with great success against U boats.*

Above: A group of 500 Sqdn officers including their CO, W/Cmdr D. Spotswood, for an investiture at Buckingham Palace.

Above: AM524 of 500 Sqdn. It was ditched on 1 July 1943 due to lack of fuel.

encounter initially two Caproni 135 aircraft but with no combat. At 1403hrs however a U boat was sighted and attacked from thirty feet. Four DCs straddled its bow and a minute later it resurfaced but down by the bow. An A/S bomb was dropped near its starboard bow. The U boat circled slowly and there was an exchange of fire resulting in at least six U boat men going into the sea. With PLE up, Ensor left the U boat circling and apparently sinking. It was U-458 which had left a French port on 1 October and now credited as damaged in this attack. The U boat diary gives it as being lost in the Mediterranean.[12]

Attacks on U-595

Seven Hudsons were involved in the sinking of a U boat on 14 November, two from 608 Squadron and five from 500 Squadron. F/O G. Williams from 608 Squadron was the first to attack, so damaging the U boat that it was unable to submerge.

F/O G. Williams and P/O C.A. Livingstone from 608 were both airborne by 0732hrs on an A/S sweep east, apparently from Gibraltar. Williams, on sighting a U boat released four DCs from thirty to fifty feet straddling the vessel which appeared to sink on a level keel. When it re-surfaced Williams attacked with machine-guns until Livingstone also straddled the vessel with DCs before circling and the Hudson firing side guns to which the U boat responded with cannon. Livingstone then climbed to 1500ft to make a diving attack with front guns. A Ju 88 came out of cloud but Livingstone's turret gunner fired a short burst and the Ju 88 returned to cloud.

Hudsons from 500 Squadron airborne from Tafaraouri now followed led by W/Cmdr D. Spotswood. His DCs straddled the stern of the vessel but his Hudson was hit by a 6lb shell. F/O Green and F/O Lord's aircraft were both hit by shells in their attacks. The U boat began to make for the shore but was sighted by F/O Barwood who was on a sweep from Gibraltar and he released DCs. Finally P/O J.H. Simpson made two attacks, one with DCs and then with an A/S bomb as the U boat was beaching itself. It was U-595 which had sailed from France on 31 October but was lost in

position 36°38′N 00°30′E.[13]

Operating from Gibraltar, P/O J. Barling of 233 Squadron was airborne at 1120hrs on 14 November. At 1620hrs he attacked a U boat in position 36°20N 01°01′W releasing three DCs with direct hits on the hull. The vessel disappeared leaving an oil patch and debris. Despite this evidence, the sinking of U-605 was credited to HMS *Lotus* and *Poppy* in position 37°04′N 02°55′E. From the U boat diary U-605 sailed from France on 4 October only to be lost in the Mediterranean.[14]

On 15 November F/O M. Ensor was airborne from Tafaraouri and while flying at 1000ft sighted a U boat fully-surfaced. He dived to attack from fifty feet. The second of four DCs gained a direct hit and was thought to have exploded a torpedo.

There was an enormous explosion with the U boat's gun flung into the air and the conning tower ripped open. The Hudson was severely damaged with rudders, elevators and trimming tabs blown off. The turret and cabin floor were blown in and six feet of each wing tip were bent upwards. Ensor climbed to 1500ft using the crew as ballast and steering with engines. The port engine cut when over Algiers Bay and the Hudson went into a spiral dive. The crew were ordered to bale out but P/O Atkinson's parachute failed to open and Sgt Prior was knocked unconscious on leaving the aircraft and he was drowned. F/O Ensor and Sgt Roe were picked up by HMS *Erne* and *Leath*. The U boat was U-259 which had sailed from France on 5 November; it sank in position 37°20′N 03°05′E.[15]

Six Hudsons from 500 Squadron were airborne from Tafaraouri on 17 November for an A/S sweep. S/Ldr Paterson first sighted a surfaced U boat and straddled it with three DCs; its bow lifted out of the water and some of the crew appeared, to be immediately machine-gunned. An A/S bomb dropped among some of the crew in the water. Sgt Young's aircraft now released three DCs. and machine-gunned the vessel. F/Lt Barwood followed by attacking with four DCs. S/Ldr Paterson remained circling while Young and Barwood left the scene. Black smoke was emitted from the U boat and the crew appeared waving white objects in surrender.

Above: A 500 Sqdn Hudson fitted with a 0.5 Browning in the nose in addition to the two fixed 0.303 Brownings; this was to counter AA fire when attacking U boats.

Paterson left the scene to warn the Navy at Maison Blanche and a destroyer was to be sent. At 1600hrs a Martlett, Swordfish and Albacore arrived. Despite Paterson's signals, the Martlett machine-gunned the water and the Albacore released a torpedo. A few of the U boat's survivors were rescued by a Walrus. It was the demise of U-331 in position 37°05′N 02°24′E captained by Kl von Tiesenhausen. No.820 Sqdn FAA was credited together with 500 Squadron RAuxAF with the kill.[16]

Below: Frank Jones of 500 Sqdn at the radio position with Bendix transmitter and receiver.

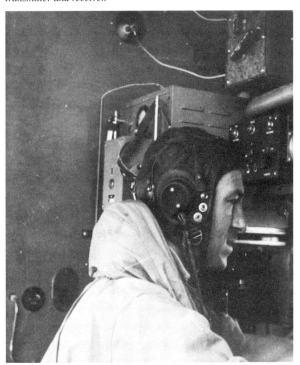

On that same day, 17 November, Sgt E.H. Smith of No.233 Squadron attacked a U boat in position 35°40′N 11°18′W. It was U-566 which had left France on 28 October and due to the damage in this attack, returned to France on 1 December.[17]

General H.H. Giraud had been brought out of France and was picked up by a Catalina, from No.202 Squadron. It was hoped by such as Churchill that he would prove useful to the Allies in perhaps rallying some of the French. On 17 November he was flown by P/O D.D. Pearce in Hudson A/608 from Maison Blanche to Bone.

F/O J.B.R. Petrie of No.608 Squadron was airborne at 0922hrs on 18 November for a patrol west of Gibraltar and at 1317hrs sighted a surfaced U boat. He dived to attack using his front guns. One man was seen trying to fire the cannon before scrambling into the conning tower. DCs were released as the vessel was submerging and ten minutes later when the U boat re-surfaced, the Hudson attacked with both front and turret guns. A shell from the U boat pierced the Hudson's elevator but without exploding. Five minutes after the attack the vessel set course on 080° at six knots. It was U-613 which had sailed from Germany on 22 October but returned to France on 27 November.[18]

The following day F/O A.F. Wilcox of 608 Squadron while on an A/S sweep west attacked a U boat in position 35°38′N 11°48′W and was credited with sinking U-98 although his DCs exploded seventy yards ahead of the swirl. Subsequent assessments give the attack as having been on

References
12. GuH p.123   13. GüH p.125; CCWR p.14; USSL p.161   14. USSL p.161
15. USSL p.161; GüH p.121   16. USSL p.161; SWR II/p.336; CCWR p.14
17. CCWR p.18; GüH p.124   18. CCWR p.18; GüH p.125

Below: Tafaraouri, near Oran, a former French base taken by the Allies during the Torch operation and here with a 500 Sqdn Hudson on fire.

Above: A 500 Sqdn Hudson flown by F/O Barwood over the Atlas Mountains, North Africa, circa early 1943.

U-413 which was only damaged.[19] The final success for Hudsons under Gibraltar's control in 1942 was achieved on 24 November by 233 Squadron. Sgt E.H. Smith was airborne in FH260 at 0916hrs and at 1135hrs attacked a U boat in position 36°40'N 11°58'W. It was recorded as having damaged U-263 which had sailed from Germany on 27 October but returned to France on 29 November.[20] After this attack there was a lull in the Hudson squadrons' offensive against U boats until another victory in February 1943.

A Parachute Descent

Hudson AM822 J/500 was airborne at 1245hrs from Blida on 6 December 1942 captained by F/O Derek Blakeley to escort a convoy including twenty troop transports for Philippeville. The convoy was left at nightfall; the weather closed in completely and it proved impossible to obtain a satisfactory fix. With the Atlas mountains in that area and then short of fuel, Blakeley gave the order to bale out. One of the crew, Terry Andrew gives this account:

Below: Bo Rizzo, Sicily, June 1944 with Hudson A/608 which crashlanded.

Above: Mount Vesuvius erupted on 18 March 1944 when 608 Sqdn was in Italy supporting Allied landings. Their Hudsons are seen here covered with volcanic ash.

My recollections of the parachute descent was the sudden quiet after the noise of the engines and a sharp jolt as my parachute opened; my descent in the dark was broken by a sudden glimpse of the dark shape of the mountains around me and within seconds I had arrived back on North African soil with a bump. Having spilled the parachute I realised that I was on high ground with a slope on my right and a chasm on my left. I made a limited exploration of the ground and found a ledge, and as there was little I could do in the way of moving in the dark I decided to stay there until daylight.

It was now about 2100hrs and I shouted to see if I could get any response from the rest of the crew but it appeared that I was completely on my own. I prepared for the night by cocooning myself in my parachute and tried to get some sleep but it was intensely cold and I did not get much. Eventually dawn came and in the half-light I could see where I was. I was halfway up the side of the mountain; I climbed to the top and found I was on a sort of plateau with a deep valley running through. I decided that it was somewhere in the Atlas Mountains which later proved correct. The North African coast runs mainly from East to West and I decided to walk north using my escape compass towards it. As I was not sure whether the locals were friendly, I proceeded with caution, but after about two hours walking saw that I had company; an Arab shepherd was walking towards me.

I thought a friendly approach was best and I spoke to him in French; he was no doubt surprised to see someone with a parachute over his arm in the mountains in the early morning, but he replied in a friendly way. I told him I was British and showed him the leaflet we all carried and asked where the nearest village was. He kept pointing back the way I had come saying: 'French soldiers in Warnier'.

I asked him to guide me there and we set off back over the mountains. After about three hours we came to a small outpost of a few huts which was manned by two French Foreign Legionnaires and a telegraphist. I said farewell to the Arab shepherd who had guided me over the mountains and opened my escape packet in which there were some French banknotes and gave him several as a token of thanks. I told the soldiers what had happened and they said that Orleanville; a bigger town was some twenty kilometres away and with the aid of my escape map I found out where I was. By now the telegraphist was very busy on a remarkable telephone of about 1914 vintage and I gathered that he was reporting my arrival and from what I could understand of the conversation, 'German parachutist', kept coming up, there was certainly doubt about me. Anyway I think I convinced them that I was British and told them that somewhere in the mountains the rest of the crew and suggested they started a search for them, this they reported to Orleanville. By now it was well into the afternoon and I had not eaten for a long time and one of the soldiers prepared me a meal of fried eggs and bread which was as good and as welcome as any I have tasted. The telephoning had now stopped but the phone interested me and I asked the telegraphist if he could get Blida *militaire Avion* base and said he would try and to my amazement after about twenty minutes he came up with 'Ullo Blida' and I was put through to a surprised operations room officer who, when I said who I was replied: 'You can't be, you went down yesterday'. My CO, W Cmdr Spotswood was there and although the line was not very clear I managed to tell him we had all baled out and were scattered around Warnier. He said they would come and get us all. It was getting quite late in the day when a police car arrived with two policemen who said they were taking me to Orleanville. I thanked my friends for their hospitality and we left in a charcoal-fuelled Citroen. After about an hour's drive we arrived at Orleanville where I was taken to a French Army barracks and to see a French officer who did not seem very happy about it all; he said there were German parachutists in the area, a fact which I later found to be correct. It was again getting late and I was given a meal and taken to a room to sleep; the door was locked and I realised that I was a prisoner.

The following morning after a breakfast I was taken to see a French officer who I believe was the Garrison Commander, he was not a particularly friendly type. He asked me what I had been doing on the flight, but I declined to give any details other than it was an operational mission, and gave him my name and squadron and asked him to contact Blida. I suppose it must be appreciated that it was only a month ago when we had been engaged in bitter fighting with the French, particularly around Oran and Algiers and I don't doubt a certain resentment against the British existed with many of the French. Not long after this the same officer told me that they had made contact with Blida and that they were out looking for the rest of the crew.

I was now handed back to the police who were the opposite of the Army; very friendly, and they said they had a surprise for me. F/Sgt Wally Cavert the wireless operator had been brought in. I was delighted to be reunited with my pal and he told me what had happened to him and that F/Lt Derek Blakeley our pilot was safe and was being brought in. When he arrived I got the sad news that our navigator had been found dead in the mountains, his parachute had not opened. News was now received that our Flight Commander S/Ldr Peter Holmes and the medical Officer were on their way to pick us up. The policeman who had brought me from Warnier took us all back to his flat and we were looked after royally; his wife prepared a meal of chicken, and a bottle of champagne was found and we all drank and toasted to better times. Towards evening S/Ldr Pete Holmes arrived and after they had had a rest we set off back over the mountains to Blida. It was a long trip and was not without incident; at about 0500hrs we ran out of fuel.

References
19. USSL p.162; CCWR p.14   20. GüH p.121; CCWR p.18

Above: Hudson A/459 at Senussi, Libya c.1942/3 together with a damaged Luftwaffe aircraft and a herd of cattle.

Following orders from Eastern Air Command No.608's detachment at Gibraltar rejoined the squadron at Blida. Hudson G/608 was escorting the liner *Strathallan* on 21 December when the ship was seen to burst into flames. It had been torpedoed at 0223hrs in position 36°52'N 00°34'W by U-562 while in convoy KMF5 when there were 5000 troops on board. It sank on the twenty-second.[21]

No.48 Squadron RAF

No.48 Squadron which had been operating from Sumburgh in the Shetlands arrived at North Front, Gibraltar just before Christmas 1942 equipped with new Mark VI Hudsons and issued with charts extending to Greece. It was said at the time, that they were held at Gibraltar because No.233's aircraft had been so depleted by the French.

On 16 January 1943 I was airborne in D/48 EW930 on an A/S sweep east with F/O Rob Beck as captain. At 1030hrs I

was in the gun turret when a Ju 88 came up directly astern and below us. The Ju 88 opened fire by bringing its nose up.

I responded with the two .303 Brownings but was limited by the tailplane and rudders and with the gun interrupter gear. There was just a chance that I may have scored the odd hit on the Ju 88's cockpit. Rob Beck turned and banked sharply to bring his two guns to bear and meanwhile 'Ricky' Richmond manned the ventral gun. We lacked the crew to man that permanently and in any case opening the ventral position would reduce the speed and range of the Hudson. The Ju 88 broke away and I felt, had some regard even for the two .303s in the turret or perhaps had no real wish to engage in combat. Hudson EW930 suffered no hits.

No.48 Squadron's first victory was gained by F/O G. Mayhew who, while flying at 3500ft on 12 February 1943 sighted a fully-surfaced U boat in position 37°32'N 11°56'W. Mayhew released DCs from forty feet when twenty to thirty feet of the stern was still visible. Two DCs exploded immediately to port of the conning tower. Oil and wood splinters appeared. They were from U-442 which had sailed from France on 20 December captained by Kl Hans Hesse and which was sunk in this attack.[22]

Sgt G. Jackimov of No.500 Squadron was airborne at 0641hrs from Blida on 4 March and at 1002hrs while flying at 3500ft sighted a fully-surfaced U boat. Three 100lb bombs were released from 1500ft and the Hudsons guns were fired before diving to thirty-five feet to release three DCs which straddled the conning tower. Fumes were emitted from near the conning tower and the U boat began to sink and there were about fifteen men in the water within an oil patch. When the vessel disappeared, the Hudson crew dropped two of their dinghies but they apparently sank. It was the demise of U-83 captained by Kl U. Woriszhoffer.[23]

Hudsons from both 48 and 233 Squadrons were involved in attacks on U-77 on 28 March. F/O Harrop of 48 Squadron was flying at 1700ft when he sighted the wash and then conning tower of a U boat. Only the periscope wake was

Below: Hudson B/459 which was flown from Lyneham, England to the Middle East and operated by the Australian squadron.

visible when he attacked with DCs in position 37°42'N 00°10'W. F/O Castell from 233 Squadron intercepted a sighting report of a damaged U boat and at 1754hrs located the damaged vessel and released DCs and A/S bombs which fell fifteen yards and ten yards from the U boat respectively. Captained by Kl O. Hartmann, U-77 was lost in position 37°42'N 00°10'E.[24]

Two captains from 233 Squadron shared the honours on 5 April. F/Sgt K.R. Dalton was airborne in AM931 at 0659hrs and at 0927hrs in position 27°48'N 14°58'W sighted a U boat heading west at six knots. He opened fire and as the U boat was submerging, released four DCs from fifty feet. Only patches of bubbling oil were seen. F/Lt Willits in V9169 was in position 27°34'N 15°18'W at 1656hrs to see a U boat on course 230° at eight to ten knots. Four DCs and an A/S bomb were released from fifty feet while the vessel was still surfaced. An oil streak was left 440 yards by fifty yards with some air bubbles. They were from U-167 captained by Kk K. Sturm and is given as being scuttled on the sixth in position 27°47'N 15°00'W.[25]

On the twenty-third W/O R. Obee of 500 Squadron was airborne from Tafaraouri and at 2309hrs obtained a radar contact. Height was lost to 200ft but at twenty yards range the U boat opened fire and a shell exploded in the Hudson cockpit fatally wounding Obee. A Wop/AG, F/Sgt Kempster, controlled the aircraft while Obee was removed from the cockpit, the navigator, Sgt Blackwell now took over the

controls and flew the Hudson back to base. The controls were set and all the crew baled out including the navigator Sgt Blackwell who set the aircraft on a westerly course. It crashed on the bank of a salt lake. Col Bob Inson the Commanding Officer of the USAAF at Tafaraouri brought the Hudson survivors back to camp. It was a feature, certainly on both numbers 48 and 500 Squadrons, that all crew members should gain some experience of the work of others in the crew, and in the writer's experience, for Wop/AGs to be at the controls on occasions. It is now understood that W/O Opee's attack sank U-602 which had sailed from France on 1 December 1942 and the U boat diary gives it being lost in the Mediterranean. Another German list gives it as 'verschollen' on 23 April 1943.

U-447 sailed from France on 27 April only to be sunk in position 35°30'N 11°55'W on 7 May. She was attacked by Sgt. J.W. McQueen of 233 Squadron in Hudson T9453 at 1845hrs with four DCs which fell fifty to seventy feet to port of the U boat. Three minutes later Sgt J.V. Holland in FH373 also from 233 Squadron straddled the U boat with four DCs with the nearest ten yards from the hull. The vessel appeared to be lifted by the explosions and an object was thrown into

References
21. SWR II/p.336; JR p.240
22. CCWR p.18; GüH p.123; USSL p.162   23. USSL p.162; HH p.280
24. USSL p.162; CCWR p.14
25. USSL p.162; CCWR p.14; GüH p.125; HH p.290

Below: A composite photograph of 48 Sqdn at North Front, Gibraltar in 1943 when commanded by W/Cmdr 'Dismal' Devitt.

the air. Buoyancy was lost and the U boat went down stern first. The Command's list credits Sgt Holland's Hudson with the kill.[26]

Rocket Projectiles

Of training in 608 Squadron an Australian pilot, Bill James, gives this account:

> We commenced rocket firing training by doing twenty degree dives from 2000ft at 200kts and pulling out at 400ft, hence wing ripples etc. Next a hand-held camera was used in the nose by the navigator to photograph the target, a painted circle in a wadi when told, as we pulled out of the dive.
>
> From the photographs the dive angle could be calculated and we adjusted the dive next time. When the angle was good enough we practised out at sea with full rocket load of eight. We would drop a sea marker and then dive at it firing single rockets and later salvoes taking photographs of the strike. We formed a habit of making violent climbing turns after firing because the rockets were unpredictable under water and sometimes after a shallow entry would emerge from the water in front of us. As a result of using rockets under the wings the flight characteristics of the Hudson changed a great deal, our cruising speed usually 120 to 140kts and we had to land at a higher speed of ninety-five knots to feel safe as they were prone to high speed flick stalls.

Two of the first successful uses of rocket projectiles by the RAF were achieved by Hudsons of Nos608 and 48 Squadrons. F/O G.A.K. Ogilvie captained AM725 M/608 on 28 May 1943 and was airborne from Blida at 1115hrs. In position 39°03′N 01°80′E he sighted a surfaced U boat which he attacked with RPs. The vessel sank after nine minutes leaving forty of its crew in the sea. They were from U-755 which had sailed from France on 1 November 1942 commanded by Kl W. Göing. An American list gives it as sinking in position 39°58′N 01°41′E.[27]

F/O H.C. 'Ginger' Bailey of 48 Squadron was flying at 4000ft on 4 June when at 1503hrs he sighted the wake of a U boat at ten miles distance. He attacked out of sun at 1506hrs from one mile at 2000ft releasing eight rocket projectiles as the U boat was diving. It appeared to attempt re-surfacing but lost way and went down on an even keel. A pale blue-green patch appeared marking the demise of U-594 in position 35°55′N 09°25′W captained by Kl F. Mumm. After this attack, no further U boats were sent into the Mediterranean until September.[28]

U-667 had left France on 18 September and between the twenty-fourth and twenty-sixth suffered a series of attacks by Coastal Command aircraft. It was first attacked by Wellingtons 'D' and 'R' of 179 Squadron followed by X/179 which on the twenty-sixth homed in AE505 captained by F/O Frandson of 233 Squadron who attacked with rockets. Frandson in turn, homed in F/O Ashbury of 48 Squadron in EW924. Ashbury sighted the U boat in position 36°14′N 09°57′W at 1150hrs and attacked with RPs released in pairs. It appears very unlikely that the Hudsons achieved any hits with their rockets as the U boat was only damaged and returned to France on 11 October.[29]

Nos 48 and 233 Squadrons remained based at Gibraltar until February 1944 before returning to the United Kingdom and converting to Dakotas.

Bill James, who had earlier ferried a Hudson from Canada to Britain, ferried another Hudson from Britain to join 608 Squadron at Blida on 1 July 1943. He left Lyneham on 26 June and flew via Portreath in a Mark VI Hudson FK682 airborne there at 0545hrs on the twenty-seventh.

> We had been briefed to fly at 10,000ft but could only climb to 7000ft. We flew over Port Lyautey on track and landed at Ras El Ma near Fez after a nine-hour trip. We had to guard our plane – all planes were parked in a large circle, tails outwards so that the turret guns could be used if necessary. Two on watch outside under the wings with outside Brownings (sic) and the two inside asleep but ready to turn on the master switch for the turret. The French Foreign Legion were doing an outer perimeter patrol. They were expecting Italian paratroopers which didn't arrive. We took off for Blida on the thirtieth and ran into a fierce dust thunderstorm but could not maintain height and after 150 miles landed at an American aerodrome, Oudja and stayed overnight.

The Auxiliary Squadrons Move to Italy

No.608 Squadron received a signal ordering it to move to Protville, Tunisia on 1 August 1943 when still based at Blida. This move was for A/S patrols and convoy escorts over Sicilian waters. The detachment at Bone was to remain there. An advance party of 82 personnel under F/Lt Penn left Blida by road in squadron transport taking tents with them. On 4 August another party of twenty under F/O S.J. Stiring left Blida in two DC-3s also for Protville. The main party of 161 under F/O Russell left by rail with squadron equipment requiring sixteen trucks.

At Protville on 22 August a party of 214 from 608 Squadron under F/Lt Crump used squadron and other transport for Bizerta where they embarked on LST 415 by 1800hrs. About eighty tons of squadron equipment was loaded that night. The following day LST 415 left its berth to anchor in the Bay of Bizerta before sailing in convoy to Augusta harbour, Sicily on the twenty-fifth. They disembarked at Augusta at 2200hrs on 26 August with unloading of equipment completed at 0630hrs on 27 August.

The squadron transport left Augusta under F/O Broughton on 28 August for Borizzo where the advance party arrived on 31 August.

Operation *Avalanche* – Salerno

Allied landings were made at Salerno on 9 September 1943 and there was a German counter-attack on the thirteenth. Additional support for the troops was by naval shelling on enemy positions with warships including the battleships HMS *Valiant* and HMS *Warspite*. On 16 September three radio-controlled bombs were aimed at *Warspite* and one of those exploded in a boiler room. As Bill James on 608 adds: 'Our squadron helped to provide cover for the damaged *Warspite*; four tugs were towing it and it was protected by eighteen warships doing anti-submarine sweeps and we were doing patrols outside their perimeter. It was travelling at four knots towards Messina.' James was airborne in AM677 at 1900hrs on the seventeenth for a patrol about twenty miles

Above: Some of General Rommel's supply barges which were bombed by 459 Sqdn Hudsons at Bardia, 1942.

Above: Servicing of 459 Sqdn Hudsons under desert conditions in August 1943.

off the coast; HMS *Warspite* arrived safely at Malta on 19 September.[30]

On 20 September when 608 Squadron was at Borizzo, a signal was received from No.242 Group for one Flight to be deployed at Grottaglie, near Taranto on 1 October and that an airlift for 8000lb would arrive at 0900hrs. Motor transport was to be sent via Messina. By 3 October sorties were being flown from Borizzo, Grottaglie and Montecorvino.

On 1 November there was a further move for No.608 Squadron with personnel under F/Lt Crump arriving at Palermo at 1630hrs. Another party using seventeen lorries from the US Army arrived at 1800hrs. At Palermo personnel were billeted at the Grand Hotel, Castello Utveggio overlooking Palermo. They embarked on the twelfth in LST 349 and LCT L76 of the USN for Nisida north of Naples later to disembark at Naples. The final part of the trip was by road to Montecorvino. Just a week later there was a signal for 608 Squadron to move to Grottaglie but leaving a Flight at Montecorvino.

Italian Caprice

In January 1944 as Bill James records:

There was quite a flap on in the squadron as we were covering the new landing near Rome so all planes and crews were ordered from Grottaglie, then our base, to Gaudo near Salerno. On the twenty-fourth I left at 1030hrs with my crew Mick Rees, Wop/Ags Norman Tonge and Len Kenny and Sgt S. Garnett, an armourer plus ground staff equipment. Our job was to patrol convoys twenty-four hours a day.

The plane S/608 FK484 was an old rocket diving trainer with badly buckled wings – we carried eight rockets under the wings and the usual turret and front guns.

It was extremely bad weather – heavy rain, very turbulent and in cloud. The plane had very sloppy controls and I could cruise at only 110kts. I was flying at 3000ft and because of bad weather, we were not flying the direct route but to the west coast via Catanzaro and Cortale through and above the gap in the mountains, all planes taking this route.

The weather became extremely turbulent and halfway

through a gale struck us, visibility became nil and I flew into a down current which dropped us like a stone and with the throttles through the gate I still had little or no control over the plane and was barely able to stop it stalling.

We were thrown out of the base of the cloud as part of the wing broke off about 100ft above the only reasonable piece of flat ground for miles and was able to plonk it down in a crash on the mountain above Cortale. The port engine caught fire immediately and before we came to rest the nose had broken off and flames were in the cockpit. Mick was unconscious from a knock on the head and was lying outside minus his flying boots. No one else was hurt except that I had hair singed from head, eyebrows, arms and chest. All the ammunition and petrol tanks went off making a spectacular bonfire. We cut up a parachute to bandage some cuts and the bump on Mick's head, inflated a dinghy and used it to carry Mick along a goat track down the mountain. The local doctor attended Mick and a few cuts that Kenny had. They were all right within a day or two. The Mother Superior of the local convent visited us to tell us she and the children had been praying for us when they heard the plane crash and that we had been reborn.

We got in touch with the squadron and on the twenty-sixth commandeered a truck to take us to Crotone where F/Cmdr S/Ldr Lewis picked us up in FK726 and flew us back to the squadron.

No.500 Squadron followed No.608 to Montecorvino in December 1943 and began conversion to Venturas. No.608 Squadron remained based at Montecorvino until July 1944.

No.459 (RAAF) Squadron Over the Eastern Mediterranean

This Australian squadron was officially formed at Burg-el-Arab LG40, forty miles west of Alexandria in Egypt. This was on 10 February 1942 when Axis forces in North Africa

References
26. CCWR p.14; GüH p.123   27. USSL p.163; HH p.292; GüH p.126
28. USSL p.163; HH p.289; SWR III/1 p.23; CCWR p.14
29. CCWR p.18; GüH p.114   30. SWR III/1. pp 177–179

Above: No.459(RAAF) Sqdn personnel with one of their white-camouflaged Hudsons.

had reached Tmimi, about seventy miles west of Tobruk in their advance towards Egypt. Although a number of North African ports were used by both Allies' and the Axis forces in Africa, Tobruk was one of particular interest to both sides.

S/Ldr P.W. 'Phil' Howson assumed temporary command of 459 Squadron whose duties were general reconnaissance over the Eastern Mediterranean area and in co-operation with the Royal Navy. At its formation it had two Hudsons with four Blenheims and their crews detached from No.203 Squadron RAF.

On 14 February sorties were flown by S/Ldr Howson and F/Lt L. Campbell, the latter sighting a Malta convoy being shadowed by a Ju 88 before then seeing a submarine's periscope which he shadowed unsuccessfully.

By the end of March the strength of the squadron included eight officers and 128 other ranks and on 19 April W/Cmdr K.S. Hennock assumed command. Operations during those two months were limited to two sorties by Hudsons from Gambut, Cyrenaica to lead formations of Hurricane fighters to Malta. A move by the unit was made five miles east from Burg-el-Arab in May to Landing Ground 40 (LG40) at Behig and where twelve more Hudsons were received.[31]

No.459 Squadron was considered fully operational on 1 June and with P/O D. Beaton flying the first sortie from LG40. Shipping recces were undertaken from Mersa Matruh to Sidi Barani with twenty sorties flown between 14–16 June when six Hudsons were fitted with extra tanks to support a Malta-bound convoy. One crew had an encounter with three Ju 88s, another was credited with two probable hits on an enemy vessel.[32]

Tobruk was attacked by Rommel on 20 June and captured on 21 June with 33,000 Allied troops made prisoners. On 28 June Mersa Matruh was lost to the Axis troops and on 1 July the Allies made their stand at El Alamein.[33]

No.459 Squadron was deployed at LG-Z in the Canal Zone on 30 June and operated from Gianaclis south of Alexandria with night recces along the coast of Cyrenaica in addition to A/S patrols. The unit commenced shipping strikes in July against enemy convoys and the 'F'-boats; barges of 200 or 250 tons, which were intent on supplying Rommel's forces and armed with 88mm, 37mm and two 20mm guns. In three weeks of July, No.459 destroyed seventeen and damaged three.

El Alamein

The Allies' 8th Army had withdrawn to El Alamein, sixty miles from Alexandria on 30 June 1942 and the Axis forces under Rommel reached that point in July. No.459 Squadron made a low-level attack against an enemy convoy bound for Tobruk on 10 July. It comprised two merchantmen with five escorts including two destroyers. One Hudson was shot down, another was badly damaged and two others crashed on take-off. Another Hudson was lost on 24 July when six of them sighted twenty-three Ju52s escorted by Me 110 fighters which attacked the Hudsons.

On 13 August General Montgomery assumed command of the Allies' 8th Army but by 15 August was under General Alexander who became C-in-C Middle East. Alexander required the Allies to attack Rommel's forces at the time of the full moon with a frontal assault against Rommel's positions and thirteen days ahead of the Operation *Torch* landings in North Africa. The intended assault at El Alamein depended on surprise for its success. Part of the RAF's duties thus became thwarting any reconnaissance flights by the *Luftwaffe* while attacks on shipping supplying the Axis forces were to be maintained.

On 4 September seven of 459's Hudsons were airborne for a strike against an Italian convoy heading for Tobruk. They located three ships together with four escorts. P/O D. Beaton in Hudson FH242 attacked an escort setting it on fire and at first thought to be a destroyer but was an MTB the *Pulluce*. Although his aircraft was damaged, he returned to base.

Six crews were briefed on 8 September to attack a merchant vessel escorted by a destroyer north of Derna. Hudson FH304 captained by S/Ldr I. Campbell crashed on take-off causing a delay. However, P/O A. Proctor in FH266 was airborne at 0359hrs and in position 32°53′N 23°39′E attacked the merchantman from thirty feet leaving the ship listing and with smoke emitted from the stern.

Hostilities by the Axis and Allied armies in North Africa were now in abeyance as they prepared for the next major battle at El Alamein where General Alexander's forces had made their stand. It was about this time that 459 Squadron reverted to its role of A/S patrols and convoy escorts covering the Red Sea and Persian Gulf and with a detachment sent to Aden commanded by S/Ldr Howson.

The Allied offensive was opened by Allied air forces on 19 October to be followed at 2140hrs on the twenty-third with an artillery barrage from about 1000 guns. This was prior to an infantry advance to make a path through minefields for the tanks.

Churchill gives figures of thirty per cent of Axis shipping supplying North Africa being sunk by largely air action with forty per cent lost in October but with the loss of sixty-six per cent of fuel supplies for Rommel's forces.

By 4 November the Axis forces were in full retreat. The 8th Army reached Tobruk on 13 November and Benghazi two days later.

Figures given are: Allied forces 195,000 men, 1029 tanks, 2311 guns; Axis forces 104,000 men including 50,000 German; 489 tanks, 1219 guns. Of serviceable aircraft: Allies 530, and the Axis 350.[34] With Tobruk and Benghazi in Allied hands shipping to those ports was covered by 459 Squadron in addition to movements of naval forces using Alexandria. The squadron was now using fields at St Jean in Palestine, Nicosia in Cyprus, LG208(formerly LG-Z), Gianaclis, Mersa Matruh and Gambut but moving from LG208 on 28 November to be based at Gianaclis. In that month the squadron achieved ninety per cent serviceabilty. Notification of awards of DFCs to F/Lt F.W. Madsen, F/Lt D.C. Beaton and F/O V.K. O'Brien were received on 7 December; two days later O'Brien was killed on crashing at Gambut. Following the Allies' successful Operation *Torch* landings in North Africa, Axis submarines became more concentrated in the Western Mediterranean and on 18 December 459 Squadron became based at Gambut about 45 miles east of Tobruk to operate under No.235 Wing RAF to cover convoys along the coast of Cyrenaica. In that month they completed 126 sorties totalling 674 hours.[35]

On 23 January 1943 the Allies' 8th Army entered Tripoli and despite severe weather which made 459's airfield u/s on

References
31. RAAF III/p.237   32. RAAF III/p.239   33. SWR II/p.34
34. AG p.163; SWR II/74, 192, 309–311; RAF II/pp.233–242; RAAF III/p.368–375; WSC IV/526–541
35. RAAF III/p.382

Below: Bardia, North Africa which was used as a leave area for 459(RAAF) Sqdn personnel from Gambut.

Above: The demise of Hudson T/459 which, captained by F/Sgt Barnard, sank U-97 on 16.6.43 in position 33°00N 34°00E.

occasions, the unit escorted convoys to Tripoli and Malta flying eighty-one sorties in that month. The 8th Army reached Tunisia on 4 February representing the end of the Desert War.[36]

The end of May 1943 marked the end of 459's first year of operations in which they had flown 1294 sorties totalling 6775 hours. The squadron's move to Gambut enabled personnel to undertake a number of diversions such as the publication of a squadron magazine *Gremloid* which included notable contributions from LAC Besier, a poem *Aero Fitter*, and *The Gospel According to 459*.

Cricket matches were arranged between RAF and RAAF personnel on the squadron; an outdoor stage was constructed with entertainment provided by various concert parties in addition to impromptu squadron shows. Tombola and whist drives were organised by Toc H; talks were given on various topics and a Squadron Brains Trust became a regular feature. A dog show was organised, the 'First Annual Western Desert Victory Dog Show'. One entry, a pet duck was led in by a rope and gained a trophy for the 'most unusual breed'. Competitors representing Britain, Australia and America were in an inter-unit athletic sports meeting organised by

459. A squadron 'Beach Club' was opened in Bardia using two renovated Italian houses with accommodation restricted to twenty personnel on forty-eight hours leave. The three padres who considered the squadron's spiritual needs, Fred McKay, Bob Davies and John McNamara, supplied also another – two truckloads of beer.

The Sinking of U-97

On 16 June 1943 F/Sgt D.T. Barnard was airborne from Lydda in FH311 at 1220hrs in a hunt for U boats in co-operation with the Navy at datum position 38°30N 34°30′E. On not locating the Navy he climbed to undertake a patrol.

Two hours later a U boat was sighted and Barnard dived to attack with DCs. One DC hit the deck and its explosion blew the Hudson up 400ft bending its mainplane, fuselage and rudder. Despite such damage to the aircraft it was safely landed back at Lydda. F/Sgt Barnard had sunk U-97 captained by Kl Hans-Georg Trox in position 33°00′N 34°00′E. U-97 had claimed sixteen ships and with Kl Trox the *Palima* of 1179 tons on the twelfth and *Athelmonarch* of 8995 tons on the fifteenth. Post-war, in 1988 a German radio operator Gerhard Dietz from U-97 was able to contact Barnard with navigator George Crisp in Melbourne but on a friendly basis.[37]

The Invasion of Sicily

At 0400hrs on 10 July 1943 Allied troops invaded Sicily at four points in Operation *Husky*. A total of 2590 ships were ultimately used including 1614 British; 115,000 troops from the British Empire and 66,000 American troops.

By 16 July four airfields had been captured and were in use and by 1000hrs on 17 August the last of the Axis forces had retreated to Italy. They had lost 1850 aircraft, 32,000 men killed or wounded, and 162,000 taken prisoner out of a

Below: No.459 Sqdn Officers' Mess, Gambut, Libya.

Above: A No.233 Sqdn Hudson connected to a trolly-acc. This was to avoid using the aircraft's own accumulators which, however, provided enough power to start the engines if necessary.

total of 405,000 troops. The Allies lost 31,158 killed, wounded or missing and less than 400 aircraft.

No.459 Squadron's Hudsons were deployed in protecting Allied shipping and none were lost in their area.

Italy was invaded on 3 September and an armistice was signed with the Italians. Major sections of the powerful Italian fleet sailed from Spezia and Taranto on 9 September ultimately for Malta but to rendezvous with the Royal Navy. On 15 and 16 September 459 Squadron Hudsons escorted convoy *Tryst* which included the battleships HMS *Howe* and HMS *King George V* with a flotilla of destroyers covering the surrender of the Italian fleet.

Winston Churchill had turned his attention to the islands in the Aegean Sea and 459's role became the bombing of enemy bases in Greece and Crete such as Kalamaki and Hereklion dropping a total of 49,050 lb bombs in 191 sorties during that month.

459's CO – W/Cmdr P. Howson – was succeeded by W/Cmdr A.D. Henderson on 5 October and in that month the squadron was attacking enemy shipping in the Aegean Sea, enemy airfields and flew on recces for enemy shipping attempting to invade islands such as Leros still in Allied hands. One ship was damaged on the tenth and another on the eighteenth, the latter left under a pall of smoke.

Leros was captured by the Germans on 16/17 November and the island of Samos was evacuated by the Allies. On 21 November the battlecruiser HMS *Renown* with three destroyers taking Winston Churchill to the Cairo conference with President Roosevelt and Marshal Chiang Kai-shek was escorted by 459 Squadron.

The harbour at Rhodes was bombed on 5 December and the air defences of Leros, now also occupied by the enemy, was tested by the Hudsons making passes at various heights.

While operating Hudsons, 459 had served under four Commanding Officers, the first of those, W/Cmdr Howson, was awarded the OBE. Other awards included nine DFCs, one DFM, and twenty-three were mentioned in dispatches (MIDs).

One of 459's navigators, Don Baird, in summing up 459's operations understates thus: 'It was one of the few squadrons operating overseas under RAAF identity rather than RAF. It had a high proportion of Australian ground staff. Operationally it had the early involvement in the extremely costly barge pranging which quickly wrote off a number of aircraft and crews.'

On Christmas Eve, 1943, No.459 Squadron received its first Venturas and by March 1944 its conversion to that aircraft was complete. For much of its service with Hudsons, it had operated under desert conditions; grim for both ground staff and aircrew.

References
36. AG p.xv   37. JR pp.296, 246; USSL p.163; HH p.281; RAAF III/p.568

Chapter 6
Other Operations

Air-Sea Rescue

The formation of No.279 Air-Sea Rescue Squadron began with the arrival on 16 November 1941 at Bircham Newton, Norfolk of F/Lt Rashleigh, DFC who found no other personnel and no aircraft for the unit. The following day Hudson V8999 was delivered from No.24 MU with some equipment including four Browning and two Vickers (VGO) machine-guns and F/Lt Rashleigh did some local flying for two-and-a-half hours. Two more personnel, F/O F. Barrett, as Gunnery Officer, and Sgt C.E. Singleton from No.407 Squadron, arrived on the twenty-first and over the next few days others came from 206, 233 and 407 Squadrons. By 19 December seventeen Hudsons had been delivered including V9046, T9408, T9898, V4044, T9401, V9042, T9402, T9399, V8993, T9405, and V9024 out of an establishment of twenty. Total personnel was then 141 including fourteen pilots, one observer, and thirty-five Wop/AGs; the observer number was made up to fourteen the following day.

Above: The rescue on 9.6.42. In position 52°07′N 02°41′E is F/Lt Henderson's Hudson, the rescue launch HSL 130, and the survivors' dinghy in the foreground.

Below: A Hudson coded OS for 279 Sqdn on a rescue mission 9.6.42 over the North Sea.

On 6 December T9401 'D' was being fitted with dual control, and by the seventeenth there was a 'full programme of flying'.

No.279's first operation was flown by F/O Tyrell in N/279 which was airborne at 0815hrs on a parallel track search for a dinghy.

The squadron was devoted to Air-Sea Rescue (ASR) operations but not infrequently encountered a hostile enemy. On 26 March 1942 F/Lt Tyrell in 'V' and P/O McKimm in 'U' were both airborne for a search. At 1412hrs a Ju88 was sighted which closed on V/279. 'U' formatted on 'V' and the Ju 88 broke away. Just under an hour later when a Ju 88 was again sighted, the Hudsons attacked with turret and side guns scoring hits and claiming damage to the enemy. There were no hits on the Hudsons.

Following a signal of a Wellington in distress, P/O Lacy was airborne at 0433hrs on 4 May from Docking. He reached the reported position at 0516hrs and released flame floats, it being too dark to search. Lacy then flew up and down the former track of the Wellington and at 0528hrs his rear gunner saw a distress signal two miles astern and five minutes later a second distress signal was seen. The position of a dinghy was located by the glow from that signal. Sight was lost and then regained at 0609hrs after seeing the tail of the Wellington above the water. Lacy flew down wind to find five or six aircrew in a dinghy. A Lindholme dinghy was dropped and at

Above: W/Cmdr Paul Lynham, CO of 279 Sqdn with his crew and Hudson OS-V. It was 279 Sqdn which pioneered the use of the airborne lifeboat in ASR missions.

0839hrs the Wellington crew was picked up by rescue launches.

There was another encounter with enemy aircraft on 2 June when Sgt S. Scott was on a rescue mission. His was one of three Hudsons to find four men in a dinghy position 52°17′N

Below: The flight plan of Hudson V9152 dated 8/9 August 1941 for a trans-Atlantic ferry flight from Gander to Prestwick by F/Lt Womersley taking 11hr 1min flying time.

02°07'E to which they had been attracted by pyrotechnics at two miles distance. While circling the dinghy to obtain a fix two Me 109F fighters attacked Hudson P/279 flown by Sgt J.G. Worrin at 2500ft closing to about 250ft before breaking away. The Hudson gunner, Sgt R. Webdell, gained strikes on the enemy in a long burst and the Me 109s kept out of range of the machine-guns but using their own cannon. Both the navigator and a gunner were wounded in the Hudson but it was thought that one Me 109 was shot down.

No.279 Squadron came to use a number of airfields from Cornwall to Caithness and on 30 June six of the Hudsons were detached to Benbecula in the Outer Hebrides. While 279 operated from the west over the North Sea, the enemy appeared to have a rescue service from the east using Dornier 24s and escorted by fighters. On 22 July F/Sgt P.G. Faux in W/279 with K/279 encountered a Do 24 with two Fw 190s in position 52°25'N 02°05'E and the gunner in Hudson K/279 fired bursts when one Fw 190 appeared to be about to attack but there was no return fire.

By August 1942 No.279 Squadron was using for ASR operations, Bircham Newton, Docking, Reykjavik, Chivenor, St Eval, Thorney Island, Ballykelly, Beaulieu, Benbecula and Stornoway. While operating from St Eval on 8 September Hudsons T and Y/279 were on a search when an Arado float plane was sighted in position 47°41'N 08°15'E. The Hudsons went into close formation to attack but no hits were seen. Weather at St Eval was bad and T/279 landed at Chivenor. Y/279 flown by Sgt H.J. Farrer crashed in flames one mile east of St Eval. With Sgt Farrer were Sgt J.D. Granger, P/O L.W. Waters and P/O J. Holloman.

Above: G-AGAR with perhaps its original serial No. N7364 at Heraklion, Crete in March, 1941 with F/Lt Potter, Al Doe of the Wright Corporation and F/Lt R.G.M. Walker.

S/Ldr R.Y. Tyrell was airborne at 0750hrs on 8 December for a CLA search. A message was received of a dinghy sighted in position 52°28'N 03°10'E. The dinghy was located with its four occupants who proved to be from No.280 Squadron. Sgt W.M. Arnold who relieved Tyrell, located the dinghy and saw the four aircrew picked up by a HSL at 1410hrs.

On Christmas Day 1942 F/O C.G. Crawford took off to relocate a dinghy and at 1251hrs saw a marine distress signal, a sea marker and then two dinghies occupied by six aircrew.

Below: A Hudson in civil guise as G-AGAR which was flown to the Middle East by F/Lt R.G.M. Walker. It was possibly from the King's Flight.

A Whitley was circling but a Lindholme rescue apparatus was dropped. When two HSLs were sighted they were given bearing and distance of the survivors and a message was flashed to them 'Boats coming Happy Christmas'.

No.279 lost an aircraft and crew on 7 January 1943. A/279 was airborne from St Eval on an ASR search but failed to return. The Hudson had been plottted but faded out at 1913hrs when off the Lizard. Three minutes later a fire was seen on the sea. The crew was Sgts W.M. Arnold, J.D. Soalter, R. Bannister and R.W. Paradise.

On 21 January F/279 flown by Sgt H.G. Mossford was returning to St Eval after completing a search 100 miles south-west of the Scilly Isles but his wireless operator was unable to make contact, the Hudson's radar failed to pick up a beacon and it was impossible to establish their position. At 2225hrs they were ordered to bale out and all the crew parachuted safely near Swansea; the Hudson crashed into a hill sixty miles inland in Radnorshire.

Another crew had cause to bale out on 5 February. V/279 T9414 was on a search from Leuchars during severe weather and on returning to base the pilot could not locate the flare path due to lack of visibilty in very heavy rain except when about to land and controlling the aircraft was difficult. He climbed to 3000ft but turned into a spin and at 1500ft the Hudson spun in the opposite direction. One of the crew, Sgt Pertus rushed to

the exit and jumped despite attempts by others to restrain him. Control of the Hudson was regained and the remainder of the crew captained by F/O A.A. Henderson baled out safely with only minor injuries. The body of Sgt Pertus was recovered from the sea and taken to Tayport.

The First Use of the Airborne Lifeboat

For the first time the airborne lifeboat was taken by a Hudson on an operational sortie. This was from Davidstow Moor on 17 February 1943 in S/279 captained by F/O C.G. Crawford who was airborne at 2240hrs on a night search. Due to modifications to the Hudson, there were some difficulties in navigation and there was heavy fuel consumption with only half the search area covered. An observer who joined the squadron about this time, Doug. Whittaker writes:

I flew regularly on Hudsons from Bircham Newton and a detachment at Harrowbeer, Cornwall until September 1944. Our main operations were scouring the North Sea and the Bay of Biscay. We usually carried a Lindholme dinghy but in early 1943 we were equipped with the first Airborne Lifeboat. This was invented by Uffa Fox a yachtsman from the Isle of Wight. I met Uffa Fox when he came to the squadron to brief us on the lifeboat. Bircham Newton was a pre-war well-built aerodrome, very pleasant with many brick buildings. A good

Below: British and Commonwealth aircrew under training at No.6 (Coastal) OTU, Thornaby, December 1941.

SGT. WALKER. SGT. ROBINSON. SGT. TURNER. SGT. SMITH. SGT. WADE. SGT. BALLARD. SGT. CHARLES. SGT. MULLEN. SGT. MEEK. SGT. JOYCE. SGT. HYAM. SGT. FORBES. SGT. HERSEY. SGT. CLIFFE. SGT. TIMBERLAKE. SGT. HANLEY. SGT. PREECE. SGT. EVANS.

SGT. JOHN. SGT. DARKE. SGT. SIMPSON. SGT. TAYLOR. SGT. O'BEIRNE. SGT. GEORGE. SGT. CORDES. SGT. BRICCS. SGT. THOMAS. SGT. DICKINSON. SGT. HANNAH. SGT. HILL. SGT. HENDRIE. SGT. COLE. SGT. WHITE. SGT. DURWOOD. SGT. MARCHAND.

SGT. DUNNETT. SGT. PARR. SGT. VERNON. SGT. BRENT. SGT. POTTER. SGT. WILLIS. SGT. BRADLEY. P/O. THOMSON. SGT. BENSON. SGT. WARREN. SGT. SUMMERHAYES. P/O. SEAL. SGT. STOW. SGT. MATTHEWS. SGT. STEWART. SGT. LEONARD. SGT. TYRREL.

Mess, outside all sports facilities available. The detachment at Harrowbeer was more Spartan; built around the village green, it was fairly near to Plymouth and Dartmoor prison was on the circuit. Often we went forward to Predannack for fighter escorts. It was dismal down there and each crew spent a month there at a time. Ju 88s from Brest were the danger.

From Bircham Newton on 28 February there was a search for a ditched Halifax of 419 Squadron from Middleton St George. A dinghy was sighted in position 54°02′N 03°35′E with seven aircrew. This was by F/Sgt J.E. Watts in K/279 who dropped a Lindholme dinghy. Watts lost sight of the ditched crew but had obtained a fix which was effectively used by No.320 Squadron and at 1958hrs the survivors were picked by by launches.

World War II aircrew invariably say that the worst enemy was the weather. S/279 was on a search from Davidstow Moor on 29 March but the weather deteriorated and No.19 Group diverted the Hudson to Exeter. It crashed in St Ives Bay. The sole survivor was its captain F/O E.G. Gibbs who was taken to hospital where he died the following day. The crew comprised F/Sgts Long, Povey, Bacon and Fletcher.

On 2 April the AOC No.16 Group presented the squadron with their new emblem which had been approved by HM The King. It depicted the sea above which were nine flashes of lightning and with the motto 'To See and be Seen'.

'The Day of Days' is the way 279 described 5 May 1943 when it had four Hudsons on a search. F/Sgt A.H. Mogridge in W/279 airborne from Bircham Newton at 0748hrs sighted a dinghy in position 53°40′N 01°29′W. An airborne lifeboat was successfully dropped from 700ft altitude at 120kts and falling thirty feet from the dinghy and a crew of seven climbed aboard.

They started the lifeboat's engine half an hour later and a course to steer for Wells was given by the Hudson crew. The

lifeboat made about six-and-a-half knots and the other Hudsons assisted in maintaining contact. When the engine failed, a mast and sails were hoisted but they were then met by an RAF launch and taken to Grimsby. Later, the crews from 279 involved in the rescue visited the survivors, who were from 1401 Met. Flight and then in the Naval Hospital, Grimsby.

No.279 had eight Hudsons flying ASR missions on 13 May from Bircham Newton and about the time when there were many bombing raids on Germany. North-west of Cromer an American Flying Fortress was seen to break up in the air but one survivor, Lt Gorse of the USAAF was picked up by a launch and taken to Wells, Norfolk. The incident arose due to the 'bubble' gunner on the Fortress having his guns run amok when he tested them and part of the tailplane was shot off. The pilot had six of the crew bale out and then headed towards the seashore with his co-pilot Lt. Gorse to avoid risk to those on land. Lt Gorse was flown to Burtonwood the next day.

On 15 May F/Sgt Mogridge flew 220 miles to thirty-nine miles NNW of Borkum. At 2016hrs a Dornier 24 was seen circling the area and as the Hudson approached the Dornier opened fire at 800 yards. Mogridge closed to 300 yards and fired two bursts and saw bullets striking the enemy on the starboard side. His navigator MacGregor was hit in the thigh and the rear gunner was wounded. Mogridge turned and broke off the engagement.

Throughout the service of the Hudson in the RAF, his late Majesty, King George VI, showed a personal interest in the operations of the aircraft and its crews. The King and Queen visited RAF North Coates on 26 May 1943 and during that morning went to Hudson A/279 and its crew, F/O Crawford, F/Sgt Postle, P/O Lerway and Sgt Jackson were presented to them. The airborne lifeboat was explained to the King and Queen by one of the officers concerned with its design, Gp/Capt Waring who was credited also with the introduction of the Lindholme dinghy. Later, 279's engineering officer,

Below: A Hudson used for demonstration at No.6 (Coastal) OTU, Thornaby.

F/O Keay, arranged a demonstration of the airborne lifeboat for Their Majesties.

No.279 Squadron played a part in the rescue of twenty-six survivors on 29 May in position 49°45′N 08°15′W about 100 miles WSW of Lands End. K/279 captained by F/O Sherwood with navigator W/O E.T. Osborne were airborne from Davidstow Moor at 0515hrs and sighted two Sunderlands, one on the sea near dinghies, the other circling at 200ft. A Whitley from No.10 OTU had ditched on the twenty-eighth and had boarded their dinghy which was found by F/Lt W.S.E. Dods in a 461 Squadron Sunderland. In attempting to land, the Sunderland crashed into a wave; Dods was killed and co-pilot Gipps, seriously injured. The Sunderland crew took to their dinghies and helped the injured Gipps. P/O G.O. Singleton captain of another 461 Squadron Sunderland landed and picked up both crews but was then so loaded that he was unable to take off. Sherwood of 279 directed a French destroyer to the scene which picked up Whitley and Sunderland survivors but leaving a skeleton crew in the Sunderland which was taken in tow. When the tow broke, the Sunderland captain successfully achieved a take-off.[1]

The Airliner from Lisbon

Much publicity was given to an event in which 279 Squadron took part on 1 June 1943.

There was a civil airline service between England and Lisbon by BOAC's DC-3s and one of those aircraft was shot down by a Ju 88 at 1100hrs while en route from Lisbon. On board was the actor Leslie Howard and another passenger was Reuter's Washington correspondent, Kenneth Stonehouse. It was thought at the time that Germany believed Winston Churchill to be on the aircraft.

H/279 captained by F/O Reade was airborne from Davidstow Moor in a search for survivors and landed at Predannack after a trip of six hours and four minutes.

No.279 Squadron received a party of nineteen USAAF officers and men who flew in with two B-17s on 11 June. This was for the Americans to gain some knowledge about ASR work.

At 1025hrs on 15 July F/O Wilson was airborne at Bircham Newton and flew to Tangmere for an escort of Spitfires before searching off Cap d'Antifer, France for a Wellington crew from 12 OTU, Chipping Warden. The Wellington's dinghy was sighted within fifteen minutes and an airborne lifeboat was released from 700ft at 140 knots. The three parachutes opened and the boat touched down fifty yards to windward of the dinghy. A rocket fired and released the drogue from the lifeboat. The Wellington crew paddled towards it. The Hudson left at 1317hrs still escorted by the Spitfires. No.279 Squadron learned later that the Wellington crew included W/Cmdr Bray, DFC and that they had made halfway across the Channel when met by a HSL which took them to Newhaven.

The dinghy from Hampden P/1401 Met. Flt was sighted by F/Sgt Mogridge on 18 July. The Hampden had ditched after the port engine failed and with the front of the aircraft sinking within ninety seconds, only the tail fin was visible

after two minutes but all the crew exited. Their dinghy was located in position 53°32′N 00°35′E at 1052hrs and at 1141hrs a HSL was sighted heading for the dinghy to pick up the Hampden crew at 1215hrs for it to be landed at Immingham. The Hampden's navigator had kept his log and Met. report which was handed in just a little later than usual!

Over the days 26 to 28 July No.279 Squadron deployed an airborne lifeboat three times. W/Cmdr Corry flew Hudson 'W' with the lifeboat and in company with 'O' captained by F/O Pederson after a dinghy had been reported sixty-five miles north of Ameland. 'W' sighted an American Fortress on the sea with its crew on the wings and getting into dinghies. The airborne lifeboat was released and F/O Pederson in 'O' returned to base for another airborne lifeboat to be flown to the original reported position. At 1505hrs crewmen from one of the Fortress's dinghies had boarded the lifeboat and paddled to their second dinghy; the Fortress sank ten minutes later but by 1525hrs ten from the ditched Fortress had boarded the lifeboat. HSLs were called by radio and a fix obtained giving position 53°14′N 02°02′E. A HSL was guided by O/279 to the lifeboat which was taken in tow at 1936hrs.

F/Lt Fitchew and Sgt Curtis were flying to the Ameland position when a Halifax was seen circling two dinghies tied together and occupied by eight Americans. Curtis remained while F/Lt Fitchew went on to Ameland. Curtis sent a message to base at 1725hrs and a Walrus arrived eighty minutes later picking up half the ditched crew; the remainder were rescued by a second Walrus at 1901hrs. F/Lt Fitchew had continued his search alone and on sighting a Halifax, followed it to see at 1846hrs five dinghies tied together and with eight Americans.

The airborne lifeboat was released from Fitchew's Hudson within thirty yards of the dinghies in position 54°33′N 05°47′E. Two survivors boarded it and paddled to the other Americans. They had the lifeboat under way at 1916hrs and were given a course to steer of 270°M. Two minutes later three Fortresses arrived; at 2030hrs the lifeboat was stationary in position 54°32′N 05°42′E and hoisted sails; the Fortresses remained and Fitchew returned to base. The lifeboat was later picked up by a Danish fishing boat together with the American aircrew and a search led by W/Cmdr Corry was flown for the Danish vessel to be located in position 54°19′N 03°21′E with the lifeboat and Americans on board; it was steering 250°T at seven knots.

The third lifeboat was used on 28 July by F/Sgt Palmer with F/Sgt Mogridge who were airborne at 1605hrs. Just over an hour later in position 54°35′N 05°08′E five or six Americans were sighted in a dinghy. The lifeboat was released fifty yards from the dinghy and boarded by the survivors. They started the engines and were under way at 1820hrs. The Hudsons gave a course to steer of 270°M before leaving but with a Mitchell aircraft circling. Frank Goff who joined 279 Squadron in November 1943 gives this account:

The airborne lifeboat was developed by Uffa Fox and I believe manufactured at Littlehampton. They were very strong – divided into many watertight compartments with an air

References   1. RAAF III/p.434

canopy fore and aft. Two Seagull engines mounted inboard provided power and sails were also carried.

The boats were carried outside the aircraft with bomb doors removed; there was very little ground clearance and it knocked about fifteen per cent off the performance. We usually reserved the boats for long range work escorted by fighters off the Dutch coast.

The longest trip made by a rescued crew was by New Zealanders from a Mosquito off Norway who defied force nine gales and finally sailed into Lerwick – it was too rough for search vessels to look for them!

The procedure was to drop a smoke marker up wind from the dinghy and then drop the boat from 700ft on its three parachutes which should release in hitting the sea.

The boats were extremely well-designed although occasionally the engines went u/s and survivors were induced to going flat out instead of going for longer range with one engine at half throttle.

Above: A No.6(C) OTU Hudson coded 'FE' at Thornaby circa 1941.

The official historian Hilary St G. Saunders gives a figure of 1684 survivors being saved by the ASR service in 1943 and 3306 Allied airmen rescued from February 1941 when the ASR service was 'systematised' up to the third quarter of 1943.[2]

No.279 Squadron converted to Warwicks in 1944 and in that year operating on ASR in Coastal Command in addition to 279, were numbers 280 and 281 Squadrons.

Meteorological Sorties

As early as 1925 'weather climbs' were undertaken by the RAF but in 1936 Bristol Bulldogs of the Station Flight at Aldergrove were flying High Altitude Met. Sorties. The Service began forming Meteorological Flights and numbers were being assigned to them. In late 1940 Coastal Command authorised the formation of three Long Range Met. Flights; No.403 at Bircham Newton, No.405 at Aldergrove, and No.404 at St Eval. Subsequently, the Flights were numbered in the 14-series.

While for the 'weather climbs' aircraft such as Spitfires and Hurricanes were used, Blenheims were operated for sorties over the Atlantic and North Sea but to be displaced by Hudsons in early 1942. An amalgamation of Flights 1401 and 1403 became 1401 Flight at Bircham Newton; at Wick 1406 amalgamated with 1408 as No.1406 Flight, and 1402 with 1405 formed 1402 Flight at Aldergrove. No.1404 Flight at St Eval replaced its Blenheims with Hudsons in late 1941 but in 1943 was operating Hampdens. On 11 August 1943 1404 Flight became No.517 Squadron.

It was customary for Coastal Command squadrons engaged in such as anti-submarine operations to give additionally a weather report, but the meteorological units in addition to providing weather reports on occasions made U boat sightings and a development was for them to be armed and out of thirty-six sightings eleven attacks were made. There were encounters with enemy aircraft and at least one was claimed to have been shot down by a Met. crew.[3] In addition to the Met. Units in the United Kingdom, some were deployed in Iceland, Gibraltar and the Azores, all within Coastal Command's jurisdiction. Initially weather observations were noted by the crew's observer or navigator but later the category of Meteorological Air Observer came into being but it was April 1945 before a brevet 'M' became available.

One of the first Tannoy broadcasts the author heard at St Eval in February 1942 was: 'All flying scrubbed except for the Met. flight!'

No.1404 Met. Flight was at St Eval during 1942 and 1943 but with some aircraft detached at Gibraltar. They flew down to the Bay of Biscay usually at 3000ft. At the extremity of the patrol readings were taken at under fifty feet and then at regular intervals of 1000ft up to 20,000 to 22,000ft. The W/T reports of some 120 groups were coded by the navigator and the wireless operator, after obtaining a fix, would be transmitting for about two hours. In addition to weather hazards there was that of being in range of German fighters when about fifty miles from Brest. A Wop/AG, Ernest Winfield, gives this account of such a trip:

We turned for home but were unable to get a fix due to atmospheric conditions and had been flying in cloud on Met. winds for five hours; we just had to break cloud and get a drift or pin-point for navigation to be checked. We began to feel our way down with everyone straining to spot the sea. We eventually broke cloud at 250ft into heavy rain right over three flak ships which opened fire with machine-guns and pom-poms. I saw tracer coming up then we were clear and vanished into the rain. I reported a bullet hole in the tail plane and port engine on fire. We used the extinguisher and the flames died down. The inner half of the wing was blazing with the flames coming almost to the tail. In the fuselage was a mass of flame with the 'chutes burning; the observer used a fire extinguisher which had no effect. He pulled both the door and dinghy release handles and away went the door.

I got rid of the parachute hatch and we took up crash positions with our backs to the fuselage tank. The bomb bay which contained petrol tanks was on fire and flames were coming up through the bomb inspection covers. We crash-landed on the beach at Cameret in Finisterre.

The escape hatch over the pilot's position had been jettisoned and Roy [the other Wop/AG], who was standing near the pilot, was catapulted out and found himself hanging by the strap of a flying boot, hooked over a gun sight. We got him free and he dragged himself away from the burning aircraft.

Above: Hudson T9422 at Gander and now removed from its plinth. It commemorates the inauguration of the WWII Trans-Atlantic Ferry which opened with a flight of Hudsons led by Captain Don Bennett.

Two Frenchmen, ignoring German threats and exploding ammunition, dragged the rest of us and took us into a nearby cottage. We were then taken to Brest Naval Hospital where the skipper died. We were then moved to the Luftwaffen Lazarette in Paris (Hospital Beaujon), and to prison camps in Poland and Germany. The crew was Sgt Charles Glover, F/O M. Butler and Sgts Roy Gilbert and Ernest Winfield.

RAF Hudsons in addition to the wing tanks taking over 500 gallons and allowing a safe endurance of typically six hours, had on occasions, additional tanks in the bomb bay and fuselage providing 200 gallons and 100 gallons respectively.

The North Atlantic Ferry

Experimental crossings of the Atlantic had been made in 1939 but in July 1940 following a suggestion by the Ministry of Aircraft production, it was decided to attempt ferrying Lockheed Hudsons. By sea, not only was valuable shipping space being taken up and with the prospect of losses due to U boats, but it was taking about three months for the Hudsons to reach an operational unit from the time of the air tests in USA. By air, that period could be reduced to less than ten days.

Below: A plaque at Gander airport naming the late Air Vice-Marshal Don Bennett who organised the first Hudson Trans-Atlantic Ferry Flight in WWII.

An Air Ferries Dept was set up by the Canadian Pacific Railway at Montreal which would be responsible for manning and despatching the aircraft after they were delivered to Montreal, but with the British Air Ministry paying all expenses and supplying flying personnel as could be spared.

Due initially to America's neutrality, Hudsons were taken to the Canadian border at Pembina, sixty miles from Winnipeg, and then drawn by horses across the border before being flown on. Following the Lease-Lend agreement, General Arnold suggested that USAAC pilots might be used to ferry the aircraft direct to Montreal, providing training for them, and releasing civilian crews thereby who might be prepared to volunteer. A condition imposed was that the USAAC crews should deliver to a military organisation and what was 'Atfero' became RAF Ferry Command under ACM Sir Frederick Bowhill.

Some BOAC captains, D.C.T. 'Don' Bennett, A.S. Wilcockson, R.H. Page, and I.G. Ross, together with S/Ldr J. Powell, RCAF arrived in July 1940. In addition to pilots however, it was essential to have trained wireless operators and Morse keys were installed at St Hubert airport to check potential operators who were being considered. Capt. Bennett sat at a Morse key and tested those being interviewed himself. Bennett and Page visited the Lockheed factory to find that the first Hudson for despatch would be ready in September. Hattie Camp, Gander in Newfoundland had been used for flying in 1937 and by the autumn of 1940 was transformed into an airport. Prestwick, Ayrshire, Scotland was found suitable as a terminus for North Atlantic flights and later, routes followed were from Dorval, ten miles from Montreal, via Goose and Reykjavik or via Botswood or Gander.

The first flight of Hudsons, with Capt. Don Bennett leading the seven aircraft, was airborne at Gander on 10 November 1940 and landed at Aldergrove in Northern Ireland, the last one arriving about noon on the eleventh. Capt. Bennett's Hudson took ten hours seventeen minutes. The ferry crews, comprising nine Americans, six British, six Canadian and one Australian, returned by sea.

Hudson T9465 which was presented by Lockheeds and their employees, was airborne from Lockheeds on 22 December 1940 and was flown by Capt. Bennett as leader in the fourth and last of the group flights. It was found that time was lost in assembling flights for the crossing.

On 25 March 1943 the organisation became RAF Transport Command under Sir Frederick Bowhill with what had been Ferry Command becoming No.45 Group. Sir Frederick moved his headquarters to Harrow, Middlesex.

With many aircrew being trained in USA and Canada it was found that the newly-trained aircrew could well serve to ferry aircraft to the United Kingdom. There were a few losses but a very small percentage, perhaps less than at an OTU. A former Flight Commander with No.224 Squadron RAF, W/Cmdr Leslie Womersley, DFC ferried Hudson V9152 from Gander to Prestwick on 8/9 August 1941 when by then he

References 2. RAF III/p.76 3. RAF III/p.77

Above: Hudson T9422 at Gander, Newfoundland. It was from Gander on 10 November 1940 that the first Hudson Trans-Atlantic flight was airborne led by Capt. Don Bennett.

would have completed a tour of operations on Hudsons. The following is based on his flight plan:

Hudson V9152 was airborne from Gander at 2037hrs on 8 August 1941 with a 22 knot wind from 270° with course set for Prestwick and climbing to 8000ft at 117 knots.

Between 2105 and 2112hrs four loop bearings were obtained and position fixed at 49°15′N 52°39′W when ground speed was 151 knots. Course was altered from 076°T to 081° with height maintained at 8000ft. Four more loop bearings were obtained and at 2310hrs another fix gave 50°12′N 44°00′W. Course was altered to 059°T when there was a wind of 24 knots from 246°.

At 0023hrs on 9 August two astro shots were taken and position fixed at 51°05′N 36°29′W, and on a course of 082°T the true airspeed was 160 knots (indicated 144 knots). Three more astro shots had been taken but seemingly without gaining a fix. Womersley 'struck cloud and showers' at 0250hrs and climbed to 9000ft with the tops at 8500ft approx. There was 4/10ths with base at 9500ft at 0407hrs and a further change of course to 075°T was made.

Barra Head was sighted twenty-eight minutes later and at 0517hrs, Womersley began losing height down to 1000ft. He had asked his navigator P/O Rowland, RAAF to notify him when they were 200 miles from Northern Ireland and while at 1000ft saw the green fields of Southern Ireland through gaps in the cloud. He asked for a QDM [course to steer] and at 0530hrs altered course for Prestwick [060°M] After two more changes of course they were over Prestwick and landed at 0738hrs completing a flight of 11 hours 1 minute. Their aircraft, V9152 a Mark III Hudson became G-AGDK.

A pilot who at the time, 1 December 1942, had very much less experience of Hudsons than Womersley, Bill James, gives this account:

The ferry trip from Dorval started off disastrously. We carried a 2000lb overload including extra petrol tanks in the bomb bay and cabin and urgently needed spares. On take-off just as we became airborne the port engine cut and I could only get enough height to scrape over the city of Montreal. I couldn't dump any petrol so I had to make an emergency single-engine landing, fortunately the smoothest landing I'd ever made and

the undercarriage didn't collapse. When the engine was tested it was found that the oil pressure and propeller were out of order. These were corrected and we took off safely. It was a Mark VI FK565 and the crew Wilf Harrison (English), 2nd pilot; Haydn 'Mick' Rees (Welsh), navigator; Norman Tonge (Australian) Wop/AG. A turret was fitted but no armaments.

Dorval to Houlton to Gander six-and-a-half hours – I still had engine trouble all the way and over Newfoundland ran into a blizzard and had to use radio range to get in. Left Dorval 1.12.42, Houlton 7.1.42. Arrived Gander 7.1.42.

We took off from Gander 0100hrs GMT. Eighteen planes took off in one-and-a-half hours most going the indirect route via Iceland etc. I had decided to go direct. Within an hour had trouble – 'George' went u/s so I flew the whole trip without leaving my seat because Wilf had no single-engine experience. He spent time pumping by hand petrol into the main tanks as required. Then I had to fly to 17,600ft to try and get above a front but couldn't for two hours and flew in the tops of the clouds and only picked up some light wing ice. We came out of clouds and flew at 15,000ft for the rest of the trip, bright moonlight enabling me to avoid cumulo-nimbus clouds. We were on oxygen all the way and eventually arrived at Prestwick at 1030hrs GMT. We were the first plane to arrive and had beaten our ETA by an hour and as no plane was expected at that time we received a check over and an escort by two Hurricanes half-an-hour before landing.

One of the fastest crossings was by a Hudson with an Australian pilot with a time of eight hours one minute. A summary for the first eleven months of the North Atlantic Ferry gives of 266 aircraft ex Montreal, 263 arrived safely in Britain. There were three crashes and one training incident

Below: A Canadian crew at Silloth OTU with their Mark V Hudson in the background.

with six killed but two crews were lost during deliveries. Other aircraft were to follow the Hudsons such as Catalinas, Fortresses and Liberators.[4]

Special Operations

In July 1940 the Special Operations Executive (SOE) was set up in London to co-ordinate subversive and sabotage activities against the enemy overseas. With much of Europe's coastline under German control there was a need for air operations in such a service.

In the RAF, No.1419 Flight became No.138 (Special Duties) Squadron on 25 August 1941 and on 15 February 1942 No.161 (Special Duties) Squadron was formed with personnel from No.138 and from the King's Flight. W/Cmdr E.H. Fielden, MVO, AFC, the Captain of the King's Flight assumed command of No.161 Squadron. This was at Newmarket but by August 1942 both squadrons were based at Tempsford near Bedford.[5]

The squadrons used a number of types of aircraft but for dropping and picking up agents in France No.161 Squadron operated Lysanders and Hudsons. The first Hudson operation was undertaken by G/Capt. Fielden on the night of 25/26 November 1942. This was Operation *Steward* to north of Toulon near Vinon-sur-Verdon with the Hudson returning at 0331hrs on the twenty-sixth.[6]

W/Cmdr Fielden was succeeded as CO of 161 Squadron by W/Cmdr P.C. Pickard, DSO, DFC in October 1942 when Fielden became Station Commander of Tempsford with the rank of Group Captain. W/Cmdr Pickard's first trips were on Lysanders but on the night of 13/14 February 1943 was on operation *Sirene Berenice* in Hudson MA-O N7263 an aircraft from the King's Flight. He had P/O Taylor as navigator and F/O Figg, wireless operator and they were airborne at 2020hrs reaching the French coast via Tangmere at 2140hrs over the entrance to an estuary west of Gabourg. Course was set for islands east of Blois and then to Nevers and following the river to the target which was St Yan with the pinpoint position of 46°24′45″N 04°01′14″E. 'This was easily found and we saw a torch flashing N. Answered with an invalid letter to see what would happen – all lights went out.'

W/Cmdr Pickard gave the correct letter and two red lights came on followed by the path being laid. He landed at 2315hrs dropping five agents and took off again at 2325hrs. The same route was followed for the return flight landing at base at 0235hrs.

W/Cmdr Pickard was airborne in N7263 at 1903hrs on 20 February from Tempsford with the same crew for Operation *Steward* taking out one agent to position 43°36′07″N 04°44′00″E. Flying at 8000ft the French coast was reached at Gabourg 2020hrs via Tangmere then setting course for islands in the Loire, Avignon and then the target area. The Hudson was on the ground only seven minutes, taking off at 2335hrs with six agents and landing at base 0335hrs.

Another successful operation by W/Cmdr Pickard was achieved on the night of 24/25th February in Hudson N7263. In addition to his normal crew, P/O Taylor, and F/O Figg, he had F/Lt Putt from No.138 Squadron. They were airborne at 2227hrs and crossed the English coast west of Tangmere,

Sussex to reach the French coast at 2351hrs at Cabourg. Course was altered to the Loire but when ETA was reached thick fog prevented Pickard locating his pinpoint position 46°33′45″N 04°59′04″E. The fog persisted until he reached Le Creusot when there was some clearance, but again on reaching the target at 0130hrs there was fog. W/Cmdr Pickard made twenty attempts before landing at 0330hrs and touching down heavily to the side of what served as a 'flarepath' [a few torches]. The Hudson became bogged but was dug out with the help of onlookers in half an hour. On again becoming bogged as is reported: 'About half the village turned out and with the help of some of the more intelligent' the aircraft was again dug out although hope was almost given up. W/Cmdr Pickard pays tribute to F/Lt Putt for his 'coolness and energy' in organising the labour. Seven passengers were taken aboard the Hudson and on take-off the aircraft barely cleared the trees as a leading edge of a wing was damaged and the auto-pilot put out of action. This was at 0530hrs and some cars were then thought to be approaching. W/Cmdr Pickard set course for base crossing the French coast north of Le Havre at 0703hrs and, as dawn was breaking, he requested fighter protection as it was likely that enemy fighters could then be expected. Neither escort nor enemy appeared however and base was reached at 0830hrs after a total flight time of eight hours forty minutes.

One of the most unusual sorties by 161 Squadron was flown by F/O John Affleck on 8/9 February 1944 who was airborne at 2115hrs on Operation *Bludgeon*. This was to the target area four kilometres from Bletterans where the Hudson landed at 2330hrs. The field was waterlogged and the aircraft became bogged while taxiing to the take-off point. The engines were cut and attempts made to manhandle it. Engines were started but the tail wheel had sunk in. By the time that was cleared the landing wheels had sunk to the hubs and again the engines were switched off.

Some horses and oxen were then brought in and attempts made to drag the Hudson out but without avail. F/O Affleck then dug channels in front of the landing wheels and tried to taxi out on engines. It was agreed that if the Hudson could not take off by 0300hrs it should be destroyed. With digging completed an attempt was made to take off but not enough speed could be gained. On taxying back, it was again bogged down but at 0205hrs after two hours thirty-five minutes on the ground, a final attempt was made to take-off; a bump in the field bounced the Hudson into the air at fifty knots and F/O Affleck managed to keep it airborne and landed at base at 0510hrs. F/O Affleck had taken seven agents into France and returned with four others.

A pilot who flew with 161 Squadron after the end of hostilities was John Bray who (via a friend as Bray was unable to speak or write clearly) gives this account:

> I did a few trips to the continent, all to evacuate ex-PoWs of all services to the UK. On 18 May I brought home some Lascar seamen. At Brussels, a Hudson of 161 Squadron crashed on

References
4. AB p.11-24; RAF II/p.46-7; RAF III/p.184-5 5. RAF I/390; JDRR p.111; JJH p.231 6. HV p.193

landing killing all those on board including a load of ex PoWs. We left Tempsford on 11 June for Frankfurt with scientists from the RAF and WAAF technical Services and a US Army major of intelligence with signed orders from Eisenhower authorising us to remove documents, equipment and personnel from German research establishments starting at Hess Lichtenhan where scientific personnel were detained for screening. Next day we went to Nordhausen to the V2 production plants. We were provided with an American 6-wheel armoured car as transport.

This caused some consternation among the local civilian population who thought we were Russians as we wore our blue uniforms, flat caps and carried side arms. We flew the boffins to Nordhausen so that the V2 construction facilities could be photographed and examined. Whilst there we arrested a German scientist who had been involved in the design of the accelerometer, an advanced feature, used on V2 rockets. He was handed over to the MPs and found to be on a 'wanted list'. We flew back to Tempsford loaded with official loot and unofficial booze.

From John Bray's log this was in a Mark III Hudson T9462 and from Mannheim on 29 June 1945 with as crew, F/O McCormick, F/O Caldwell and F/Sgt Turner and his last ever flight.

Photo-Reconnaissance

The development of photo-reconnaissance in the Royal Air Force in World War II owed a great deal to an Australian aeronautical engineer – F. Sidney Cotton. In 1938 Cotton was flying his own aircraft on behalf of British Intelligence over Germany, ostensibly as a businessman but equipped with RAF cameras. After war broke out losses amongst Blenheim reconnaissance aircraft were so high that the Air Ministry approached Cotton.

Up to that time, the RAF had had difficulty in taking series of photographs from the air for two reasons: 1. The pictures had been taken from a high altitude; 2. The cameras froze due to condensation. Cotton was prepared to operate from a low altitude and to prevent freezing of the cameras, he ensured that a current of air from the aircraft flowed over the cameras.

He began his work at Heston on 23 September 1939 using a spare hangar for his 'No.2 Camouflage Unit' as it was known. For this purpose his own two civil aircraft were used and he was allotted Bristol Blenheims to adapt and two Spitfires. He was granted the honorary rank of Wing Commander. The Unit came under the control of the new Photographic Development Unit at Heston. He gave first priority to the taking of photographs of high quality and did not wish his aircraft to be involved in aerial combat. Thus to fly over enemy territory with reasonable safety, it was essential that the aircraft used could outpace the enemy. The Blenheims in France were far too slow and had suffered enormous casualties. By removing all armament and 'rubbing down' the speed of the aircraft could be increased. The disadvantage of a one-man fighter was the difficulty of navigating over long flights in bad weather. Cotton therefore developed his 'H' plan. For this he requested Hudsons which were heated and provided good facilties for the crew who were thus better able to concentrate on their task.

His first Hudson arrived in February 1940 and the Heston unit was joined by an ex-airline pilot – F/O Denis 'Slogger' Slocum. In the 'H' plan, a Hudson would fly out on the proposed Spitfire route and send back a radio message if the weather was unsatisfactory. Slocum carried out eight sorties up to 29 February taking excellent pictures and successfully evaded enemy aircraft, suffering only slight damage on one occasion. In the same month Winston Churchill, then First Lord of the Admiralty, saw Cotton's photographs of Wilhelmshaven and the *Tirpitz* and realised their value. He stated that if the Air Ministry would not formally take over Cotton's organisation, then the Admiralty would. Negotiations immediately began and in April the Air Ministry officially took Heston over. On 3 March 1940 Slocum's Hudson was shot down in flames over Meopham, Kent possibly by No.32 or No.79 Squadron.[7]

After the end of the phoney war, 'Cotton's Club', came under the auspices of Coastal Command. Hudsons of the Photo Reconnaisance Unit (PRU) as it was now known, were used in the evacuation of embassy staff from France on 21 June. By now the original PDU unit had split into two: PIU under S/Ldr Hemming concerned with interpretation and the PRU under W/Cmdr Tuttle with recce sorties. PR units operated from a number of Coastal Command stations such as St Eval and Wick, and from Leuchars on 30 June, a PRU Hudson covered the Bergen, Haugesund, Stavanger region of Norway.

In German bombing of St Eval in August, a PRU Hudson was damaged, and when Heston was also bombed, an alternative base was sought. In December the PRU unit moved to Benson from Heston.

In April 1940 F/O R.G.M. Walker was posted from No.224 Squadron to the Photographic Development Unit at Heston and found the Hudsons were required to serve a dual purpose; one to provide communications between base and the advanced Spitfire flights, carrying films, spares, etc; the other was to cover targets in the event of inclement weather. This was achieved by approaching the target in cloud, to break cloud over the target, photograph as much as possible, escaping back into cloud and then returning to base. Many such sorties were made but were not very successful.

An additional task for the Hudsons was to provide coverage of areas not then in the war and following damage to a British Airways Lockheed 14 which had been on continental service, a modified Hudson emerged from a hangar as G-AGAR looking like a Lockheed 14 but with six seats in the cabin and a concealed camera. On 4 June 1940 it was flown out from the United Kingdom by F/O Walker and H.C. McPhaill. They were in civilian clothes and were ostensibly directors of a company 'Aircraft Sales & Research'. They intended being abroad for three weeks and took their own ground crew. With the collapse of France and the entry of Italy in the war they became stranded in the Middle East. They established No.2 PRU and as that unit became equipped with Hurricanes and Beaufighters, the Hudson was used for communications. It received its original serial number 'N7364' and another Hudson, N7357 which had escorted Hurricanes was received.

N7364, piloted by F/O Walker became based at Heliopolis in Egypt and covered the Middle East from Malta to Aden and from Greece to Khartoum. It was a Mark I with Wright Cyclone engines and was operated at about 20,000ft and rarely higher than 25,000ft. When operating over Italian Somaliland targets for the Hudson were the airfields Gura and Mai Edaga. When Greece entered the war it became more convenient to use Crete and Athens as bases. Photo-recces were however taken over more and more by the Hurricanes.

On 17 March 1941 N7364 was airborne from Heliopolis with a PRU Hurricane; their targets were three airfields on Rhodes. The Hurricane was refuelled at Mersa Matruh and they were held up for five days due to weather. On 22 March the Hurricane was airborne but returned to Heraklion on Crete having passed out at 20,000ft recovering after spinning down to 10,000ft. He was followed by by four Italian CR42s which attacked the airfield and the Hudson became a write-off.

General Wavell at Khartoum

No.2 PRU provided a Hudson aircraft for Generals Wavell and Maitland-Wilson with their ADCs on 3 September from Heliopolis to Maaten Bugush for a conference with their Desert Army commanders shortly before Italy invaded North Africa. Wavell's great desert victories followed in late 1940 and early 1941. F/O Walker (now W/Cmdr) recalls General Wavell as a 'charming person, full of humour and devilment'. General Wilson was left at Maaten Bagush, but ten days later on the fourteenth, General Wavell was taken with three of his staff to Khartoum. The following day, with the addition of the AOC Khartoum, Air Commodore Slatter, the Hudson was flown to Azaza to gain an escort of Gladiator fighters. This was to enable General Wavell to make his own visual reconnaissance of Gedaref, Khashm El Girba bridge over the Atbara river, and the river up and down stream of the bridge. The General appeared well satisfied with the flight and although tired, had time to thank the Hudson crew.

Winston Churchill wrote to Anthony Eden, then Minister for War, on 24 September reviewing the Middle East situation and asking him to make a personal inspection of the Middle East. Mr Eden arrived in Cairo on 15 October. The Italians had been halted at Sidi Barrani and in addition to having discussions with Generals Maitland-Wilson and Wavell, Eden arranged to meet General Smuts at Khartoum on 28 October and to fly back to Lagos after that meeting.

F/Lt Walker was at Port Sudan when he was instructed to proceed to Khartoum as soon as possible for that Top Secret mission. He took off immediately at 1530hrs and signalled Khartoum that he would land at Atbara where he intended staying the night. While refuelling and the crew having some refreshment, a further signal instructed them to proceed to Khartoum and that night-landing facilties would be available. When over Khartoum only three paraffin flares could be seen but lacking a further flare to indicate which side of the line to land. As he was touching down, shapes of other aircraft could be seen flashing down but he was able to follow a jeep flashing a green light. He made a few comments about the clot who laid the flarepath and the one who advised of night landing facilities only to find he was speaking to the AOC! However, A/Commodore Slatter was full of apologies.

On the thirty-first the Hudson crew took on board Anthony Eden with Mr Casey who represented the Australian Government. Their first flight was to Port Sudan, and after a short conference in the aircraft, its crew was required to stand by. The Hudson was refuelled, the crew had lunch, and, after another conference, Mr Eden and his party returned to Khartoum. The Hudson was on stand-by until 5 November when its passengers were taken to Port Sudan via Carthage.[8]

References
7. AH S&S p.81   8. Letters to Author from W/Cmdr R.G.M. Walker, DFC

Chapter 7
The Far East

Malaya

Following the fall of France in June 1940 Japan applied pressure on the Vichy government and on Thailand for bases in Indo-China and on 30 August French Indo-China agreed to Japan using airbases and having troops there.[1]

Germany urged Japan to attack Malaya and the Dutch East Indies but a prerequisite was considered either a settlement with USA or an attack on American bases.[2] Japan's assets were frozen by the Americans on 24 July 1941 followed by the British and the Dutch and these actions effectively cut off much of Japan's vital oil supplies and according to Churchill, brought matters to 'a head'. On the same day Japanese warships were off Camranh Bay, French Indo-China, and four days later Japanese troops landed at Saigon. On 29 July a pact was signed at Vichy giving Japan the use of eight airfields in Indo-China.[3]

Air Chief Marshal Sir Robert Brooke-Popham, the C-in-C Far East had operational control of the Army and Air Forces but with instructions to avoid provocation of Japan. At a conference on 16 October 1940 Far Eastern Commands specified 566 aircraft but by 8 December 1941 only 362 RAF aircraft were available and of those, 233 were serviceable. In Malaya there were twenty-two airfields and four on Singapore but they lacked suitable defence systems.[4]

The Admiralty's war plans approved on 30 January 1939 had given the Far East as third after Home Waters and the Mediterranean in its priorities and by December 1941 the Royal Navy was notably lacking in aircraft carriers in the Far East. The naval historian Capt. Roskill adds that the one who held the coast of Indo-China with Camranh Bay base, would control the South China Sea.[5]

Six Hudsons from No.1 Squadron RAAF were airborne from Laverton on 30 June 1940 bound for Singapore. After a flight via Adelaide, Alice Springs, Darwin and Sourabaya they arrived at Sembawang on 4 July. The squadron completed a move from Sembawang to Kota Bharu on 5 August 1941. No.8 Squadron at Canberra had by 30 July 1940 collected twelve aircraft and on 5 August began their flight to Singapore arriving at Sembawang on 9 August. The remainder of their personnel arrived on 26 August disembarking from RMS *Strathallan*.

The duties for the two Hudson squadrons became primarily armed recces over the sea and to attack any seaborne forces; for No.8 it was to patrol between Kota Bharu and Kuantan and 'to report and shadow any convoy of more than three ships.' No.8 Squadron made a number of moves; but on 2 December 1941 commenced transferring

Above: No.194 Sqdn served in India and Burma supporting Wingate's 'Chindits'. Here, three of their number on 2 July 1944 at Dubalia.

Below: Sgt Birchall of No.194 Sqdn with one of their Hudsons having the 'Dumbo' motif on the nose.

from Sembawang to Kuantan with the movement completed on 8 December with the arrival of the ground party which had travelled by sea.

On 6 December No.1 Squadron made a number of sightings of Japanese forces including a battleship, five cruisers, seven destroyers and twenty-two transports 265 miles from Kota Bharu and apparently heading for that base.[6]

About that time the operational strength of the RAF Command, Malaya included No.1 Squadron RAAF's twelve Hudsons at Kota Bharu, and eleven Blenheims of No.62 Squadron (RAF) at Alor Star. Twelve Hudsons of No.8 were at Kuantan and as G/Capt. H.C. Plenty adds: '. . . the precise number we flew to attack the Japanese landing at Kota Bharu on the morning of 8 December . . .'

At about 0200hrs on 8 December Kuantan received a signal of the Japanese attempting landings at Kota Bharu. No.8 formed four flights of three Hudsons with the first airborne at 0630hrs; the Japanese forces reached Kota Bharu at 1030hrs. The Hudsons attacked but some were damaged including A16-43 captained by F/Lt G. Hitchcock which suffered forty-three bullet holes but returned to Kuantan. 'Spud' Spurgeon in A16-41 bombed a ship but crash-landed at Kota Bharu due to damage to the Hudson. F/Lt Russell Bell had the hydraulics made u/s by bullets in his Hudson A16-81 and flew it to Seletar from Kota Bharu. The assault on Kota Bharu represented only a small part of Japan's advance; in twelve hours it had attacked Hong Kong, the Philippines, Wake Island, Guam, Siam and Pearl Harbor.

The attack on Pearl Harbor on the seventh was by about 460 carrier-borne aircraft resulting in the disabling or sinking of eighteen warships but many shore installations remained intact and three vital aircraft carriers were not in port. The attack on Pearl Harbor brought America into the war which Japan was now bound to lose.[7]

The battleship HMS *Prince of Wales* and the battlecruiser HMS *Repulse* sailed from Singapore at 1735hrs on 8 December intending to attack Japanese forces believed heading for Kuantan. Both ships were sunk by bombing and torpedo attacks on 10 December. It had been intended for that force to include an aircraft carrier and additionally for air cover to be provided. Neither materialised.

As the Australian historian John Robertson records: 'So ended British sea power based on Singapore'.[8] It was to be June 1942 before the tide turned in favour of the Allies following the Battle of Midway.

The First Sinking of a Japanese Ship in WWII

On the night of 7/8th the enemy had achieved landings at Singora and early on the eighth enemy troops were reported. Another Japanese force including two cruisers, seven destroyers and three transports was reported heading for Kota Bharu. The Hudsons of Nos 1 and 8 Squadrons were actively engaged They were armed with four 250lb bombs and one of the first to attack was F/O A.B. Lockwood of No.1 who sighted three transports. He was followed by F/Lt J.C. Ramshaw who saw two of Lockwood's bombs gain direct hits on a transport.

F/Lt O.N. Diamond of No.1 Squadron selected the largest merchantman which he dive-bombed. From his own account two 250lb bombs released in his first attack scored direct hits and on his second run his remaining two bombs also struck the vessel which was then machine-gunned and left on fire. It was the *Awajisan Maru* of 9794 tons which sank in position 06°08′N 102°16′E. It was the first Japanese ship of any type to be sunk in World War II.[9]

Other attacks by Hudsons followed and the other two transports *Sakura Maru*, 7170 tons, and *Ayatosan Maru*, 9788 tons, were damaged but F/Lt Ramshaw failed to return from a second sortie.

No.1 Squadron's base at Kota Bharu was subject to air attacks, there was a lack of communication and anti-aircraft defences. Both crews and aircraft were overworked; the squadron had only five airworthy Hudsons and it was decided to evacuate Kota Bharu; aircraft which could not be flown off were destroyed including two from No.1 and one Hudson from No.8 Squadron. Those able to fly went to Kuantan. F/Lt O'Brien while taking seventeen passengers in a damaged Hudson was subjected to ground fire and then managed to evade six Zero fighters. The remaining seven Hudsons of No.8 Squadron at Kuantan were ordered to

References
1. JRob. p.60; DG RAAF I/p.169   2. WSC III/p.160
3. WSC III/p.521; DG RAAF I/p.169   4. RAF II/pp.4 & 5
5. SWR I/pp.41 & 560   6. RAAF III/p.200
7. JRob. p.72; JK p.68; DG RAAF III/p.207; AH *FC* pp.113–114
8. JRob. p.73; SWR I/566   9. JN &Msp.29; RAAF I/p.210

Below: Maintenance on a Pratt & Whitney 'Wasp' engine of a 194 Sqdn Hudson.

Above: Servicing Hudsons at Batchelor Field, NWT, Australia in 1942.

Above: KO-X A16-160 of No.2 Sqdn RAAF at Drysdale. It crashed on 23.5.45 when with another unit.

Sembawang; they were A16-11, -17, -48, -76, -82, -85, and A16-87.[10] Of this evacuation G/Capt. Plenty writing to the author states: 'I remained at Kuantan for about ninety minutes after the last seven Hudsons of No.8 had departed for Singapore. My CO had given approval to find a "serviceable" Hudson to fly. Four or five abandoned ones stood on the airfield.' Plenty found A16-23 and flew it to Singapore single-handed.

No.8 flew operations the next day, the tenth. G/Capt. Plenty adds: 'I watched Japanese torpedo-bombers sink the battleship *Prince of Wales* and the battlecruiser *Repulse*.' He continues: '. . . at Kota Bharu the previous day there were eight separate attacks by formations of enemy aircraft. No.1 Squadron lost two-thirds of their machines there, including two shot down by enemy ships. Had No.8 Squadron remained at Kuantan there would have been similar destruction.'

On 24 January 1942 F/Lts 'Spud' Spurgeon in Hudson A16-11 and 'Herb' Plenty in A16-87 of No.8 Squadron were airborne from Sembawang on a patrol over the South China Sea. They flew together heading north-east before turning west for their datum north of Kuantan. It was G/Capt. Plenty's rear gunner F/Sgt Jacobson who reported four Zero fighters. The Hudsons broke formation and the Zeros headed for Spurgeon's aircraft in line ahead as Plenty headed for cloud cover. Spurgeon headed for sea level but the Hudson was sprayed with bullets and it crashed. Only Spurgeon and his second pilot, F/O S.N. Chesterman, escaped finishing up drifting south in their Mae Wests. Chesterman succumbed during the night and was drowned. Spurgeon drifted ashore on Pulo Tioman island. After care by Chinese who took him to the mainland he attempted to move southwards but was made PoW by a Japanese patrol. Plenty had escaped into cloud but after assuming the Zeros had gone he broke cloud and the fighters attacked.

Plenty made for sea level taking evasive action but the starboard engine was hit, the wing dipped and the Hudson struck the sea, bounced a few times and began to sink. The aircraft dinghy in a Hudson was normally in the door and

would release and inflate automatically but No.8 Squadron had opted to keep it separate and it required inflation after ditching. The Zeros circled but did not fire; as Plenty adds 'they were Navy pilots from the 22nd Air Flotilla and found to be more gentlemanly than those in the Japanese army.' This was near Palau Sri Buat Island and after inflating the dinghy, Plenty's crew paddled to the island where they met a Chinese fisherman.

The next day he took the Hudson crew to Malays on another island who agreed to sail them in a *prahu* towards Mersing for fifty dollars. En route it was suspected that the boatmen might sell them to the Japs and Hewett drew his revolver and took over the tiller.

Beyond Mersing the money was paid and the Australians waded to the beach and later found a *prahu* which could be made seaworthy and set sail reaching an Allied signals post near Point Ramunia on the twenty-eighth. The Navy was radioed and they were taken to Singapore by a minesweeper.

As A/Cmdre Spurgeon in writing to the author says: 'In the final incident in Malaya, when we were both shot down . . . my crew was lost, his survived in an incident of traumatic proportions, certainly at the time!'[11]

Singapore

The Japanese had made a further landing at Endau on 26 January and on the twenty-eighth General Wavell decided that Allied troops should withdraw to Singapore. The island's defences had been prepared for any attack from seaward, not from the land and about a third of Singapore's water supplies came from Johore. By 9 February the Japanese had gained a foothold on the island and on the twelfth ships were leaving the harbours with personnel not required for defence. On 15 February General Percival informed General Wavell that due to losses, lack of food, ammunition, petrol and water he was unable to continue the defence.[12]

The Japanese had used three divisions to capture Singapore in sixty-eight days with 10,000 casualties including 1793 killed in Malaya and 1714 on Singapore.

Above: No.6 Sqdn RAAF Hudsons FX-G, E, and F, flying over Milne Bay, Papua in early 1943.

They captured 130,000 troops and about 8000 Allies were killed or wounded. These included Australian causualties of 1789 killed, 1306 wounded and 15,395 captured. About a third of the Australian PoWs died in captivity.

For Winston Churchill it was the largest capitulation and worst disaster in British history; for the Australian historian professor John Robertson, 'The Empire strategy based on Singapore had been shattered'.[13]

Sumatra

No.62 Squadron, RAF equipped with Blenheims was posted to the Far East in August 1939 and by February 1941 was based at Alor Star on the north-west coast of Malaya. About the time of the attack on Pearl Harbor it moved down to Butterworth. In late December there was a further move south to Tengah on Singapore.

At Kemble in England, Hudson crews from Nos 53 and 59 Squadrons were being prepared to reinforce No.62 in the Far East and as one of their Wop/AGs, John Tubb adds:

Eighteen aircraft left Kemble via Portreath for Singapore in January 1942 and fifteen aircraft arrived in the Far East. One crashed at Bombay, I'm not sure of the other two. Three aircraft survived to reach Buitenzong in Java, these were then destroyed by a Jap air-raid.

Living conditions in Singapore and Sumatra were very poor – low rations, very poor morale of the RAF who had retreated through Malayan heat and humidity, living in tents in the Sumatra jungle.

John Tubb left Kemble on 2 January in Hudson AE529 captained by a New Zealander, F/O Henry; their route was via Gibraltar, Malta, Egypt, Iraq, India, Burma, and the Andaman islands arriving at Palembang II in Sumatra on 27 January 1942 having flown eighty-one-and-a-half hours in twenty-five days. Their arrival coincided with the remnants of the Blenheim-equipped crews.

From Tubb's log, F/O Henry's first sortie was a recce of the coast of Sumatra in AE551 on 1 February and on the third in AE521, a trip to Singapore to find the island shrouded in smoke from burning oil. John Tubb remarks: 'I went to Raffles Hotel and signed for a case of beer, nobody very interested in money – most of the staff had fled.'

On 4 February six Hudsons were detailed for a dawn strike

References
10. HP; RAAF I/pp.214; 217–8   11. CHS; HCP; RAAF I/343; JB pp.67–75
12. SWR II/p.9; WSC IV/p.94   13. WSC IV/p.94; JRob. p.89

Below: An engine change for a No.2 Sqdn Hudson circa 1940/41.

Above: Turnbull airstrip, Papua on 8 April 1943 taken from A16-131.

on Kluang aerodrome then occupied by the enemy. They included AE529 which was airborne at 0545hrs with F/O Henry who released bombs from about 6000ft. He was attacked by three Zero fighters but as Tubb comments: 'The older Hudsons in Malaya had a rear turret and side guns only. Our Hudson had a ventral gun below the turret to wind down and with a single .303 Browning which slid forward on rails, the gunner lying half in and half out. The Zeros made classic attacks behind and below the Hudson, and were, I imagine, very surprised by my return fire. One came up to about fifty yards astern – I must have hit him! We lost no aircraft.'

The Hudsons had been due for a Hurricane escort but the fighters' guns had been sabotaged. A recall had not been received as the wireless operators were on guns. AE529 returned to Palembang II.

While still with No.62 Squadron, Tubb had one more notable trip. This was on 13 February in AE521 captained by F/O Henry who dive-bombed a Japanese convoy of two cruisers, four destroyers and one merchant vessel.

On 27 and 29 January Hudsons of No.8 and No.1 Squadrons left Singapore for what was considered a secret landing field in Sumatra, Palembang II. From there recces were made to the east and north-east of Sumatra. They made bombing attacks on Alor Star and an enemy-occupied airfield at Kluang. By 10 February part of Singapore had been taken by the Japanese and Allied forces surrendered on 15 February.[14] On that day No.1 Squadron aircraft in Java were sent to Palembang, Sumatra to evacuate personnel and, from the very limited squadron record, the evacuation was achieved without loss. No.8 Squadron which had withdrawn to Sumatra on 27 January after handing over its remaining Mark I Hudson to No.1 had begun to rearm with Mark III Hudsons from England. Its recces over the South China Sea had continued to 12 February.

F/O P.J. Gibbes of No.1 Squadron was airborne from Palembang II on 6 February for a recce over the South China Sea and in the Anambas islands after evading fighters, sighted four destroyers and four transports. Because of lack of fuel he landed at Kallang, Singapore.

On 13 February a lone Hudson from No.1 Squadron was on a recce when a possible landing on Sumatra was anticipated. He reported a force north of Banka Island of twenty-five to thirty transports heavily escorted. On the fourteenth aircraft from both the RAF and RAAF made attacks including five Hudsons from No.8 Squadron. They were intercepted by fighters but were able to use cloud cover. One flown by F/Lt Douglas crashed but hits on transports were claimed by F/Lts O'Brien, Diamond, Williams and Brydon. From the official RAF account six transports were sunk or damaged for the loss of seven aircraft.

On that same day the Station CO at Palembang II was advised of the Japanese landing at Palembang I and Palembang II was to be evacuated. Four Hudsons were flown to Batavia, Java leaving two aircraft to patrol the Palembang river. They flew to Java on the fifteenth. Other personnel reached Java by land and sea arriving at Batavia on 17 February.[15]

ABDA had ordered all British units to leave Sumatra for Java on the fifteenth and by the eighteenth the evacuation was considered complete with over 10,000 men having arrived in Java.[16]

Of the evacuation from Sumatra to Java, John Tubb believed that his captain achieved something of a record by taking twenty-one passengers in addition to his Hudson crew of three. (Seven more than one would anticipate.)

Darwin is Bombed

A Japanese force of four aircraft carriers, two battleships, five cruisers and about twenty destroyers sailed from Kendari, Celebes and entered the Banda Sea on 19 February 1942. Ten P40s of the 33rd Pursuit squadron led by Major Floyd Pell of the 5th Army Air Force were airborne from Darwin and headed for Koepang. An unfavourable weather report decided Major Pell to return. When a report of enemy aircraft fifty miles north-west of Darwin was received, the P40s took off again and nine of the ten were shot down, only Lt Robert G. Oerstreicher returning to make a safe landing.

On the four carriers were eighty-one aircraft and at 1000hrs there was the first air-raid on Darwin with twenty-seven bombers flying in from the south-east to attack the harbour and town; it was over by 1030hrs. At 1200hrs there was a second raid, now directed against the Air Force base and by fifty-four land-based bombers from Celebes. It lasted twenty minutes and aircraft lost on the ground included six RAAF Hudsons from No.2 Squadron, which had recently returned from Koepang; they were A16-6, -57, and -35; and from No.13 Squadron, A16-72, -63 and -141.

The Americans lost in addition to their P40s, three ships; the destroyer USS *Peary,* a transport *Meigs* and the merchantman *Mauna Loa.*

The RAAF history gives a total of 238 killed and 248 wounded; eight ships sunk with twenty-three aircraft including those of the Americans destroyed. The Japanese lost, at most, ten aircraft.

For the Australian historian Professor Robertson it was 'Japan's biggest single strike since Pearl Harbor'; for the British naval historian Capt. Roskill, 'the last reinforcement link with Java broken' and for the American historian Richard L. Watson, the Japanese had achieved their objective in bombing Darwin – the isolation of Java.[17]

Java

Of the Hudson-equipped squadrons on Java, Nos 1 and 8 RAAF and No.62 RAF were based at Semplak due south of Batavia. No.1 with thirteen Hudsons, and Nos 8 and 62 each with six aircraft. On 20 February Nos 8 and 62 were instructed to hand over their Hudsons to No.1 Squadron and leave Java. Five officers and forty-six other ranks from No.8 and four RAF crews became attached to No.1 while tired crews from No.1 went to No.8 Squadron. Ten complete crews from No.8 then flew to Darwin to reinforce Nos 2 and 13 Squadrons. Remaining personnel of No.8 comprising fourteen officers and 132 other ranks sailed on *Orchades* from Batavia on 22 February disembarking at Adelaide on 15 March.

No.1 Squadron Hudsons attacked a Japanese 10,000-ton ship on the Musi river on 22 February claiming two direct hits and setting it on fire. On the same date Zero fighters strafed Semplak for thirty minutes setting six Hudsons on fire and shooting up three others.

On the twenty-third six Hudsons flew from Semplak to Kalidjati where there was stronger AA defences. Kilidjati was bombed the following day with two more Hudsons lost. During a further raid on Kilidjati on the twenty-sixth five enemy aircraft were believed to have been shot down by the AA Bofors guns.

Of his experiences in Java John Tubb remarks: [By contrast with those in Singapore and Sumatra] 'Conditions in Java were good with excellent food and billets. Evacuated Java by Dutch steamer *Kota Gede*, although most ground crew were taken PoW.'

Western Java was invaded at Merak and Bantam Bay, and Eastern Java was invaded at Eretanwetan and Kragen all on 1 March. Of four airworthy Hudsons, two took off for Andir, east of Semplak. By then Japanese forces had reached the area but F/O Gibbes took off a third Hudson and opened fire on the enemy before flying to Andir. The following day all airworthy Hudsons were ordered to Australia. They each carried an extra 100 gallons of petrol in four-gallon cans. For refuelling in mid-air, a window was broken open to feed a tube fitted with a funnel through to the wing tanks.[18]

Timor

For General Wavell, Timor provided bases for an air link from Australia to Singapore. With the loss of Singapore and Sumatra it still provided a link to Java and that link was broken with the Japanese occupation of Bali. A base on Timor then served for air strikes against the enemy.

No.2 Squadron RAAF had been based at Laverton but on 5 December 1941 'A' Flight with four aircraft moved to Darwin under F/Lt R.B. Cuming. Two days later it was deployed at Koepang on Timor. On 10 December the remainder of No.2 Squadron then at Darwin followed them to Koepang. At the end of December 'A' Flight under F/Lt R.B.

Cuming was transferred to Namlea on Buru island.

A flight of No.2's Hudsons led by F/Lt Cuming on 11 January was en route from Namlea to attack shipping at Menado, Celebes. It was intercepted by Zero fighters and Hudsons captained by F/Lt P.H.R. Hodge and F/O P.C. Gorrie were shot down. Living conditions for No.2 Squadron were such that as much as thirty per cent of the unit were reporting sick with malaria, dengue fever, dysentery and tropical sores. F/Lt Cuming was airborne at Penfui, Timor on 20 January but his Hudson stalled and crashed.

The aircraft was heavily loaded with stores for Namlea and F/Lt Cuming was killed with the nine others in the Hudson. Another Hudson was lost on 14 February when F/O G.G. Mitchell of No.13 Squadron was airborne from Penfui. The aircraft was struck by lightning and he crashed.

The Japanese were making recces of Timor during 16 to 20 February and W/Cmdr F. Headlam, No.2's CO but acting as base commander at Koepang, was ordered to evacuate all RAAF personnel except small maintenance and signals parties. Six officers and twenty-three other ranks were selected out of volunteers. This was on 18 February when six Hudsons arrived to take the main staff to Darwin. En route four of them attacked a Japanese submarine with guns having no other armament.

The remaining personnel apart from the rear party were flown out the following day. The Koepang garrison received warning of a Japanese convoy approaching through the Semau Strait on 19 February and later there was news of enemy landings at Dili on the north coast of Portuguese Timor and on the south coast near Koepang.

F/Lt B. Rofe in charge of No.2 Squadron's rear parties had two portable radios and headed initially for Babau but when paratroopers were sighted being dropped, headed for Champlong where an army force was based. Later he joined the second party under F/O Cole both then going to the hills overlooking Koepang. Two Hudsons sent to ferry the rear party, on sighting the enemy landings returned to Darwin. F/Lt Rofe then took both parties to Nuatutu which was reached on 25 February. Ultimately on 15 April they received a signal to light a fire on the beach on the seventeenth. This was repeated on the eighteenth and No.2's personnel were picked up by the USS submarine *Sea Raven* returning to Fremantle on 26 April.

It was to be in February 1945 when the Japanese in turn found themselves isolated on Timor and with the wish to withdraw.[19]

Reconnaissance to Truk

No.6 Squadron RAAF based at Richmond, NSW in April 1940 had four Hudsons, A16-5, -6, -32 and A16-56. Another four, A16-33, -34, -35, and A16-46, were on charge by 1 May. Their operations comprised convoy escorts and anti-submarine patrols. By 11 December 1941 six of their

References

14. JRob. p.88 15. RAF II/43; RAAF III/390; No.8 RAAF Sqdn record
16. RAF II/p.45 17. SWR II/p.12; JRob. pp.93–4; RAAF I/pp.431–2; C&C I/p.394
18. RAAF I/pp.441–2 19. RAAF II/p.403

Hudsons were at Richmond and four at Laverton.

A special reconnaissance of the Truk Islands was requested in January 1942 and two Mark IV Hudsons captained by F/Lt R.A. Yeowart and F/O R.M. Green were selected for the mission. Each one of the Hudsons was fitted with two 105 gallon fuel tanks in the main cabin and two cameras, one forward, one aft.

They first flew to Townsville and received their final briefing there on 3 January before being airborne the following morning on course for Rabaul. When one hour's flying from Rabaul they were warned that the base was being bombed and they diverted to Lae on New Guinea for refuelling. On reaching Rabaul on the fifth it was closed in by weather and the Hudsons landed at Namatanai on New Ireland before flying to Rabaul on the sixth. F/O Green's aircraft had a faulty carburettor and he had to withdraw leaving F/Lt Yeowart to proceed alone. Yeowart with his crew, F/O P.R. McDonnell, and Sgts M.C. Ellis and E.C. Marriner was airborne at 0544hrs on 8 January 1942 from Kavieng, New Ireland and four-and-a-half-hours later was over Toll, one of the Truk islands where in harbour were twelve or thirteen enemy warships including a carrier with cruisers and destroyers. Seen also were flying boats, float planes and twenty-seven bombers on an airstrip. A photo run was made at 13,000ft and while on a second run the Hudson was subjected to AA fire and was attacked by enemy fighters. Yeowart evaded them by diving into a rain squall; he had been over the target for twenty-five minutes but the Hudson suffered little damage and seemingly, via Kavieng, Rabaul and Milne Bay returned to Townsville where the films were processed.

Later that year McDonnell and Ellis were killed in action with No.32 Squadron, and Marriner with No.24 Squadron.[20]

No.6 Squadron were still based at Richmond commanded by S/Ldr A.A. Barlow on 21 August but moved via Townsville on the twenty-third to Horn Island.

The Battle of the Java Sea

Following the sighting of a Japanese invasion force in the Macassar Strait heading for Java on 26 February, the Dutch naval commander, Vice-Admiral Doorman sailed from Surabaya to intercept. He commanded what was ostensibly a powerful force comprising three Dutch cruisers with HMAS *Hobart*, HMS *Exeter*, four Dutch and six American destroyers. Both crews and ships, were well worn and tired and, unlike the Japanese forces lacked integration. They lacked air support and, from the official British naval account, Admiral Doorman attacked in line ahead, thus all his ships could not bring their guns to bear.

On 27 February 1942, in what came to be known as the Battle of the Java Sea, the Allied naval forces were defeated and Admiral Doorman went down with his ship the *De Ruyter,* one of ten Allied ships lost in the battle. Allied forces in Java had been put under the command of General ter Poorten who had 25,000 troops and 40,000 militia plus 8000 British and Australian troops.

General ter Poorten surrendered Java to the Japanese on 9 March. As Churchill recorded, the conquest of the Netherlands East Indies was complete. Of the 8000 British and Australian forces taken prisoner, 3462 survived the war. In addition to Malaya, Singapore, Sumatra and Java, the Japanese, by 20 February 1942, made assaults on the Philippines, Borneo, Celebes, Bali, Amboina and Timor.[21]

New Guinea

The Japanese had made landings on the northern coast of New Guinea at Finschhaven (9 February) and Lae and Salamaua on 8 March 1942 and intended taking Port Moresby together with Tulagi in the Solomon Islands, the latter covering the waters near Guadalcanal. Such moves would have cut communications between America and Australia, they would also form part of Japan's intended extension of its conquests to include part of the Aleutians, Midway Island, New Hebrides, New Caledonia and the Fiji Islands.[22]

Forces at Port Moresby were strengthened and included the Hudson-equipped composite unit under W/Cmdr J.M. Lerew. Attached to the base was F/Lt D.W.I. Campbell who undertook a recce of New Britain on 6 February. While over Rabaul his Hudson was attacked by a fighter and Campbell suffered a shattered wrist due to an explosive bullet which severed a finger. His second pilot, P/O J.E. Lauder, had fractures to a leg and an arm plus a wounded hand. Sgt G.A. O'Hea in the turret suffered a wounded leg. Sgt G. Thompson, a fourth crew member, assisted in flying the Hudson back 500 miles with both altimeter and air speed indicator u/s. On landing at Port Moresby it was found that only five gallons of fuel remained.[23]

On 9 February a Japanese force was sighted at Gasmata, New Britain and that night W/Cmdr Lerew led five Hudsons in addition to three Catalinas from No.4 Squadron to attack two transports and a destroyer inshore and four destroyers outside Gasmata harbour. W/Cmdr Lerew led another strike on 11 February with F/Lt W.A. Petrina and F/O G.T. Gibson flying two other Hudsons. They attacked from mast height and scored hits on two transports. The Hudsons were then attacked by five or six fighters. Pedrina's gunners shot down one in flames and claimed another probable. Gibson's aircraft was seen with an engine on fire and diving into a hillside. With Gibson was P/O F.L.O. Thorn and Sergeants A.E Quail and B.I. Coutie. They were all killed. Lerew's Hudson was also on fire and he ordered his crew to bale out. Lerew landed in a tree from which he broke free to live off the jungle, evading Japanese troops and ultimately was guided by natives to a coastwatcher before being returned to Port Moresby nine days later in a schooner. His three crewmen were lost.[24]

While on a reconnaissance to New Britain on 19 February, F/Lt Pedrina's Hudson was attacked by two fighters when he was near the south-west coast. His rear gunner after firing what was probably most of his ammunition, saw one fighter diving out of control. The wireless operator was fatally wounded and the Hudson extensively damaged but was flown back to base.

On 21 February the composite Hudson unit was designated No.32 GR-Bomber Squadron and its commanding

Above: A16-12 of the RAAF. This underside view shows clearly the wing slots, landing lights, bomb doors, and the wing flaps which are fully retracted. A16-12 crashed over Celebes on 12.1.42 after combat with Zeros.

officer, W/Cmdr Lerew, was succeeded by S/Ldr D.W. Kingwell. The first daylight attack by Japanese bombers on Port Moresby was on 24 February.

The Hudsons had been dispersed to Horn Island but one which remained was destroyed together with buildings and motor transport.

F/O A.S. Hermes on 7 March sighted an enemy force of transports escorted by a cruiser and four destroyers heading for Lae and Japanese landings were made at both Lae and Salamaua when No.32 Squadron's Hudsons were dispersed on Horn Island. An American carrier force heading for Rabaul diverted two carriers with escorting cruisers and destroyers to south of New Guinea. After briefing by the Australians on how to fly over the Owen Stanley Range, aircraft from a carrier attacked Japanese shipping at Lae and Salamaua with ultimately a cruiser and three destroyers confirmed as damaged.[25]

At Port Moresby on 31 March when a reconnaissance of Salamaua was considered imperative, No.32 Squadron had only one Hudson available and which was considered unserviceable. W/Cmdr Kingwell opted to fly it in place of F/O R.M. Green who had been detailed. During the sortie the Hudson was attacked by three Zeros; Kingwell's gunner shot down one and possibly a second. W/Cmdr Kingwell shot down

the third Zero with his front guns, this in a twelve-minute combat. Both Kingwell and Green were wounded as also was one of the gunners, Sgt J.V. Townshend.[26]

The Battle of the Coral Sea

On 20 April 1942 a Japanese task force sailed from Truk in the Caroline Islands, and on 3 May, Tulagi an island in the southern Solomons forty kilometres west of Guadalcanal was occupied.

An invasion force of transports and destroyers intended for an assault on Port Moresby sailed from Rabaul, New Britain on 4 May to be joined at midnight of the fifth/sixth by the light aircraft carrier *Shoho* with four cruisers. Meanwhile a Japanese strike force comprising the carriers *Shokaku* and *Zuikaku* with two cruisers and six destroyers was sailing southwards east of the Solomons.

Admiral Nimitz was aware of Japan's intentions and had deployed forces including notably the carriers *Lexington* and *Yorktown* under Rear-Admiral F.J. Fletcher supported by Rear-Admiral Fitch and Rear-Admiral J.G. Crace, RN.

The Japanese objective of taking Port Moresby in addition to Tulagi would have cut communications between Australia and America and pose a serious threat to Australia itself.

On 6 May S/Ldr G.E. Hensworth in a RAAF Catalina reported two Japanese destroyers south-east of Misima in the Louisiade Archipelago before being shot down by fighters. A further report by P/O P.T.E. Pennycuick from a 32 Squadron Hudson was of a carrier with a transport and two destroyers followed by a sighting of three merchantmen and four destroyers. Attacks were made on the ships by land-based aircraft but with no real success but on the morning of the seventh an American carrier aircraft sank the *Shoho* north of Misima and the invasion force intended for Port Moresby retreated.

The Allies' cruiser force under R/Admiral Crace which had been deployed to cover the Jomard Passage had been attacked by shore-based aircraft but suffered no damage. In what came to be known as the Battle of the Coral Sea the Japanese carrier *Shokaku* was severely damaged but the American carrier *Lexington* later suffered an internal explosion and had to be sunk. The battle was fought by carrier aircraft with no exchange of gunfire and the opposing forces out of sight of each other. It was considered a tactical victory for the Japanese but a strategic one for the Allies. It was the first time that the enemy had been thwarted in his moves southwards. Japan still hoped to capture Port Moresby but in an overland operation. [27]

The Australian Hudson Squadrons

By May 1942 No.2 Squadron was based at Darwin and No.6 was operating from Richmond, NSW. Serving as an

References
20. RAAF I/pp.315
21. SWR II/14–15, Map 2; RAAF I/p.400; RAF II/pp.45 &54; WSC IV/p.131
22. WSC IV p.214 chart; JRob. p.131; JK p.75   23. RAAF I/pp.449–50
24. RAAF I/p.451   25. RAAF I/p.456   26. RAAF I/p.462–3
27. RAAF I/pp.519–527; SWR II/pp.35–36; WSC IV/pp.215–20; JRob. pp.130–32; JK p.75

Above: A16-12 devoid of a turret but showing the main door which contained the dinghy (although some RAAF units elected to have the dinghy separate from the door).

Operational Training Unit (OTU) at Bairnsdale, Victoria was No.7 Squadron. No.13 which had withdrawn from forward bases at Laha and Penfui was deployed at Hughes, south of Darwin. No.32 Squadron remained at Port Moresby. No.8 had been disbanded and Nos 23 and 24 served to reinforce No.32. No.2 Squadron operating from Darwin was undertaking anti-shipping and anti-submarine sorties extending to 300 miles for the first two weeks of May.

On the thirteenth at 0455hrs S/Ldr A.B. McFarlane in A16-172 led a strike force of eight Hudsons to Ambon. Five of the aircraft captained by McFarlane, F/Lt Frazer, F/O McCombe, F/O Sharp and P/O Venn attacked ships from mast height with 250lb GP bombs with an eleven-second delay each selecting his own target ship. The other three Hudsons flown by F/Lt Dalkin, P/O Alcock and P/O Jacques used five 250lb SAP bombs with a one-second delay from 1000ft. P/O C.C. Venn made a direct hit on a 3000-tonner which exploded and his Hudson was seen to explode. Hits were claimed on two other ships. Complete surprise had been achieved in the raid.

S/Ldr McFarlane led another strike to Ambon at 0545hrs on the twenty-second. The eight Hudsons included some from No.13 Squadron, the plan being for all to dive from a height. The enemy was prepared and AA fire was encountered immediately and with a destroyer and two merchantmen under way. All thirty-two bombs overshot.

F/O P.G. Brooks in A16-177 from No.13 and P/O C.W. Alchin flying A16-187 were seen to hesitate in selecting targets and were attacked by Zero fighters with [probably Brooks], going down in flames. The other Hudson was last seen with a Zero on its tail.

The gunner in one of No.2's aircraft flown by F/O A.J. Sharp shot down one Zero and scored hits on two others which then broke off.[28]

The Battle of Midway

On 5 May 1942 Japan ordered the invasion of Midway Island (28°13′N 172°22′W) and the western Aleutians; the latter intended to divert American forces and to fight a decisive

naval battle to destroy the United States' carrier force. It was decisive however in favour of the Americans in a battle which took place on 4 June between approximate positions 29°30′N, 32°N and 176°W and 180°W.

Although some land-based aircraft were used, successes were achieved by carrier-borne aircraft and for the USN, their dive bombers which attacked the Japanese carriers when their own aircraft were on board. The opposing forces included the carriers USS *Enterprise, Hornet* and *Yorktown* with a total of 233 aircraft; for Japan, the carriers *Akagi, Kaga, Hiryu* and *Soryu* with 272 aircraft.

Sunk by aircraft from the USS *Enterprise* were *Akagi, Kaga,* and *Hiryu; Soryu* by aircraft from USS *Yorktown. Yorktown* was damaged by aircraft from *Hiryu* and was subsequently torpedoed.

Although Japan still retained a very powerful fleet, for the British naval historian Captain Roskill, the dominance of the Japanese navy in the Pacific which had lasted almost six months was destroyed in a few hours. For the Australian historian Professor John Robertson, the battle was the major turning point in the Pacific war. Winston Churchill records a similar opinion and adds that the enemy had lost his highly trained aircrews.

Additionally the Japanese lost a cruiser and 258 aircraft; the Americans, the destroyer *Hamman,* ninety-two carrier-based aircraft and forty shore-based machines.[29]

The New Guinea Land Campaign

For the American General MacArthur, New Guinea represented his only route to the Philippines which he was committed to recover. For the Australians, New Guinea was too close to their home to tolerate its occupation by the Japanese. To achieve their goal – Port Moresby – the Japanese attempted an overland route from New Guinea's northern coast and subsequently, landings at Milne Bay.

On the night of 21/22 July 1942 over 2000 troops were landed in the Gona area and by 1100hrs on 22 July their ships were sailing away. Only one transport the *Ayatosan Maru* of 9788 tons was sunk in position 8°50′S 148°50′E. Only one RAAF aircraft was involved in the strike, a Hudson from No.32 Squadron flown by F/Lt L.W. Manning.

On 30 July Manning flew the final combat sortie for his squadron from New Guinea; to attack the enemy in the Buna area. The Hudsons were then involved in supplying the Allied troops in defence operations. By 29 July the Japanese had taken Kokoda, 100km from their beachhead and a key point in the overland route from the Gona/Buna area to Port Moresby.

The Allies' air strength in August for the campaign is given by the Australian historian as 481 with 151 serviceable for the USAAF and 215 RAAF with 149 serviceable.

Those with the RAAF included 73 Hudsons of which 52 were serviceable.[30]

In the same month there were 9000 Allied troops at Milne Bay including RAAF and AIF plus 1400 Americans.

No.6 Squadron commanded by S/Ldr A.A. Barlow had fifteen Hudsons at Richmond on 21 August but flew via Charlesville and Townsville for Horn Island with seven aircraft arriving there on the twenty-third. F/Lt Manning in A16-230 was on a recce the following day from 1115 to 1626hrs and on the twenty-fifth A16-205 was used for a further recce. At 1749hrs an enemy convoy of three cruisers leading four other ships was sighted followed by minesweepers in position 10°17'S 151°19'E north-east of Milne Bay. A16-205 flown by P/O M.S. Law attacked at 1800hrs with four 250lb GP bombs with eleven seconds delay and three 100lb A/S bombs from 100ft obtaining a near miss on a 2000-tonner. There was intense AA fire and the Hudson's front port tank was holed.

On the twenty-sixth F/Lt R.A. Yeowart in A16-239 attacked a ship in Mullins Harbour position 10°26'S 149°37'E. At 1620hrs oil drums in the water and on the beach six miles east of Fall river were bombed in a shallow dive from 500ft causing large fires. There was no AA or enemy aircraft and enemy positions were machine-gunned. Six burning barges were seen on the beach to Fall river. On the same date No.6 Squadron records a Japanese landing at 0140hrs on the North Shore, Milne Bay four miles east of Fall River.

Japanese shipping was attacked in Milne Bay between 0820hrs and 1455hrs on 3 September by Hudsons captained by F/O Hughes, F/Lt Lower. F/Sgt Wheeler from No.6 Squadron and later the same day there was a further strike by No.6 Squadron including Hudsons flown by P/O Glenwright and F/O De Salis. On 11 September F/O R.W. Shore in A16-231, F/Sgt Wheeler (A-16-211), F/Lt H.A. Robertson (A16-230) and F/O De Salis flying A16-246 were on a search from 1420hrs to Dawson Island. At 1610hrs two destroyers were sighted in position 09°55'S 151°31'E steaming at thirty knots on course 160°. The Hudsons attacked releasing nineteen 250lb SAP bombs with one second delay. It was later confirmed that a hit was scored by A16-229 flown most likely by P/O Glenwright. The Hudson crews confirmed a direct hit by a B-17 on a destroyer, leaving it down by the stern and on

Below: No.6 Sqdn RAAF operations room at Milne Bay, Papua in January 1943.

fire.

The enemy found themselves against strong resistance and outnumbered 4:1, and with the Australians controlling the air. By 6 September they were defeated at Milne Bay; it was a strategic victory for the Allies with the Japanese repulsed on one of their two routes to Port Moresby. Overland they reached within fifty kilometres of Port Moresby at Imita Ridge on 28 September. The Australians advanced eight kilometres and met no resistance; the enemy had retreated.[31]

No.6 Squadron had in January 1942 sent four Hudsons and crews to Port Moresby to form part of No.32 Squadron. In August when No.6 was deployed on Horn Island, a flight had been detached to Milne Bay using the Turnbull Strip. No.6 used also, the seven-mile strip near Port Moresby. They became fully engaged in supporting the Allied ground forces.

One of their Hudson captains, Ray Kelly, was undertaking such sorties in support of forward troops in November then in the Buna area and writes regarding a trip on 21 January:

. . . you could see the native carriers and troops standing by. The flight took two hours five minutes crossing the Owen Stanley Ranges being made through the Kokoda Gap. Later in the day it took three hours thirty-five minutes . . . as the day progressed the cloud built up over the Owen Stanleys and invariably closed the Kokoda Gap. This meant climbing to over 12,000ft to find a clear passage across the Range. I remember carrying items such as picks and shovels and all had to be pushed out at low altitude.

On 22 November I did a trip with my own crew, F/O Green, navigator and Sgts E.A. Prime and I. Warwick Wop/AGs in A16-239 on a supply-dropping mission to the forward troops at Gona. It lasted two hours five minutes because it was morning and the Kokoda Gap was open. During the drop stage our flight path took us over the Gona Mission and in three passes I noted the large white out-door cross set in the gardens and thinking how peaceful things looked from 300ft. Yet there was a fierce struggle taking place on the ground. Our circuits were planned to keep away from the Gona wreck because of its AA batteries.[32]

Ray Kelly returned to flying A/S patrols on the twenty-fourth, twenty-sixth and twenty-eighth using Hudsons A16-239, -203, and -239 respectively although supply dropping continued by others such as F/O Turner-Walker who crashed on take-off from Ward's Strip with all the food intended for troops lost; he escaped with his crew. Kelly flew more sorties to Buna from Ward's Strip, Port Moresby on 1 December in A16-177 armed with flares and four 250lb bombs with delay fuses to attack Japanese positions.

There were other trips for him on the third, fifth and thirteenth. For the latter A16-203 was used in a flight of five hours and twenty minutes for a recce from Buna to Salamau. He adds:

All the four trips involved take-off from Ward's Strip after midnight, proceeding across the Owen Stanley Range at about 12,000ft and letting down through overcast on the north side

References
28. RAAF I/pp.238 &282
29. RAAF I/pp.533–36; SWR II/pp.38–41; WSC IV/p.224; JRob, p.23
30. RAAF I/pp.574–75 31. JRob. pp.141–44; No.6 Sqdn RAAF record
32. See also RAAF I/pp.668–9

of New Guinea. The latter was always hazardous in view of storms and lack of navigational facilities. There was the discomfort from the releasing of flares from other aircraft in the area in a confined space. They were to counter the enemy barge traffic. In these harassing missions we were briefed to be out of the area shortly after first light because of possible enemy fighter attacks but we had to make the return flight to Port Moresby in daylight so that we could get through the Kokoda Gap at relatively low altitude.

On 8 December No.6 Squadron had been warned of an intended move from Ward's Strip, Port Moresby; preparations began on the twentieth and they arrived at Turnbull Field, Milne Bay on the twenty-seventh. The squadron prepared a camp site in a coconut grove clearing dense undergrowth and erecting tents.

The main party arrived by ship on 29 December and two days later buildings were being erected with what material was available and native labour was employed for roofing the buildings. No.6's establishment was then fifty-four officers, 417 other ranks and nineteen aircraft.

On 17 January 1943 the Japanese raided Milne Bay in which No.6 lost one Hudson, six were severely damaged and all others were damaged to some degree. Three Hudsons were detailed for a search towards Bougainville and New Britain on 24 February including A16-245 captained by F/O Ray Kelly who was airborne at 0600hrs from Turnbull Strip. Bad weather forced the other two Hudsons to return but Kelly managed to get through to clear weather for his recce. On his return flight, 100 miles from Milne Bay the weather closed in and to climb to 30,000ft above the clouds was impracticable; flying low there was the hazard of striking one of the many islands. With limited fuel he headed for Milne Bay attempting to follow the shore line at 100ft, Flying Control giving no alternative but to attempt landing there. With almost nil visibility he opted to ditch the Hudson. Probably the safest position for his crew would have been to sit on the floor in the cabin with their backs to the bulkhead. The wireless operator stayed at his post holding the key down to transmit, the other Wop/AG went to the main door and the navigator remained behind the pilot's seat. They ditched at eighty knots and the Wop/AG near the door was thrown forward striking his head but they all managed to exit. The dinghy had broken lose and Prime swam for it while the others were on the wings. The Hudson sank within three to four minutes leaving three supported by Mae Wests. Native canoes appeared and took them all ashore. Later the USS *Tulsa* came and the natives ferried the crew to the ship. Post-war Ray Kelly sent me a photograph of Hudson A16-245 now under fifty feet of water in Milne Bay.

The Battle of the Bismarck Sea

On 28 February 1943 a Japanese convoy sailed from Rabaul to reinforce their base at Lae on the northern coast of New Guinea. It had been expected by the Allies and strong air forces were ready including Mitchells, Beaufighters, Fortresses, Bostons, Beauforts and Lightnings. They were from the US 5th Army Air Force and the RAAF. The convoy was sighted at 1500hrs on 1 March by a Liberator forty miles

Above: No.13 Sqdn RAAF Hudsons over Timor. During the years 1940–1946, No.13 Sqdn served at Darwin, Ambon, Namlea, Canberra, Gove, and Labuan.

north-west of Ubili. Lae was bombed by the RAAF on 2 March to counter Japanese air support and on the fourth Malahang airfield near Lae was bombed.

In a series of attacks on the convoy with bombs, torpedoes, and cannon, all eight transports were sunk, plus a special service vessel *Nojima* and four of the eight escorting destroyers. Accounts vary regarding casualties but a Japanese one gives that of 5000 troops plus the ship's crews, 2734 were saved in rescue operations. Of aircraft, the same account gives the Allies losing six against the Japanese losing ten Zeros shot down and five damaged.[33]

Admiral Yamamoto set up his headquarters on Guadalcanal in an attempt to destroy the Allied air forces in the area of New Guinea and Guadalcanal with a total of 350 aircraft for raids beginning on 7 April against Allied ships at Guadalcanal. On 12 April Port Moresby was bombed and Milne Bay on the fourteenth when No.6 Squadron's record reports thirty-six medium bombers, twenty-five dive bombers and thirty fighters attacking Turnbull Field. They achieved one hit on the strip and some on dispersal with one fuel dump destroyed. They lost at least fourteen bombers and three fighters.

Ray Kelly was airborne that day at 0800hrs in A16-134 on a recce towards Bougainville and when about 100 miles north of Milne Bay his radio operator Sgt E.A. Prime reported a large number of aircraft ahead indicated by blips on the radar screen. Ray Kelly continues:

Within a matter of minutes, a large number of aircraft appeared ahead and slightly above to starboard when I was at about 2000ft. In the excitement that followed I cannot recall if we ever heard the all-clear from Milne Bay. Very quickly three aircraft of the formation ahead peeled off and stationed themselves one on each side and one behind. Then the three attacked in unison, pulled away and then made a second pass. I could only see the Zero coming in at an angle of about forty-

References
33. MO p.191

Picture: GRAHAM TIDY

Retired Flight-Lieutenant "Spud" Spurgeon with a damaged Hudson aircraft engine, of the type which he flew in World War II.

'Spud' copped the first war damage

By PETER CLACK

A World War II pilot has told how he was blown up while attacking invading Japanese "before" the attack on Pearl Harbour 50 years ago.

Flight-Lieutenant "Spud" Spurgeon was on a mission to Kota Bharu in northern New Guinea to repel a large invading Japanese force.

He piloted his Hudson bomber low over three Japanese escort ships and troop carriers but his bombs sent splinters through the bottom of the aircraft which, coupled with ground fire, forced him to limp back to base and crash-land, thereby saving his crew.

For Mr Spurgeon and his crew it was the first blow of the war with Japan. He said the official time of the attack on Pearl Harbour was December 7, 1941. In Australia, across the international date line, it was December 8. By his reckoning he was blown up one hour and 38 minutes before the first bombs fell on the American fleet.

Mr Spurgeon is one of the first surviving Australian veterans returning to their former battlefields and prisoner of war camps this year to commemorate the 50th anniversary of the war in the Pacific. In a small ceremony in the Australian War Memorial, the Department of Veterans' Affairs launched the 1992 calendar, outlining events to commemorate the fall of Singapore, the bombing of Darwin, the battles of the Java Sea and Coral Sea, and of Kokoda, the Owen Stanleys and El Alamein.

Before graphic, enlarged wartime photographs of Australian servicemen, several prominent former servicemen gave details of many of the battles, struggles and terrible consequences, leading to the loss of many Australian lives.

Perhaps the most moving talk was by the national president of the Returned and Services League, Brigadier Alf Garland, who said simply that 1942 was "a dark year for Australia".

Brigadier Garland said it was "most appropriate" to be flanked by the photographs, in particular one of the "fuzzy wuzzy angels" transporting a wounded soldier.

The ordeal Mr Spurgeon recounted captured the drama and dangers of the start of the war in the Pacific.

Standing next to the distorted prop of a Hudson bomber, he said that by January, 1942, he was again on a mission when his Hudson was attacked by Japanese fighter planes. The defenceless bomber was shot down and he and one surviving crew member were thrown into the sea.

He floated for 24 hours, during which he lost contact with his companion, eventually floating on to a small island, where he stayed for 2½ days without food.

Local Chinese took him to the mainland but he was captured by the invading Japanese. By then Singapore had fallen. He spent time at Padu prison, before going to Changi POW camp for a month before being taken to Formosa, where he ran the cookhouse for 18 months.

"We kept each other going because we were Aussies. We stole for each other and looked after each other while we were sick. That's how I survived."

Eventually he was taken to Mukden where he was released by Russian soldiers. He recalled seeing the Anzacs marching in Melbourne's Swanson Street as a child. "I never dreamed it would happen to me," he said. In December, Mr Spurgeon and his squadron members and their wives returned to Padu prison.

Above: A cutting from the Canberra Times *about A/Cmdre C.H. 'Spud' Spurgeon, DFC. The then F/Lt Spurgeon of No.8 Sqdn RAAF operating from Malaya engaged the enemy on 8.12.41 but on 24.1.42 was shot down by Zeros in Hudson A16-11 in the South China Sea.*

five degrees from behind on the port side and the only re-assurance I could take was from seeing the tracers of the single .303 Browning operated by the navigator in the nose. The turret guns were being fired by Sgt J.H. Clark alternately at the other two aircraft. In the time available Sgt Prime was unable to do more than send a quick radio message as to the attack. By the time he could man the rear side gun the action had been broken off by the enemy. I had dived down to sea level.

Normanby Island and its rugged foreshore gave protection on the starboard side and the background of the island would have made it difficult to see in attacks from port. Flying at sea level was intended to save us from attacks from below and help against attacks from port and starboard.

The enemy would have been heavily involved in the raid against Milne Bay and were probably short of both fuel and ammunition and with some distance to reach their base in New Britain. The attacks however, were made at close range – I can still recall seeing the outline of the pilot of the Zero attacking from the port side and the smoke from his guns but thinking of the effect of the navigator's Browning causing damage to the Zero. We received not one hit and made no claim of hits on the enemy. Given unfavourable circumstances, it is hard not to accept that A16-134 would have been another victim of the enemy.

We were met on approaching Milne Bay by a Kittyhawk sent out as escort, but the two Kittyhawk squadrons had been very busy that afternoon and most would have been out of fuel and ammunition.

We saw evidence of the raid on Milne Bay with smoking ships and our own bombed airstrip requiring us to land at Gurney.

History has shown that the series of Japanese raids between 7 and 14 April 1943 further depleted the enemy's diminishing resources and from then on he was on the defensive in that area.

Bill Pacey who served as Engineering Officer with No.6 Squadron gives this account:

Being a bomber unit we were posted early 1942 to Horn Island. As we were the first RAAF squadron equipped with radar our mission was to seek out the enemy movements in the Rabaul, New Britain area, mostly in fiendish tropical weather. The radar proved its worth and many sightings were made and one included sighting a large invasion force heading for Milne Bay.

General Kenney ordered our 'A' and 'B' Flights, twelve aircraft in all to go and help stem the invasion. This they did with great courage and effect. Flaps were torn off most of our aircraft due to the depth of water covering the strip. Yet they managed to fly without them. As the enemy had landed only twelve miles away at K.B. Mission, it enabled our aircraft to take off with very little fuel, the unstick speed was much greater minus the flaps.

The enemy was so sure of victory that they sent Zero fighters as they were convinced that our strip would be in their hands. Our Army boys made short work of them as they could not carry enough fuel to return to their base at Gasmata. This was the first occasion the Japanese were defeated in the Pacific area and I feel that this example of 'WE CAN DO IT' was just what the Allies needed and we never retreated on any front after that.

We then moved as a body from Horn Island to Milne Bay and it was from there that we constantly bombed Gasmata airfield. The Japanese retaliated at night by regular bombings and got their revenge in a massive raid in which we lost twenty of our twenty-four bombers on the ground. It was on 17 January 1943.

Burma

The Allies had not anticipated Burma being attacked by the Japanese but the enemies' forces reached Victoria Point in the extreme south of Burma by 9 December 1941 and on 23 December they were bombing the capital, Rangoon. It was estimated that over 100,000 escaped by sea to Calcutta. Rangoon was to suffer thirty-one bombing raids up to 25 February 1942 and by 27 March the RAF had been bombed from its last Burma base.

Earlier defence arrangements in Burma had included the construction of airfields under the direction of an Australian, Group Captain E.R. Manning. Runways and accommodation had been included in these works, and by the end of 1941 seven had been completed. They lacked however an efficient defence system including anti-aircraft guns and an effective early-warning system. They lacked also aircraft both in terms of numbers and performance.

Against the estimated 400 Japanese fighters and bombers the Allies could deploy Buffalo fighters together with twenty-one P40s of the American Volunteer Group. These fighters were subsequently reinforced by thirty Hurricanes and a squadron of Blenheims. There was also a flight of No.139 Squadron Hudsons. The fighters were progressively depleted until only about twenty-seven remained. This number included four of the Americans' P40s and three Buffaloes.

Orders for a general withdrawal were made on 7 March and main bases were established at Magwe, a civil aerodrome and without accommodation for Air Force personnel. The other base to be used was on the island of Akyab lying just off the Arakan coast. The Air Force units at this latter base formed collectively 'Akwing' and included No.139 Squadron Hudsons. Akwing was commanded by a Scotsman, Group Captain N.C. Singer.[34]

The Japanese attacked Magwe on 21 March using 230 aircraft and dropping over 200 tons of bombs. This was followed on 23, 24 and 27 March with attacks on Akyab in which the Allies lost twenty aircraft. Akwing was then withdrawn to India, at Chittagong which became the location for No.221 Group. Akyab was to remain a base of some significance serving to refuel Hudsons on long reconnaissance flights and for other sorties. Port Blair in the south of the Andaman Islands was captured by the Japanese on 23 March. The enemy then used Port Blair as a base for flying-boats. This deployment of enemy flying boats in the Andaman Islands was also of particular significance as the British Naval forces were being reinforced in Ceylon where there was a concentration of Allied shipping, and the presence of enemy reconnaissance aircraft in the Andaman Islands would have rendered the movements of Allied shipping difficult to hide. On 14 April two Hudsons from No.139 Squadron's remaining three, attacked the enemy base at Port Blair sinking one flying boat and setting two others on fire. The remaining eleven were then damaged by machine-gun fire. For this raid refuelling was undertaken at Akyab. Port Blair was again attacked by Hudsons on the eighteenth when Zero fighters were encountered. Despite this opposition, running attacks were made at thirty-feet altitude and two more Japanese flying-boats were destroyed. One

Hudson was lost, the second returned to base badly damaged. As a result of these raids, no Japanese flying-boat reconnaissance flights were made for a few months over the Bay of Bengal and the sailing of about seventy Allied ships through those waters proved possible.

In the evacuation of Burma in May 1942, some aircrew and ground staff used road transport and one route followed by some was via Lashio to Myitkyina. From there some were flown to Dinjan. It was from Myitkyina, that the Governor of Burma, Sir Reginald Dorman-Smith, was flown out on 4 May by a Hudson sent in from India.

The supply lines to China's Nationalist's forces through Burma were cut and there was a potential threat to Ceylon. It was to be 3 May 1945 before Rangoon was regained by the Allies.[35]

The Loss of Hudson FH267

F/O Herries of No.62 Squadron RAF was airborne from Dum Dum on 3 September 1942 for a recce of the Arakan coast south of Akyab. There were rain squalls and with cloud base down to 500ft. Suddenly without any warning, the aircraft was in rain so heavy that it was difficult to maintain height. Bombs were jettisoned and height was gained to 5000ft. In climbing, the engines overheated and Herries throttled back to glide. With no improvement in the weather or the engines, an SOS was transmitted when the Hudson was estimated ninety miles west of the Arakan coast and an attempt was made to achieve landfall and then reach Chittagong.

Eventually the navigator recognised the Naf River through one of the clearer patches in the weather but the engines were still giving trouble and the weather was closing in. Preparations were made for ditching in the river as they were now in rough hilly country.

Ditching was safely achieved and the crew realised that the Hudson was resting on the river bed. They climbed onto the wing, checked the dinghy and then returned to the cabin to shelter from the rain and decide what to do. It was estimated that they were ten miles from the river mouth and on the Burma side but by this time there were a number of native boats circled about the Hudson. Eventually one boat came

References
34. RAF II/pp.56–63; SWR II/20   35. RAF II/pp.56–70; JK p.162

Below: A cutting from an Australian paper illustrating the memorial at Khota Bharu for Australians killed in the initial stages of the war with Japan which included personnel from the two RAAF squadrons Nos 1 and 8.

Memorial marks opening battle of Japanese war

A memorial has been officially opened at Khota Bharu in the Malaysian State of Kelantan to honour Australians killed in the opening battle of the war against Japan.

The battle, in the early hours of December 8, 1941, began 80 minutes in real time before the Japanese attack on Pearl Harbour.

Lockheed Hudson aircraft and crews of the RAAF operated against the Japanese seaborne invasion force. Seven Australians were killed when two Hudsons were shot down. The sole survivor was Flying Officer D.A.Dowie (now Dr Don Dowie, of Willunga SA), who was among 15 RAAF veterans who attended the opening of the massive granite block memorial on September 21.

F.O. Dowie's Hudson, under the command of Flight Lieutenant J C Ramshaw, attacked a Japanese cruiser but was badly damaged by retaliatory fire and crashed into the water. Dowie injured where he received treatment

The memorial at Khota Bharu honouring Australians killed in the opening battle against Japan in WWII. Seven RAAF crew members lost their lives when two Lockheed Hudsons were shot down by the Japanese invaders.

of RAAF No.1, 8, 21 and 453   contributed $2,000 toward

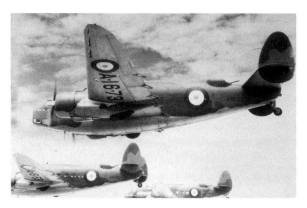

Above: A16-73, A16-55 and A16-42 of No.6 Sqdn RAAF without turrets. A16-42 was lost at Semplak, Java due to enemy action on 22.2.42.

close and with the mention of 'backsheesh' two natives understood what was wanted. Herries and a wireless operator stayed in the aircraft to destroy secret equipment, while the navigator and the other Wop/AG went up the river with the natives.

After half-an-hour they reached a large village, Villa, from the navigator's map. There were many natives on the bank gathered on a platform and the navigator asked if any spoke English. 'Yes,' came the answer from a Burmese man. The navigator asked to get in touch with the police and was told of one at Teknof and with an offer to send a runner there.

The two aircrew were taken into one of the buildings and given coffee and cigarettes. Shortly afterwards, the police inspector himself came in a boat and introduced himself as Abdul Khaliqun. A note was written to the Miltary Commander at Ukhia, which was the nearest point with a telephone, requesting the RAF to be informed of the situation. Following the despatch of the message by runner, the two aircrew returned to the aircraft with the police inspector. The other wireless operator Sgt Welch with F/Lt Herries were now on the Bengal side of the river with a forestry officer and were joined by the navigator with Sgt Shelley. The police arranged for a guard on the aircraft and for the crew to stay the night at the Teknof police post. It was now evening and about six hours after the ditching; the forestry officer provided a meal of curried chicken and rice. After a journey of two hours by boat, the aircrew reached Teknof and were given another meal of chicken and a fermented drink. Their beds were bare boards with blankets and sheets.

The following day, the crew returned to the Hudson by sampan and removed as much of the equipment as possible including guns, ammunition, radio, instruments and parachutes and flying kit. This was loaded in sampans and taken back to Teknof. An unsuccessful attempt was made to fire the plane. Another Hudson flew over and signalled by Aldis lamp, 'Will report position, help from Chittagong'. On return to Teknof the navigator made an inventory of the equipment and the guns were cleaned. The following day, 5

September, a military patrol of Punjabis arrived from Ukhia, having travelled during the night. They provided an escort for the aircrew and a relief guard for the Hudson. The Burmese went out of their way to help in every way possible and provided yet another meal for the aircrew, accepting no payment. The party left by 1130hrs using sampans on the river for the nearest point to Ukhia. Their four sampans with seven Punjabis and four aircrew plus equipment covered about forty miles until nightfall when the wind dropped and reliance was placed on oars. The aircrew swam on occasions alongside the boat and at intervals ate the remaining dinghy rations. At about 2100hrs they moved inshore and saw other boats and a landing stage.

'Good evening, gentlemen,' said a pleasant English voice out of the darkness. It was an English Army officer who, while on patrol, had heard from the runner about the Hudson crew. They followed him along a ridge above the muddy fields to Grondah where the Army officer had arranged for a hot meal of meat and vegetables to await them. The next day the Punjabi escort distributed the equipment into coolie loads and the next six miles were covered in two hours. This was through wooded country but rough and uphill on occasions. At Ukhia, the aircrew again met the Army captain and stayed in his bungalow where advice was gained regarding the next twenty-one miles to Cox's Bazar. For this, they needed to traverse a beach for much of the way and waited until 1700hrs so that one particular section of the beach would be reached at midnight when there was low tide which would be impassable at high tide.

They left with a new escort and coolies, twenty-four in all. One river was crossed by sampan, a second by wading to a sampan and then from the sampan to the bank. By now it was dark and a halt was made at a native village for a meal. The Army captain had given them a tin of corned beef which was opened with a bayonet. By 2030hrs the coast was reached and by lantern light they crossed wet sand and waded through streams. A halt was made at a coastguard station at about 2100hrs until the tide was low enough to pass the next stretch of beach but even so needed to wade waist deep through an inlet in the cliffs. At 2200hrs a very narrow stretch of beach was reached where the cliffs of 200ft would be washed at high tide and they approached as a section of the cliff collapsed and they waited for the tide to recede. At midnight they were clambering over wet rocks and wading.

It now started to rain and they pressed on. Cox's Bazar was reached at 0330hrs where a hot meal awaited them at the house of the military commander. The aircraft equipment was loaded onto a steamer at Cox's Bazar to be handed over to the RAF at Chittagong. The return of the crew of Hudson FH267 of No.62 Squadron was completed to Calcutta by train and steamer.[36]

Shipping Strike to Akyab

On 9 September 1942 flights of Hudsons from No.62 Squadron at Dum Dum led by S/Ldr Henderson and Blenheims from Ondal led by W/Cmdr Cox, were detailed for a shipping strike to Akyab. They were briefed that if enemy fighters were seen before reaching the target, the bombers were not to attack and if weather separated them, they were to attempt to reach the target individually and to fly at low level, pull up to bomb, and then return to sea level.

They flew at 50 to 100ft over the Bay of Bengal and visibility was five miles although cloud covered most of the Baronga Islands. When a mile from the target a ship of 1700 tons was seen at the jetty with stacks of shells each about a foot long nearby. At 400 yards the leading aircraft saw two fighters circling overhead but he was committed to attack which was made at 1015hrs from fifty feet. He suffered no fire from either ship or fighters. A third aircraft reported seeing bombs from either the first or second aircraft strike the larger ship. A second flight attacked a minute later and the rear gunner of F/O Bassingthwaite's aircraft saw bomb bursts amidships of a vessel.

Four Navy Zeros were seen and P/O Mockridge's aircraft was lagging behind. The leader of the flight throttled back to maintain formation as they headed out to sea. For the next ten minutes they were subjected to continuous attacks by the Zeros. At this point they made for cloud cover at 800ft but on emerging a figher was close on P/O Loane's tail and his aircraft was not seen again.

The Zeros attacked from more than one direction simultaneously closing to eighty yards. The Blenheim crews helped each other by firing at Zeros attacking others.

When W/Cmdr Cox with Blenheims from Ondal attacked at 1035hrs he found the larger ship at Akyab severely damaged listing and down by the bows. His flight saw the Zeros but were not attacked by them. The two vics of Hudsons from Dum Dum which arrived at Akyab at 1245hrs found a large ship sunk and dropped bombs on the jetty from 1500ft after a low level approach. The Hudsons were attacked by two fighters; these were made head on and beam closing to forty yards. Fire from the Hudsons struck one of the fighters which broke off in a combat lasting ten minutes. The second vic of Hudsons was attacked by only one Zero fighter; two of these returned safely to Dum Dum, the other crash-landed at Chittagong. No.62's record gives the armament of the Zeros being four guns with two firing through the propeller and two from the wings – the latter apparently cannon.

The balance sheet was one ship sunk, one Zero shot down, another damaged against three Blenheims and one Hudson missing with a second Hudson crashing on landing at Chittagong.

No.194 Squadron

No.194 Squadron ('The Friendly Firm') was formed as a transport unit at Lahore on 13 October 1942 under the command of W/Cmdr Alec C. Pearson a highly experienced pilot from No.31 Squadron. S/Ldr Thirwell arrived on 27 October in Hudson FK457 and was to become 'A' Flight commander. He was followed two days later by P/O McLauchland with Hudson FK4ll. By the end of October thirteen aircraft were on charge but with only sixty-two personnel.

From the log of Jack Foster, on 194, Hudson FK485

captained by Ken Wilson must have been one of the first to arrive, this was on 19 September and after a total of twenty-six hours and twenty minutes flying spread over nine days en route from Bilveis, Egypt. Jack Foster, a navigator who flew with Ken Wilson as pilot, and Anderson as wireless operator, gives this account:

We arrived at Lahore in Hudson FK485 on 22 September 1942 having flown from Bilbeis, Egypt via Habbaniyah, Shaiba, Sharjah, Karachi and Delhi, in twenty-six hours and twenty minutes spread over nine days.

Wingco Pearson met us on the runway and almost his first words were that he wanted all aircrew commissioned. We had come together at 13 OTU Bicester, very new sergeants, flying Blenheims and were to stay together until March 1946 some 1500 flying hours later. During the autumn of that year, more crews arrived and we did some fairly routine mail runs mainly in FK605 and FK477, then in December we made a routine flight to Colombo with F/O Champion and Ken Wilson as co-pilots. I spent Christmas in hospital with malaria. In January I returned to Lahore in easy stages with Bill Harris and Eric Woodwiss and by February we were way up in Tezpur, Assam dropping supplies on the tennis-court at Sumprbum in the Kachin Hills.

These were marvellous days, the dense jungle below, scorching sun above, the long flights home finishing low over the Brahmaputra with the sky a thousand colours, conviviality of the Mess, comradeship of the air and ground crews; the hospitality of the tea planters; a world which can never be recaptured.

In March, to Agataria, attached to 31 Squadron flying FK567, 687 and 642. New names for the dropping zones – Buthidung, Tigyaing, Taguang – and contact with the characters of 31 Squadron.

By the end of April we had done a fair whack of operations and returned to Delhi (Palam) and to the mail run. It was about this time that we went on leave to Mussoorie in the foothills of the Himalayas.

Most of that summer was taken up with mail runs to Bombay, Calcutta, Madras etc. in the same old loveable aircraft, EW963, FK584, FK946. War?

Yes, we were brought back to reality in October when we went to Basal in the North West Punjab to convert to Dakotas, to practise dropping parachutes, first with containers, then with soldiers, and to usher in a new world. I remember with affection the old Hudson, the pilots I flew with, and the friends and colleagues, the last of the 'landmark and dead reckoning' navigation before the days of radar.

One of the first supply drops by Foster's crew was in FK584 from Tezpur to Dinjan on 7 February another on 15 February in FK607 was to Auchtaung when a fighter escort was provided.

One of their first passengers for a transport flight from Karachi to Delhi on 27 May in FK596 was General Claude Auckinleck who had served as C-in-C Middle East against General Rommel whose advance towards Egypt was halted by Auckinleck at El Alamein.

From October 1942 No.194 Squadron's duties became

References
36.Based on No.62 Sqdn RAF's record with permission

largely internal flights over India transporting freight, mail and passengers but with some supply-dropping to troops.

On 24 November Hudsons FK485, FK493, FK474 and two other aircraft were detached from 194 Squadron to Dum Dum with five crews and nine ground staff; not only to carry freight but for supply-dropping and troop-carrying. One of their first encounters with the enemy was on 16 December 1942 when Hudson FK474, captained by F/O Salvesen was over Sitakund. He was intercepted by two Japanese Zero fighters which in four attacks, damaged the Hudson's port engine and the undercarriage. Salvesen made a forced-landing on a beach at low tide. The crew then walked seven miles to a police station at Sitakund and were taken to Chittagong hospital. They were later ferried back to Dum Dum in FK481.

The following day, a 194 Squadron crew, sergeants Tempest, McLean, Cameron and Kerswill then attached to No.31 Squadron at Tezpur, were reported missing from a supply-dropping sortie for Wingate's troops in the Fort Hertz area on 15 December. This was in Hudson FK431 of 353 Squadron. The burnt out wreckage of this Hudson was located by the 16th Brigade five miles west of Talakkok in January 1943. No.194 Squadron undertook practice supply-dropping with the 77th Brigade during January in anticipation of supporting General Wingate whose forces were due to cross the Chindwin River in February.

On 18 February 1943, 194 Squadron was posted to Palam, Delhi with the move made by road, rail and air from Lahore. By the end of the month the squadron had on its strength twenty officers, and 246 other ranks. Nine aircraft were at Palam with three unserviceable (u/s), one u/s at Bangalore, two u/s at Lahore, one u/s at Cuttack, one at Jessore, one at Dhubalia and five at Tezpur.

By the end of March, the squadron had eleven aircraft at Palam, two at Lahore and seven at Dhubalia. In that month, with a total flying of 505.55hrs, 203 passengers had been carried and freight and mail of 14,130lb. Part of the squadron's flying to support the Chindits, was over 'the hump', mountains 15,000ft to 20,000ft and so dubbed by the Americans who were involved in supplying the Chinese by air. F/Lt Doug Williams, a Wop/AG with 194 gives his experience with 194 Squadron:

In the Far East during the Burma Campaign we not only had the deadliest of enemies, the suicidal Japanese but the world's worst terrain, weather conditions and diseases. Flying supplies from India over the 7000ft Chin Hills to our troops in Burma crews frequently encountered fearsome electrical storms over the mountain barrier and the cumulo-nimbus cloud could be many thousands of feet high from the tops of the hills making it impossible to fly under or over. While flying on a night drop to a Chindit column at 16,000ft trying to avoid the worst of the weather we suddenly hit one hell of a storm with lightning flashing along the wings and torrential rain hitting the cockpit. We were buffeted like a cork in a broiling sea. Suddenly there was a terrible *wooshing* sound and we dropped like a stone from 16,000ft to 12,000ft. Joe Curtis by brute force brought us out safely to complete a successful sortie of 3500lb supplies to Chindits.

The RAF's official history gives Nos 31 and 194 Squadrons flying 178 sorties both day and night in support of General Wingate's seven columns of Chindits and dropping thirty-one tons at Myene on three nights 15, 16 and 17 February for the Northern group of the 77th Brigade.[37]

In May 1943, 194 Squadron was advised that it would be converting to DC-3s/C-47 Dakotas and the first of those aircraft to arrive was FD812 K/194 on 29 May. Hudsons FK587, FK596, FK606, FK586, FK411 and FK946 were being allotted away but some remained in service in July when their highest monthly flying total was achieved of 637 hours, carrying 715 passengers and 115,891lb freight.

On 20 September 1943, 194 was reclassified (Airborne Forces) Squadron under No.177 Wing with Dakotas. From Jack Foster's log however, one of 194's last Hudson flights was by FK481 on 16 October when it was flown from Basal to Lahore.

With the arrival of the monsoon period, the first Chindit expedition came to an end in June 1943 but troops were still being supplied from the air in the Chin Hills and at Goppe Bazar.[38]

Post-war, 194 organised an active association and retained its quite unofficial title 'The Friendly Firm' with its equally unofficial emblem of 'Dumbo', the flying elephant.

References
37. RAF III/p.302   38. RAF III/p.305

Chapter 8
The South Pacific

Guadalcanal

In July 1942 both the Americans and the Japanese intended occupying Guadalcanal, one of the larger islands in the southern Solomons.

On 4 July an Allied recce aircraft sighted the Japanese constructing an airfield on Guadalcanal. The Americans sent a task force under Vice-Admiral Fletcher and the airstrip on Guadalcanal was captured on 7 July and to be dubbed 'Henderson Field'. Tulagi Island was taken by the Allies on 8 July.

Over the next few months there were land battles on Guadalcanal land with notably the Americans' 'Glorious Marines' as Churchill describes them. At sea there were five major battles namely of Savo Island, Eastern Solomons, Cap Esperance, Santa Cruz and finally, on 30 November, The Battle of Tassafaronga. Allied naval losses of 126,000 tons included two carriers, eight cruisers and fourteen destroyers; the Japanese lost one carrier, two battleships, four cruisers eleven destroyers and six submarines totalling 134,000 tons.

Above: A Mark V of the RNZAF coded ZX-Z for No.1 OTU and flying near Mount Egmont.

Below: Hudsons of the RNZAF in the Solomon Islands 1942/43.

Above: Nelson, New Zealand 1942 with NZ2083 (FH434) in the foreground and coded W-UH for No.2 Sqdn.

To support their landings the Japanese sailed down 'The Slot' between the islands fast warships, dubbed *The Tokyo Express* at night in attempts to land additional troops and supplies. They tended to be notably more successful than the Americans in night naval engagements, and their torpedoes were more efficient. On land the Americans deployed 60,000 troops and Marines with 1600 killed and 4200 wounded. Japan had 36,000 on the island from which 14,000 were killed or missing, 9000 died from disease and 1000 were captured.[1]

An Australian historian gives seven squadrons being established on Henderson Field during 20 to 30 August and including two from the USS *Enterprise* but by 2 February 1943, thirty-seven squadrons including two from the RNZAF.[2]

A New Zealander, James Parkinson, who served as a wireless mechanic with the RNZAF on Guadalcanal for four months from June 1943 and who serviced equipment on Hudsons for Nos 2 and 3 Squadrons gives this account:

Living conditions on Guadalcanal were rather harsh at first as only temporary accommodation was provided in the living area which was situated on a ridge about one mile from Henderson Field. This was later improved by the provision of wooden framed and floored structures with a canvas roof. The six men who lived in each of these were provided with camp stretchers and slept under individual mosquito nets.

Nearby was a tunnel through the ridge to provide an air-raid shelter; it was much more interesting however to watch activity from the ridge or motor to the airfield.

Food was rather short to commence with and consisted of rations supplied by the US Forces. This was mainly Spam and other tinned foods with a greasy substance called Carter Spread used as butter on bread. There was only one slice per man but sometimes a crust could be obtained in addition with jam to complement. There was a big improvement when the No.40 Transport squadron began flying in supplies from New Zealand by DC-3. We looked upon eggs, fresh meat and butter

as a valuable addition to our diet. A whole shipment of eggs was lost when they fell off a truck negotiating a steep hill.

There were a large number of American units based on the island which in June 1943 represented the most advanced base held by the Allies. The RNZAF operated fighter aircraft from Russell Island by day only. There were defence units consisting of anti-aircraft gun and searchlight crews in the vicinity of our camp. At various units there was provision for movie films with a screen and projection box, but seating was provided by patrons. It was always wise to take some waterproof gear because it often rained, sometimes so heavily that the sound was lost. The greatest threat was the air-raid warning which immediately stopped the show and there was a scattering of men to AA defence which often resulted in Kiwis sitting on their boxes contemplating a deserted scene. If the alert was short the show would resume.

The first servicing area operated by the squadron was adjacent to a taxiway which also served as a road. This was formed on an earth base which became very muddy when wet. It was so bad that vehicles often became bogged and had to be towed out. When dry we had tremendous volumes of dust in our workshop area from the taxying aircraft. Later we moved about half-a-mile to a surfaced area, the rainy season ended and workshops were provided for each trade instead of rather poor tents at the first site.

The island electricity supply in the Henderson Field area came from a Diesel generator left by the Japanese. Our ground radio communication for aircraft on patrol was located in a Japanese tunnel which had been dug into a low hill adjoining Henderson. The equipment was US Navy and used 400 cycle power with a motor driven inverter at the tunnel entrance. The Americans on Henderson were mainly carrier-based Naval units with a small number of Army Air Force units. The former operated TBF, SDB and Catalinas while the latter used B-24 Liberators and Flying Fortresses.

The Army moved to Carney Field when it became established. We had very good relations with the Americans and they readily made available any equipment we needed. This was most helpful with regard to ASV radar used in the

Hudsons because it was directly interchangeable with that in the Catalinas. I made friends with some men from a Carrier Air Servicing Unit (CASU 11).

During my tour of duty we lost two Hudsons due to enemy attack, (7/8 July) one was lost on flare duty for a bombing raid and resulted in a number of Americans losing their way in returning to Henderson. The other loss occurred on the X-ray patrol.

The Hudsons were equipped with Bendix radio and consisted of Ta 12J transmitter, Ra 1B receiver, Mn 26C compass receiver and intercom set. There was also the RAF TR9D which did not like the tropics. While I was there a transponder beacon was installed on Henderson. This worked in conjunction with the ASV. We also had a VHF beacon which transmitted a letter code for each sixty degrees and was received by means of a converter ahead of the Ra1B. The planes were fitted with IFF which gave some problems in serviceability due to high humidity.

Above: NZ2031 at MOTAT with the late Barry East.

Hudson Attacks on Timor

In August 1942 the Allies had a guerrilla force on Timor *Sparrow Force* and the enemy attempted encircling them with troops already deployed and with others landed at Beco. It was the task of Nos 2 and 13 Squadrons of the RAAF at bases south of Darwin to harass the enemy and support the guerrilla force. Additionally they would attack other enemy bases north of the Timor and Arafusa Seas.

On 7 August, W/Cmdr A.B. McFarlane, CO of No.2 Squadron led nine Hudsons to attack enemy ships off Suai and as they approached the Timor coast three were sighted one of which was an *Akikazi* class destroyer of 1300 tons. The Hudsons attacked from 6000ft in three flights of three and a 2000-ton merchantman and another smaller vessel was left burning.

A move of the squadron begun on the fifth to Batchelor Field was completed on the sixteenth. Six of their Hudsons captained by F/Lt Frazer, F/O Badger, F/Sgt Hawkesford, F/Lt McCombe, F/O Hay and F/O S.G. Wadey were airborne at 2335hrs on 20 August to attack Maubisse and then to undertake a recce. One Hudson had to return due to a u/s turret but five in formation crossed the Timor coast at Kilan River and bombed Maubisse town. While on the recce the formation was attacked by two Zeros, with one passing at 400 yards and firing without effect before diving over the Hudsons at 200 yards. Hits were suffered in the auxiliary tanks of A16-209, F/O Wadey's aircraft and apparently only he was able to bale out. A16-209 crashed on a hill. Wadey was able to reach the Sparrow force. F/O N.T. Badger in A16-241 was tailed by the second Zero which made various attacks. Finally while the Hudson was flying at eighty feet above the sea, the Zero flew lower and was promptly raked with fire from the Hudson's ventral gun and crashed into the sea. The four Hudsons returned at 0600hrs on the twenty-first.

W/Cmdr McFarlane in A16-160 led a flight of three Hudsons on 14 September to attack shipping in Saumlaki Bay. They dived from 3000 to 600ft and bombs fell within ten feet of a ship. F/O K.L. McDonell's aircraft A16-172 was hit by AA fire, it was thought to have been hit in the auxiliary

Above: A16-199 coded SF-R for No.2 Sqdn RAAF at Hendon Museum and now stripped of all guns and turret. It was flown for No.2 Sqdn RAAF's last Hudson sortie by F/O Roger Kuring on 8 April 1944.

tank in the cabin and the others saw a 'flaming mass hurtling towards the water'. The first attack had been with each releasing five 100lb bombs. In a second attack McFarlane scored a direct hit on a ship but suffered a splinter from his bombs in the starboard nacelle.

One Hudson Versus Four Zeros

F/Lt Hay, P/O Daniels and P/O James from No.2 Squadron were detailed for a shipping strike to Dili harbour on 25 September and left in formation but due to a port engine fault, James who was on his first sortie, arrived four minutes after the other two had released their bombs scoring hits on a fuel dump with no sightings in the harbour. While leaving Dili P/O R.R. James was attacked by two Zeros from below and on the port and starboard quarters. His turret gunner held fire while a side gunner warned of any approach. James flew into cloud, stall turned and was attacked by a third Zero. He dived back into cloud and then on coming out again saw a fourth Zero.

During the next twenty minutes a side gunner called the

References
1. J. Rob pp 140–141; SWR II/pp.222–233
2. RAAF I/p.581

Above: W/Cmdr R.H. Moran congratulating the No.2 Sqdn RAAF crew captained by F/O R.R. James which shot down two Zero fighters when on their first sortie on 25.9.42.

position of the main attack and evasion was so made that the attacker came into the turret gunner's line of fire although his port gun was u/s after the first fifteen rounds. James' tactics appeared to be using cloud and a series of stall turns which apparently confused the Zeros.

One Zero which had kept at a distance using cannon finally attempted a belly attack and was sent down and smoking in a spin from a sustained burst from the ventral gun.

Cloud cover was again reached but with intermittent attacks from two remaining Zeros. After thirty minutes combat the main tanks were almost empty and ventral gun, and side guns out of ammunition. The turret became u/s. P/O James dived for water on a southerly course while his side gunner took 100 rounds from the front guns. James zigzagged and the side gunner just gave short bursts to counter attacks from the starboard quarter. The turret gunner recovered the use of his port gun and fired a short burst at a Zero which broke off and headed for Dili. James, on reaching the Timor coast flew through valleys so the Zero could only attack from astern although his turret gunner had to load by hand and fire single shots or odd bursts of up to five rounds. After losing the Zero in fog it re-appeared, the gunner fired a short burst of five rounds into its engine and the Zero broke off. The whole combat had lasted forty-five minutes. The No.2 Squadron record concludes with: 'This being the first strike by this crew, it is considered a particularly good show. P/O James excelled in air tactics and the turret and tunnel gunners Sgts Reilly and Reen showed coolness under constant attack.'

The crew of Hudson A16-177 which suffered only seventeen bullet holes was P/O R.R. James (capt), Sgt R.D. Ryan (obs), turret gunner, Sgt P.S. Reen, tunnel gunner, Sgt H. Reilly, side gunner Sgt K.G. Keech. By 24 December 1942 No.2 Squadron had eighteen Hudsons based at Batchelor Field while No.13 Squadron was at Hughes Field with eighteen Hudsons.

On 27 December six of No.2's aircraft were detailed to bomb Japanese stores in position 08°25'S 126°44'E in the Lavai area of Timor. They flew in two flights with the second to bomb transport at the Lavai river crossing. When five miles over Timor a Zero attacked F/O M.W. Johns while two other Zeros attacked the other Hudsons. Other Hudsons attempted to protect him but another Zero raked John's aircraft and it burst into flames, went out of control, and spiralled into the sea. As F/O J.W. Robertson was approaching cloud a Zero moving in to attack passed within fifty yards of his ventral gunner who got in a long burst. The Zero turned over on its back with flames coming from its engine and cowling. It was last seen still on its back and falling away. In the affray which lasted at least fifteen minutes, the Hudsons fired 6800 rounds. By April 1943 No.2 was still operating from Australia northwards towards Timor and other islands but with raids notably on Penfui, a base for enemy aircraft.

On 18 April S/L K.M. Kemp led thirteen Hudsons after staging at Drysdale for an attack on Penfui near Koepang and in conjunction with Mitchell bombers from No.18 Squadron. A Hudson captain on No.2 who had earlier served with No.608 Squadron RAuxF, F/O J.S. Austin, flew from Koepang to Penfui and back at 20,000ft to confuse the enemy while other Hudsons bombed Penfui.

Hudsons A16-236, -227, -195 and A16-181 were on another night attack over Penfui on 20 June. They were flown by S/L Kemp. P/O Griffiths, F/O Hornby and F/O Kilgariff. They bombed from about 14,000ft but fires were started and there were some large explosions.

On 20 July F/O Hornby of No.2 Squadron had as navigator on a Penfui raid, F/O Murray Kidman. In 1942 Murray was a navigator with No.48 Squadron RAF operating from Wick in Scotland and Sumburgh in the Shetlands. The author had a number of trips with him.

Another No.2 Squadron navigator was Ian Moyes who flew with F/O Gordon Sprigg in A16-199 on 19 August 1943 taking off at 1720hrs for a strike on Doelah, an airfield in the Kai Islands. Moyes gives this account:

I well recall that flight: the targets were the harbour facilities, stores, buildings used to construct a new airbase. We were to drop flares and take photographs of the area. I recall the flash of AA batteries and the glow reflected from the landing lights of aircraft taking off to intercept.

I flew once more in A16-199 on 11 September in a search for enemy shipping in the Banda Sea. There were volcanoes on Nila, Romang and Seroea Islands and fertile soil with coconut plantations and Nip observation posts. Sometimes a floatplane version of the Zero was lurking in a bay ready to knock off a lone Hudson. So we used to swing round the headlands into sheltered bays looking for ships and then climb steeply up the flanks of the volcanoes to use the orographic cloud cover if necessary. There was a strong down-draught over the crater that day and the Hudson fell like a stone.

Fred Waterer was also a navigator on No.2 Squadron who flew on Hudson A16-199 (which is now in the RAF Museum at Hendon). On 28 August 1943 the Hudson was armed with eight bombs and thirty incendiaries for a strike on Atabua on the north coast of Timor. It was a seven-and-a-half hour trip. As Dr Waterer adds: 'The strike on Atambua was a reprisal at dusk after the crew of a Liberator returning from Macassar was shot down and the crew murdered. During this trip many thousands of rounds of .303 were also fired and the bombing etc at low level on barracks and a bridge.'

The last Hudson sortie for No.2 Squadron RAAF was flown by F/O Roger Kuring in A16-199 on 8 April 1944. By then the unit was converting to Beauforts and with the prospect of a further conversion to B-25 Mitchells.[3]

Other Australian Units

In addition to the combatant squadrons there were a number of units used for transport and other duties such as the Survey Flight. In the years 1944–1945 the survey unit was operating Hudsons such as A16-47 and A16-130 as far north from Australia as Merauke in Dutch New Guinea and south to Port Lincoln. In Queensland, bases at Iron Range, Townsville and Brisbane were used and flights were made as far west as Broome and Wyndham.

These aircraft were stripped of armament and the bomb bays were adapted to carry spares. Four cameras were carried, one fixed forward in the nose for vertical shots, two were used for obliques, one of which operated from the port side and one from starboard. A fourth camera was carried as a spare. Additional spares for the aircraft included two sets of plugs for the engines, tyres for all three wheels and any odd pieces which could be acquired.

Flights were prepared by Headquarters months in advance, and thereafter each crew with its individual aircraft became virtually a self-contained unit. The crew of A16-47 (SU-R) was captained by F/Lt 'Nobby' Clark, a fitter 2E, Cecil Fitzhenry, and fitter 2A Keith Chew. The navigator P/O Tom Steele, also served as wireless operator and camera operator. There was also a fifth member, a photographer, John Newbiggin. Survey flights were made typically from an altitude of 12,000ft but also from 20,000ft. Representative of such surveys was one made in October 1944 when, operating from 20,000ft in Northern Territory, the area of Darwin and the Alligator Rivers were covered. Another survey was completed in South Australia during the following January and again operating from 20,000ft. A flight of some 17,000 miles was made from Brisbane to Darwin. For refuelling, except at main squadron bases, a semi-rotary hand-pump was used. Tyres were inflated with a foot pump. For routine maintenance, the crew would climb onto the nacelles and use improvised stands. For shelter and accommodation, crews relied on the hospitality of cattle stations. The usual hazards of flying were accentuated by being so often far from established bases and with the need to improvise. Thus while on the trip from Brisbane to Darwin, smoke was seen pouring from the port engine of A16-47. An emergency landing was made at Alexandria Downs cattle station where there was a short but rough landing strip two miles from the homestead. A station truck was backed up to the aircraft and using that as a stand the two fitters in the aircrew found one stud holding the oil pressure governor had sheared resulting in oil being pumped over the hot engine cylinders. This area was very isolated and with American threads the fitters wondered how they could manage. Keith Chew found the cattle station's workshop 'fantastic' and he was able to make a temporary

stud from a high tensile steel bolt using the station's lathe and other equipment. Chores on such trips were shared but what they most missed were engine stands.[4]

The Survey Unit must have been one of the last of the RAAF units to use Hudsons although No.2 Squadron had them in strength up to March 1944.

RNZAF Squadrons

Seven New Zealand squadrons were ultimately to receive allocations of Hudsons wholly or as part of their equipment. Initially however, out-dated machines such as Baffins, Vincents and Vildebeests were used. New Zealand was dependent on Britain for allocations of aircraft and in July 1941 six Hudsons per month were authorised from RAF allocations for New Zealand. Thirty were to be delivered before the end of the year, and the balance out of a total of sixty-four which had been ordered by New Zealand in 1942 between March and May.

On the outbreak of war with Japan, thirty-six Hudsons represented an important part of New Zealand's first line aircraft. By February 1942 thirty-two Hudsons were included in the operational strength distributed between the reconnaissance squadrons. No.1 based at Whenuapai, had twelve; there were eleven Hudsons with No.2 at Nelson, and based at Nandi in Fiji were nine with No.4 Squadron.

Allied plans for the South Pacific in 1942 included provision for a defence line of bases extending from Northern Australia eastwards through New Caledonia, the New Hebrides, the Fiji Islands through to Tonga and the Samoa Islands.

New Zealand was very aware of the Fijis lying directly north but in practice extended its operations with Hudsons further north to the Ellice Islands and north-west to the Solomons. One of its most important potential bases was Suva on Viti Levu, one of the Fiji Islands and early in 1939 proposals were made for bases to be constructed on Viti Levu for land-based aircraft. In view of the foreseen threat from Japan, it was also proposed that New Zealand should cover the line by air reconnaissance from the New Hebrides to Tonga. Plans were made for landing fields at Nandi on the west coast of Viti Levu and at Nausori fifteen miles from Suva. Following the arrival in Fiji of advanced parties of RNZAF personnel, No.4 Squadron was formed as a GR unit on 8 October 1940.

The first six Hudsons for New Zealand arrived in September 1941 and No.4 Squadron on Fiji received six Hudsons in December, to be increased to nine in the following February. On 14 February 1942 a Japanese task force was reported approaching and Hudson crews were briefed to bomb from 9000ft on sighting the enemy. A recce was made of the Ellice Islands area but no contact was made.

In addition to its recce and escort duties, No.4 served as a training unit for forward-based squadrons. On 25 May 1943 while escorting an American convoy, a Hudson crew sighted

References
3. JB p.196   4. From Keith Chew's letters

Above: Hudson NZ2003 (AM591) a Mark V with the RNZAF.

Above: Hudsons of No.3 Sqdn RNZAF on Norfolk Island.

a submarine 180 miles south-west of Suva and attacked with four DCs apparently causing some damage. No.4 Squadron made another attack on a submarine on 7 September while escorting an American ship *Saugatuck* but no lethal damage was claimed. While operating from Fiji No.4's tasks remained anti-submarine and anti-shipping patrols. In January 1944 a detachment of six Hudsons was made to Tonga, followed by two more aircraft in February. During the following months they patrolled the Friendly Islands group area. A further detachment was made to the Ellice Islands in September followed by an additional four a fortnight later. From there until November, based at Funafuti, they operated on A/S searches. During this period, No.4's Hudsons were being replaced by Venturas.

No.3 Squadron RNZAF was re-formed at Harewood in April 1941 with obsolete aircraft and the Hudsons it received at the end of the year were withdrawn to reinforce No.4 Squadron in the Fijis. From February 1942 No.3 was based at Whenuapai but on 22 September was posted to Espiritu Santo in the New Hebrides with then a total strength of 300 officers and men commanded by W/Cmdr G.H. Fisher. An airstrip was developed at Pallikulo and in the two weeks following No.3's arrival, there was American help in bulldozing the site; the squadron erected messes, servicing facilities etc to become operational on 16 October. The squadron came under the operational control of USS *Curtiss* which was deployed in the Segond Channel and sorties were undertaken up to 400 miles from Pallikulo; A/S patrols within short range of the Segond Channel.[5]

In November 1942 six of the unit's Hudsons were detached to Guadalcanal where they came under the control of General L.E. Woods of the US Marine Corps. They were engaged on armed recces both day and night along the coastlines in the approaches to Guadalcanal which might be used for Japanese movements of troops and supplies. From the official USAF history, No.3 Squadron RNZAF 'had opened operations on Guadalcanal with twelve Hudsons on 24 November 1942'.[6]

In the south-west Pacific the aircrews of both the RAAF and RNZAF appeared adept at undertaking long-range recces, often to the extreme limits of their Hudson aircraft. From Guadalcanal the New Zealanders fulfilled this role alongside the American dive-bombers and torpedo aircraft. They flew on patrols north over the area including New Georgia, Santa Isobel and Choiseul. Although briefed to avoid encounters with the enemy except submarines, when attacked the Hudsons quitted themselves well. Thus on 24 November F/O G.E. Gudsell while operating south of Vella Lavella sighted an enemy convoy but was attacked by three Japanese float planes but after a combat of about twenty minutes, Gudsell escaped with none of his crew wounded.

A fully-surfaced submarine was sighted by Sgt I.M. Page of No.3 Squadron on 2 December. He attacked with two bombs and two 350lb DCs. A large patch of oil appeared after the vessel dived. The following afternoon, with reports of an enemy force steaming south from Buin, a Hudson shadowed four cruisers and six destroyers which were later attacked by an American strike force off New Georgia. Ten enemy aircraft were reported shot down and four of the vessels hit in bombing attacks.

After an American photo-recce confirmed the enemy constructing a landing strip on Munda Island 150 miles north in the Solomons group, a New Zealand Hudson bombed the runway from 7000ft on 9 December to be followed by American strikes. The field on Munda Island posed a constant threat and was then shelled by cruisers and destroyers with Hudsons providing air cover.

On 15 January 1943 a No.3 Squadron Hudson on patrol west of Choiseul and near an enemy base at Ballale 230 miles north of Guadalcanal, sighted a Japanese cargo vessel and six destroyers. Base was signalled and the Hudson shadowed the ships for one-and-a-half hours. On reaching PLE nine enemy fighters appeared; the Hudson used cloud cover and flew north before turning back for Henderson Field. The Americans sent a strike force to attack the ships. During this month No.3 Squadron undertook 213 sorties despite night raids on their base and made sightings of ninety-five enemy ships. F/O M.W. McCormick of No.3 Squadron while on patrol north of Choiseul Island on 2 April 1943 attacked a Japanese submarine with bombs and DCs only twenty-five seconds after it had dived. While still on patrol a Japanese float-plane was sighted and McCormick shot it down with his forward guns. He was later attacked by two float-planes but the combat was broken off with no hits on either side.

On 7 July F/Lt W.O. Rutherford of No.3 Squadron acted as pathfinder for American torpedo-bombers by dropping flares over the enemy harbour in southern Bougainville and assisting their navigation with more flares off Vella Lavella. He failed to return and was thought to have been shot down by a night-fighter.

A Hudson Versus Eight Zero Fighters

F/Lt W.G.C. Allison while on patrol on 24 July was attacked by eight Zero fighters off Baga Island near Vella Lavella. In a combat lasting forty minutes one of the Hudson gunners shot down two Zeros. The Hudson caught fire and three of the crew were wounded including Allison who managed to ditch the aircraft two miles off the coast of Baga. The crew were able to exit but were then strafed by the fighters; Trevor E. Ganley was the sole survivor. He managed to swim ashore, contact a coastwatcher who treated his wounds and with whom he stayed before being picked up by a US Catalina on 21 September and returned to Henderson Field.

The Allies had occupied New Georgia in August 1943; No.3 Squadron moved to Espiritu Santo in the New Hebrides in October being replaced by No.1 Squadron on the twenty-third on Guadalcanal. By 1 November a base depot was established at Espiritu Santo with facilities for servicing and repairs, serving also for fighters and flying boats and as a staging post. Duties for Hudsons remained of northerly patrols searching particularly for enemy shipping from Truk and Rabaul. Additionally, No.3 would raid enemy barges and shore installations and have an aircraft on standby for any submarine reported. No.3 withdrew from Espiritu Santo in January 1944 but returned in May for a few months before being posted to Guadalcanal. In August it moved to Bougainville before a further move north to Emirau in the New Ireland group.

Norfolk Island

When Japan entered the war No.1 Squadron sent five Hudsons to Nandi, on Viti Levu in the Fijis; an additional five following on 29 December. In July 1942 three of their Hudsons were sent to Norfolk Island about halfway between New Zealand and New Caledonia. From there searches were made for two enemy submarines thought to be in the area.

This arrival on Norfolk Island was thought to be the first time that aircraft had landed there and in September 1982 a set of three postage stamps was issued depicting RNZAF Hudsons on Norfolk Island. In May 1943 No.1 Squadron began re-equipping with Venturas and by 17 October 1943 was fully operational on them.

No.2 Squadron was supplied with Hudsons in 1941 and in February 1942 was based at Nelson with eleven Hudsons but six were sent to Nandi where they became attached to No.4 Squadron. When Nelson ceased to be an operational base in 1943, No.2 Squadron moved to Ohakea on North Island for convoy escorts and A/S patrols. Some were sent on detachment and at Gisborne during June to October 1943, No.2 re-equipped with Venturas.

Following a request to the New Zealand Government to send six aircraft to New Caledonia in 1942, Hudsons were despatched from Fiji with additional aircraft from Nos 1 and 2 Squadrons. The Hudson unit so formed was initially considered from No.4 but was designated No.9 GR

Above: Postage stamps issued in Norfolk Island commemorating the arrival of RNZAF Hudsons at Christmas 1942.

Squadron. An advance party was taken by USS *Mackinac* arriving at Noumea, New Caledonia on 5 July 1942 but the report of a Japanese task force delayed disembarkation until the sixth. They were accommodated in tents 180 miles from Noumea and relied initially on the Americans for a number of services and shared messing facilities at Plaine des Gaiacs. A further request in August was for No.9 Squadron to replace an American one in a forward area but No.9 Squadron remained on New Caledonia. The following year they transferred to Espiritu Santo providing reserves for No.3 Squadron. It was replaced in October at Espiritu Santu by No.3 Squadron and returned to New Zealand.

With New Zealand units operating in forward areas there was a need for transport to carry both personnel and equipment. With shipping there were delays and Hudsons were used carrying in early 1943 forty-five personnel on average every month in each direction. DC-3s or Dakotas and Lockheed Lodestars were also used.

No.40 Squadron was formed on 1 June 1943 with W/Cmdr J. Adams as CO. By August 1943 it had an establishment of twelve Hudsons, nine Lodestars and sixteen Dakotas and by November it was making regular flights to Samoa, Fiji Islands and Guadalcanal.

A second transport squadron was formed on 15 August 1944, No.41 which, like No.40, was based at Whenuapai, Auckland. Commanded by S/Ldr E.F.H. Tye, DFC, it was equipped with thirteen Hudsons and nine Lodestars. By September it had a schedule of ten flights per week to the Solomons, Bougainville and Guadalcanal. In 1945, No.40 re-equipped with Dakotas.

With the end of hostilities, the transport squadrons were employed with the repatriation of Allied prisoners-of-war and some aircraft were converted to ambulances.

References
5. See also AH FC p.168   6. C&C IV/p.203

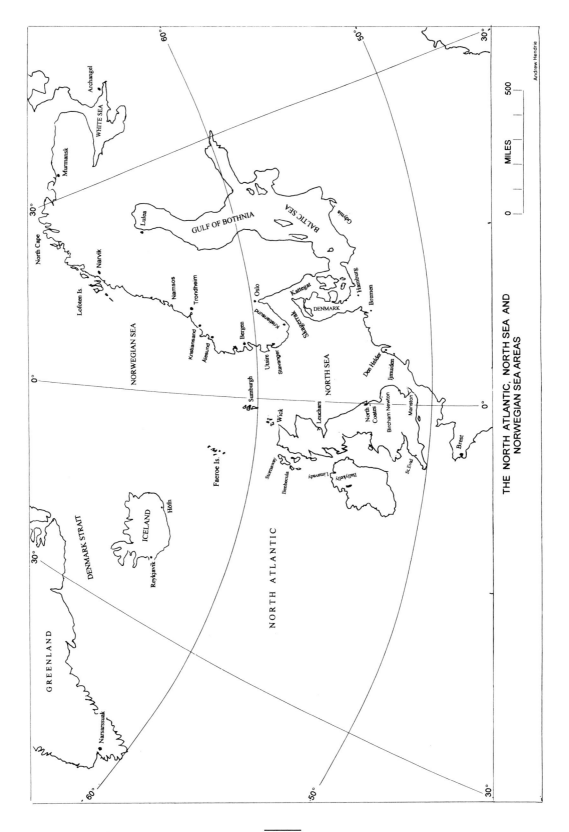

THE NORTH ATLANTIC, NORTH SEA AND
NORWEGIAN SEA AREAS

Andrew Hendrie

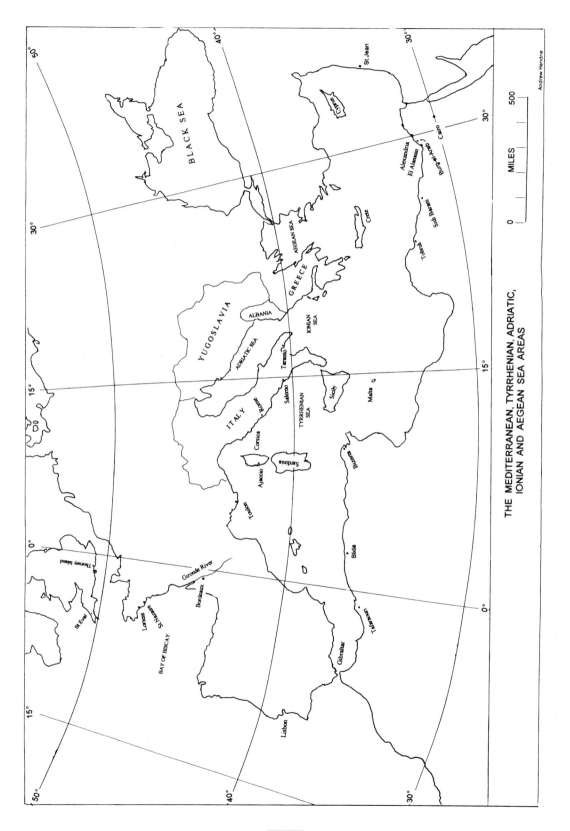

THE MEDITERRANEAN, TYRRHENIAN, ADRIATIC,
IONIAN AND AEGEAN SEA AREAS

Andrew Hendrie

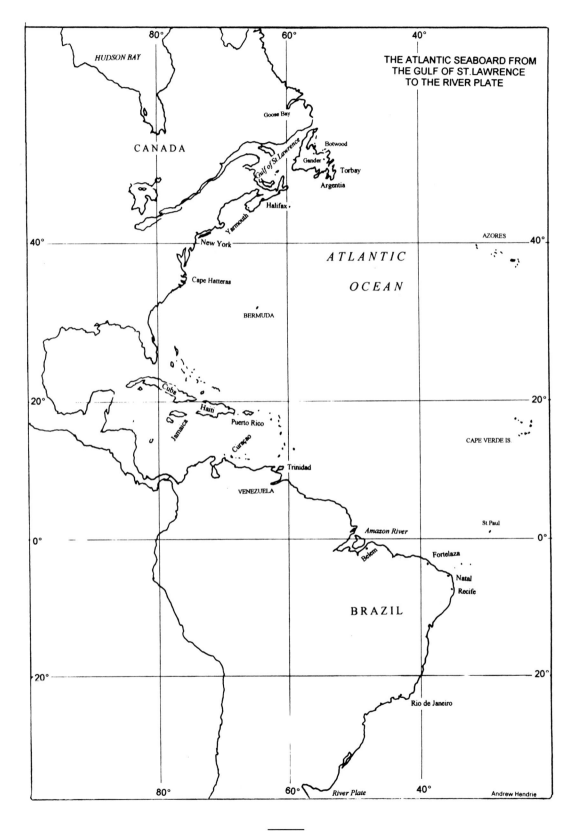

THE ATLANTIC SEABOARD FROM
THE GULF OF ST.LAWRENCE
TO THE RIVER PLATE

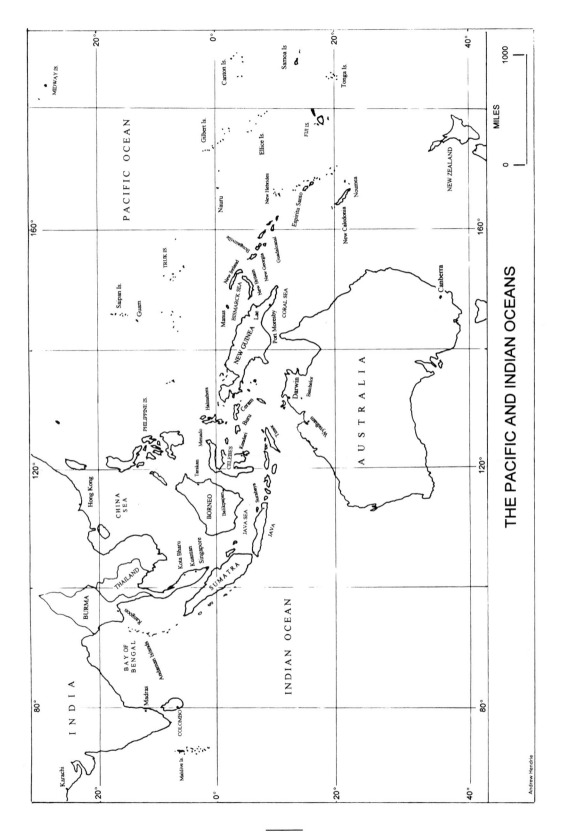

THE PACIFIC AND INDIAN OCEANS

Andrew Hendrie

Appendix A

U boats Sunk or Damaged in Attacks by Hudson Aircraft

Date	U boat	Captain	Squadron	Captain	Position	Remarks
25.10.40	U-46	Kl E. Endrass	E, K, L/233	P/O Baudoux		damaged
27.8.41	U-570	Kl Rahmlow	S/269	S/L Thompson	67°15′N 18°35′W	captured
30.10.41	U-81	Kl Guggenberger	H/53 & Z/209	P/O Henry	48°00′N 09°10′W	damaged
1.3.42	U-656	Ol Kröning	VP-82	Ens. W. Tepuni	46°15′N 53°15′W	sunk
15.3.42	U-503	Kl Gericke	VP-82	Lt D. Mason	45°50′N 53°15′W	sunk
1.5.42	U-573	Kl Heinsohn	M/233	Sgt Brent	37°00′N 01°00′W	damaged
7.7.42	U-701	Kl H. Degen	AAF 396	2nd. Lt Kane	34°50′N 74°55′W	sunk
31.7.42	U-754	Kl Oerstermann	RCAF 113	S/L N.E. Small	43°02′N 64°52′W	sunk
27.8.42	U-173	Kl Beucke	W/53	F/S Sillcock	09°21′N 53°25′W	damaged
20.9.42	U-217		F/53	F/S Jesty	11°02′N 57°05′W	damaged
22.9.42	U-512	Kl W. Schultz	C/53	P/O Rickards		damaged
26.9.42	U-262	Kl H. Franke	Z, A/48	P/O Horney P/O Thammes		damaged
5.10.42	U-619	Ol Makowski	N/269	F/O Markham	58°41′N 22°58′W	sunk
30.10.42	U-658	Kl H. Senkel	RCAF 145	F/O Robinson	50°32′N 46°32′W	sunk
10.11.42	U-505	Kl P. Zscech	L/53	F/S Sillcock	10°10′N 59°04′W	damaged
13.11.42	U-458	Kl Diggins	S/500	F/O M. Ensor		damaged
13.11.42	U-411	Kl Spindlegger	D/500	S/L J.B. Ensor	36°00′N 09°35′W	sunk
14.11.42	U-595	Kl Q-Faslem	C, D/608 S/500	F/O Williams P/O Livingstone W/C Spotswood	36°38′N 00°30′E	sunk
14.11.42	U-605	Kl H. Schultz	B/233	P/O Barling	36°20′N 01°01′E	sunk
15.11.42	U-259	Kl K. Köpke	S/500	F/O M. Ensor	37°20′N 03°05′E	sunk
17.11.42	U-331	Tiesenhausen	Z, L, C/500	S/L Patterson	37°05′N 02°24′E	sunk
17.11.42	U-566	Kl H. Hornkohl	U/233	Sgt E.H. Smith	35°40′N 11°18′W	damaged
18.11.42	U-613	Kk H. Köppe	U/608	F/O J. Petrie		damaged
19.11.42	U-413	Ol Poel	C/608	F/O A.L. Wilcox	35°38′N 11°38′W	damaged
24.11.42	U-263	Kl K. Nölke	Q/233	Sgt E.H. Smith	36°34′N 12°00′W	damaged
12.2.43	U-442	Kl H. Hesse	F/48	F/O Mayhew	37°32′N 11°56′W	sunk
4.3.43	U-83	Kl Wörtszhoffer	U-500	Sgt G. Jackimov	37°10′N 00°05′E	sunk
28.3.43	U-77	Kl O. Hartmann	L, V/48 & 233	F/O J. Harrop	37°42′N 00°01′E	sunk
5.4.43	U-167	Kk K. Sturm	W, L/233	F/S K. Dalton F/L W. Willets	27°47′N 15°00′W	Sunk
7.5.43	U-447	Ol F. Bothe	X, T/233	Sgt J. Holland Sgt J. McQueen	35°30′N 11°55′W	sunk
17.5.43	U-646	Ol H. Wulff	J/269	Sgt F.H. James	62°10′N 14°30′W	sunk
19.5.43	U-273	Ol H. Rossmann	M/269	F/O J.N.P. Bell	59°25′N 24°33′W	sunk

28.5.43	U-755	Kl W. Göing	M/608	F/O G. Ogilvie	39°58′N 01°41′E	sunk
4.6.43	U-594	Kl F. Mumm	F/48	F/O H.C. Bailey	35°55′N 09°25′W	sunk
8.6.43	U-535	Kl Elmenreich	K-269	Sgt Couchman	60°40′N 20°55′W	damaged
16.6.43	U-97	Kl H. Trox	459 RAAF	F/S Barnard	33°00′N 34°00′E	sunk
14.7.43	I-29	Izu	8 RAAF	F/S N. Miller	12°13′N 51°13′E	damaged
31.7.43	U-199	Kl Kraus	BAF & USN	Lt S. Schoor	23°54′S 42°54′W	sunk
3.8.43	U-489	Ol A. Schmankt	J/269	F/S E. Brame	62°03′N 12°52′W	damaged
17.8.43	U-403	Kl K. Heine	O/200	F/O Horbat	14°11′N 17°40′W	damaged
26.9.43	U-667	Kl Schoeteler	T/233, N/48 & 179 Sqdn	F/O Frandson F/O Ashbury	36°10′N 09°48′W	damaged
4.10.43	U-731	Ol A. Keller	S/269	P/O H.M. Smith	62°02′N 28°27′W	damaged
5.10.43	U-336	Kl H. Hunger	F/269	F/S G. Allsop	62°43′N 27°17′W	sunk

Appendix B
Ships Sunk or Damaged by Hudson Aircraft

Date	Ship	Sunk/dmgd	Tonnage	Squadron	Captain	Position
29.4.40	*Theodor* MV	D	1939	233		Grimstad fjord
8.7.40	*Kristine* fv	S	29	220		Danish coast
25.7.40	*William Blumer* MV	D	3604	233	F/O Fuller	SW Norway
30.7.40	*Anna Sofie* MV	D	3100	224	P/O Lynn	SW Norway
3.9.40	*Heinrich Gunter* [UJ124]	D	475	206		Terschelling
7.10.40	*Clipper* fv	D	50	233	F/Lt Hopkins	SW Norway
27.12.40	*Arfinn Jarl* MV	S	1159	224		SW Norway
4.1.41	*Snyg* MV	S	1326	224	F/Lt Davies	SW Norway
5.7.41	*Advance* MV	S	881	220	Ainsworth	W Norway
24.9.41	*Tiger* MV	D	3941	220		SW Norway
11.10.41	*Mucke* [Aux]	S	245	220	Tate	Nr Bergen
13.10.41	*Brategg* MV	D	480	220		W Norway
13.10.41	*Hamm 109 dgr*	S	100	407	S/L Lynham	Terschelling
18.10.41	*Ingeren* MV	D	6123	500		Borkum
29.10.41	*Barcelona* MV	S	3101	220		Ålesund
"	*Vesla* MV	D	1108	220		"
29.10.41	*Svanefjell* MV	D	1371	220		Ålesund
"	*Archimede* MV	S	?	220		"
31.10.41	*Solskin* MV	S	372	220		SW Norway
1.11.41	*Braheholm* MV	D	5676	407	S/L Lewis	Dutch coast
2.11.41	*Hornelen* MV	D	257	220		SW Norway
7.11.41	*Bamse* tug	D	210	608		S Norway

11.11.41	*Vios IV* [IJM96]	S	190	407	W/C Styles	IJmuiden
28.11.41	*Vindafjord* MV	S	142	220	Ramsey	Stavanger
4.12.41	*Vestri* MV	S	499	220	Sanderson	W Norway
9.12.41	*Bjonn* MV	S	5509	220	F/S Stone	W Norway
9.12.41	*Burgermeister Smidt* [Aux. M1203]	S	500	224	Sgt Crewe	Off Brest
9.12.41	*Madrid* MV	S	8777	407/217	W/C Styles	IJmuiden
14.12.41	*Topaz* fv	S	142	220		SW Norway
21.12.41	*Karmsund* MV	D	287	220	Clark or Carpenter	W Norway
5.1.42	*Cornelia Maersk* MV	S	1892	407	S/L Anderson	IJmuiden
17.2.42	*Eber* N.S.21	S	226	48		SW Norway
27.4.42	*Inga* MV	S	1494	53	Hastie/Guthrie	Hornsriff
3.5.42	*Konsul Carl Fisser* MV	S	5843	608		Off Ålsund
4.5.42	*Klaud Fritzen* MV	S	2936	608	Scholefield	W Norway
4.5.42	*Taarnholm* MV	D	1420	53	Puckeridge	IJmuiden
4.5.42	*Jantje Fritzen* MV	D	6582	59		IJmuiden
4.5.42	*Troma* MV	D	5029	59		IJmuiden
4.5.42	*Sizilien* MV	S	4647	407	W/C Brown	Terschelling
5.5.42	*Alice Freyman* MV	D	1377	608		W Norway
8.5.42	*Burgundia* MV	D	1668	320		Emden
8.5.42	*Ruth* MV	S	3726	407	W/C Brown	Texel
8.5.42	*Namdo* MV	D	2860	407	W/C Brown	Texel
13.5.42	*Tampa* MV	D	4694	608		Off Ålesund
15.5.42	*Selje* MV	S	6698	407	F/L Christie	Terschelling
16.5.42	*Madeleine Louise* [VP2002]	S	464	407	F/L Christie	Terschelling
29.5.42	*Niels R. Finsen* MV	S	1850	407	F/L Christie	Ameland
29.5.42	*Veriato* [Sperrbrecher]	S	750	320		Ameland
29.5.42	*Nordcap* [VP1103]	S	285	59		Ameland
30.5.42	*Varmdo* MV	S	2956	407	P/O O'Connell F/S Honey	Terschelling
2.6.42	*Dietrich Oldendorff* MV	D	1876	608		SW Norway
3.6.42	*Worth* MV	D	6256	608		SW Norway
12.6.42	*Senta* MV	S	1497	407	P/O Taylor	IJmuiden
25.10.42	*Emma* fv	D	150	407		Biscay
27.10.42	*La Mouette*	D	303	407		Biscay
27.11.42	*Haarlem* fv	S	431	320		IJmuiden
18.1.43	*Algeria* MV	S	1619	320/407	de le Haye	Terschelling
8.12.43	*Awajisan* Maru	S	9794	1 RAAF	F/L Diamond	06°08′N 102°16′E
8.12.43	*Sakura* Maru	D	7170	1 & 8 RAAF		06°08′N 102°16′E
8.12.43	*Ayatusan* Maru	D	9788	1& 8 RAAF		08°08′N 102°16′E

Appendix C
Royal Air Force Serial Numbers

No.	Unit	Remarks
N7205	AAEE/RAE	S.O.C. 17.12.43.
N7206	AAEE/1 OTU/6 OTU	Crashed Gainsford, Co. Durham 1.5.42.
N7207	AAEE/ 1 OTU	Crashed 3m N of Abbeytown, Cumberland.
N7208	AAEE/ 1 OTU/ 320/ 1 OTU/ 2 TAF CF	To 4587M 3.44.
N7209	CFS/320/233/ 1 OTU 2 TAF CF	S.O.C. 13.12.44.
N7210	224	Swung on landing, u/c collapsed, Leuchars 8.9.39.
N7211	RAE/224/1 OTU/ 1 PRU Abbotsinch/Film Unit	S.O.C. 25.5.44.
N7212	224	Spun into ground 1m SW of Leuchars 14.3.40.
N7213	224	Swung on t.o. crashed Leuchars 19.11.39.
N7214	224	Dived into ground 1m N of Leuchars 4.10.39.
N7215	224/PDU/PRU/1 OTU/ 6 OTU/ 1 OTU/ATA	
N7216	224	Shot down by Me 109, Brunsbüttel, 30.9.39.
N7217	224	Shot down by Me 109s, Stavanger, 15.6.40.
N7218	224/233/1 OTU	S.O.C. 19.4.45.
N7219	224	Shot down by AA near Sylt 30.9.39.
N7220	GRU/1 OTU/24/ 1 OTU/ 24/MCS	To Dutch Govt, 23.6.44.
N7221	224/220/161	Crashed 28.3.44; S.O.C. 16.8.44.
N7222	224	Missing over North Sea 21.12.40.
N7223	233/ 1 OTU	Dived into ground, Silloth 14.12.41.
N7224	233	Shot down by Me 109s off Norway, 31.7.40.
N7225	233/6 OTU/1 OTU/ 5 OTU	S.O.C. 17.12.43.
N7226	233/ 1 OTU	Engine cut on t.o. Silloth, crashed-landed, Beckfoot, Cumb. 13.1.43.
N7227	233	Flew into high ground 1½ m S of Freuchie, Fife, 10.10.39.
N7228	233/ 6 OTU	Stalled on approach to Thornaby, hit ground W Ackham, Yorks. 6.11.41.
N7229	224	Forced landing on ferry flt, Prestwick – crashed 5.1.40.
N7230	220/320	To 3076M 27.4.42.
N7231	220	Hit balloon cable, crashed Boldon Colliery, Co. Durham 11.7.40.
N7232	220	Damaged by return fire from Ju 88, crashed in sea 20m E of St Abbs Head, 1.1.40.
N7233	220	Lost height after t.o. flew into ground, Thornaby 15.9.40.
N7234	220/ 3 FFP	Sideslipped into ground Hullavington 30.5.40.
N7235	220/224	Missing on training flt; presumed crashed in Loch Bradan 4.3.41.
N7236	220	S.O.C. 14.6.45.
N7237	220	Undershot in forced landing; hit construction plant, Thornaby 30.3.40.

N7238	220/320/BN/320/1 OTU/ ATA	Engine caught fire on t.o. belly-landed Littlewick, Berks. 13.8.44.
N7239	233	Stalled on t.o. crashed in river, Leuchars 4.9.39.
N7240	233/224	Missing over Atlantic 25.10.40.
N7241	233	Shot down by Me 110 on Stavanger recce W of Hestholmen 13.4.40.
N7242	233	Missing from patrol 21.7.40.
N7243	233/6 OTU	Elevator jammed on approach to Thornaby and crashed on Brambles Farm, Middlesbrough, 22.12.41; one engine torn off. [Sgt Dunnet].
N7244	233/224	Crashed in river, near Leuchars 23.8.40.
N7245	233	Props. hit ground on t.o.; flew into wood, Leuchars 15.1.40.
N7246	233	Shot down in flames during attack on *Scharnhorst* off Utsire 21.6.40 [S/L Feeny].
N7247	233/224	Dived into sea 3m NE of North Carr L.V. 7.9.39.
N7248	233/224	Crashed in sea off Norway 31.8.39.
N7249	224	Shot down by AA from cruiser HMS *Curacoa*, Andalsness 23.4.40.
N7250	224	Stalled on attempted overshoot and hit ground, Prestwick 5.1.40.
N7251	224/233/1 OTU/83 Gp	To 4266M 31.10.43.
N7252	233/224/ 1 OTU	Swung on t.o. Silloth 16.2.42. D.B.R.
N7253	233/24/233/233/24	Control lost in cloud and wing broke off, Tyn-y-Bryne, Glam. 17.7.42.
N7254	233/6 OTU/ 1 OTU	S.O.C. 31.5.45.
N7255	233	F.T.R. from patrol 5.6.40.
N7256	233	Flew into hill, bad vis. Nant-y-Moel, Glam. 7.1.40.
N7257	233/FTU	Engine cut on t.o.; swung and hit Spitfire X4411, Kirkbride 3.2.43.
N7258	233	Shot down by Me 109s SW of Kristiansand while shadowing *Scharnhorst* 12.4.40.
N7259	233/1 OTU/6 OTU/ 7 RS/ 10 RS	To 3652M 11.6.43.
N7260	Lockheed	Broke up in air and crashed Thurstaston, Wirral 28.7.39.
N7261	224/220	S.O.C. 3.12.41.
N7262	224	Shot down by AA from destroyers off Horns Reef 11.1.40.
N7263	24/63/12 OTU/King's Flt/161	Swung on landing, hit building, Tempsford 1.8.44.
N7264	224/1 OTU/ATA	S.O.C. 30.11.45.
N7265	224	F.T.R. 9.12.40.
N7266	224	Damaged during attack on Fw 200, 27.10.40; S.O.C. 1.11.41.
N7267	224/220/6 OTU/83 Gp/RS	To 4768M 17.4.44.
N7268	224	F.T.R. From North Sea patrol 8.9.40.
N7269	224/233/1 OTU/6 OTU	S.O.C. 29.10.47.
N7270	224	Shot down by Me 109s off Stavanger 15.6.40.
N7271	233	Swung on t.o. and hit Anson K6268, Leuchars 18.10.39.
N7272	224	Abandoned out of fuel 3m NW of Luss, Dunbartonshire 20.11.40.
N7273	1 OTU/206/ 1 OTU	Stalled at low altitude and crashed Cummertrees, Dumfries 30.9.40.
N7274	269/1 OTU/269/6 OTU 608/1 OTU	S.O.C. 29.11.45.
N7275	1 OTU/206/220/ATA 24/CCDU/1 OTU/24 Hutton Cranswick /ATA	*Spirit of Brussels;* S.O.C. 28.4.45.
N7276	269/1 OTU/269/CCTDU RAE/CCDU/1 OTU 6 OTU/ 2 TAF CF	To 4799M 18.5.44.

N7277	1 OTU	Swung on t.o. u/c collapsed, Silloth 8.7.40.
N7278	206/269	Shot down by Me 109s off Stavanger 1.5.40.
N7279	224	Shot down by Me 109s off Stavanger 15.6.40 .
N7280	224/233/1 OTU/AAEE/. 1 OTU/6 OTU/ATA	S.O.C. 28.6.45.
N7281	220/83Gp/220	Engine cut and crashed in forced landing, Newgale, Pembs. 17.6.41.
N7282	224	Shot down off Bergen by Me 110 7.8.40.
N7283	220	F.T.R. from North Sea patrol 24.4.40.
N7284	220	Crashed in sea 4½ m E of Seaham, Co. Durham 19.11.39.
N7285	220	S.O.C. 3.5.40.
N7286	220	Damaged by Me 109s and ditched in Skagerrak 24.4.40.
N7287	220/224/233	F.T.R. From recce 20.6.40.
N7288	220/320/6 OTU	Engine cut; ditched off Hartlepool 30.4.42.
N7289	220	Shot down by Me 109s over Skagerrak 24.4.40.
N7290	220	Stalled on approach Thornaby and spun into house in Middlesbrough 8.11.39.
N7291	220	Abandoned; crashed near Sancreed, Cornwall 7.11.40.
N7292	220/6 OTU/ATA	S.O.C. 28.4.45.
N7293	220/206/6 OTU/RAE	S.O.C. 7.11.46.
N7294	220	Flew into hill when windscreen iced up after t.o., Great Ayton, Yorks. 11.2.40.
N7295	220	Overshot landing into ditch St Eval 7.11.40.
N7296	233	Brakes seized, swung and u/c collapsed, Nutts Corner 21.5.41.
N7297	220/6 OTU	To 3467M 24.12.43.
N7298	224	Flew into high ground during bad vis., Kildare, Eire 11.1.41.
N7299	269/1 OTU/206	Flew into runway when flarepath extinguished without warning, Bircham Newton 29.6.40.
N7300	206	Flew into wood in fog, West Raynham Hall, Norfolk 19.11.40.
N7301	2 FPP/PDU/PRU	F.T.R. From mission to Scheldt Estuary 26.10.40.
N7302	206/320	Engine power lost on nav. ex. Ditched 26.10.42.
N7303	1 OTU/269/Wick/1 AAS	*Snow White*; S.O.C. 23.5.44.
N7304	220/1 OTU	Stalled and spun into Solway Firth 4.5.41.
N7305	224	Shot down by Me 110s W of Hestholmen 10.7.40.
N7306	224	Shot down by Me 109 14.4.40.
N7307	224/1 OTU	Stalled on circuit hit ground and overturned, Silloth 9.6.42.
N7308	224/1 OTU	Engine power lost, stalled and spun in Silloth 4.1.43.
N7309	220	Destroyed in air raid Thornaby 6.6.40.
N7310	220	Flew into hills in cloud 4½ m NW of Tor Ness, Orkney Is. 19.3.41.
N7311	269/220/6 OTU/1 OTU	S.O.C. 29.11.45.
N7312	CC Pool/206	Tyre burst on landing, swung and u/c collapsed 25.4.40.
N7313	1 OTU/6 OTU/5 OTU	S.O.C. 29.11.44.
N7314	220	Hit HT cable in fog crashedlanded; bombs blew up, Maltby, Yorks. 2.8.40.
N7315	224	Engine cut, attempted to overshoot and spun in. Wick 5.3.41.
N7316	220	Engine cut after t.o. crashlanded, Thornaby 16.8.40.
N7317	RAE/ PDU	Destroyed 30.6.40.
N7318	206/6 OTU	Overshot landing and hit air-raid shelter, Thornaby 16.8.40.
N7319	206	Damaged by Me 109s off Elbe estuary; belly-landed Bircham Newton 3.5.40.

N7320	1 OTU	To 2176M 18.7.40.
N7321	1 OTU/PDU/PRU	Hit by AA Cuxhaven; short of fuel and ditched 15m off Sherringham, Norfolk 27.8.40.
N7322	1 OTU	Overshot landing and hit truck, Kirkbride 13.4.42.
N7323	233	Shot down by Me 110 off Stavanger 13.4.40.
N7324	233/ Malta	F.T.R. 1.9.40.
N7325	1 OTU	Crashed near Appleby, Cumberland 6.9.42.
N7326	233/ 1 OTU/ATA	S.O.C. 28.4.45.
N7327	269/1 OTU/206/1 OTU ATA/TU/1 OTU	S.O.C. 20.12.43.
N7328	269/1 OTU/269/6 OTU 1 OTU/ATA	S.O.C. 28.6.45.
N7329	206	F.T.R. from Hamburg 18.5.40.
N7330	1 OTU/269	Shot down by Me 109 off Norway 27.6.40.
N7331	206/269/1 OTU/6 OTU	S.O.C. 19.7.43.
N7332	1 OTU/SFPP/12 STT	S.O.C. 28.2.46.
N7333	206	Crashed after t.o. from Bircham Newton 20.12.40.
N7334	2 Cam Unit	Shot down by Hurricanes [32 or 79 Sqdn] Meopham, Kent 3.3.40.
N7335	1 OTU/269	Shot down by Me 109 off Stavanger, 29.5.40.
N7336	RAE/233/1 OTU/6 OTU ATA/ Benson	S.O.C. 3.1.45.
N7337	1 OTU	Flew into hill in fog 2m S of Ramsey, I.O.M 9.9.41.
N7338	CC pool/1 OTU/2 TAF/ATA	S.O.C. 28.4.45.
N7339	CC pool	Overshot landing and u/c collapsed Silloth 15.1.40; to 2168M 5.8.40.
N7340	233/1 OTU	Overshot at Acklington19.4.42.
N7341	220/1 OTU/8th USAAF	S.O.C. 9.4.45.
N7342	224/1 OTU/ATA	S.O.C. 28.4.45.
N7343	206/220/608/6 OTU	F.T.R. from North Sea Met. Flt 18.5.42.
N7344 to N7350		Direct to R.C.A.F as 759–765.
N7351	206	Hit trees on t.o. belly-landed Docking 3.9.40.
N7352		Direct to R.C.A.F. as 766.
N7353	206	Shot down by Me 109s N of Baltrum off German coast 12.5.40.
N7354 to N7356		Direct to R.C.A.F. as 767–769.
N7357	224/267	Lost 16.8.42 NFD.
N7358	224	S.O.C. 28.1.41.
N7359	224	F.T.R. from convoy escort 21.6.40.
N7360		Direct to R.C.A.F. as 770.
N7361	1 OTU/269	Shot down by Me 109s over Trondheim 11.6.40.
N7362	206	F.T.R. 14.10.40.
N7363	206	F.T.R. From Hamburg 20.5.40.
N7364	24/PDU/267/2 PRU	Used G-AGAR damaged in air raid Heraklion, 22.3.41 abandoned.
N7365	269	Undershot landing and hit ground, Ringway 17.5.40.
N7366	1 OTU/ATA	S.O.C. 30.11.45.
N7367	206	Swung on t.o. and u/c collapsed, caught fire, bombs exploded, Bircham Newton 1.9.40.

N7368	206	F.T.R. from ASR for Hampdens off Texel 4.7.40.
N7369	206/1 OTU/269/224	Overshot landing in bad vis. u/c collapsed, Aldergrove 16.3.41.
N7370		To R.C.A.F. direct as 771.
N7371		To R.C.A.F. direct as 772.
N7372	233	Overshot and u/c collapsed, Aldergrove 13.2.41 DBR.
N7373		To R.C.A.F. direct as 773.
N7374	233	Shot down by fighters while bombing Lister airfield, 3.11.40.
N7375		To R.C.A.F direct.
N7376	206/1 OTU/269/224/220/1 OTU	Engine cut on t.o.; hit gunpost, Silloth 7.1.42.
N7377	233	Shot down by Me 110 off Shetlands 9.7.40.
N7378	206/1 OTU	Short of fuel when lost; stalled attempting forced landing, hit trees Hamilton, Lanarkshire 16.7.40.
N7379	220/206/1 OTU/5 OTU	S.O.C. 17.12.43.
N7380 to N7391		R.C.A.F. direct as 774, 775, 777, 778, 781, 780, 782, 783–786.
N7392	206/1 OTU/269/224/1 OTU	Crashed Solway Firth 3m S of Silloth; presumed collided with AM699 25.3.42.
N7393	269/1 OTU/206/220/6 OTU	To 3468M 23.12.43.
N7394	1 OTU/ATA	S.O.C. 28.4.45.
N7395	269/1 OTU/206	Overshot, swung and u/c collapsed, bombs exploded, Bircham Newton 7.8.40.
N7396	206/320	Crashed low flying 3m W of Dunino, Fife 10.8.41.
N7397	1 OTU	S.O.C. 6.6.45.
N7398	1 OTU/ECFS	S.O.C. 26.9.44.
N7399	1 OTU/Benson/PRDU	Abandoned t.o. swung and u/c collapsed, Benson 23.6.44.
N7400	206	F.T.R. from Hamburg 18.5.40.
N7401	206	Control lost in circuit after t.o.; dived into ground Sunderland Farm, Docking, 14.8.40.
N7402	206	F.T.R. Recce off German coast 22.5.40.
N7403	206	Crashed on landing and blew up, Bircham Newton 25.4.40.
N7404	RAE/CGS	Swung on t.o. and u/c collapsed Sutton Bridge 9.12.42.
P5116	220/407/PRU/6 OTU/1 OTU	Overshot at Silloth 26.10.41.
P5117	233	Abandoned in bad weather Scremerston, Berwick 5.10.40.
P5118	1 OTU/269/1 OTU/5 OTU	S.O.C. 7.44.
P5119	1 OTU/269/6 OTU/1 OTU 5 OTU	S.O.C. 17.12.43.
P5120	206	Hit ridge on approach, bounced, stalled & u/c collapsed, Bircham Newton 20.6.40.
P5121	269/1 OTU/269/1 OTU/ ATA/Newmarket	S.O.C. 17.7.44.
P5122	224/6 OTU/ATA	S.O.C. 28.6.45.
P5123	233	Force landed Sligo, Eire 25.1.41; to Irish Air Corps 13.4.42 as No.91.
P5124	220	Out of fuel crashlanded on beach 1m N of Hayle, Cornwall 7.11.40; to 2429M.
P5125	1 OTU/269/PRU/1 FU	S.O.C. 9.7.44.
P5126	1 OTU/269/1 OTU/ATA	S.O.C. 7.7.44.
P5127	220	Swung after t.o. and dived into ground 1m from Thornaby, bombs exploded 11.6.40.
P5128	1 OTU/269	F.T.R. from patrol 8.2.41.
P5129	1 OTU/269	F.T.R. from patrol 28.9.40.
P5130	1 OTU/269	Lost 26.10.40.

P5131	1 OTU/269	Shot down by AA over Trondheim 11.6.40.
P5132	269	F.T.R. 24.10.40.
P5133	206	Stalled after steep turn, hit ground and blew up, Syderstone, Norfolk 5.8.40.
P5134	1 OTU	Stalled on approach Scorton 9.6.43.
P5135	220	Crashed in sea off Hartlepool Co. Durham 4.12.40.
P5136	224/233/1 OTU	Crashed on overshoot Kirkbride 31.1.42.
P5137	206/PRU/220/1 OTU/ 1444 Flt/1 OTU	S.O.C. 19.1.45.
P5138	1 OTU/6 OTU/1 OTU/ATA	S.O.C. 9.5.44.
P5139	FDU/220/1 OTU	S.O.C. 29.11.45.
P5140	206/1OTU/ATA 1 OTU/ATA	S.O.C. 14.5.45.
P5141	206/220/608/6 OTU 1 OTY	S.O.C. 9.4.45.
P5142	1 OTU	Turned after t.o. and dived into sea, Solway Firth 29.11.40.
P5143	206/1 OTU/ATA	S.O.C. 28.4.45.
P5144	1 OTU	Swung on landing and wrecked, Silloth 4.9.40.
P5145	AAEE & MAEE	Trials a/c; to 4555M 2.44.
P5146	220	F.T.R. 2.4.41.
P5147	269/1 OTU/269/ 1 AAS/1 OTU	F.T.R from '1000 bomber raid', Bremen 26.6.42.
P5148	269/1 OTU/206/1 OTU	Damaged while taxying, Thornaby 23.9.43.
P5149	320/1 OTU/Benson/ Melton Mowbray	S.O.C. 28.12.44.
P5150	220/ 1 OTU	S.O.C. 29.11.45.
P5151	220	Engine cut; lost height and ditched off Redcar, 16.1.41.
P5152	269/1 OTU/269	Collided with Hurricane P2863 on t.o. Wick 23.7.40.
P5153	269/1 OTU/206	Crashed on landing, bombs exploded, Bircham Newton 6.8.40.
P5154	1 OTU	S.O.C. 2.6.42.
P5155	1 OTU	Swung on landing, u/c collapsed, Silloth 2.8.41.
P5156	233/1 OTU	S.O.C. 1.12.44.
P5157	220	Destroyed in air raid, Thornaby 6.6.40.
P5158	220/6 OTU/5 OTU	To 4466M 1.44.
P5159	224/6 OTU/1 OTU	Crashed on landing Thornaby 31.5.43.
P5160	PDU/PRU/1 OTU	Engine cut; forcelanded on sandbank, Solway Firth 3.5.42.
P5161	269/224/1 OTU	Ditched off Jurby Head, Isle of Man 14.4.42.
P5162	206	F.T.R. from ASR search for Hampdens off Texel 4.7.40.
P5163	SAAF/267/CF	N.F.T.
P5164	SAAF/267	Engine cut; hit obstacle and crashed near Abbassia, Cairo 5.10.41.
P5165		Sunk in Pacific on delivery.
R4059	220	Swung on t.o. and u/c collapsed, Wick 5.7.41.
T9266	AAEE/1 OTU	S.O.C. 12.40.
T9267	1 OTU	Crashed on t.o., Silloth 17.3.41.

T9268	1 OTU	Stalled and dived into sea off Skinburness, Cumberland 28.7.41.
T9269	1 OTU/320/ATA	S.O.C. 28.4.45.
T9270	1 OTU/233/1 OTU	S.O.C. 17.12.43.
T9271	1 OTU/269/SFP/FTU/ 6 MU/12 MU/ATA	S.O.C. 14.5.45.
T9272	1 OTU/206	Heavy landing, Aldergrove 5.8.40 DBR.
T9273	1 OTU/224/233/1 OTU	Collided with AE646 and crashed in Solway Firth 20.8.42.
T9274	206/220/6 OTU	Ditched with engine fire 14m NE of Hartlepool, Co. Durham 6.5.42.
T9275	269/6 OTU/1 OTU	To 4822M 6.44.
T9276	206	Stalled on landing avoiding Hurricane, Bircham Newton 7.9.40.
T9277	224	F.T.R. 9.12.40.
T9278	224/233/6 OTU/ATA	S.O.C. 28.5.45.
T9279	1 OTU/320/6 OTU	F.T.R. From North Sea 31.5.42.
T9280	1 OTU	Crashed on landing, Worthy Down 23.8.40.
T9281	206/407/6 OTU	F.T.R. 29.10.41.
T9282	206	F.T.R. 3.8.40.
T9283	206/6 OTU/1 OTU	Overshot at Thornaby 23.6.43.
T9284	233/6 OTU/279/ATA	S.O.C. 28.5.45.
T9285	1 OTU/PRU/224/233 1 OTU/ ATA	S.O.C. 28.6.45.
T9286	320	Overshot at Penrhos 5.6.42.
T9287	206	Hit barn low flying near Langham 1.1.41.
T9288	206/1 OTU/5 OTU	S.O.C. 5.1.45.
T9289	206	F.T.R. 12.2.41.
T9290	PRU/PDU/220/6 OTU 1 OTU/ATA	S.O.C. 28.5.45.
T9291	269/224	S.O.C. 15.7.42.
T9292	1 OTU/269	Abandoned in fog off Brora 30.4.41.
T9293	1 OTU/269/1 OTU ATA/ECFS	S.O.C. 27.7.45.
T9294	1 OTU/269/6 OTU	U/c collapsed on landing, Thornaby 18.12.41.
T9295	1 OTU	Crashed on t.o., Silloth 10.3.42.
T9296	1 OTU	Dived into ground, Dalbeattie, Dumfries 11.2.41.
T9297	1 OTU	Crashed in forced landing 4m E of Annan, Dumfries 21.11.42.
T9298	206/1 OTU/6 OTU/ECFS	S.O.C. 27.7.45.
T9299	1 OTU/269	Stalled on overshoot and spun in, Wick 23.8.40.
T9300	206/220/1 OTU/ATA	S.O.C. 7.7.44.
T9301	220/1 OTU	Ditched off Grune Point 1.9.41.
T9302	206/1 OTU/Hendon/ECFS	Crashed on landing, Farnborough 16.3.44.
T9303	206	F.T.R. 16.10.40.
T9304	206	Crashed at Castle-on-Dinas 21.4.41.
T9305		Lost at sea en route to UK.
T9306		〃 〃
T9307		〃 〃
T9308	269/1 OTU	Hit house low flying near Carlisle 31.1.42.

T9309	RAE/Cunliffe-Owen 1 OTU/RAE	Swung on landing and u/c collapsed, Farnborough 5.5.44.
T9310	206/6 OTU	S.O.C. 29.11.45.
T9311	206/1 OTU	S.O.C. 29.11.45.
T9312	269/1 OTU/ECFS	S.O.C. 21.2.46.
T9313	233/1 OTU/5 OTU	To 4465M 1.44.
T9314	224/220/6 OTU 1 OTU/Benson	S.O.C. 3.1.45.
T9315	224	Crashed on landing, Leuchars 22.2.41.
T9316	1 OTU/320/1 OTU/ATA	S.O.C. 30.11.45.
T9317	1 OTU/220/407/6 OTU ATA	S.O.C. 28.3.45.
T9318	6 OTU	S.O.C. 30.11.45.
T9319	1 OTU	Crashed in forced landing Crosby 10.10.42.
T9320	1 OTU	Hit balloon cable on t.o. and crashed, Eastleigh.
T9321	1 OTU/ATA	S.O.C. 30.11.45.
T9322	1 OTU	Crashed on t.o. Silloth 13.1.43.
T9323	220	Shot down by ship's AA off Danish coast 6.10.40.
T9324	206	Crashed on beach N Sheppey in forced landing 17.5.41.
T9325	1 OTU	Crashed on t.o., Thornaby 29.3.43.
T9326	224	Crashed after t.o., Aldergrove 30.9.40.
T9327	223/1 OTU/RAE	S.O.C. 20.3.46.
T9328	224	Flew into Slievenanee Mountain, N Ireland 16.10.40.
T9329	1 OTU	Crashed on landing, Silloth 15.6.42.
T9330	220/6 OTU/1 OTU/ATA	S.O.C. 15.9.44.
T9331	206	F.T.R. 4.2.41.
T9332	206/1 OTU/ATA	S.O.C. 16.5.45.
T9333	269/6 OTU	F.T.R. 8.3.42.
T9334	269	Abandoned at sea 8.3.41.
T9335	269/1 OTU/5 OTU	S.O.C. 16.12.43.
T9336	320/ATA	S.O.C. 30.7.45.
T9337	269/224/269/1 OTU	Nosed over taxying, Thornaby 21.9.43 DBR.
T9338	224	Crashed on t.o. due to icing, Aldergrove 15.11.40.
T9339	320/FTU	S.O.C. 21.6.45.
T9340	RAE/AAEE/220 1 AAS/ATA	S.O.C. 14.5.45.
T9341	233/ 1 OTU	Crashed on landing, Silloth 19.7.41.
T9342	1 OTU	Crashed on t.o., Silloth 23.5.42.
T9343	233	F.T.R. 14.10.40.
T9344	224/1 OTU/ATA	S.O.C. 16.5.45.
T9345	224	Stalled on circuit, Leuchars 20.4.41.
T9346	206	Abandoned in fog 2m off Sarclet, Caithness 12.2.41.
T9347	269/6 OTU/ATA	S.O.C. 30.11.45.
T9348	206/407/6 OTU	Swung on t.o., Thornaby 24.8.41.
T9349	269/1 OTU/Benson	S.O.C. 3.1.45.

T9350	206	Abandoned in fog off Caithness 12.2.41.
T9351	224/233/6 OTU/ATA	S.O.C. 14.6.45.
T9352	RAE/AAEE/5 OTU	F.T.R. from training flt 30.10.43.
T9353	1 OTU	Dived out of cloud into Solway Firth 11.7.42.
T9354	220/1 OTU/ATA	S.O.C. 16.5.45.
T9355	220 6 OTU	Crashed after t.o., Thornaby 11.8.42.
T9356	233/320	Crashed on t.o., Carew Cheriton 8.3.41.
T9357	206	Hit hedge landing at Docking 10.10.40 DBR.
T9358	1 OTU/5 OTU	S.O.C. 14.6.45.
T9359	1 OTU/6 OTU/1 OTU/ATA	
T9360	269	Crashed on t.o., Wick 15.5.41.
T9361	1 OTU	Crashed on landing 3.5.41.
T9362	233/320/1 OTU/Hendon	S.O.C. 30.11.45.
T9363	1 OTU	To synthetic trainer 8.41. Became 3653M 8.43.
T9364	233/320	Crashed on t.o. into hangar, Carew Cheriton 25.2.41.
T9365	233	Crashed on t.o., Leuchars 4.12.40.
T9366	PRU/220	F.T.R. from shipping sweep 1.6.41.
T9367		Retained in Canada.
T9368	206/ 6OTU	Overshot landing and u/c collapsed, Thornaby 28.1.42.
T9369	220/1 OTU/ATA	S.O.C. 28.6.45.
T9370		Retained by R.C.A.F.
T9371	220	Flew into high ground during bad vis. Osmotherly, Lancs. 22.1.41.
T9372	233/6 OTU/1 OTU	Crashed on landing, Silloth 9.6.42.
T9373	220	S.O.C. 27.12.42.
T9374	269/1 OTU	Crashed on t.o., Silloth 9.6.42.
T9375	24	Crashed on t.o., Sydenham 10.1.42.
T9376	224/233/6 OTU	Crashed on landing, Thornaby 25.7.42.
T9377	233	Shot down by AA off Lister, Norway 31.10.40.
T9378	233/6 OTU	Undershot and hit tree, Thornaby 17.4 .42.
T9379	PRU/233	Dived into ground in circuit, Aldergrove 8.1.41.
T9380	233/320	F.T.R. 30.8.41.
T9381	RAE/233/320	S.O.C. 18.9.41.
T9382	206	Damaged by AA and abandoned off Birchington 10.11.40.
T9383	206/1 OTU	Collided with N7307 on landing, Silloth 24.2.42.
T9384	206/1 0TU	S.O.C. 29.11.45.
T9385		Believed retained in U.S.A.
T9386		Retained in Canada.
T9387	269/500/233/1 OADU 233/1404 Flt/ATA	S.O.C. 25.4.46.
T9388	269	Hit snowdrift on t.o. and u/c collapsed, Kaldadarnes 26.1.42.
T9389	269/ATA	S.O.C 14.6.45.
T9390	269/500	F.T.R. 13.3.42.
T9391	269	Ditched 66°35′N 24°40′W 30.4.42.
T9392	269/500/48/269	S.O.C. 28.3.46.

T9393	269	Crashed on t.o., Kaldadarnes 10.10.42.
T9394	279	S.O.C. 11.12.44.
T9395	6 OTU	Crashed on t.o., Thornaby 13.3.42.
T9396	320/Lee	S.O.C. 25.4.41.
T9397	203/459	Crashed in forced landing, L.G. 05 17.4.42.
T9398	279/269/233	Crashed in forced landing, Aoreora, French Morocco 30.3.43.
T9399	279	Crashed in sea 24.8.43.
T9400	279/48/233	Crashed on t.o., Aoreora, French Morocco 6.4.43.
T9401	279/139/1428 Flt/ATA	S.O.C. 25.2.46.
T9402	279	S.O.C. 23.8.42.
T9403	6 OTU/608/48/269/1407 Flt	S.O.C. 23.8.46.
T9404	6 OTU/521/ATA/519	S.O.C. 30.1.45.
T9405	279/269/161	F.T.R. 22.2.45.
T9406	6 OTU/ 279	S.O.C. 5.3.45.
T9407	6 OTU/279	Crashed on t.o., Bircham Newton 27.11.42.
T9408	279	Crashed in forced landing, Docking 24.12.43.
T9409	6 OTU	Stalled and crashed, Newham Hall, Nunthorpe, Yorks. 14.10.41.
T9410	6 OTU/269/Lee	S.O.C. 25.4.46.
T9411	6 OTU/279	S.O.C. 31.3.46.
T9412	459	S.O.C. 27.10.44.
T9413	320	F.T.R. 18.8.41.
T9414	279	Abandoned when lost 6m NW of Kinross 5.2.43.
T9415	279	S.O.C. 19.4.45.
T9416	224/269	Flew into hill in bad vis. 8m SW of Kaldadarnes 7.12.41.
T9417	224/53	Crashed on t.o., Manby 28.3.42.
T9418	Cunliffe-Owen/AAEE	Swung on t.o. and u/c collapsed, Boscombe Down 20.4.45.
T9419	224/269	S.O.C. 1.11.41.
T9420	224/269/ATA/1407 Flt/279	S.O.C. 25.4.46.
T9421	269	S.O.C. 28.3.46.
T9422	AAEE/279/500/233/59 269/ 1407 Flt	Ditched in Sanagerd Harbour, Iceland 20.3.44.
T9423	RAE	S.O.C. 30.5.46.
T9424	6 OTU/271/24/1 OADU/ME	S.O.C. 14.3.46.
T9425	224/269	S.O.C. 22.2.43.
T9426	224/269/ATA/48/15 FPP	Crashed on t.o., Gosport 15.3.44.
T9427	224/269	Crashed in forced landing 7m E of Eshvalfgard, Iceland 12.2.43.
T9428	320/48/269	S.O.C. 28.3.46.
T9429	6 OTU/24	Ditched on approach, Gibraltar 3.10.42.
T9430	233/ATA	S.O.C. 11.3.46.
T9431	220/206	Crashed on t.o., Aldergrove 8.4.42.
T9432	233	Flew into hill in bad vis., Ben Laoigh, Perthshire 15.4.41.
T9433	RAE/206/279/RAE	S.O.C. 28.6.45.
T9434	233/206/233/59	Crashed on t.o., North Coates 5.4.42.
T9435	320	F.T.R. 26.6.42.

T9436	269/ATA/161	S.O.C. 25.4.46.
T9437		Retained in Canada.
T9438	224/53/1401 Flt 521/1404 Flt	Engine cut, belly-landed, St Mary's, Scilly Isles 27.8.42.
T9439	139/1428 Flt/1444 Flt/161	Force-landed when lost, Göteborg, Sweden, 19.4.44.
T9440	320	S.O.C. 29.11.41.
T9441	220/269/ATA/279	S.O.C. 28.3.46.
T9442	233	Flew into hill 3m S of Geafch Goch, Glamorgan 20.8.44.
T9443	206/279	Crashed on t.o. Bircham Newton 28.2.43.
T9444	206/1401 Flt	S.O.C. 4.12.44.
T9445	220/269/233/161	F.T.R. 21.3.45.
T9446		Crashed before delivery.
T9447	233	Crashed in forced landing 1m SW of Coleraine, N Ireland 18.6.41.
T9448	220/269	Ditched 10m N of Skagi, Iceland 24.6.42.
T9449	OADF	Crashed on delivery flt 35m NE of Gander 21.2.41.
T9450		Crashed on delivery flight.
T9451	206/279/233/MCS	S.O.C. 25.4.46.
T9452	220/269	F.T.R. from convoy escort 11.7.41.
T9453	206/233/269/233/161	S.O.C. 25.4.46.
T9454	206/224/500/269	S.O.C. 30.5.46.
T9455	220/269/233/5 OTU	Ditched 52°21′N 04°56′W 25.7.44.
T9456	269	Undershot landing and u/c collapsed, Kaldadarnes 28.4.41. Cannibalised.
T9457	224/53/MCS	S.O.C. 25.6.46.
T9458	224/206/48/233	F.T.R. 9.11.42.
T9459	233/10ADU /233	Ditched 36°07′N 05°12′W 13.10.42.
T9460	224/53/1404 Flt	Crashed into cliffs, Port Quin, Cornwall 21.7.42.
T9461	224/53	To 3623M 6.42.
T9462	269	U/c collapsed on landing, Kaldadarnes 18.4.41.
T9463	206/48/1404 Flt/161	F.T.R. 27.11.44.
T9464	220/269	Crashed on t.o., Kaldadarnes 29.1.43.
T9465	269/161	S.O.C. 21.7.43.
V8975	6 OTU	Swung on t.o. and hit N7267 Thornaby 18.6.42.
V8976	269/279	S.O.C. 31.3.46.
V8977	269/ATA	S.O.C. 28.3.46.
V8978	269	S.O.C. 18.12.42.
V8979	279/RAE	S.O.C. 25.4.46.
V8980	6 OTU/1404 Flt	S.O.C. 31.3.46.
V8981	320	F.T.R. 8.5.42.
V8982	320/269/1407 Flt/279	S.O.C. 30.5.46.
V8983	320/Bircham Newton/24	Flew into hill in cloud, Bordon Wood, Wendover, Bucks 30.10.42.
V8984	459/1 OADU	Crashed on landing, Portreath 28.3.42.
V8985	6 OTU/48/Gosport/233	F.T.R. off Casablanca 8.11.42.
V8986	6 OTU/1404 Flt	F.T.R. from 30m SE of Scilly Isles 10.2.43.

V8987	269/279	Hit hill in cloud E of St Eval 8.9.42.
V8988	6 OTU/279/Bircham Newton/279/251	S.O.C. 9.1.46.
V8989	269/519	S.O.C. 25.4.46.
V8990	1 FTU/1 OADU/353	Crashed on landing, Dum Dum 13.7.42.
V8991	1 OADU/459	Crashed in forced landing, Romani, Iraq 28.3.42.
V8992	1 OADU/459/METS	S.O.C. 1.11.43.
V8993	279	F.T.R. from ASR search 13.2.42.
V8994	1 OADU/459	Crashed in circuit, Gambut 9.12.42.
V8995	FTU	Stalled at low altitude in circuit, Honeybourne 10.3.42.
V8996	279	Crashed in forced landing 3m W of Docking 13.4.42.
V8997	FTU/459	Crashed at L.G.40 1.6.42.
V8998	1 OADU/459	Crashed on landing L.G.208 6.9.42.
V8999	279/251	S.O.C. 4.1.46.
V9020	6 OTU	Crashed on landing, Thornaby 9.6.42.
V9021	6 OTU/521	S.O.C. 7.10.44.
V9022	1 OADU/459	D.B.R. 18.6.42.
V9023	6 OTU/48/Gosport/233 1 OADU/233	S.O.C. 1.5.44.
V9024	279	Crashed on landing, Stornoway 16.7.42.
V9025	1 OADU	Stalled on approach, Luqa 30.3.42.
V9026	1 OADU	Crashed in Western Desert 1.4.42.
V9027	OADU/459	Crashed in sea off Edku 10.7.42.
V9028	269	S.O.C. 25.6.46.
V9029	6 OTU/1404 Flt	S.O.C. 1.2.43.
V9030	1444 Flt/OADU/459	Crashed on landing L.G. 228 8.7.42.
V9031	279	F.T.R. from ASR mission 7.1.43.
V9032	6 OTU	Stalled after t.o., Thornaby 18.12.41.
V9033	320/279/269	S.O.C. 12.7.45.
V9034	6 OTU/1404 Flt/48/ 269/RAE	
V9035	1 OADU/459	U/c collapsed in dust storm L.G. 07 27.7.43.
V9036	320	F.T.R. 2.12.41.
V9037	FTU/OADU/ME	S.O.C. 18.10.45.
V9038	285	Crashed on t.o., Wrexham 16.2.42.
V9039	6 OTU/5 OTU	S.O.C. 31.3.46.
V9040	1 OADU	Crashed on t.o., Gibraltar 31.3.42.
V9041	320/521/1401 Flt	Crashed on t.o. 27.7.43.
V9042	279	Out of fuel, abandoned 4m N of Bodmin, Cornwall 22.1.43.
V9043		S.O.C. before delivery.
V9044	279	F.T.R. from ASR mission approx. 52°40′N 02°35′E.
V9045		S.O.C. before delivery.
V9046	279	Abandoned in bad weather near Swansea 21.1.43.
V9047	233/279/269/ATA	S.O.C. 28.4.46.

V9048		S.O.C. on arrival in UK 3.10.41.
V9049	OADU/India	S.O.C. 31.7.44.
V9050	6 OTU/Wick/269	S.O.C. 31.3.46.
V9051	269	S.O.C. 25.4.46.
V9052	1444 Flt/OADU/459	F.T.R. from patrol 24.7.42.
V9053	269/Wick	S.O.C. 28.3.46.
V9054	269	Ditched SW of Iceland 11.2.42.
V9055	269	Swung on t.o. and crashed, Kaldadarnes 5.8.41.
V9056	269	Swung on t.o. and crashed, Reykjavik 30.7.41.
V9057	269/279	S.O.C. 31.3.46.
V9058	320/269/279/520	S.O.C. 7.1.46.
V9059	1444 Flt	Crashed on t.o., Kemble 25.4.42.
V9060	1444 Flt/1 OADU/459	Crashed on t.o., Gambut 3 D.B.R. 3.5.43.
V9061		S.O.C. on delivery 5.43.
V9062	6 OTU/48/269	Crashed on landing, Höfn, Iceland 11.10.42.
V9063	320	F.T.R. from sweep off Norway 30.8.41.
V9064	269/519	Swung on landing at Wick and u/c strained BER 24.2.45.
V9065	320	F.T.R. from sweep off Norway 30.8.41.
V9066	220	F.T.R. from sweep 4.10.41.
V9067	1444 Flt/1 OADU/ 353/355	Crashed on t.o., Bishnupur 24.3.44.
V9068	53/224/48/1406 Flt/ 1402 Flt/Aldergrove/MCS	To Royal Netherlands A.F. 16.5.46.
V9069		Retained in Canada.
V9090	53/224/48/53/233	Crashed in sea 15m E of Gibraltar 30.11.43.
V9091	53/224	Overshot landing at St Eval 25.12.41.
V9092	53/224/233/519/521	S.O.C. 28.3.46.
V9093	1 OADU/200/CF Takoradi/276	Crashed on landing, Abbassia 2.6.42.
V9094	500/233/1 OADU/233	U/c collapsed on landing, Gibraltar 29.3.43.
V9095	407/Thorney Is./Bircham N.	Ditched with AA damage off Oran 9.11.42.
V9096	500/53/269/1407 Flt	S.O.C. 31.3.46.
V9097	500	Flew into ground near North Walsham 16.1.42.
V9098	59/1428 Flt	Failed to t.o. due to icing, Dulton 28.1.42.
V9099	59/233/1 OADU/233	S.O.C. 29.2.44.
V9100		Not delivered.
V9101	1 OADU/459/75 OTU/ Gianaclis	S.O.C. 1.2.44.
V9102	407/Thorney Is./Bircham N. 1401 Flt	Crashed on landing, Bircham Newton 4.6.42.
V9103		Not delivered.
V9104	48	Stalled on approach, Odiham 26.9.41.
V9105	220/48/53	Crashed at Rio Claro, Trinidad 28.9.42.
V9106	407/1444 Flt/1 OADU/ 217/353	Stalled and crashed, Mauripur 18.7.44.
V9107	407/1401 Flt/407/279	Crashed on t.o., Leuchars 11.2.43.

V9108	608/48/53	S.O.C. 7.6.43.
V9109	500.	
V9110	608	Crashed in forced landing 1m N of Skitton 10.2.42.
V9111	48/1404 Flt	Flew into ground in bad vis., St Eval 4.7.42.
V9112	1527 Flt	Crashed in forced landing, Ballycastle, N. Ireland 12.4.42.
V9113	48/608/279/500/269	Crashed on t.o., Kaldadarnes 20.11.42.
V9114	1527 Flt/139/62/353	Crashed on landing, Cuttack 24.10.42.
V9115	24	Crashed in sea off Corunna, Spain 16.12.41.
V9116	59	Crashed on t.o., Thorney island 14.10.41.
V9117	1 OADU	Crashed on t.o. L.G. 224 31.1.42.
V9118	1527 Flt/1444 Flt/FTU/ 1527 Flt/6 OTU/407/48/ 269/279/519	S.O.C. 28.3.46.
V9119	200/Med ME CS	S.O.C. 22.11.45.
V9120	1 OADU/FE	Lost at Singapore 18.1.42.
V9121	1 OADU/FE	Lost at Singapore 18.1.42.
V9122	320	Lost 30.5.42.
V9123	1527 Flt/1428 Flt/1527 Flt 6 OTU/407/48/1404 Flt/517	S.O.C. 28.3.46.
V9124	139/1444 Flt/62	Crashed in forced landing near Agartala 17.4.43.
V9125		Crashed on ferry flt in icing conditions off Newfoundland 9.1.42.
V9126	1 OADU	Flew into high ground, Siggewi, Malta 18.1.42.
V9127	FTU	Crashed into hill in bad vis., Brayspool, Cardigan 10.2.42.
V9128	608/233/608/233	F.T.R. 15. 3.42.
V9129	233/53/233/1 OADU/233	Swung on landing and u/c collapsed Lagens 15.2.44.
V9150	48/1407 Flt/Thornaby/ 1407 Flt/ 519	S.O.C. 28.2.46.
V9151	267/1428 Flt/Gosport	S.O.C. 28.3.46.
V9152		Became G-AGDK on arrival.
V9153	1 OADU/FE	Lost at Singapore 18.1.42.
V9154	1405 Flt/6 OTU/1407 Flt	Crashed on t.o., Reykjavik 16.12.42.
V9155	286/289/233/1404 Flt/161	F.T.R. 1.6.44.
V9156	1405 Flt/1402 Flt	F.T.R. 16.9.42.
V9157	200	Crashed on t.o., Robertsfield, Liberia 16.12.42.
V9158	289/279/269/279/269	S.O.C. 8.8.45.
V9159	1405 Flt/1402 Flt	Swung on t.o., Aldergrove 13.4.42.
V9160	287/269	F.T.R. 1.9.42.
V9161	1405 Flt/1403 Flt/500/ 269/279	Overshot on landing, Bircham Newton 23.8.44.
V9162	139/62/CF Lydda/CF Aden	Caught fire after t.o., Beihan, Saudi Arabia 30.6.45.
V9163	608/233/59	F.T.R. 11.5.42.
V9164	287/1404 Flt/1 OADU/ ALS India	Abandoned when lost near Jessore 22.3.43.
V9165	1403 Flt/6 OTU/30MU	Crashed on t.o., Sealand 3.1.42.
V9166	301 FTU/1 OADU/200	Crashed on landing, Hastings, Sierra Leone 1.8.42.

V9167	BOAC/1444 Flt/200	
V9168	287/233	S.O.C. 1.5.44.
V9169	59/233/161	Crashed on overshoot, Evere 18.5.41.
V9170	289/500/269	Crashed on t.o., Kaldadarnes 4.9.42.
V9171		Retained in Canada.
V9172	1444 Flt/459	F.T.R. 18.8.42.
V9173	1403 Flt/6 OTU/1407 Flt/ Thornaby/1407 Flt	S.O.C. 30.5.46.
V9174	1404 Flt	Caught fire while refuelling, St Eval 10.7.42.
V9175	139/1 OADU	Crashed on landing, Luqa 11.4.42.
V9176	287/1444 Flt/233	
V9177	59/24/MCS/RAE	S.O.C. 18.6.48.
V9178	1 OADU/62	S.O.C. 1.1.45.
V9179	1 OADU/200/Med ME CS	Crashed in forced landing, Ile de Mourmoutier, France 24.1.45.
V9180	1 OADU	Lost at Singapore 1.42.
V9181		Lost on delivery flight.
V9182		Lost on delivery flight.
V9183	1444 Flt/1 OADU/FE	S.O.C. 28.9.44.
V9184		Lost on delivery flight.
V9185	1404 Flt/1403 Flt/1401 Flt 1406 Flt/269/1407 Flt/269 1407 Flt/251	S.O.C. 25.4.46.
V9186	1444 Flt/62	Crashed on landing, New Delhi 12.6.42.
V9187	1 OADU/459	Crashed near Gianaclis 1.7.42.
V9188	1444 Flt/62	S.O.C. 28.9.44.
V9189	139/12	S.O.C. 30.11.44.
V9190	139/62	Flew into sea and D.B.R. 16.7.42.
V9191	139/1444 Flt/1 OADU/459	Crashed on landing, Abu Sueir 2.7.42.
V9192	139/62	Abandoned when lost 15m N of Cox's Bazar 17.3.43.
V9193	285/1444 Flt/1 OADU/62	S.O.C. 28.12.44.
V9194	1444 Flt/62	Crashed on landing, Dhubalia 20.1.43.
V9195	407/519	Ditched off Shetlands 60°47′N 01°31′W 10.10.44.
V9196	1404 Flt	F.T.R. 18.12.42.
V9197	53/ 16 FU	Crashed on t.o., Kirkbride 31.5.43.
V9198	1 OADU/62/353	Crashed on landing, Asansol 20.9.42.
V9199	1 OADU/ ALS India	Crashed on firing range, Peshawar 19.4.43.
V9220	1444 Flt/200/MCCF /Med ME CS	Crashed on t.o., Bari 9.9.45.
V9221	1 OADU/India	
V9222	287/233/1403 Flt/520/AAEE	S.O.C. 28.3.46.
V9223		Retained in Canada.
V9224	1 OADU	S.O.C. 26.1.42.
V9225	139/62	S.O.C. 9.8.42.
V9226	233	S.O.C. 17.1.46.
V9227	200/267	Crashed on landing, Luqa 21.5.42.

V9228	AFE/AFEE	Crashed on t.o., Sherburn-in-Elmet 11.8.43.
V9229	1 OADU/200/CF/ Takoradi/ME	S.O.C. 12.7.45.
V9230	139/1428 Flt/6 OTU/24	Crashed on t.o., Luqa 2.9.42.
V9231	139	Crashed on t.o., Oulton 18.12.41.
V9232	289/53	Crashed on landing, Guantanamo, Cuba 4.8.42.
V9233	1 OADU	Lost at Singapore 1.42.
V9234	1 OADU	Hit obstruction on landing L.G.224 3.3.42.
V9235 to V9246		To R.N.Z.A.F. 21.8.41.
V9247 to V9252		To R.N.Z.A.F. 30.8.41.
V9253	288/53	S.O.C. 7.6.42.
V9254	1444 Flt/139	Crashed on t.o., Chittagong 23.4.42.
AE485	FE	Lost at Singapore 1.42.
AE486	62	S.O.C. 21.6.45.
AE487	3 FPP	Iced up and crashed in forced landing 3/4 ml NE of Speke 7.2.42.
AE488	FE	Lost in Malaya 1.42.
AE489	8 FPP	Flew into ground in fog 4m N of Stewarton, Ayrshire 26.12.41.
AE490		To R.N.Z.A.F. as NZ2025.
AE491	1 OADU	Ditched on ferry flight from Gibraltar to Malta 16.1.42.
AE492	FTU/200	S.O.C. 25.1.45.
AE493	India	
AE494 to AE504		To R.N.Z.A.F. as NZ2026 to NZ2036.
AE505	288/289/1405 Flt/233/161	F.T.R. 21.2.45.
AE506	1 OADU	Lost on ferry to Malta 1.42.
AE507		F.T.R. 16.2.42.
AE508	62	S.O.C. 18.12.44.
AE509	286/53/51	S.O.C. 21.12.44.
AE510	1 FTU/459	Crashed on night landing L.G.226 26.7.42.
AE511		Lost in Malaya 1.42.
AE512	62	S.O.C. 10.42.
AE513	139/1328 Flt/1444 Flt/ 301 FTU/279	Stalled at low alt. and crashed in sea 20m E of Great Yarmouth 19.8.44.
AE514	62/353	Crashed in forced landing Shortt's Island 1.8.42.
AE515	139/1428 Flt	Crashed on night training flt 3.6.42.
AE516	139/1444 Flt	Crashed in forced landing, Lakeham, Norfolk 9.2.42.
AE517	59/139	Swung off runway, Allahabad 15.1.42.
AE518	139/62/357	
AE519	139/1428 Flt/279	Crashed in sea off St Ives, Cornwall 29.3.43.
AE520		Not delivered.
AE521	FE	Lost in Malaya 1.42.
AE522	233	D.B.R. 7.12.43.

AE523	287/289/62	Shot down by Ki 43 Akyab 9.9.42.
AE524	1444 Flt	Crashed on t.o. Luqa 9.4.42.
AE525	320	F.T.R. from attack on convoy off Terschelling 16.5.42.
AE526	286/ATA	S.O.C. 28.3.46.
AE527		Not delivered.
AE528		Not delivered.
AE529	FE	Lost in Malaya 1.42.
AE530	FE	Lost in Malaya 1.42.
AE531	139/1428 Flt/1406 Flt/279	F.T.R. From nav. exercise 13.11.43.
AE532	286/217	Spun into ground on approach Minneriya 29.1.43.
AE533	24	Hit by bomb, Luqa 29.6.42.
AE534	139/1428 Flt/1408 Flt/ 279/519	S.O.C. 25.4.46.
AE535	285/233/1 OADU/233	S.O.C. 10.10.43.
AE536		To 2917M 1.42.
AE537	286/ATA/161	S.O.C. 25.4.46.
AE538	288/1444 Flt/FE	D.B.R. 6.5.42.
AE539	FE	Lost 30.6.42.
AE540	139/62	Flew into high ground near Jitpur 29.3.43.
AE541	285/139/62	S.O.C. 28.9.44.
AE542		No record.
AE543		" "
AE544	1444 Flt/353	S.O.C. 1.1.45.
AE545		Missing between Gander and UK 21.9.41.
AE546	288/289/1444 Flt/FE	Crashed 14.6.42.
AE547	285/1 OADU/200	S.O.C. 1.5.43.
AE548	286/24	Dived into sea off Gibraltar 20.5.42.
AE549	1444 Flt	D.B.R. 25.4.42.
AE550	OAPU	Crashed 11.3.42.
AE551	FE	Lost in Malaya 1.42.
AE552	20	Crashed in forced landing 2m E of Port Bouet, Senegal 18.5.42.
AE553	FE	Lost in Malaya 1.42.
AE554	139/ME	S.O.C. 14.11.42.
AE555	FTU/1 OADU/217	S.O.C. 28.9.44.
AE556	139/FE	S.O.C. 9.8.42.
AE557	287/1444 Flt/200/62/353	S.O.C. 28.9.44.
AE558	139/1428 Flt	Crashed near Biggleswade, Beds. 1.4.42.
AE559	287/279/161	S.O.C. 28.3.46.
AE560	1 OADU/53	S.O.C. 18.8.42.
AE561		To R.C.A.F. direct.
AE562	1444 Flt/62	
AE563	48/233	F.T.R. off Casablanca; presumed shot down by USN 9.11.42.
AE564	139/1428 Flt/279	S.O.C. 24.4.46.
AE565	139/1428 Flt/200	Crashed 6.4.42.

AE566	1444 Flt/1 OADU/FE	S.O.C. 8.1.45.
AE567		Not delivered.
AE568	1402 Flt/200/500	S.O.C. 25.1.45.
AE569	285/62/353	S.O.C. 26.10.44.
AE570		Not delivered.
AE571		Not delivered.
AE572		Not delivered.
AE573	Cunliffe-Owen	D.B.R. 29.1.42.
AE574	62	F.T.R. 7.5.42.
AE575	FTU/200	Crashed 16.9.42.
AE576	285/48/269/519	Damaged 21.12.44. & S.O.C.
AE577		Flew into mountain, Dundalk, Eire, on delivery flt 27.9.41.
AE578	FTU/24	Out of fuel, force landed Cintra, Portugal 9.12.42. Interned.
AE579	24	Crashed on t.o., La Senia 17.7.43.
AE580	286/289/62	Ditched 8m NE of Puri 8.1.43.
AE581	BOAC/24/1 OADU/24	G-AGDU with BOAC; Swung on landing, Castel Benito 1.4.43. With 24; D.B.R.
AE582	1 OADU	Crashed on landing, Luqa 21.2.42.
AE583	FE	
AE584		Not delivered.
AE585	288/1406 Flt/279	Engine caught fire, crashed in forced landing Norfolk 6.5.44.
AE586	287/289/1428 Flt/ 1402 Flt/ATA/RAE	S.O.C. 3.9.47.
AE587	1 OADU/53	S.O.C. 2.4.43.
AE588	TU/24/MCS	S.O.C. 19.2.45.
AE589	OADU	F.T.R. 11.4.42.
AE590		Not delivered.
AE591	288/233/1 OADU/233	F.T.R. From patrol 1.11.42.
AE592	1 OADU/FE	Lost in Malaya 1.42.
AE593	139/1444 Flt/62	S.O.C. 24.12.44.
AE594	286/1428 Flt/279	Crashed 4.11.42.
AE595 to AE600		Not delivered.
AE601	139/62	S.O.C. 9.8.42.
AE602	OADU	D.B.R. 26.1.42.
AE603	OADU	Crashed in sea near Villa Corrente Is. 17.2.42.
AE604	FE	Lost in Malaya 1.42.
AE605	287/1444 Flt/200	S.O.C. 26.9.46.
AE606	288/233	Crashed into sea after t.o., Gibraltar 22.9.42.
AE607	FE	Lost in Malaya 1.42.
AE608		Not delivered.
AE609	206	F.T.R. From patrol 1.7.41.
AE610	AAEE/RAE/TFU/CCDU	S.O.C. 28.6.45.
AE611	206	Dived into ground after night t.o., Aldergrove 20.3.41.
AE612	206	F.T.R. from ASR search 13.6.41.

AE613	206	Ditched on A/S patrol 8.7.41.
AE614	206	F.T.R. From ASR search 12.6.41.
AE615	206/200	S.O.C. 18.10.45.
AE616		Lost at sea en route to UK.
AE617	206/ 2 SAN	S.O.C. 29.11.45.
AE618	200/2 SAN	Crashed 28.4.42.
AE619	206/200	S.O.C. 28.3.46.
AE620	206/200/CvIII/St Eval	S.O.C. 25.4.46.
AE621		Lost at sea en route to UK.
AE622	206/200	Ditched on patrol off Gambia 10.10.41.
AE623	206/200	S.O.C. 26.7.46.
AE624	206/200/CF Iraq/CF Lydda	S.O.C. 31.5.45.
AE625	206/200	Crashed on t.o., Gibraltar 10.9.41.
AE626	206/200/MECF/CF Iraq	
AE627	6 OTU	Crashed 5.9.42.
AE628	206/200/ATA/Heston	To Admiralty 7.1.45.
AE629	206/200	S.O.C. 15.4.42.
AE630	206/200	Swung on t.o. and hit Blenheim, Takoradi 23.1.42.
AE631	206	S.O.C. 10.11.42.
AE632	206/1404 Flt/1 OTU	S.O.C. 29.11.45.
AE633	206/200/608/CF Iraq	S.O.C. 9.8.45.
AE634	206/24/6OTU/301 FTU/ 1 OADU/200	S.O.C. 26.7.45.
AE635	PTS/29MU/Heston/ Admiralty Flt	S.O.C. 30.5.46.
AE636	PTS/24/6OTU/301 FTU/ 1 OADU/200	S.O.C. 1.10.44.
AE637	200/CF Takoradi	D.B.R. 14.5.44.
AE638	200/ CF Takoradi	S.O.C. 2.8.45.
AE639	53/224/53/301 FTU/ 1 OADU/608	S.O.C. 12.7.45.
AE640	OADF	Flew into high ground in bad vis., Mull of Kintyre, Argyll 25.7.41.
AE641	233/608	Hit tree and crashed near Cheraga, Algeria 16.5.43.
AE642	608	S.O.C. 25.1.45.
AE643	53/224/53/301 FTU/ 1444 Flt/1 OADU/608	S.O.C. 25.1.45.
AE644	608	S.O.C. 21.6.45.
AE645	48	F.T.R. from patrol 11.4.42.
AE646	1 OTU	Crashed 20.8.42.
AE647	500	Crashed on Brancaster Beach, Norfolk 17.2.42.
AE648	48/220/206/1 OTU/ 301 FTU/1 OADU/ME	S.O.C. 25.1.45.
AE649	407	F.T.R. from Dutch coast sortie 31.1.42.
AE650	AAEE/233/53	S.O.C. 18.8.47.
AE651	224/407/301/FTU/ 1 OADU/162 MU	Swung on landing and u/c collapsed, Setif 2.12.43.

AE652	48	F.T.R. from shipping strike, Bergen 7.1.42.
AE653	608/1 OTU/5 OTU	Dived into Strangford Lough, Co. Antrim, during gunnery practice 18.11.43.
AE654	48	F.T.R. 9.2.42.
AE655	407	F.T.R. from shipping strike off Terschelling 5.11.41.
AE656	53	F.T.R. from shipping sortie off Brittany 12.12.41.
AE657		Crashed on approach to Moncton on ferry flight 3.8.41.

AM520	53/1 OTU	
AM521	224/53	Crashed 16.5.42.
AM522	224/53/48/407/1 OADU/ 1 OTU/5 OTU	Engine cut on t.o.; ditched off Turnberry, 22.8.44.
AM523	6 OTU/608	F.T.R. from attack on Thisted seaplane base 20.10.41.
AM524	407/59/500	Out of fuel; ditched 1.7.43.
AM525	224/48/407	F.T.R. from shipping strike off Dutch coast 16.5.42.
AM526	AAEE/CCDU/2 FIS/RAE	S.O.C. 23.2.49.
AM527	224/53/59/407/301 FTU/ 500/608	S.O.C. 25.1.45.
AM528	224/301 FTU/1 OADU	Swung on t.o., Portreath 5.2.43.
AM529	224/608/408/5 OTU	S.O.C. 28.3.46.
AM530	224/53	Shot down by AA from convoy 4.5.42.
AM531	224/1428 Flt/1406 Flt/ 224/6 OTU	Crashed 4.11.42. D.B.R.
AM532	224/53/6OTU/301 FTU/500	Dived into ground 3m W of Tafaraouri 2.8.43.
AM533	220	F.T.R. From anti-shipping sortie 19.7.41.
AM534	1 OTU	Spun into Solway Firth 14.11.41.
AM535	407/233	Crashed 1m N of St Merryn, Cornwall 8.3.42.
AM536	233	Ditched off Gibraltar 19.4.42.
AM537	224/53/407/233/407/ 1 OTU/27th TG USAAF	S.O.C. 29.11.44.
AM538	224/48/220/407/ 27th TG USAAF	S.O.C. 29.11.44.
AM539	224	Swung on t.o.; u/c collapsed, Limavady 16.9.41.
AM540	224/53	Damaged by Me 110 and crashlanded at Langham, Norfolk 8.5.42.
AM541	233	Stalled while circling destroyer and crashed into sea 70m SW of Tory Is. 27.7.41.
AM542	224/53	F.T.R. from sortie 22.4.42.
AM543	233	Swung on t.o. and u/c collapsed Gibraltar 19.12.41.
AM544	407	Undershot at night, Donna Nook 12.8.41.
AM545	233	Swung on t.o. and u/c collapsed, Gibraltar 19.12.41.
AM546	233/48	Damaged by Fw 190s off Norway 14.7.42. S.O.C.
AM547		Not delivered.
AM548	233	F.T.R. from sortie 14.9.41.
AM549	224/53	F.T.R. from sortie 8.4.42.
AM550	224/608	To USAAF 29.1.44.
AM551	407/233/407	F.T.R. from shipping strike off Dutch coast 21.1.43.
AM552	608/407/500/301 FTU/608	S.O.C. 12.2.43.

AM553	233/608/407/1 OTU/CNS	D.B.R. 12.9.45.
AM554	59/407/320/279	Crashed on t.o., Bircham Newton 26.3.44.
AM555	233/500/301 FTU/ 1 OADU/500	S.O.C. 25.1.45.
AM556	407	F.T.R. from shipping strike off Borkum 5.12.41.
AM557	220/1 OTU/5 OTU	S.O.C. 25.4.46.
AM558	233/59/407	Swung on t.o., Docking 12.3.43.
AM559	233/407/301 FTU/ OADU/608/500	S.O.C. 2.8.45.
AM560	224/53	F.T.R. from sortie 11.4.42.
AM561	608/1 OTU	S.O.C. 28.3.44.
AM562	407/1OTU/5 OTU	Spiralled into sea 2m off Maidens, Ayrshire 21.1.45.
AM563	224/53	F.T.R. From anti-shipping sortie 24.2.42.
AM564	233/59/407/301 FTU/ OADU/500	Crashed in sea during thunderstorm off Cape Tenes, Algeria 26.4.43.
AM565	224/53	Shot down by AA when attacking convoy 4.5.42.
AM566	206/407/27thTG USAAF	S.O.C. 29.11.44.
AM567	233/48/407	Crashed after rudder jammed by broken aerial North Coates 17.2.42.
AM568	224/53/59/500	
AM569	233	Lost power and ditched off Gibraltar 28.12.41.
AM570	206/224/53/320	To U.S.A.A.F. 23.1.44.
AM571	608/407	F.T.R. from Dutch coast 29.4.42.
AM572	233/1OTU/301 FTU/ 1 OADU/608	Crashed on approach in bad weather, Blida 6.3.43.
AM573	233	Hit balloon cable; crashed in Falmouth Harbour 31.10.41.
AM574	6 OTU/48/6 OTU/1 OTU	To U.S.A.A.F. 6.2.44.
AM575	233	Ditched off Tarifa, Spanish Morocco, 5.5.42.
AM576		To R.C.A.F. 20.7.42.
AM577		Crashed on delivery flight.
AM578	233/CCDU	To U.S.A.A.F. 27.7.44.
AM579	220/48	To U.S.A.A.F. 4.2.44.
AM580	269/59/27thTG USAAF	To 5779M 1.46.
AM581	233/206/ATA/CNS	Crashed 30.5.44.
AM582	233/407/301 FTU/ 1 OADU/Med ME CS	S.O.C. 6.12.45.
AM583	269/220	F.T.R. from anti-shipping sortie 6.8.41.
AM584	220/53	Crashed on landing, Donna Nook 25.3.42.
AM585	1 OTU	S.O.C. 28.3.46.
AM586	407	F.T.R. from anti-shipping sortie 10.10.41.
AM587	407/206/500	Crashed 18.9.42.
AM588	206	Flew into hill at night 4m NE of Ladyhill, Co. Antrim 16.8.41.
AM589 to AM594		Diverted to R.N.Z.A.F.
AM595	1 OTU/301 FTU/OADU/500	S.O.C. 25.1.45.
AM596	1 OTU/5 OTU/7FIS	S.O.C. 1.8.45.
AM597	407/1444 Flt/1 OADU/500/459	Crashed 16.2.45.

AM598	407	F.T.R. from attack on *Scharnhorst* and *Gneisenau* off Belgian coast 12.2.42.
AM599	608	F.T.R. from sortie off Norway 2.9.41.
AM600	1 OTU	Overshot landing at Thornaby 30.5.43.
AM601	608	Overshot night landing at Thornaby 7.9.41.
AM602	407	Stalled on overshoot, North Coates 22.1.42.
AM603	206/233/53/500/608	S.O.C. 25.1.45.
AM604	206	Hit trees low flying near Aldergrove 1.2.42.
AM605	206/500	Ditched on shipping sortie 20.8.42.
AM606	206	F.T.R. from sortie 26.6.42.
AM607	1 OTU/24/RAE	Engines cut; dived into ground near Tackley, Oxon. 27.4.45.
AM608	1 OTU	Crashed 22.9.42.
AM609		D.B.R. during shipment S.O.C. 7.5.41.
AM610	608/407/301 FTU/ 1 OADU/500	
AM611		Lost at sea en route.
AM612	233/206/233	F.T.R. from attack on convoy 17.2.42.
AM613	220/206	U/c collapsed on t.o., Aldergrove 1.2.42.
AM614	407/233	F.T.R. 15.5.42.
AM615	220	Hit tree during dummy attack and crashed, Nutts Corner 1.2.42.
AM616	220	Crashed on landing Stornoway 7.8.41.
AM617	407	F.T.R. from Dutch coast 8.2.42.
AM618	220	F.T.R. From shipping sortie 31.1.41.
AM619	407/6 OTU/48/6 OTU	Crashed 1.10.42.
AM620	608	F.T.R. 22.5.42.
AM621	608/407/27thTG US	S.O.C. 25.4.46.
AM622	206	Crashed on t.o., Aldergrove 14.2.42.
AM623	220/224/53/59/500	Flew into hill near Couragra, Algeria 7.1.43.
AM624	1 OTU	Flew into hill near Egremont, Cumberland 21.12.41.
AM625	220	F.T.R. 4.8.41.
AM626	407/24/301 FTU/OADU 500/MAC CU	S.O.C. 26.4.45.
AM627	407	To U.S.A.A.F 10.1.44.
AM628	1 OTU	Crashed 26.7.42.
AM629	1 OTU/608/500/MAC CU	S.O.C. 26.4.45.
AM630	608/407	To U.S.A.A.F 18.1.44.
AM631	53/224/407/301 FTU/ 608/ 4 PTS	S.O.C. 27.6.46.
AM632	59	F.T.R. from training flight 17.5.42.
AM633	220/6 OTU	To U.S.A.A.F. 23.1.44.
AM634	1 OTU/233/206	Ditched on patrol 11.12.41.
AM635	206/407/AFDU/5 OTU	S.O.C. 13.6.45.
AM636	220	F.T.R. from anti-shipping sortie 13.10.41.
AM637	6 OTU	S.O.C. 30.5.46.
AM638	608/407/AFDU/5 OTU	F.T.R. from sortie 13.1.42.
AM639	59	F.T.R. 28.4.42.

AM640	500	F.T.R. 8.10.42.
AM641	220/224/53/59/48/59/ 6 OTU/407/320/407/279	To U.S.A.A.F 4.2.44.
AM642	608	F.T.R. from shipping strike off Frisians 5.11.41.
AM643	224/59/500/301 FTU/500	Crashed on landing, Tafaraouri 19.7.43.
AM644	608	Crashed 9.8.43.
AM645		S.O.C. for spares 1.6.42.
AM646	407	Crashed in sea off Newquay, Cornwall 3.11.42.
AM647	220/500/220/53/608/500	S.O.C. 25.1.45.
AM648	53/224/48/206/224/48/407	Flew into hill near Carew Cheriton 3.11.42.
AM649	59/407/5 OTU	To U.S.A.A.F 3.1.44.
AM650	206/407	F.T.R. from Dutch coast 29.5.42.
AM651	53	Ditched in flames off Falmouth Bay 27.10.41. (F/Lt Bunce).
AM652		Lost at sea en route.
AM653	1OTU/608/1 OTU/5 OTU	To U.S.A.A.F. 24.1.44.
AM654	1 OTU	To U.S.A.A.F. 20.1.44.
AM655	48/1 OTU	D.B.R. 8.8.42.
AM656		Lost at sea en route.
AM657	608	F.T.R. from shipping strike off Frisians 5.11.41.
AM658	59/608/500	F.T.R. 6.12.42.
AM659	500	F.T.R. from anti-shipping sortie 6.12.42.
AM660	500	Crashed on t.o., Portreath 6.11.42.
AM661	1 OTU	Crashed 15.6.42.
AM662		Lost at sea en route to UK.
AM663	59/500	Crashed on Brancaster Beach after t.o. from Bircham Newton 17.2.42.
AM664	206	Stalled at low altitude on approach, Aldergrove 24.9.41.
AM665	1 OTU	To U.S.A.A.F. 20.1.44.
AM666	53/59/48/59/6 OTU/ 1 OTU/5 OTU/RAE	S.O.C. 31.5.47.
AM667	48	To U.S.A.A.F. 10.1.44.
AM668	1 OTU	To U.S.A.A.F. 11.1.44.
AM669	53	F.T.R. 26.12.41.
AM670	220	Crashed in forced landing in snowstorm, Larne, Co. Antrim 4.1.42.
AM671	1 OTU/RAE	D.B.R. 20.7.45.
AM672	53	Shot down by AA when attacking convoy 10.8.41.
AM673	608/48/6 OTU/301 FTU/500	Swung on t.o., Blida 18.1.43.
AM674	500	To U.S.A.A.F. 3.1.44.
AM675	1 OTU	D.B.R. 15.2.42.
AM676	1 OTU	Crashed 25.8.42.
AM677	53/224/500	Crashed at Docking 8.2.42.
AM678	220	F.T.R. from sortie off Norway 23.12.41.
AM679	608/407	F.T.R. from shipping strike off Dutch coast 15.5.42.
AM680	1 OTU	S.O.C. 10.11.42.
AM681	53/224/1 OTU/279/5 OTU	S.O.C. 25.3.46.

AM682		Lost at sea en route to UK.
AM683	53/224/53	F.T.R. from sortie 8.5.42.
AM684	407/233/407	F.T.R. from sortie 5.4.42.
AM685	608	D.B.R. 29.8.42.
AM686	53/224/53/48/407/ 320/279/ATA	S.O.C. 26.8.45.
AM687	1 OTU	F.T.R. believed ditched in Irish Sea 5.2.42.
AM688	608/6 OTU/1 OTU	To U.S.A.A.F. 28.1.44.
AM689	206/500	Shot down by U boat 27.12.42.
AM690	206	D.B.R. 31.1.42.
AM691		Lost at sea en route to UK.
AM692	53/224	F.T.R. 6.2.42.
AM693		Lost at sea en route to UK.
AM694	53/224/53/59407/5 OTU	Flew into ground Loushamore, Co. Antrim 29.1.43.
AM695	53/224/53/407	F.T.R. from anti-shipping sortie off Dutch coast 23.12.42.
AM696	48/407/233	F.T.R. 10.4.42.
AM697	59/500	Ditched on patrol 22.8.42.
AM698	53/224	F.T.R. 8.1.42.
AM699	1 OTU	S.O.C. 29.3.42.
AM700	53/224/53/224/608/ 6 OTU/279/5 OTU	S.O.C. 5.3.45.
AM701	233/407	F.T.R. from shipping strike off Dunkirk 7.9.42.
AM702	53/224/279/6 OTU/407/ 1 OTU/5 OTU/ATA	S.O.C. 25.4.46.
AM703	233	Engine cut on t.o., Gibraltar 18.2.42.
AM704	59	F.T.R. 3.10.41.
AM705	233	D.B.R. 17.2.42.
AM706	206	Crashed on overshoot, Aldergrove 5.2.42.
AM707	SFP/ATA	To U.S.A.A.F 4.2.44.
AM708	1 OTU/48	Crashed on anti-sub sweep 23.4.42.
AM709	1 OTU	Crashed 12.3.42.
AM710	6 OTU/233/6 OTU/48/608	Crashed in sea after engine fire off Sicily 14.9.43.
AM711	206/407	Crashed in sea off Thorney Island 13.6.42.
AM712	407	F.T.R. from attack on *Scharnhorst* and *Gneisenau* off Belgian coast 12.2.42.
AM713	608	F.T.R. from sortie off Norway 20.4.42.
AM714	SD Flt/TFU/CCDU/53/ 224/500/608	S.O.C. 12.7.45.
AM715	608	F.T.R. 23.11.41.
AM716	407	Damaged on landing at Ibsley 14.3.42. S.O.C.
AM717	24/1 OADU/24	Crashed on landing, Portreath 28.10.42.
AM718	53/500	Spun into ground after night t.o., Docking 1.12.41.
AM719	407	Dived into ground $\frac{1}{2}$ mile S of North Coates 30.7.41.
AM720		Diverted to R.C.A.F.
AM722	206/500/21/500	S.O.C. 29.2.44.
AM723		Diverted to R.C.A.F.

AM724	220	F.T.R. 19.10.41.
AM725	3 FPP/24	Destroyed in hangar fire, Hendon 22.4.42.
AM726		Diverted to R.C.A.F.
AM727	59/53	
AM728	407	F.T.R. from anti-shipping sortie off Texel 22.12.41.
AM729		Diverted to R.C.A.F.
AM730	220/48	Crashed NW of Wick on returning from sortie 14.4.42.
AM731	407	F.T.R. from sortie off Terschelling 16.12.41.
AM732	407/59/608/500	Crashed on t.o., Maison Blanche 22.2.43.
AM733		Diverted to R.C.A.F.
AM734	206/6 OTU/608	S.O.C. 26.4.45.
AM735	233/407/608	Ditched on ferry flight 5.6.43.
AM736		Diverted to R.C.A.F.
AM737		Diverted to R.C.A.F.
AM738	45 Group	S.O.C. 22.11.45.
AM739	608	S.O.C. 21.6.45.
AM740	59	F.T.R. 16.10.41.
AM741	53/224	Hit by AA from ship and abandoned near Princetown, Devon 27.1.42.
AM742	53/224/59/608	S.O.C. 28.2.43.
AM743	59/301 FTU/1 OADU/ME	S.O.C. 12.7.45.
AM744	1 OTU/608	S.O.C. 2.8.45.
AM745		Diverted to R.C.A.F.
AM746	2 SAN/CNS/ATA	S.O.C. 18.8.45.
AM747		Diverted to R.C.A.F.
AM748	31 OTU/45 Group	S.O.C. 22.11.45.
AM749		Diverted to R.C.A.F.
AM750	1 OTU	Crashed 17.11.41.
AM751		Diverted to R.C.A.F.
AM752		Diverted to R.C.A.F.
AM753	AAEE/RAE/CCDU/ AAEE/RAE/5 OTU	S.O.C. 25.4.46.
AM754	1 OTU	Swung on t.o. and u/c collapsed, Thornaby 3.6.43.
AM755		Diverted to R.C.A.F.
AM756		Crashed on delivery flight.
AM757	53/223/6 OTU/301 FTU/ 1 OADU/500	S.O.C. 29.2.44.
AM758	1 OTU	
AM759		Diverted to R.C.A.F.
AM760	1 OTU	F.T.R. from training flight 26.6.42.
AM761		Diverted to R.C.A.F.
AM762	206	F.T.R. 26.6.42.
AM763 to- AM767		Diverted to R.C.A.F.
AM768	48	F.T.R. 7.1.42.
AM769		Diverted to R.C.A.F.

AM770		Diverted to R.C.A.F.
AM771	1 OTU	Crashed 1.9.42.
AM772		Diverted to R.C.A.F.
AM773		Diverted to R.C.A.F.
AM774	ATA	To U.S.A.A.F 24.1.44.
AM775	301 FTU/1 OADU/500	S.O.C. 25.1.45.
AM776	608	F.T.R. 17.3.42.
AM777	53	F.T.R. 14.9.41.
AM778	407	F.T.R. 1.12.41.
AM779	53/224	Crashed 4.8.42.
AM780	407/301 FTU/1 OADU/608	S.O.C. 25.1.45.
AM781	53/224/500	Hit by AA from U boat and abandoned near Tafaraouri 24.4.43.
AM782	59	F.T.R. 21.4.42.
AM783	500	Crashed on t.o., Bircham Newton 9.5.42.
AM784	59	F.T.R. 29.5.42.
AM785	206/500	S.O.C. 21.6.45.
AM786	1 OTU	Crashed in forced landing near Maryport, Cumberland 28.12.41.
AM787		Not delivered to RAF.
AM788	206/301 FTU/1 OADU	Crashed on t.o., Ras-el-Ma 25.7.43.
AM789	59/53	S.O.C. 7.6.43.
AM790	500/301 FTU/1 OADU/608	S.O.C. 25.1.45.
AM791	608	Crashed in forced landing on shore Ardmore Bay, Skye 21.7.42.
AM792	206/500	F.T.R. 14.9.42.
AM793	1 OTU/27th TG US	S.O.C 13.3.45.
AM794	1 OTU	F.T.R. 25.5.42.
AM795	53	S.O.C. 18.8.42.
AM796	59	F.T.R. 3.3.42.
AM797	53/59/500/53	Crashed 22.4.44.
AM798	1 OTU	D.B.R. 26.8.42.
AM799	220	F.T.R. Engine cut during attack on ship near Stavanger 28.11.41.
AM800	1 OTU/301 FTU/1 OADU/ 500	Swung on t.o. and u/c collapsed, Tafaraouri 11.10.43.
AM801	206/48/220/1 OTU/5 OTU	S.O.C. 2.5.45.
AM802	608	F.T.R. 11.11.42. Presumed shot down by Naval AA off Algiers.
AM803	48/220/53	F.T.R. from recce 17.4.42.
AM804	6 OTU	Crashed 17.3.42.
AM805	206	F.T.R. 28.7.42.
AM806	224/53	D.B.R. 3.1.42.
AM807	1 OTU	F.T.R. 21.4.43.
AM808	48	Crashed in forced landing near Helmsdale on return from Bergen 7.1.42.
AM809	48/608	Crashed on landing, Gosport 25.8.42.
AM810	608	F.T.R. 20.4.42.
AM811	407/233	F.T.R. 23.3.42.
AM812	407/233	F.T.R. 16.5.42.

AM813	1 OTU/5 OTU	S.O.C. 28.3.46.
AM814	220/48	F.T.R. 24.2.42.
AM815	220/48	Crashlanded at Wick on return from patrol and blew up 21.7.42.
AM816	271/6 OTU/407/608/233/ 6 OTU/301 FTU/1 OADU/608	Crashed on landing Borizzo, 22.5.44. D.B.R.
AM817	1 OTU/500/608/4PTS	Stalled off turn and crashed 5m NW of Gioia 3.3.45.
AM818	48/608	Short of fuel, force landed on beach near Taher 11.1.43.
AM819	TFU/301 FTU/1 OADU/608	S.O.C. 21 10.43.
AM820	233/301 FTU/1 OADU/608	S.O.C. 25.1.45.
AM821	608/301 FTU/1 OADU/ 608/500/608	S.O.C. 26.4.45.
AM822	206/500/608/500	Crashed 12.12.42.
AM823	AAEE/608/1 OTU/ 5 OTU/RAE	S.O.C 18.12.47.
AM824	220/48	F.T.R. from shipping strike 1.5.42.
AM825	1 OTU	Stalled and spun into sea off Allonby, Cumberland 18.2.42.
AM826	59/53/1 OADU/500/608	S.O.C. 28.9.44.
AM827	53/224/608	F.T.R. 28.11.42.
AM828	500	Crashed in bad weather 3m NE of Kolea, Algeria 3.4.43.
AM829	6 OTU	Crashed 11.7.42.
AM830	59/407/1 OTU/301 FTU/ 1 OADU/608	S.O.C. 26.4.45.
AM831	500/301 FTU/1 OADU/608	S.O.C. 26.4.45.
AM832	1 OTU	Flew into mountain at night, Beddgelert, Caernarvon, 4.2.43.
AM833	1 OTU/301 FTU/ 1 OADU/608	S.O.C. 26.4.45.
AM834	1 OTU	Crashed in sea off Cahore, Ireland 24.2.42.
AM835	6 OTU/608/1 OTU	S.O.C. 25.4.46.
AM836	59/500	S.O.C. 28.2.43.
AM837	206	F.T.R. 21.12.41.
AM838	407	To 3151M 6.42.
AM839	220/48	F.T.R. from shipping strike Bergen 7.1.42.
AM840	1 OTU/407/1 OTU	Ditched off West Hartlepool, Co. Durham 19.9.43.
AM841	407/233/407/608/500/608	S.O.C. 29.3.45.
AM842	48/59/220/59	30.5.42.
AM843	608/5 OTU/RAE	S.O.C. 17.6.48.
AM844	53	S.O.C. 7.6.43.
AM845	500	Stalled on overshoot, Docking 8.2.42.
AM846	1 OTU/ 5 OTU	S.O.C. 28.3.46.
AM847	6 OTU	Crashed 27.3.42.
AM848	224/407/279/5 OTU	S.O.C. 20.7.45.
AM849		Crashed on delivery flight.
AM850	24/MCS	S.O.C. 7.10.45.
AM851	220/48/407/608	Crashed on t.o., Gaudo 7.12.43.
AM852	59	F.T.R. 11.5.42.

AM853	220/48/608/459	Crashed on landing in sandstorm, Gambut 3, 20.10.43.
AM854	1 OTU/ATA	Spun into ground near Taplow, Berks. 20.4.45.
AM855	59/53/500/301 FTU/ 1 OADU/ 608	S.O.C. 25.1.45.
AM856	59	Overshot landing at Roborough 20.11.41.
AM857	59/608/500	Flew into sea off Cap Serrat, Algeria 2.9.43.
AM858	220/48/608/500	Crashed on t.o., Tafaraouri 14.11.43.
AM859	608/6 OTU/1 OTU	D.B.R. 12.5.43.
AM860	407	Short of fuel and crashlanded near Bircham Newton 30.7.42.
AM861	220/48	F.T.R. from sortie 27.3.42.
AM862	59	F.T.R. 24.10.41.
AM863	220/48/1 OTU	Crashed in sea on approach to Silloth 11.1.43.
AM864	407	Crashlanded at Coningsby on return from shipping strike 15.5.42.
AM865	233/407/301 FTU/RAE	S.O.C. 15.8.47.
AM866	48/220/48/53/301 FTU/ 1 OADU/500	S.O.C. 25.1.45.
AM867	59	Swung on t.o. and blew up, Thorney Island 29.9.41.
AM868	1 OTU	S.O.C. 25.4.46.
AM869	48	F.T.R. from sortie 24.2.42.
AM870	6 OTU/407/608/1MECCU	Swung on landing and D.B.R., Bilbeis 21.1.44.
AM871	48	F.T.R. from Norway 10.2.42.
AM872	6 OTU	Crashed 25.3.42.
AM873	220/48	F.T.R. from sortie 16.2.42.
AM874	608	F.T.R. 15.5.42.
AM875	206/6 OTU/608	D.B.R. and S.O.C. 30.6.44.
AM876	608	F.T.R. from sortie 6.2.42.
AM877	224/53	F.T.R. 9.3.42.
AM878	407/233	F.T.R. 18.4.42.
AM879	48/608/500/1 MECCU	Crashed on t.o., Bilbeis 19.6.44.
AM880	608	D.B.R. 30.12.41.
AM881	48	F.T.R. from strike 17.5.42.
AM882	224/269/224/608/500	S.O.C. 29.4.45.
AM883	608	Flew into high ground in bad weather 2m W of Lurnsden, Aberdeenshire 16.11.41.
AM884	1 OTU/5 OTU/7 FIS	S.O.C. 30.5.46.
AM885	59/48/53/301 FTU	Crashed at Ballyyellame, Eire 16.9.43.
AM886		Diverted to R.C.A.F.
AM887	31 OTU/231/6 FU	Crashed on landing, Miami 1.11.45.
AM888 to- AM896		Diverted to R.C.A.F.
AM897		Crashed before delivery.
AM898		Not delivered to R.A.F.
AM899		Diverted to R.C.A.F.
AM900		Crashed before delivery.
AM901	45 Group	S.O.C. 30.5.46.
AM902		Diverted to R.C.A.F.

AM903		Diverted to R.C.A.F.
AM904	45 Group	
AM905		Diverted to R.C.A.F.
AM906	48/220/407	Shot down by AA off Dutch coast 15.5.42.
AM907	TFU	S.O.C. 14.8.44.
AM908	48	Crashed in sea off Aberdeen on return from sortie 27.2.42.
AM909	500	F.T.R. 9.9.42.
AM930		Not delivered to RAF.
AM931	233/161	D.B.R. 19.1.45.
AM932		Ditched off Newfoundland in ferry flight 24.1.42.
AM933	200	S.O.C. 25.1.45.
AM934	62	F.T.R. 16.6.42.
AM935	45 Group/ 6 FU	Both engines cut; crashlanded 1m SW of Dorval 20.7.45.
AM936	24/AFE/1444 Flt/FE	S.O.C. 22.2.45.
AM937	FE	
AM938	287/289/1444 Flt/62	Crashed on t.o., Jessore 17.3.43.
AM939	320	F.T.R. from shipping strike 30.5.42.
AM940		Missing between Gander and Prestwick 27.9.41.
AM941	62	Lost 24.5.42.
AM942	FE	Destroyed by enemy action 29.4.42.
AM943	139	S.O.C. 14.11.42.
AM944	1444 Flt/200	S.O.C. 11.10.45.
AM945	1 OADU/FE	Lost at Singapore 1.42.
AM946	1 OADU	Missing between Portreath and Gibraltar 29.1.42.
AM947	1444 Flt/353	Crashed 31.5.42.
AM948	62	Crashed 31.5.42.
AM949	1444 Flt/357	Crashed into hill on supply drop 23°44′N 98°48′E 15.3.44.
AM950	459/CF Aden	Crashed on landing, Djibouti 11.7.45.
AM951	1444 Flt/200	Lost 22.11.42.

417 Lockheed Hudson Mark IIIAs [BW361 – 777] were diverted before delivery as follows and with the remainder to the R.C.A.F.:

BW361 to BW380	To USN.
BW386 to BW398	To China.
BW409	To 45 Group, Canada.
BW411	To 45 Group, Canada.
BW413 to BW421	To R.A.A.F.
BW445	To 45 Group, Canada.
BW461 to BW613	To U.S.A.A.F.
BW661 to BW681	To R.A.A.F.
BW684	To 45 Group, Canada.

BW699		To 45 Group, Canada.
BW736 to BW755		To R.A.A.F.
BW756 to BW767		To R.N.Z.A.F.
EW873		Diverted to R.C.A.F.
EW874		Diverted to R.C.A.F.
EW875	117/CF Iraq	S.O.C. 14.3.46.
EW876	216	S.O.C. 31.5.45.
EW877	117	Lost power on t.o. and crashed, El Adem 5.2.43.
EW878	45 Group	S.O.C. 30.5.46.
EW879	4 METS	Swung on landing and u/c collapsed, Kabrit 8.12.42.
EW880		Crashed on ferry flight to Middle East 10.42.
EW881	216/117/1 MECCU/Aden CF	Dived into ground, Riyan 25.9.44.
EW882	45 Group	S.O.C. 30.5.46.
EW883	45 Group	S.O.C. 30.5.46.
EW884	163/267	S.O.C. 20.9.45.
EW885		Crashed on delivery flight.
EW886		Crashed before delivery.
EW887	163/267/117/EACF	Stalled on t.o. and u/c collapsed, Eastleigh 15.1.45.
EW888	267/BOAC/MECF	S.O.C. 1.3.46.
EW889	267/117	S.O.C. 14.3.46.
EW890	AAEE &COA/1 OAPU	Swung on landing and u/c collapsed, Kemble 7.8.43.
EW891	48/1 OTU/48/ATA	S.S. 3.9.47.
EW892		Crashed before delivery.
EW893	320/48/1 OTU/48/RAE/48	S.O.C. 30.5.46.
EW894	45 Group	Engine cut on t.o.; swung and u/c collapsed, North Bay 19.7.43.
EW895	320/48/320/1 OTU/48	S.O.C. 30.5.46.
EW896	45 Group	Swung on landing and tipped up, North Bay 10.7.43.
EW897	320/279/48	F.T.R. 20.1.44.
EW898	45 Group	Crashed on delivery flight 6.8.43.
EW899	320/279	S.O.C. 30.5.46.
EW900	216	Engine cut on t.o.; stalled and crashed, El Khanka 4.11.42.
EW901	407/1 OTU/48	S.O.C. 30.5.46.
EW902	1444 Flt/217/353	S.O.C. 25.1.45.
EW903	59/320	F.T.R. from night sortie off Dutch coast 23.11.42.
EW904	59/320/279	Swung on t.o. and cartwheeled, Bircham Newton 17.8.43.
EW905	595/407/320/279/48	S.O.C. 21.3.46.
EW906	320/48/1 OTU/48	Flew into ground, Estrella Mountains, Portugal, 22.2.44.
EW907	48/1 OTU/48	S.O.C. 31.3.46.
EW908		Crashed on delivery flight.
EW909	TFU	S.S. 3.9.47.
EW910	320/279/48/ATA	S.S. 3.9.47.

EW911	48/1 OTU/48	S.O.C. 31.3.46.
EW912	59/320	F.T.R. from night shipping strike off Dutch coast 9.11.42.
EW913	320/279/48	S.O.C. 28.3.46.
EW914	320/279	S.O.C. 31.3.46.
EW915	59/320/1444 Flt/1 OADU	Short of fuel, force landed 17°25′N 16°02W and interned 3.11.42.
EW916	59/407/320/48/1 OTU/48	N.F.D.
EW917	320/48/1 OTU/2 FIS/7 FIS	S.S. 3.9.47.
EW918	59/320	Damaged by AA 12.10.42 S.O.C.
EW919	59/407/320	F.T.R. 27.1.43.
EW920	1 OADU/ATA	S.O.C. 30.5.46.
EW921	407	F.T.R. from Bay of Biscay 20.10.42.
EW922	320/279	S.O.C. 30.5.46.
EW923	320	Failed to climb on t.o. and crashlanded, Thorney Island 7.9.42.
EW924	59/320/279/48/ATA	S.O.C. 30.5.46.
EW925	320/301 FTU/1 OADU/ MACAF/ CF	S.O.C. 14.3.46.
EW926	163/BOAC/MACCU	S.O.C. 7.44.
EW927	163/BOAC	S.O.C. 30.5.46.
EW928	45 Gp/313 FTU	
EW929	48/1 OTU/48/ATA	S.O.C. 30.5.46.
EW930	59/407/1 OTU/48	S.O.C. 31.3.46.
EW931	45 Group	S.O.C. 30.5.46.
EW932		Crashed on ferry flight.
EW933	45 Group	S.O.C. 30.5.46.
EW934	216/Ferry convoy Flt	S.O.C. 28.9.44.
EW935	163/Iraq CF	Swung on t.o. and u/c collapsed, Jiwani 2.6.43.
EW936	163/267	S.O.C. 2.8.45.
EW937	163/267/459/75 OTU	S.O.C. 14.3.46.
EW938		Crashed on ferry flight.
EW939	267/Ferry convoy Flt	S.O.C. 30.9.45.
EW940	163/EACF	S.O.C. 27.3.47.
EW941	117/4 METS	S.O.C. 29.3.45.
EW942	267	S.O.C. 20.5.47.
EW943	163/267/Aden CF	U/c collapsed on t.o., Hargeisa, Italian Somaliland 18.5.45.
EW944	267	Swung on t.o. and u/c collapsed, Kabrit 5.9.42.
EW945	117	Missing on transport flight 25.11.42.
EW946	194	S.O.C. 15.1.45.
EW947	117/4 METS	S.O.C. 22.2.45.
EW948	267/117	S.O.C. 31.8.44.
EW949		To R.N.Z.A.F. as NZ2091.
EW950		To R.N.Z.A.F. as NZ2092.
EW951	117/1 ASR Flt NA	
EW952		To R.N.Z.A.F. as NZ2093.
EW953		To R.N.Z.A.F. as NZ2094.

EW954	216/Ferry Convoy Flt	S.O.C. 28.9.44.
EW955	267/117/1ASR Flt NA	S.O.C. 22.2.45.
EW956		Diverted to R.C.A.F.
EW957	117/459/Aden CF	U/c jammed; belly-landed at Masirah 14.2.45.
EW958	163/BOAC	S.O.C. 29.3.45.
EW959	163/117/ALS[I]/ Ferry Convoy Flt	S.O.C. 29.3.46.
EW960	163/267/117	S.O.C. 22.2.45.
EW961	267	Hit by bomb in air raid, Kufra 14.10.42.
EW962	216	S.O.C. 16.1.45.
EW963	216/353	S.O.C. 25.1.45.
EW964	117	Swung on t.o. and u/c collapsed, Asmara 7.9.42. D.B.R.
EW965	216/MECF	S.O.C. 1.12.43.
EW966	163/117/31/194	S.O.C. 4.9.43.
EW967	163/267/459	S.O.C. 25.5.44.
EW968	216	Swung on t.o. and u/c collapsed, Khartoum 14.10.42.
EW969	267/Iraq CF	Crashed in bad weather on ferry flight, Iran 18.1.43.
EW970	117	S.O.C. 30.11.44.
EW971	163/267/BOAC/459/ 1 MECCU/117/1 MECCU	Engine cut; crashed on overshoot 4m NW of Bilbeis, 16.3.44.
EW972	163/267/194/353/135 RSU	Blown over in gale, Gaya 30.6.44.
FH167	24/MCS	S.S. 3.9.47.
FH168	AFEE/38 Wg	Engine cut; crashed in forced landing 7m S of St Eval 19.5.43.
FH169 to FH174		Diverted to R.A.A.F.
FH175		Diverted to R.N.Z.A.F. as NZ2049.
FH176 to FH214		Diverted to R.A.A.F.
FH215 to FH226		Diverted to R.N.Z.A.F.
FH227	1444 Flt/459	Crashed on t.o. in bad weather, Gambut 3, 12.3.43.
FH228		Crashed on acceptance flight 22.2.42.
FH229	217/353	Swung on t.o. and u/c collapsed, Yalahanka 13.3.44.
FH230	1444 Flt/AAEE/1 OADU	Engine cut on approach, Luqa 26.6.42.
FH231	1444 Flt	Overshot landing and u/c collapsed, Sharjah 12.7.42.
FH232	1444 Flt/FTF/1444 Flt/217	Crashed on landing, Dum Dum 5.12.44.
FH233		Crashed on ferry flight 23.5.42. Doncgal, Eirc.
FH234	1444 Flt/62	S.O.C. 24.12.44.
FH235	45 Group	Flew into high ground near Wilmington, NY. 8.2.43.
FH236	200	S.O.C. 21.6.45.
FH237	48	Swung on t.o. and u/c collapsed, Sumburgh, Shetlands 21.10.42.
FH238	1444 Flt/353/India CU	S.O.C. 28.9.44.
FH239	1444 Flt/ME	S.O.C. 31.8.44.
FH240	48/233/3502 SU	U/c collapsed on landing, Gosport 18.10.43; to 4257M.

FH241	1444 Flt/353/62	S.O.C. 22.2.45.
FH242	1444 Flt/459/75 OTU	S.O.C. 24.4.45.
FH243	1444Flt/353/129 RSU	Overshot, abandoned t.o. and u/c collapsed, Cuttack 12.12.42.
FH244	1444 Flt/459/4 METS	S.O.C. 31.8.44.
FH245	1444 Flt	Swung on t.o. and u/c collapsed, Portreath, Cornwall 29.5.42.
FH246	1444 Flt	Crashed on ferry flight off Newfoundland 8.4.42.
FH247	1444 Flt/459	Hit trees on t.o. and blew up, Edku 10.7.42.
FH248	1444 Flt	Crashed on approach, Luqa 19.6.42.
FH249	1 OADU/459	S.O.C. 26.9.46.
FH250	1444 Flt/459/Aden CU/1330 CU	S.O.C. 4.4.46.
FH251	1444 Flt/353	Nosed over on landing, Colombo racecourse 29.2.44.
FH252	50 MU	Destroyed by fire on ground Cowley, 30.9.42.
FH253	1444 Flt/233/3502 SU	Stalled on approach 1m SW of St Athan 30.7.43.
FH254	1444 Flt/353	Engines cut in cloud; crashlanded on mudflat 10m W of Surat 5.7.44.
FH255	200/MedME CS	Crashed in circuit during storm, Linate 1.7.45.
FH256	1444 Flt/FE	S.O.C. 22.2.45.
FH257	1444 Flt/459	Stalled off turn and crashed 5m W of L.G. 'Z' 25.8.42.
FH258	1444 Flt/459	S.O.C. 23.8.45.
FH259	1444 Flt/253	S.O.C. 24.12.44.
FH260	59/48/233	Out of fuel; forcelanded, Portella, Portugal, 3.10.43; sold to Portugal.
FH261	1444 Flt.	Swung on t.o. and u/c collapsed, Gibraltar 22.6.42.
FH262	1444 Flt/353	S.O.C. 6.7.44.
FH263	251	S.S. 3.9.47.
FH264	FTU/459	Engine lost power on t.o.; swung and u/c collapsed, Kasfareet, 1.7.42.
FH265	200	Lost height on t.o. and flew into ground, Jeswang 16.9.42.
FH266	1444 Flt/459	S.O.C. 15.10.45.
FH267	1444 Flt/62/353	Damaged in accident 7.42.
FH268	ARC Karachi	Swung on t.o. and u/c collapsed Ahmedabad 9.9.42.
FH269		Engine cut on ferry flight, Gander-Reykjavik 12.5.42.; failed to arrive.
FH270	45 Group	S.O.C. 30.5.46.
FH271	53/48	S.O.C. 31.3.46.
FH272	200/ Hudson Flt	Swung on t.o. and u/c collapsed, Robertsfield, Liberia 13.9.43.
FH273	1444 Flt/353	Swung on t.o. and u/c collapsed, Cuttack, 3.2.43.
FH274	1444 Flt/217/353	Engine cut on t.o., Dum Dum 24.12.43.
FH275	353	Engine cut, undershot landing at Palam 9.9.43.
FH276	200/ARC Karachi	Swung on landing and u/c collapsed, Juhu 5.10.42.
FH277	1 OADU/1444 Flt	Swung on t.o. and u/c collapsed, Gibraltar 1.9.42.
FH278	1444 Flt/62	Swung on landing, Cuttack 12.9.42.
FH279	163/Aden CF	U/c collapsed on t.o. Salalah 11.5.45.
FH280	200/SF Gibraltar	Both engines cut, ditched 4m S of Gibraltar 9.4.46.
FH281	1444 Flt/353	F.T.R. from offensive recce 1.1.43.
FH282	200/ME	S.O.C. 25.1.45.
FH283	1444 Flt/353	Swung on t.o. and u/c collapsed, Vizagapatam 12.10.42.

FH284	1444 Flt/459	Crashed landing at Gambut 3 on return from patrol, 9.12.42.
FH285	1444 Flt/459/8	Flew into cliffs in bad weather and blew up 8m W of Balalah, Saudi Arabia 10.7.43.
FH286	353	S.O.C. 31.8.44.
FH287	1444 Flt/1 OADU	Spun into ground on ferry flt, Habbaniya 12.7.42.
FH288	200	Force landed on patrol, Port Guinea 16.9.42. Interned.
FH289	1 OADU/FE	D.B.R. in accident 4.10.42.
FH290	62	Engine cut; bellylanded 3m SW of Manteswar 25.3.43.
FH291	1444 Flt/353	Dived into sea off Gannavaram 28.4.43.
FH292	1444 Flt/459	Hit by AA from convoy off Mersa Matruh and ditched 28.7.42.
FH293	353	Hit trees after t.o., Feni 2.1.43.
FH294	1444 Flt/459	F.T.R. from shipping strike off Libyan coast 13.8.42.
FH295	459/353	S.O.C. 28.9.44.
FH296	1444 Flt/459/108 MU/2 METS	U/c collapsed on t.o. LG.237 21.1.43.
FH297	217/Ferry Convoy Flt	S.O.C. 22.2.45.
FH298	1444 Flt	Swung on t.o. and u/c collapsed, Lyneham 29.6.42.
FH299	1444 Flt	Crashed on landing in dust storm, H.3, Iraq 6.6.42.
FH300	1444 Flt/459	F.T.R. from attack on convoy off Tobruk, 10.7.42.
FH301	200/ME	D.B.R. in accident 25.7.44.
FH302	1444 Flt/ 459	F.T.R. from shipping strike, 5.8.42.
FH303		Crashed before delivery.
FH304	1444 Flt/459	Wing hit ground on t.o. and u/c collapsed LG.226, 8.9.42.
FH305	1444 Flt/353	Swung on t.o. and hit concrete mixer, u/c collapsed, Cuttack 1.8.42.
FH306	1444 Flt/459	U/c collapsed on landing, LG226, on return from shipping strike 8.7.42.
FH307	24	Stalled on approach and crashed 1m NNW of Chivenor 29.4.43.
FH308	459/1 MECCU/1330 CU	S.O.C. 29.3.45.
FH309	1444 Flt	Swung on t.o. and u/c collapsed, Horsham St Faith 7.6.42.
FH310	1444 Flt	Engine cut on t.o., Horsham St Faith 7.6.42.
FH311	459	S.O.C. 18.10.45.
FH312	1444 Flt/353	Flew into ground in storm, Luagundi 2.8.42.
FH313	200/353	S.O.C 22.2.45.
FH314	1444 Flt/459/75 OTU	S.O.C. 11.10.45.
FH315	313 FTU	Swung on landing and hit bank, North Bay 3.8.44.
FH316	45 Group	Crashed in Newfoundland on ferry flight 18.10.42.
FH317	FC Trg Flt	Crashed 5m W of Dorval, 22.7.42.
FH318	45 Group/313 OTU	S.O.C. 30.6.46.
FH319	1444 Flt	Dived into sea after t.o., Gibraltar 10.7.42.
FH320 to FH328		Diverted to R.N.Z.A.F.
FH329	459	Swung on landing and u/c collapsed, Heliopolis 12.11.42.
FH330	1444 Flt/233	S.O.C. 7.10.44.
FH331	459	Stalled on t.o., Socotra 8.12.42.
FH332	608/48/233	S.S. 3.9.47.
FH333	217/1576 Flt	S.O.C. 26.4.45.
FH334	OADU	Engine cut, jetttisoned fuel and bellylanded on ferry flt, Gibraltar–Jeswang 26.7.42.

FH335	45 Group	Out of fuel and crashed on delivery flt 1m W of New Carlisle, PQ, 22.4.42.
FH336	1444 Flt/200/French Hudson Flt	Crashed at Ouakam, Senegal, 6.8.43.
FH337	1444 Flt/1 OADU	Bounced on landing and wing hit ground, Kemble 9.6.42.
FH338	1444 Flt/353	Out of fuel in bad weather and ditched in river, Salipur 2.8.42.
FH339	1444 Flt/353	Swung on t.o., Asansol 17.9.42. D.B.R.
FH340		Crashed in Canada on delivery flt.
FH341	62	Swung on landing and u/c collapsed, Dum Dum 3.2.43.
FH342	217	S.O.C. 19.7.45.
FH343	OADU	Crashed in sea on ferry flt off Gibraltar 1.11.42.
FH344		DBF at No.12 MU, Kirkbride 29.5.42. NFD.
FH345	1444 Flt/500	S.O.C. 26.9.46.
FH346	407	F.T.R. from shipping strike off Dutch coast 21.6.42.
FH347		Crashed before delivery.
FH348	1442 Flt/200	S.O.C. 5.45.
FH349	217	S.O.C. 16.1.45.
FH350	59/233	Ditched on operations east of Gibraltar 24.4.43.
FH351	459/1 MECCU/1330 CU	S.O.C. 2.8.45.
FH352	459	S.O.C. 18.10.45.
FH353	200	To F.F.A.F 1.4.43.
FH354	1444 Flt/FE	S.O.C. 14.2.46.
FH355		Crashed on delivery flt.
FH356	53/279/1407 Flt/251	U/c jammed; bellylanded at Wick 2.5.45.
FH357	407/233/1403 Flt/520/161	S.S. 3.9.47.
FH358	459	S.O.C. 29.9.45.
FH359	1444 Flt/459/1MECCU	Lost power on t.o. and wing dug in, Bilbeis 15.6.44.
FH360	608/48	F.T.R. 18.10.42.
FH361	407/48/1404 Flt/48/ 1404 Flt/1407 Flt	Stalled and dived into ground 8m NE of Reykjavik 16.7.44.
FH362	48	Swung on t.o.; wing hit ground, Keflavik 24.9.42. Crashed in sea off Horn Is.
FH363	500/269/233/269	Lost 2.3.43.
FH364	1444 Flt/62/353	S.O.C. 8.10.42.
FH365		Stalled on t.o., Oakes Field, Bahamas, on ferry flt 29.4.43.
FH366	200	F.T.R. from convoy escort 27.8.43.
FH367	1444 Flt/200	F.T.R. from patrol 19.7.43.
FH368	FC Trg Flt	Crashed 2m W of Dorval 16.7.42.
FH369	24/MCS	S.S. 3.9.47.
FH370	353	S.O.C. 22.2.45.
FH371	1444 Flt/ 353	Hit donkey on runway and swung, Karachi 15.9.42 D.B.R.
FH372	459	S.O.C. 23.8.45.
FH373	59/233/Defford	S.S. 3.9.47.
FH374	459/FE	Failed to become airborne, Dum Dum 29.12.43. D.B.R.
FH375	500	F.T.R. from test 1.8.42.
FH378	48	F.T.R. 16.7.42.
FH379	1401 Flt/521	Swung on t.o.; hit building and crashed, Bircham Newton 4.10.42.

FH380	1401 Flt/521/279	S.S. 3.9.47.
FH381	200/3 FU	U/c jammed, bellylanded at Blida, 14.2.45.
FH382		Crashed on delivery flight.
FH383	62/353	Broke up in storm near Jodhpur 2.7.44.
FH384	407/48/233/1403 Flt/520	S.O.C. 31.3.46.
FH385	500/269	F.T.R. presumed ditched 1.9.42.
FH386	353	S.O.C. 30.11.44.
FH387		To China 25.5.43.
FH388	459/Levant CF	Engine cut, bellylanded near Lydda 12.4.45.
FH389		Diverted to R.N.Z.A.F. as NZ2071.
FH390	217	Swung on landing and u/c collapsed, Minneriya 31.1.43.
FH391		Diverted to R.N.Z.A.F. as NZ2072.
FH392	FE	S.O.C. 22.2.45.
FH393		Diverted to R.N.Z.A.F. as NZ2073.
FH394	1444 Flt/200	S.O.C. 25.1.45.
FH395	FC Trg Flt	Stalled and spun into ground, Lake St Louis PQ 6.7.42.
FH396		Diverted to R.N.Z.A.F.
FH397		Crashed before delivery.
FH398	233	Flew into hill during bad weather and blew up near Gibraltar, 11.9.42.
FH399	62	S.O.C. 16.1.45.
FH400	200/FFAF/MedME CS	Swung on t.o. and u/c collapsed, Rabat-Salé 18.3.45.
FH401		Diverted to R.N.Z.A.F. as NZ2075.
FH402		Diverted to R.N.Z.A.F. as NZ2076.
FH403	459/1330 CU	S.O.C. 6.12.45.
FH404	1402 Flt	Bounced on landing, swung and crashed, Aldergrove 3.10.42.
FH405		Diverted to R.N.Z.A.F. as NZ2077.
FH406	24/161/24	Engine cut; bellylanded near Tougourt, Algeria, 22.3.43.
FH407	1402 Flt	F.T.R. from Atlantic Met. Flight 30.12.42.
FH408		Diverted to R.N.Z.A.F. as NZ2078.
FH409	353	To China 29.3.45.
FH410	200/500	S.O.C. 14.3.46.
FH411	353	S.O.C. 24.12.44.
FH412		Diverted to R.N.Z.A.F. as NZ2079.
FH413		Diverted to R.N.Z.A.F. as NZ2080.
FH414	ARC Karachi	Wing hit ground on attempted overshoot, Hakimpet 15.11.42.
FH415		Diverted t.o. R.N.Z.A.F. as NZ2081.
FH416		Diverted to R.C.A.F.
FH417	217/353	Engine cut on t.o., Palam 30.5.44.
FH418	353	N.F.T. 3.43.
FH419	608/48/279	S.O.C. 20.11.44.
FH420	24/200/WACF	S.O.C. 15.8.44.
FH421	53/269/1407 Flt/521	S.O.C. 28.6.45.
FH422	1444 Flt/1576 Flt	Engine cut on t.o. crashed in swamp near Dum Dum 17.10.43.

FH423	48/269	N.F.T. 12.42.
FH424	608/233	S.O.C. 1.5.44.
FH425	217/1576 Flt	S.O.C. 28.9.44.
FH426	59/48/233	F.T.R. 28.12.42.
FH427	48	F.T.R. 11.8.42.
FH428	459	S.O.C. 28.9.44.
FH429	1444 Flt/FE	S.O.C. 30.4.44.
FH430	217	Wings folded recovering from dive, Vavuniya, 30.4.43.
FH431	31/India CU/353/194	F.T.R. from supply drop, Fort Hertz 17.12.43.
FH432		Diverted to R.N.Z.A.F. as NZ2082.
FH433	53/279/520	S.O.C. 23.1.46.
FH434 to FH441		Diverted to R.N.Z.A.F. as NZ2083 to NZ2090.
FH443	62	S.O.C. 22.2.45.
FH444	353	S.O.C. 22.2.45.
FH445	200	Swung on t.o. and hit Wellington HD970, Jeswang.
FH446	459/1330 CU	S.O.C. 11.4.46.
FH447	353	S.O.C. 24.12.44.
FH448	233	Swung on t.o. and hit excavator, Gibraltar 30.1.43.
FH449	Lyneham	Swung on t.o. and u/c collapsed, Lyneham 26.7.42.
FH450	FE	To China 25.5.43.
FH451	200	Crashed on ferry flight 10m N of Marshall, Liberia 26.7.42.
FH452	OADU/FE	S.O.C. 3.9.47.
FH453	48/233	F.T.R. from Casablanca sortie, presumed shot down by USN F4Fs 8.11.42.
FH454	1444 Flt/MAC CU	Swung on t.o. and u/c collapsed, Treviso 16.5.45.
FH455	24/MCS	S.O.C. 27.6.46.
FH456	1442 Flt/459	S.O.C. 9.8.45.
FH457		Diverted to R.C.A.F.
FH458		Crashed in Canada on delivery flight.
FH459	459	U/c collapsed on landing, Lydda 30.6.43.
FH460	RAE/24	Flew into high ground in bad visibility, Wendover, Bucks. 4.8.44.
FH461	353	Lost power on t.o. and u/c raised to stop, Dum Dum 4.5.44.
FH462	48/1404 Flt	Swung on t.o. and u/c collapsed, Gibraltar 16.2.43.
FH463	1 OADU/407/48/233	S.S. 3.9.47.
FH464	?/24	Caught fire refuelling, Gibraltar 17.9.42.
FH465	45 Group	Missing on Atlantic delivery flight 30.5.42.
FH466	521	Sank back on t.o., Bircham Newton 1.11.42.
FK381	117/459/ECAF	S.O.C. 29.8.46.
FK382	117	S.O.C. 1.12.43.
FK383	117/1 ASR Flt NA	S.O.C. 14.3.46.
FK384	216/117	Hit by Baltimore AG779 while parked, Luqa 6.4.43.
FK385	117/459/4 METS	S.O.C. 2.8.45.
FK386	24/117/1 OADU	Missing on ferry flight 3.6.43.

FK387	216	Swung on t.o. and u/c collapsed, LG.224 4.12.42.
FK388	117	Engine caught fire, crashlanded and u/c collapsed near Soluch 29.11.42.
FK389	117	Shot down by US fighters, Thelepte 27.12.42.
FK390	117	Crashed in circuit, Monastir 28.4.43.
FK391	163	Swung on t.o., LG224, 22.12.43. D.B.R.
FK392	163	Swung on t.o., skidded and wing dug in, Asmara 7.9.42.
FK393		Diverted.
FK394	48/ATA/ 1 FP	S.O.C. 25.4.46.
FK395	48/1 OTU/48/AFEE	S.O.C. 27.6.46.
FK396	301 FTU	S.O.C. 21.3.46.
FK397	163/117	S.O.C. 29.3.45.
FK398	48	Dived into sea on RP practice 15m E of Gibraltar 23.10.43.
FK399		Diverted.
FK400	45 Group	S.O.C. 30.6.46.
FK401	301 FTU/500	Shot down by Beaufighter off Algiers, 13.4.43.
FK402	320/279/ATA	S.S. 3.9.47.
FK403	45 Gp/313 FTU	U/c collapsed taxying at North Bay, Ontario, 30.3.45. Not repaired.
FK404		Crashed before delivery.
FK405	48	Blew up in air off Gibraltar 11.5.43.
FK406	24/AAEE/5 OTU	U/c collapsed on landing, High Ercall 9.7.45.
FK407	163/267	Crashed in bad weather 10m S of El Agheila 13.12.42.
FK408		Diverted.
FK409		Diverted.
FK410	48/29MU/1 FPP	Found to be unstable after rebuild, 6.4.44. S.O.C.
FK411	163/117/194	Stalled on t.o., Palam 16.4.43.
FK412		Diverted.
FK413		Missing on ferry flight Gander-Reykjavik, 14.7.42.
FK414	1 OTU/48	S.O.C. 30.5.46.
FK415	Hdlg Sqdn/ATA	S.O.C. 27.6.46.
FK416	ME	S.O.C. 11.4.46.
FK417	48/1 OTU/48	Crashed in sea during ASR patrol approx. 90m E of Gibraltar 29.5.43.
FK418	1 OTU/48	Swung on landing and u/c collapsed, Gibraltar 9.2.43.
FK419		Diverted.
FK420 to FK440		Diverted.
FK441	1444 Flt/217/Ferry Convoy Flt/India CF	S.O.C. 22.2.45.
FK442	45 Group	Hit trees and dived into ground, St Adolphede Howard 23.6.43.
FK443		Diverted.
FK444	1444 Flt/500/608/353	S.O.C. 28.9.44.
FK445 to FK449		Diverted.
FK450	320/279	S.O.C. 31.2.46.
FK451		Diverted.
FK452	163/267	Swung on t.o., Marble Arch 23.6.43.

FK453		Diverted.
FK454	163/267/MedME CS	S.O.C. 1.3.44.
FK455	163/267/117/459/EACF	Stalled on t.o., Eastleigh 12.7.45.
FK456	163/BOAC	S.O.C. 28.2.43.
FK457	163/117/194	S.O.C. 28.12.44.
FK458	320/1 OTU/48	S.O.C. 30.5.46.
FK459	163/BOAC	Spun into ground on approach, Khartoum 16.6.43.
FK460		Diverted.
FK461	163/117/267	S.O.C. 28.9.44.
FK462	48	S.O.C. 7.10.44.
FK463		Crashed on ferry flight 15.3.43.
FK464 to FK468		Diverted.
FK469	163/117/194	S.O.C. 28.9.44.
FK470		Diverted.
FK471	163/267	Tyre burst on landing and u/c collapsed, Gardabia Main 12.5.43.
FK472	45 Group	Overshot night landing into ravine, Burlington, Vermont 21.11.45.
FK473	117	S.O.C. 26.9.46.
FK474	163/117/194	Damaged by Ki 43s and crashlanded on beach near Sitakund, 16.12.42.
FK475	1444 Flt/217	S.O.C. 28.9.44.
FK476	267/163/267/117/Ferry Convoy Flt/EACF	S.O.C. 31.10.46.
FK477	163/117/31/194/17/1 MECCU	S.O.C. 26.4.45.
FK478	163/1 MECCU	Failed to become airborne and u/c raised to stop, Bilbeis 16.5.44.
FK479	53/301 FTU/608	S.O.C. 31.10.46.
FK480		Crashed on ferry flight, 1.43.
FK481	163/117/194	S.O.C. 15.1.45.
FK482	24/MCS	Bounced on landing, drifted off runway and hit Auster, Eindhoven 7.11.44.
FK483	217/ALS(I)/BAFSEA CS	S.O.C. 10.1.45.
FK484	500/608	D.B.R. in accident 18.2.44.
FK485	163/117/31/194	Bounced on landing, bellylanded and hit DC-2 and B17, Bangalore 21.2.43.
FK486	163/BOAC/MECF/CF Iraq	S.O.C. 10.1.45.
FK487	ME	To U.S.A.A.F 1.11.42.
FK488	163/117/194	Swung on t.o., Bangalore 7.12.42. D.B.R.
FK489	301 FTU/500	S.O.C. 26.9.46.
FK490	163/117/4 FC	Overshot landing at Sharjah 16.9.42.
FK491	163/117/267	Swung on t.o. and u/c collapsed, Bilbeis 1.10.42.
FK492	163/117/Aden CF	Swung on t.o. and u/c collapsed, Asmara 13.8.44.
FK493	163/267/194/353	S.O.C. 28.9.44.
FK494	10 MU	Engine cut on t.o.; hit trees near Chippenham, Wilts. 10.10.42.
FK495		Diverted.
FK496	301 FTU/1444 Flt/353	S.O.C. 28.9.44.
FK497	200	Stalled on t.o. and spun into ground, Cape St Mary, near Jeswang 6.1.43.
FK498	163/267/353	S.O.C. 18.12.44.

FK499		Crashed in sea on delivery flight 1.10.42.
FK500	301 FTU/500/608	S.O.C. 28.11.46.
FK501	267	Engine cut on overshoot, crashlanded LG125, 12.11.42.
FK502	48/5 OTU	Crashed in sea after night t.o. in bad weather, 2m off Turnberry, 11.2.45.
FK503	216/117/1ASR Flt NA	D.B.R. in accident 14.1.44.
FK504	194/India CU/ACSEA CS	S.O.C. 28.9.44.
FK505	117	S.O.C. 29.2.44.
FK506		Diverted.
FK507	267	Engine cut on t.o., bellylanded, El Adem 28.4.43.
FK508	267	S.O.C. 1.4.44.
FK509	31	Engine cut on t.o. crashed 5m W of Karachi 8.10.42.
FK510	48/1 OTU/48/5 OTU	S.O.C. 15.5.45.
FK511		Diverted.
FK512		Diverted.
FK513	48	To 4588M 1.3.44.
FK514		Diverted.
FK515	1444 Flt/BAFSEA CS	S.O.C. 18.12.44.
FK516	1444 Flt/200	S.O.C. 26.4.45.
FK517		Crashed before delivery.
FK518		Diverted.
FK519	FE	S.O.C. 1.1.45.
FK520	301 FTU/500/608	S.O.C. 26.4.45.
FK521	1444 Flt/ 200	S.O.C. 29.2.44.
FK522	1444 Flt/ 1 OADU	Flew into cliffs after night t.o. Portreath, Cornwall 6.12.42.
FK523	233/45 Gp/313 FTU	S.O.C. 30.5.46.
FK524	45 Group	S.O.C. 1.7.44.
FK525	267/117	S.O.C. 23.8.45.
FK526	267/117/75 OTU	S.O.C. 31.5.45.
FK527	117	Overshot, abandoned t.o. and u/c collapsed, Marble Arch 6.3.43.
FK528	267	S.O.C. 1.4.44.
FK529	WA	S.O.C. 22.2.45.
FK530	301 FTU/608	S.O.C. 26.9.46.
FK531	48/1 OTU/48	S.O.C. 30.5.46.
FK532		To F.F.A.F.
FK533		Crashed before delivery.
FK534		Diverted.
FK535	301 FTU/608	Engine cut; crashlanded at La Chiffa near Algiers 26.6.43.
FK536	1444 Flt/200/1314 Flt	S.O.C. 2.8.45.
FK537	AFEE	Engine cut on approach, hit embankment, Sherburn-in-Elmet 16.12.43.
FK538	1 OADU	Out of fuel and ditched off Cape Roca 29.8.43.
FK539		Diverted.
FK540	45 Gp/313 FTU/	S.O.C. 30.8.46.
FK541		Diverted.

FK542	62 OTU/301 FTU/608	Engine caught fire; swung on landing and u/c collapsed, Tingley 18.4.43.
FK543	301 FTU/608	S.O.C. 26.4.45.
FK544 to FK548		Diverted.
FK549	194	S.O.C. 26.10.44.
FK550 to FK557		Diverted.
FK558		Crashed before delivery.
FK559		Crashed before delivery.
FK560 to FK564		Diverted.
FK565	301 FTU/500	D.B.R. in accident 26.1.44.
FK566	ME	S.O.C. 22.2.45.
FK567	194	Out of fuel and crashlanded, Nirmatud 26.3.43.
FK568	117	S.O.C. 29.3.45.
FK569	608	Crashed on t.o., Grottaglie 15.1.44.
FK570	194	To GI airframe 18.12.44.
FK571	301 FTU	Engine cut; stalled while forcelanding, Ashton-under-Hill, Worcs. 16.7.43.
FK572		Crashed before delivery.
FK573	216/117	Swung on landing and u/c collapsed, Lentini West 28.7.43.
FK574	9 FU	U/c jammed; crashlanded at Kanchrapara 19.11.44. D.B.R.
FK575	268/75 OTU	S.O.C. 29.3.45.
FK576	194/353/Ferry Convoy Flt	S.O.C. 30.11.44.
FK577	ME	S.O.C. 31.12.43.
FK578	200	Flew into ground on t.o. at night, Takoradi 7.1.43.
FK579	117/459	S.O.C. 29.8.46.
FK580	267/117	S.O.C. 31.8.46.
FK581	459	Swung on landing and u/c collapsed, LG.07 29.8.43.
FK582	45 Gp/313 FTU	S.O.C. 12.7.45.
FK583	200.MACAF CF	S.O.C. 5.45.
FK584	194	Stalled on approach Bamrauli, 27.8.43.
FK585	Ferry Convoy Flt	S.O.C. 22.2.45.
FK586	194/353	S.O.C. 28.9.44.
FK587	USAAF/194/Ferry Convoy Flt	S.O.C. 24.12.44.
FK588		Crashed before delivery.
FK589	200	U/c collapsed in heavy landing, Waterloo 19.4.43. D.B.R.
FK590	India CU/ACSEA CS	S.O.C. 6.7.44.
FK591	200	S.O.C. 1.3.43.
FK592	608/117	Tyre burst on t.o. and u/c collapsed, Castel Benito 21.6.43.
FK593	194	S.O.C. 28.9.44.
FK594	295 Wg	Swung on t.o. and u/c collapsed, Hastings, Sierra Leone 6.3.43.
FK595	FE	S.O.C. 31.8.44.
FK596	194/ALS(I)/307 MU	Swung on t.o. and u/c collapsed, Lahore 11.10.43.
FK597	India CU	S.O.C. 24.12.44.
FK598	Med	S.O.C. 22.2.45.

FK599	8 AFU	Swung on t.o. and crashed, Hastings, Sierra Leone, 15.11.42.
FK600	216	S.O.C. 3.1.45.
FK601	117	S.O.C. 22.2.45.
FK602	Ferry Convoy Flt	S.O.C. 1.1.45.
FK603	AFU	Overshot landing at Takoradi 21.10.42.
FK604	301 FTU/608	Lost height on t.o. and hit ground 1m E of Tafaraouri 9.4.43.
FK605	194	Crashed in jungle 6m NE of Talablok 25.12.42.
FK606	22 FC	Swung on t.o. and u/c collapsed, Bamrauli 15.1.44.
FK607	194/353	S.O.C. 15.1.45.
FK608	194/117/1 ASR Flt NA/ MATAF CF	Engine cut after t.o. spun into ground, Peretola 19.2.45.
FK609	Ferry Convoy Flt	S.O.C. 25.10.45.
FK610		Crashed on ferry flight.
FK611	Ferry Convoy Flt	S.O.C. 28.9.44.
FK612	Ferry Convoy Flt	S.O.C. 31.5.45.
FK613	117/459	S.O.C. 20.5.47.
FK614	117	S.O.C. 7.2.43.
FK615	117	Swung on landing and u/c collapsed, Castel Benito 13.3.43.
FK616	200	S.O.C. 22.2.45.
FK617	India CU	S.O.C. 22.2.45.
FK618	BOAC	Spiralled into ground near Khartoum 30.6.43. Presumed overloaded.
FK619	22 FC	Dived into ground after t.o., Trichinopoly 22.5.44.
FK620	Ferry Convoy Flt	S.O.C. 10.1.45.
FK621	OADU	Crashed after t.o. from Gibraltar on ferry flight 12.3.43.
FK622	FE	S.O.C. 16.1.45.
FK623	301 FTU/608	Swung on landing and u/c collapsed, Blida 15.7.43.
FK624	India CU	To GI airframe 14.12.44.
FK625	8/75 OTU	S.O.C. 18.7.46.
FK626	301 FTU/608	Crashed on t.o. Blida, 5.4.43.
FK627	301 FTU/500	Engine cut on t.o. hit pole and crashedlanded, Tafaraouri 30.6.43.
FK628	8/75 OTU	S.O.C. 29.3.45.
FK629		Crashed on delivery flight.
FK630		Crashed on delivery flight.
FK631	Ferry Convoy Flt	S.O.C. 24.12.44.
FK632	353	S.O.C. 28.9.44.
FK633	301 FTU/Med	S.O.C. 22.2.45.
FK634	India CU/ACSEA CU	S.O.C. 28.9.44.
FK635	FE	S.O.C. 8.1.45.
FK636	500	S.O.C. 28.9.44.
FK637	301 FTU/75 OTU	S.O.C. 29.3.45.
FK638	FE	S.O.C. 2.8.45.
FK639	200/Hudson Flt WA	S.O.C. 26.4.45.
FK640	301 FTU/500/608	S.O.C. 14.3.46.
FK641	Ferry Convoy Flt/353	To GI airframe 14.12.44.

FK642	194/353/22 FC	Crashed on ferry flight 1m W of Gurgeon 27.11.43.
FK643	1 OADU	Stalled on t.o., Accra 26.11.42.
FK644 to FK655		Diverted.
FK656	301 FTU/608	S.O.C. 26.4.45.
FK657	301 FTU/500	S.O.C. 26.4.45.
FK658	459/75 OTU	S.O.C. 2.8.45.
FK659		Crashed on delivery flight.
FK660	ATA	S.OC. 30.5.46.
FK661	301 FTU/500/MedME CS	S.O.C. 14.3.46.
FK662	608/500	S.O.C. 12.2.45.
FK663	301 FTU/608/MedME CS	S.O.C. 14.3.46.
FK664	8/75 OTU	D.B.R. in accident 3.3.44.
FK665		Crashed on delivery flight.
FK666	200	Swung on t.o. and u/c collapsed, Waterloo 4.6.43.
FK667	301 FTU/500	F.T.R. from A/S search off Cape Rosa 2.9.43.
FK668	301 FTU/608/EACF	Swung on t.o. and u/c collapsed, Tabora, Tanganyika, 29.8.46.
FK669	301 FTU/500/608	S.O.C. 29.8.44.
FK670	500	S.O.C. 26.4.45.
FK671	608	Swung on t.o., Blida 2.6.43.
FK672	301 FTU/608/500/MedME CF	Swung on t.o. and u/c collapsed, Marcianese 25.10.45.
FK673	301 FTU	Caught fire in hangar, Lyneham, Wilts. 24.2.43.
FK674	301 FTU/608/MedME CF	Engine failed on icing conditions, abandoned 10m E of Innsbruck 19.9.45.
FK675	301 FTU	Swung on t.o., Lyneham 2.4.43.
FK676	301 FTU/608	S.O.C. 20.5.47.
FK677	301 FTU/608	D.B.R. in accident 10.3.44.
FK678	301 FTU/500	Drifted off strip on landing and u/c collapsed, Bone 3.10.43.
FK679	301 FTU/608	Crashed on t.o., Bone 4.6.43.
FK680	301 FTU/608/500	Engine cut on t.o. swung and u/c collapsed, Blida 12.9.43.
FK681	301 FTU/117/500/608	S.O.C. 26.4.45.
FK682	301 FTU/608/500/608	S.O.C. 14.3.46.
FK683	301 FTU/500	S.O.C. 22.2.45.
FK684	62 OTU/301 FTU/608/500	S.O.C. 26.4.45.
FK685	301 FTU/608	D.B.R. in accident 10.3.44.
FK686	301 FTU/608	Both engines cut; forcelanded 4m SW of Bone, 21.5.43. D.B.R.
FK687		Crashed on delivery flight.
FK688	301 FTU/608	S.O.C. 19.7.45.
FK689	AAEE/301 FTU/500	S.O.C. 26.4.45.
FK690	45 Group	Stalled on t.o. on delivery flight, Gander 6.12.42.
FK691	301 FTU/608	F.T.R. from patrol 7.5.43.
FK692	10 MU	Engine cut on test flight, bellylanded and hit wall, Bollinger farm, Glos.4.2.43. D.B.R.
FK693	45 Group	Missing on delivery flight Gander–Reykjavik 28.11.43.
FK694 to FK703		Diverted.

FK704	608/500	S.O.C. 26.4.45.
FK705	301 FTU/500	S.O.C. 26.4.45.
FK706	301 FTU/500/608	S.O.C. 5.45.
FK707	301 FTU/500	S.O.C. 22.2.45.
FK708	301 FTU/500/608/500	Stalled on landing, swung and u/c collapsed, Tafaraouri 19.7.43.
FK709	608	S.O.C. 14.3.46.
FK710	301 FTU/608	Both engines cut; crashlanded in Algeria 10.6.43.
FK711	608	F.T.R. from A/S sweep 13.7.43.
FK712	301 FTU/608/500	S.O.C. 22.2.45.
FK713	FE	S.O.C. 18.12.44.
FK714	1 OADU	Force landed on ferry flt Portella 11.4.43. Transferred to Portuguese AF.
FK715	301 FTU/608	Flew into ground after t.o., Blida 23.5.43.
FK716	301 FTU/608	S.O.C. 26.4.45.
FK717	301 FTU/608	Force landed in fog returning from patrol, 11.6.43. D.B.R.
FK718	301 FTU/Med	S.O.C. 26.4.45.
FK719	301 FTU/608/MedME CS	S.O.C. 31.10.46.
FK720	1 OADU	Swung on t.o. and u/c collapsed, Ras el Ma 30.5.43.
FK721	ME	S.O.C. 2.8.45.
FK722	1 OADU	Crashed in sea on night t.o., Gibraltar 12.3.43.
FK723		Crashed before delivery.
FK724	113 Wg	Control lost on attempted overshoot on ferry flt, Jeswang 9.1.43.
FK725	301 FTU/500/608	U/c jammed, bellylanded at Borizzo 27.9.43.
FK726	301 FTU/608	S.O.C. 29.2.44.
FK727	301 FTU/608/500	S.O.C. 29.8.46.
FK728		Crashed on delivery flight.
FK729	608/MACAF CF	S.O.C. 5.45.
FK730	FE	S.O.C. 8.1.45.
FK731	233/48/519	S.O.C. 25.4.46.
FK732	301 FTU/608	S.O.C. 30.5.46.
FK733	301 FTU/608	F.T.R. from patrol off Anzio 31.1.44.
FK734	301 FTU/608	26.9.46.
FK735	233	Crashed in bad weather 6m W of Lagens, returning from patrol 13.12.43.
FK736	269/45Gp/192 Wg	Engine cut, stalled and crashed, Ellenburg, NY 22.6.44.
FK737	269/SF Heston/FCCS/SF Northolt/ Sigs Dev Flt/SFU/CSE	S.O.C. 15.8.47.
FK738	233/269	Hit by Wellington NB908 at dispersal, Chivenor, 19.12.44.
FK739	233/48/1407 Flt/251	F.T.R. From Met. flt. Presumed iced up, 17.3.45.
FK740	269/521	F.T.R. from Met flt 7.2.45.
FK741	301 FTU/500	S.O.C. 21.5.45.
FK742		Stalled on t.o. on ferry flight, Reykjavik 28.5.43.
FK743	269/519/251	Flew into mountains in Iceland 27.3.45.
FK744	269/521	S.S. 3.9.47.
FK745	48/FCCS/CCCF/SF Benson/ SF Thorney Is./ASWDU	S.O.C. 23.4.48.

FK746	269/519	Swung on landing and u/c collapsed, Turnberry 19.10.44.
FK747	269/251	S.S. 3.9.47.
FK748	279/251	Tyre burst on t.o. and u/c collapsed, Kaldadarnes 11.12.44.
FK749	301 FTU/608/DAF CS	S.O.C 21.6.45.
FK750	233	S.S. 3.9.47.
FK751	301 FTU/608	S.O.C. 26.9.46.
FK752	269/279/1407 Flt/251	F.T.R. presumed iced up and ditched off Iceland 10.11.44.
FK753	301 FTU/608	S.O.C. 25.1.45.
FK754	113 Wg	Swung on landing B.W.1, Greenland 2.6.43. D.B.R.
FK755	269/AAEE	S.O.C. 29.10.47.
FK756	10 MU	Stalled on approach 2m N of Kemble, 23.7.43.
FK757	279/519/251, Tempsford	S.S. 3.9.47.
FK758	269	Crashed during RP practice off Kaldadarnes, 22.11.43.
FK759	269/521	F.T.R. from Met. Flt 23.10.44.
FK760	301 FTU/608	S.O.C. 26.9.46.
FK761	301 FTU	Damaged by enemy aircraft off Cape Finisterre; forcelanded, Grandola, Portugal, 31.12.43.
FK762	301 FTU/608/MedME CS/Italy CS	S.O.C. 26.9.46.
FK763	161	Engine caught fire; abandoned over Dorking, Surrey, 12.4.45.
FK764	269/519/RAE	S.O.C. 31.5.48.
FK765	269	S.O.C. 25.4.46.
FK766	269	To R.C.A.F. 19.6.44.
FK767	161	Dived into ground at night during practice parachute drop, Arlesey, Beds. 28.3.44.
FK768	269	Abandoned t.o. overshot and u/c collapsed, Reyjavik 29.10.43.
FK769	45 Group	To Canadian Pacific Railways 28.3.46.
FK770	45 Group	To Canadian Pacific Railways 28.3.46.
FK771	45 Group	To Canadian Pacific Railways 28.3.46.
FK772	301 FTU/608/MACAF CF	S.O.C. 26.9.46.
FK773	45 Group	Swung on t.o. and hit snowbank, Dorval 17.2.45.
FK774	45 Gp/521	To Canadian Pacific Railways 28.3.46.
FK775	233	S.O.C. 31.3.46.
FK776	301 FTU/608	Crashed at Borizzo 23.5.44.
FK777	269/1407 Flt	S.O.C. 9.1.46.
FK778	45 Group	Swung on landing, Dorval 3.5.44. D.B.R.
FK779	45 Group	To Canadian Pacific Railways 28.3.46.
FK780	45 Group	Flew into hill in bad weather near Machrihanish 10.6.43.
FK781	301 FTU/608	S.O.C. 25.1.45.
FK782	269/251	S.O.C. 25.4.49.
FK783	269	Swung on t.o. and crashed on ferry flight, Wick, 10.10.43.
FK784	269	To R.C.A.F. 19.6.44.
FK785	269/4 FPP	Engine cut on t.o. crashlanded, Prestwick 17.1.43.
FK786	269	Caught fire during refuelling at Lagens 25.3.44.
FK787	259/521/Staff College Flt/RCCS	S.O.C. 12.8.47.
FK788	301 FTU/608	F.T.R. from patrol off Anzio 31.4.44.

FK789	45 Group	Swung on t.o., Dorval 10.6.43.
FK790	161	F.T.R. 5.7.44.
FK791	269	Engine cut on ferry flight, crashed in forced landing, near Mira, Portugal, 6.3.44.
FK792	45 Group	Swung on t.o., Goose Bay 15.6.43.
FK793	301 FTU	To R.C.A.F. 19.6.44.
FK794	45 Group	Swung on t.o., Goose Bay 15.6.43. D.B.R.
FK795	45 Group	Swung on landing and u/c collapsed, Prestwick 20.6.43.
FK796	301 FTU	Swung on t.o. and crashed, Lyneham 7.10.43.
FK797	161	S.O.C. 18.4.45.
FK798	301 FTU/608	S.O.C. 25.1.45.
FK799	269/1407 Flt/251	S.S. 3.9.47.
FK800	301 FTU/500	S.O.C. 31.5.44.
FK801	301 FTU/608	S.O.C. 4.4.46.
FK802	301 FTU/500/608	S.O.C. 29.9.46.
FK803	161	F.T.R. 21.3.45.
FK804	301 FTU/608	F.T.R. presumed ditched SW of Sicily 28.1.44.
FK805	301 FTU	S.S. 3.9.47.
FK806	301 FTU/608/MedME CS	S.O.C. 26.9.44.
FK807	269/251	Sold in Iceland 18.7.46.
FK808	301 FTU/608	Swung on t.o. and u/c collapsed, Montecorvino 9.12.43.
FK809	301 FTU/608/MedME CS	Tipped up on t.o., Innsbruck 30.5.45.
FK810	301 FTU/500	S.O.C. 25.1.45.
FK811	301 FTU/Med	S.O.C. 25.1.45.
FK812	301 FTU/ 1 FU/519	S.O.C. 25.4.46.
FK813	301 FTU/608/500	S.O.C. 31.8.44.
VJ416	Ex G-AGDC (ex V9061)	S.O.C. 25.4.46.
VJ421	Ex G-AGDK (ex V9152)	S.O.C. 28.3.46.

Lockheed Hudson Marks

Mark I
RAF Serial Numbers N7205–N7404; P5116–P5165; R4059; T9266–T9365
Mark II
RAF Serial Numbers T9366–T9385
Mark III
RAF Serial Numbers T9386–T9465; V8975–V9254; AE485– AE608; AM930– AM953; VJ416 & VJ421
Mark IIIA
RAF Serial Numbers BW361–BW777; FH167–FH466; FK731–FK813
Mark IV
RAF Serial Numbers AE609–AE638
Mark V
RAF Serial Numbers AE639–AE657; AM520–AM909
Mark VI
RAF Serial Numbers EW873–EW972; FK381–FK730

RAF Unit Codes

24 Squadron	ZK	220 Squadron	NR
48	OY	224	QX
53	PZ	233	ZS
59	TR	269	UA
62	PT	279	OS
161	MA	320	NO

194		407	RR
200		459	BP
206	VX	500	MK
217	MW	608	UL
		6(C)OTU	FE

Appendix D

Royal Australian Air Force Hudsons

Units Equipped with Hudsons

Squadron	Code Letters	Operational areas
No.1	US and NA	Australia and Malaya
No.2	KO	Australia and Timor (Keopang)
No.6	FX	Australia and New Guinea
No.7	KT	Australia and New Guinea
No.8	UV	Australia and Malaya
No.13	SF	Northern Territory, Celebes (Namlea and Laha)
No.14	PN	Pearce, Western Australia
No.23	NV	Australia and New Guinea
No.24	GR	Australia, New Guinea and Rabaul
No.25	SJ	
No.32	JM	Horn Island (Torres Straits)
No.38	PK	Australia and New Guinea
No.459	BP	North Africa and Palestine
No.464	SB	

Communications Units

No.1	EV	Essenden, Victoria
No.3	DB	Mascot, NSW
No.4	VM	Archerfield, Queensland
No.6	XJ	Northern Territory
Survey Flt	SU	" "
No.2 (Air Ambulance)		Australia and SW Pacific

The RAAF received 247 Hudson aircraft:

Mark I	Numbers 1	to 50
Mark II	Numbers 51	to 100
Mark III	Numbers 153	to 162
	Numbers 170	to 247
Mark IV	Numbers 101	to 152
	Numbers 163	to 165

Serial No.	Received	Abbreviated History
A16-1	9.2.40	No.1 Sqdn 15.2.40. Sembawang 17.7.40. No.1 OTU 31.5.42. W/o12.11.46.
2	26.1.40	No.8 Sqdn 10.5.40. No.6 Sqdn 3.7.40. No.1 OTU 19.3.42. Damaged by e/a Dobodura 26.12.42. W.o 3.9.46.
3	26.1.40	No.6 Sqdn 1.4.40. No.23 Sqdn 1.7.40. No.1 OTU 16.2.42. Crashed Hariko Bay, during c/a combat, Dobodura, New Guinea 26.12.42.
4	26.1.40	No.6 Sqdn 1.4.40. No.8 Sqdn 27.6.40. Destroyed Kuantan by e/a 9.12.41.
5	26.1.40	No.6 Sqdn 1.4.40. No.2 Sqdn 3.1.42. Crashed Drysdale 7.3.42.
6	26.1.40	No.6 Sqdn 1.4.40. No.2 Sqdn 24.6.40. W/o 20.3.42.
7	26.1.40	No.14 Sqdn 4.4.40. No.13 Sqdn 18.12.41. F.T.R. from Manado, Celebes 12.1.42.
8	26.1.40	No.13 Sqdn 8.6.40. Crashed near Darwin 15.8.41. Conversion to components 4.9.41.

A16-9	26.1.40	No.2 Sqdn. 5.7.40. Lost by e/a Koepang 30.1.42.
10	26.1.40	No.8 Sqdn 4.5.40. No.13 Sqdn 3.7.40. No.1 OTU 29.11.45. Disposed 26.3.48.
11	7.2.40	No.8 Sqdn 4.8.40. Shot down by Zeros (22 Air Flotilla) 24.2.42. S. China Sea (F/L Spurgeon).
12	7.2.40	No.7 Sqdn 12.8.40. No.2 Sqdn 21.8.40. Crashed in Kema Bay during shipping strike and attack by e/a 12.1.42.
13	7.2.40	No.24 Sqdn 9.9.40. Set on fire by enemy bomb burst Rabaul 8.1.42.
14	7.2.40	No.8 Sqdn 4.8.40. Force landed on beach Knala Kemasik 45m N of Kuantan 23.7.41. (F/Lt N. Lampe).
15	7.2.40	No.8 Sqdn 4.8.40. Bombed by e/a Kuantan 9.12.41.
16	7.2.40	No.24 Sqdn 9.9.40. No.4 Com. Flt 26.3.43. Converted to instruction frame and to No.1 Engineering school 9.10.44. Disposed 9.4.46.
17	7.2.40	No.8 Sqdn 4.8.40. Lost due to e/a Bandoeng 7.3.42.
18	7.2.40	No.7 Sqdn 11.8.40. No.2 Sqdn 21.8.40. Force landed Coffi Harbour, NSW 15.11.41. No.2 Sqdn 10.5.42. No.1 OTU 30.7.42. F.T.R. Flinders Island 11.10.42.
19	6.2.40	No.1 Sqdn 15.4.40. F.T.R. from sortie over enemy c/v Kota Bharu 7.12.41.
20	9.2.40	No.1 Sqdn 1.4.40. Hit by AA over enemy c/v Kota Bharu 8.12.41. Destroyed by e/a on ground 9.12.41.
21	9.2.40	No.1 Sqdn 1.4.40. F.T.R. from shipping strike Banka Island 12.2.42.
22	9.2.40	No.14 Sqdn 4.4.40. Force landed Moore River Native Mission 12.12.41. No.14 Sqdn 23. 2.42. No.1 OTU 23.6.42. No.1 Com. Flt 30.10.43. No.1 Com Flt 25.1.45. Guinea Airways 27.2.46.
23	9.2.40	No.1 Sqdn 1.5.40. Lost through e/a Java 20.3.42.
24	14.2.40	No.1 Sqdn 1.5.40. Hit by AA from enemy c/v Kota Bharu 8.12.41. Destroyed on ground by e/a 9.12.41.
25	15.4.40	No.1 Sqdn 1.5.40. Crashed in Jahore Strait, Singapore 7.5.41.
26	16.2.40	No.1 Sqdn 1.5.40. No.7 Sqdn 13.4.42. No.1 OTU 3.8.42. Landed Cooktown 17.12.42. No.1 OTU 21.5.43. For components 7.8.44.
27	20.2.40	No.23 Sqdn 1.7.40. F.T.R. 12.8.40 ex Archerfield.
28	14.2.40	No.14 Sqdn 2.5.40. No.151 MU 18.12.41. No.1 Sqdn 3.1.42. Damaged by bomb blast Kilidjati, Java 24.2.42.
29	9.3.40	No.14 Sqdn 4.4.40. No.13 Sqdn 28.12.41. Crashed in sea near Amboina 1.1.42.
30	20.2.40	No.14 Sqdn 2.5.40. No.13 Sqdn 28.12.41. No.1 OTU 21.1.44. Sold 23.6.46.
31	9.3.40	No.14 Sqdn 4.4.40. Crashed at Pearce 16.5.40. No.14 Sqdn 13.9.41. Crashed Lukenai Rabaul 22.11.41. To components.
32	16.2.40	No.6 Sqdn 10.4.40. No.2 Sqdn 24.6.40. No.1 OTU 30.7.42. F.T.R. 6.7.43.
33	15.2.40	No.6 Sqdn 2.5.40. Damaged on t.o. Canberra 23.5.40. Lost by e/a Timor 25.1.42.
34	9.2.40	No.6 Sqdn 2.5.40. No.2 Sqdn 24.6.40. No.1 OTU 30.7.42. Components 7.8.44.
35	9.2.40	No.6 Sqdn 2.5.40. No.1 Sqdn 3.1.42. Destroyed on ground by e/a Semplak, Java 22.2.42.
36	9.2.40	No.14 Sqdn 2.5.40. No.13 Sqdn 28.12.41. No.1 OTU 9.6.42. Shot down by AA Seputa airstrip 15.12.42.
37	22.2.40	No.6 Sqdn 15.9.40. No.1 Sqdn Singapore 3.1.42. Destroyed by direct bomb hit, Bandoeng, Java 2.3.42.
38	22.2.40	No.23 Sqdn 15.9.40. No.24 Sqdn 17.1.42. No.32 Sqdn 26.2.42. No.1 OTU 17.9.42. Crashed Bairnsdale 27.10.42.
39	22.2.40	No.24 Sqdn 2.9.40. No.32 Sqdn 19.2.42. No.1 OTU 23.3.42. No.7 Sqdn 5.5.42. Crashed Long Point 5.6.42.
40	22.2.40	No.8 Sqdn 29.6.40. Lost due to e/a 13.1.42. Seletar or Tengah.
41	22.2.40	No.8 Sqdn 29.6.40. Crashed on Kota Bharu 8.12.41[F/Lt Spurgeon].
42	22.2.40	No.6 Sqdn 25.8.40. Destroyed on ground by e/a Semplak, Java 22.2.42.
43	22.2.40	No.8 Sqdn. 29.6.40. Lost due to e/a Kuantan 8.12.41. [F/L G. Hitchcock].
44	22.2.40	No.8 Sqdn 29.6.40. No.1 Sqdn 22.1.42. Lost through e/a Semplak, Java. W/o 20.3.42.
45	7.3.40	No.14 Sqdn 2.5.40. No.13 Sqdn 28.12.41. No.7 Sqdn 6.4.42. No.1 OTU 29.6.42. ERD 9.8.44. Conversion to components.
46	4.3.40	No.6. Sqdn 2.5.40. No.2 Sqdn 3.1.42. F.T.R from Menado, Kerna area, NE Celebes 12.1.42.
47	4.3.40	No.6 Sqdn 28.5.40. No.23 Sqdn 29.6.40. No.24 Sqdn 6.12.41. Damaged by e/a Rabaul 7.1.42. No.1 OTU 3.3.43. Survey Flt 21.8.44. Lost between Lowood and Bowen 23.7.45.
48	12.3.40	No.8 Sqdn 11.6.40. Damaged in shipping strike; crashlanded Palembang 14.2.42.[F/L Diamond].

A16-49	7.3.40	No.8 Sqdn 13.6.40. Crashed in sea 3mls NW of Palau Redang, Malaya 14.2.41. [P. Barnes].
50	7.3.40	No.8 Sqdn 11.6.40. Force landed on beach Kuala Kemanan 32 mls N of Kuantan 23.7.41. [F/L P. Parry].
51	13.3.40	No.1 Sqdn 28.5.40. Lost due to e/a Far East. W/o 20.3.42.
52	12.3.40	No.1 Sqdn 28.5.40. Shrapnel damage over enemy c/v Kota Bharu 8.12.41. Destroyed on ground by e/a 9.12.41. Kota Bharu.
53	7.3.40	No.1 Sqdn 28.5.40. Shrapnel damage over enemy c/v Kota Bharu 8.12.41. Destroyed by e/a on ground Kota Bharu 9.12.41.
54	3.3.40	No.2 SFTS 29.7.40. No.1 Sqdn 11.2.41. Destroyed on ground by e/a Semplak, Java 23.2.42.
55	3.3.40	No.6 Sqdn 28.5.40. No.4 Conversion Flt 12.4.43. For disposal 20.2.46.
56	2.3.40	No.6 Sqdn 10.4.40. No.8 Sqdn 3.1.42. No.1 Sqdn 22.1.42. Damaged beyond repair by e/a Semplak, Java 22.2.42.
57	8.3.40	No.6 Sqdn 28.5.40. No.2 Sqdn 6.1.42. Destroyed on ground by e/a Darwin 19.2.42.
58	8.3.40	No.6 Sqdn 28.5.40. Crashed N of Windsor 17.6.40.
59	2.3.40	No.14 Sqdn 1.6.40. No.13 Sqdn 12.1.42. Crashed on landing Namlea 27.1.42. Destroyed on ground by e/a 30.1.42.
60	10.3.40	No.14 Sqdn 1.6.40. No.8 Sqdn 3.1.42. No.1 Sqdn 22.1.42. Lost by e/a Bandoeng, Java w/o 20.3.42.[Flown by F/L Jim Marshall to P2 7.2.42.].
61	7.3.40	No.14 Sqdn 1.6.40. No.13 Sqdn 28.12.41. Crashed Koepang 14.2.42.
62	10.3.40	No.14 Sqdn 1.6.40. No.1 Sqdn 25.12.41. Lost by e/a Java, w/o 20.3.42.
63	11.3.40	No.13 Sqdn Destroyed on ground by e/a Darwin 4.3.42.
64	7.3.40	No.13 Sqdn F.T.R. Ex Amboina, last seen near Tondawa 19.1.42.
65	11.3.40	No.2 Sqdn 12.6.40. Destroyed on ground by e/a 15.1.42. Or Darwin 4.3.42.
66	30.3.40	No.13 Sqdn 8.6.40. Destroyed on ground by e/a at Laha 20.1.42.
67	31.3.40	No.13 Sqdn 8.6.40. F.T.R. from Manado area, Celebes 12.1.42.
68	29.3.40	No.13 Sqdn 24.6.40. Crashed on approach, Richmond NSW 20.12.44.
69	30.3.40	No.13 Sqdn 24.6.40. Crashed in sea after t.o. Darwin 10.12.41.
70	31.3.40	No.1 Sqdn 13.6.40. Destroyed on ground by e/a Kota Bharu 9.12.41.
71	29.3.40	No.13 Sqdn 24.6.40. Destroyed on ground by e/a Halong 20.1.42.
72	21.4.40	No.13 Sqdn 24.6.40. Destroyed on ground by e/a Darwin 19.2.42.
73	4.4.40	No.6 Sqdn 3.7.40. No.2 Sqdn 3.1.42. No.1 OTU 28.6.42. W/o 11.12.46.
74	3.4.40	No.6 Sqdn 1.7.40. No.2 Sqdn 3.1.42. No.1 OTU 17.4.42. W/o 12.11.46.
75	5.4.40	No.8 Sqdn 27.6.40. Shot up over Malacca St.[F/L Arnold] Crashed Sembawang 18.1.42.
76	3.4.40	No.8 Sqdn 27.6.40 Bombed at Sembawang 17.2.42. W/o 20.3.42.
77	4.4.40	No.2 Sqdn 5.7.40. No.13 Sqdn 26.5.42. No.1 OTU 21.12.42. Crashed 11.10.43.
78	5.4.40	No.2 Sqdn 5.7.40. Destroyed at Darwin by e/a 19.2.42
79	2.4.40	No.2 Sqdn 3.7.40. Crashed on t.o. Koepang 20.1.42.
80	3.4.40	No.2 Sqdn 23.7.40. No.13 Sqdn 26.5.42. No.1 OTU 17.8.42. Components 23.1.45.
81	2.5.40	No.8 Sqdn 2.6.40. Destroyed on ground by e/a Semplak, Java 22.4.42.[F/L J. Lockwood].
82	1.5.40	No.8 Sqdn 29.6.40. Bombed at Sembawang 19.2.42.
83	1.5.40	No.13 Sqdn 3.7.40. Crashed on t.o. Broome 7.9.40.
84	2.5.40	No.13 Sqdn 3.7.40. No.4 Com. Flt 21.3.42. W/o 12.11.46.
85	17.5.40	No.8 Sqdn 9.7.40. No.1 Sqdn 22.1.42. Lost on shipping strike, Banka Is.[F/L J.K. Douglas].
86	17.5.40	No.1 Sqdn 9.7.40. Crashed Sembawang 30.7.41.
87	17.5.40	No.1 Sqdn 9.7.40. Shot down by Zeros 24.2.42 near Sri Buat Is.[F/L H.C. Plenty].
88	17.5.40	No.23 Sqdn 11.9.40. No.1 OTU 15.2.42. No.32 Sqdn 30.4.43. No.1 OTU 4.5.43. W/o 12.11.46.
89	17.5.40	No.1 Sqdn 9.7.40. No.7 Sqdn 24.3.42. No.1 OTU 29.6.42. Crashed Bairnsdale 9.8.42.
90	17.5.40	No.1 Sqdn 9.7.40. Destroyed on ground by e/a Kota Bharu 9.12.41.
91	17.5.40	No.24 Sqdn 22.9.40. Lost in shipping strike Gasmata 11.2.46. [& A16-126].

A16-92	20.6.40	No.1 Sqdn 9.7.40. Destroyed on ground by e/a 9.12.41.
93	20.6.40	No.1 Sqdn 9.7.40. No.8 Sqdn 28.10.41. Destroyed on Java 6.3.42.
94	20.6.40	No.1 Sqdn 9.7.40. F.T.R. from sortie against enemy c/v Kota Bharu 8.12.41.
95	20.6.40	ATS 21.8.40. No.2 Sqdn 23.12.40. No.14 Sqdn 21.6.41. No.8 Sqdn 3.1.42. Bombed at Seletar 12.1.42.
96	20.6.40	ATS 20.11.40. No.2 Sqdn 17.5.41. No.13 Sqdn 21.6.41. Bombed at Darwin. W/o 19.2.42.
97	20.6.40	No.2 Sqdn 2.8.40. Crashed 2 miles E of Canberra 13.8.40. As components 27.8.40.
98	20.6.40	No.14 Sqdn 9.9.40. No.13 Sqdn 2.2.41. Damaged by e/a Laha 9.1.42. No.7 Sqdn 12.5.42. No.1 OTU 27.6.42. No.1 Com. Flt 3.7.42. W/o 12.11.46.
99	20.6.40	No.6 Sqdn 16.9.40. No.2 Sqdn 3.1.42. No.1 OTU 8.5.42. No.4 Com. Flt 19.10.42. Conversion 7.8.44.
100	20.6.40	No.2 Sqdn 15.9.40. Force landed off Bathurst Is. 20.3.42.
101	5.12.41	No.14 Sqdn 28.12.41. No.32 Sqdn 19.2.42. F.T.R. from Gasmata area 3.3.42.
102	5.12.41	No.6 Sqdn 28.12.41. No.32 Sqdn 19.2.42. No.1 OTU 25.8.42. Ground-looped Bairnsdale 28.2.43.
103	5.12.41	No.6 Sqdn 3.1.42. Damaged on Rabaul recce 19.2.42. No.32 Sqdn 19.11.42. No.6 Sqdn 15.8.43. No.1 OTU 25.9.43. Ground-looped Bairnsdale 28.7.44.
104	5.12.41	No.14 Sqdn 28.12.41. U/c collapsed during t.o. Albany 19.1.42. Conversion 3.2.43.
105	5.12.41	No.1 OTU 20.12.41. Landing accident in Tasmania 19.1.42. Became VH-BKY.
106	5.12.41	No.6 Sqdn 3.1.42. F.T.R. from Salamaua–Rabaul flt 24.1.42.
107	5.12.41	No.1 OTU 10.1.42. Crashed during t.o. Mildawa 27.9.43. Conversion 14.10.43.
108	5.12.41	No.6 Sqdn 3.1.42. No.13 Sqdn 19.5.42. Crashed on Timor at Halneoelik 2.6.42.
109	5.12.41	No.7 Sqdn 2.2.42. No.13 Sqdn 19.3.42. Attacked by e/a and spun into sea Timor 23.3.42.
110	5.12.41	No.1 OTU 21.12.41. Attacked by e/a after t.o.; landed and was strafed Dobodura 26.12.42. No.1 Com. unit 30.7.44. No.1 OTU 14.7.45. Sold 1.4.47.
111	5.12.41	No.6 Sqdn 28.12.41. No.13 Sqdn 13.4.42. No.14 Sqdn 16.6.42. No.32 Sqdn 13.1.43. Special Duties Flt 17.9.43. Survey Flt 6.12.43. Crashed landing Flinders Is. 12.1.44.
112	5.12.41	No.1 OTU 28.12.41. No.14 Sqdn 17.7.42. No.32 Sqdn 23.12.42 No.6 Sqdn 9.6.43. Survey Flt 19.5.44. Sold 10.9.47. Became VH-BNJ.
113	8.12.41	No.14 Sqdn 28.12.41. No.32 Sqdn 31.12.42. No.6 Sqdn 25.7.43 No.1 OTU 1.10.44. Crashed into sea 3 miles from Paynsville 4.5.45.
114	5.12.41	No.7 Sqdn 9.2.42. No.1 OTU 29.6.42. No.1 Com. unit 3.8.44. Sold 31.3.47. Became VH-SMK.
115	5.12.41	No.14 Sqdn 5.1.42. No.32 Sqdn 14.1.43. No.6 Sqdn 24.4.43. No.3 Com. Unit 26.5.44 No.1 OTU 18.7.45. Sold 31.3.47. Became VH-BDN.
116	8.12.41	No.14 Sqdn 28.12.41. No.32 Sqdn 28.12.42. No.4 Com. Unit 4.12.43. No.1 OTU 14.4.45. No.1 Com. Unit 19.10.45. Sold 1.4.47.
117	5.12.41	No.1 OTU 28.12.41. No.6 Sqdn 23.3.42. No.13 Sqdn 8.5.42. No.14 Sqdn 1.8.42. No.1 OTU 13.3.43. Force landed Laverton 17.1.45. Sold 31.3.47.
118	5.12.41	No.7 Sqdn 9.2.42. No.13 Sqdn 23.3.42. No.6 Sqdn 3.4.43. No.4 Com. Unit 7.4.44. Crashed into sea 2 1/4 miles N of Cairns 5.3.45.
119	5.12.41	No.14 Sqdn 28.12.41. Destroyed at Broome by e/a 3.3.42.
120	8.12.41	No.7 Sqdn 9.2.42. No.6 Sqdn 22.5.43. No.1 Com. Flt 7.12.43. Sold 10.2.48.
121	8.12.41	No.14 Sqdn 28.12.41. No.2 Sqdn 25.1.42. Destroyed Laha, Koepang 30.1.42.
122	5.12.41	No.14 Sqdn 25.1.42. No.32 Sqdn 15.1.43. No.6 Sqdn 29.5.43 No.38 Sqdn 20.3.44. Sold 24.7.47.
123	8.12.41	No.14 Sqdn 24.12.41. No.13 Sqdn 25.1.42. Lost by e/a Laha, Koepang 30.1.42.
124	8.12.41	No.14 Sqdn 28.12.41. No.32 Sqdn 14.1.43. No.37 Sqdn 5.9.43. Special Duties Flt 1.11.43. No.38 Sqdn 16.12.43. No.1 Com. Flt 10.9.45. Sold 21.6.48.
125	5.12.41	No.14 Sqdn 28.12.41. No.13 Sqdn 25.1.42. Lost by e/a Koepang 20.1.42.
126	15.12.41	No.6 Sqdn 3.1.42. Lost in enemy action Gasmata 11.2.42.
127	15.12.41	No.1 OTU 10.1.42. No.13 Sqdn 28.3.42. No.1 OTU 10.10.42. No.1 OTU 13.2.43. Sold 24.9.47.
128	15.12.41	No.6 Sqdn 28.12.41. No.1 OTU 25.10.42. No.32 Sqdn 30.4.43. Lungatha 5.8.43 landed without u/c down.

A16-129	15.12.41	No.6 Sqdn 3.1.42. No.13 Sqdn 13.4.42. No.14 Sqdn 20.7.42. No.32 Sqdn 3.2.43. No.6 Sqdn 27.4.43. Crashed Woodlark Is.17.8.43. Conversion 14.9.43.
130	15.12.41	No.6 Sqdn 3.1.42. No.32 Sqdn 6.2.43. No.6 Sqdn 27.4.43. Special Duties Flt 10.11.43. Survey Flt 3.2.44. Fishing Survey Flt 16.7.46. No.1 Com. Unit 19.8.46. Sold 24.9.47.
131	15.12.41	No.6 Sqdn 3.1.42. No.32 Sqdn 5.3.42. No.1 OTU 18.8.44. Crashed East Sale 12.9.45.
132	15.12.41	No.6 Sqdn 3.1.42. No.13 Sqdn 20.5 42. F.T.R. from flt Darwin-Buro 18.6.42.
133	15.12.41	No.13 Sqdn 9.2.42. No.1 OTU 4.3.43. Crashed on t.o. Bairnsdale 11.6.43.
134	15.12.41	No.6 Sqdn 3.1.42. No.32 Sqdn 18.3.42. No.13 Sqdn 19.9.42. No.32 Sqdn 7.2.43. No.6 Sqdn 9.4.43. No.38 Sqdn 7.11.43. No.1 OTU 10.6.44. Sold 24.9.47.
135	15.12.41	No.14 Sqdn 28.12.41. No.2 Sqdn 25.1.42. Destroyed on ground Darwin 19.2.42.
136	15.12.41	No.14 Sqdn 28.12.41. No.32 Sqdn 21.2.42. Destroyed on ground by e/a Seven Mile, Port Moresby 14.3.42?
137	15.12.41	No.7 Sqdn 9.2.42. No.13 Sqdn 19.3.42. F.T.R. from Koepang area 14.4.42.
138	15.12.41	No.7 Sqdn 1.2.42. No.13 Sqdn 6.4.42. No.32 Sqdn 18.10.42. No.3 Com Unit 4.2.44. No.1 OTU 2.5.45. Sold 24.9.47.
139	26.12.41	No.7 Sqdn 9.4.42. Force landed Kilsyth 26.3.42. Conversion.
140	26.12.41	No.1 OTU 17.1.42. Crashed at Sale, Vic. 26.2.42. Conversion.
141	26.12.41	No.7 Sqdn 25.1.42. No.13 Sqdn 18.2.42. Destroyed by e/a Darwin 19.2.42?
142	26.12.41	No.7 Sqdn 25.1.42. Crashed between Darwin and Daly Waters 1.3.42.
143	29.3.42	No.13 Sqdn 17.5.42. No.32 Sqdn 3.2.43. No.1 OTU 19.3.43. Special Duties Flt 25.11.43. 1 APU 30.11.43. Sold 24.9.47.
144	26.12.41	No.14 Sqdn 18.1.42. Crashed Ceduna 17.1.42. Conversion.
145	26.12.41	No.24 Sqdn 12.1.42. F.T.R. from Lae-Rabaul sortie 21.1.42.
146	26.12.41	No.24 Sqdn 12.1.42. Destroyed by e/a Rabaul 3.2.42.
147	26.12.41	No.14 Sqdn 25.1.42. No.1 OTU 28.3.43. No.6 Sqdn 15.8.43. No.1 Com. Unit 23.11.43. No.38 Sqdn 8.1.44. No.1 OTU 17.6.44. Sold 24.4.47.
148	26.12.41	No.14 Sqdn 25.1.42. No.32 Sqdn 25.12.42. No.6 Sqdn 1.5.43. No.38 Sqdn 8.2.44. No.1 OTU 21.6.44. Sold 24.9.47.
149	26.12.41	No.13 Sqdn 9.2.42. No.14 Sqdn 31.12.42. No.6 Sqdn 10.6.43. No.4 Com. Unit 29.11.43. No.1 OTU 5.8.44. Sold 24.4.47.
150	26.12.41	No.7 Sqdn 25.1.42. No.14 Sqdn 27.7.42. No.32 Sqdn 16.2.43. No.6 Sqdn 1.6.43. Ground-looped Turnbull Field, Milne Bay 5.9.43. Conversion.
151	26.12.41	No.1 OTU 17.1.42. No.7 Sqdn 23.3.42. Crashed Christmas Hill, Vic. 15.4.42.
152	26.12.41	No.7 Sqdn 25.1.42. No.14 Sqdn 30.5.42. No.32 Sqdn 13.1.43. Crashed Victoria Park, NSW 26.1.43. Conversion.
153	16.3.42	No.32 Sqdn 8.4.42. Crashed on t.o. Seven Mile, Port Moresby 28.4.42.
154	16.3.42	No.32 Sqdn 22.4.42. No.6 Sqdn 14.9.42. No.2 Sqdn 20.8.43. Conversion 7.8.44.
155	16.3.42	No.32 Sqdn 22.4.42. No.1 OTU 29.11.42. Sold 10.9.47.
156	16.3.42	No.2 Sqdn 6.4.42. No.13 Sqdn 31.5.42. AAU 18.11.44. Sold 24.9.47.
157	16.3.42	No.32 Sqdn 27.4.42. No.6 Sqdn 27.8.42. No.1 OTU 2.4.43. Sold 2.7.46.
158	16.3.42	No.32 Sqdn 23.4.42. Damaged Horn Island 28.7.42. Conversion 27.8.43.
159	16.3.42	No.2 Sqdn 6.4.42. Crashed in sea Koepang Bay 13.4.42.
160	16.3.42	No.32 Sqdn 20.4.42. No.2 Sqdn 8.9.42. No.1 OTU 5.6.44. No.2 AAU 12.5.45. Crashed 23.5.45.
161	16.3.42	No.2 Sqdn 6.4.42. No.1 OTU 16.7.44. Crashed at Cressy 24.3.45.
162	16.3.42	No.32 Sqdn 23.4.42. Crashed at Hinchinbrook Passage 5.5.42.
163	26.12.41	No.23 Sqdn 18.1.42. No.32 Sqdn 23.2.42. No.6 Sqdn 19.12.42. No.1 OTU 31.3.43. Sold 24.9.47.
164	8.1.42	No.7 Sqdn 1.2.42. Crashed on t.o. Laverton 2.4.42.
165	8.1.42	No.23 Sqdn 24.1.42. No.32 Sqdn 23.2.42. F.T.R. from Gasmata op. 3.3.42.
166	8.1.42	No.7 Sqdn 1.2.42. No.13 Sqdn 29.8.42. F.T.R. from Laivai, Timor op. 24.12.42.
167	8.1.42	No.23 Sqdn 25.1.42. No.32 Sqdn 23.2.42. Destroyed by e/a Seven Mile, Port Moresby, 24.2.42.
168	8.1.42	No.7 Sqdn 2.2.42. Collided with 2 × Wirraways Laverton 26.3.42. Conversion.
169	8.1.42	No.23 Sqdn 2.1.42. No.32 Sqdn 23.2.42. No.2 Sqdn 2.4.43. Shot down over Keaukwa 3.4.43.

A16-170	16.3.42	No.32 Sqdn 14.4.42. No.2 Sqdn 5.9.42. F.T.R. from Koepang op. 25.10.42.
171	8.1.42	No.7 Sqdn 1.2.42. No.1 OTU 29.6.42. No.6 Sqdn 6.3.43. No.2 Sqdn 3.5.43. Shot down by e/a Maikdoor 6.5.43.
172	16.3.42	No.2 Sqdn 6.4.42. Shot down into sea by AA fire Saumlaki Bay 14.9.42.
173	16.3.42	No.32 Sqdn 20.4.42. Crashed 25 miles W of Port Kembla, NSW 4.11.42.
174	16.3.42	No.2 Sqdn 13.4.42. Destroyed in shipping strike Ambon 22.5.42.
175	23.3.42	No.2 Sqdn. Engine failure; force landed 18.6.42.
176	21.3.42	No.2 Sqdn 11.4.42. Crashed on t.o. Darwin 7.5.42. Conversion 13.8.43.
177	23.3.42	No.2 Sqdn 21.4.42. No.6 Sqdn 28.11.42. No.2 Sqdn 29.3.43. No.2 AAU 10.7.44. Sold 26.8.46.
178	23.3.42	No.2 Sqdn 17.4.42. F.T.R. from Arafura Sea op. 15.10.43.
179	23.3.42	No.32 Sqdn 13.4.42. Destroyed on ground by e/a Port Moresby 20.7.42.
180	23.3.42	No.32 Sqdn 13.4.42. No.1 OTU 14.4.43. No.2 Sqdn 12.10.43. No.6 Com. Unit 10.2.44. No.3 Com. Unit 14.3.44. No.1 OTU 8.5.45. Sold 24.9.47.
181	23.3.42	No.2 Sqdn 24.4.42. F.T.R. from Keaukwa 15.8.43.
182	21.3.42	No.2 Sqdn 23.4.42. F.T.R. from Koepang op. 23.4.42.
183	21.3.42	No.2 Sqdn 23.4.42. Crashed after t.o. Millingimbi 19.4.43. Collided with A16-197.
184	29.3.42	Ground-looped Darwin and destroyed 30.5.42. Conversion.
185	29.3.42	No.32 Sqdn 1.6.42. No.6 Sqdn 27.8.42. No.2 Sqdn 3.6.43. Conversion 22.11.43.
186	29.3.42	No.32 Sqdn 27.4.42. No.13 Sqdn 28.12.42. No.2 Sqdn 9.43. Crashed 12.6.43.
187	29.3.42	No.2 Sqdn 11.5.42. F.T.R from shipping strike Halong Bay, Ambon 22.5.42.
188	29.3.42	No.32 Sqdn 4.5.42. Crashed on landing Cooktown 13.5.42. Conversion.
189	29.3.42	No.6 Sqdn 18.5.42. No.32 Sqdn 27.8.42. No.6 Sqdn 19.12.42. No.2 Sqdn 15.5.43. No.6 Com. Unit 12.2.44. Sold 24.9.47.
190	29.3.42	No.32 Sqdn 11.5.42. Crashed into sea Beverlac Island 23.5.42.
191	29.3.42	No.6 Sqdn 8.4.42. No.32 Sqdn 11.5.42. Crashed at Giru Is. after air collision with A16-194 24.5.42.
192	5.4.42	No.32 Sqdn 8.4.42. No.13 Sqdn 25.9.42. No.2 Sqdn 4.4.43. No.4 Com. Unit 31.7.44. No.1 OTU 16.8.44. Sold 24.9.47.
193	5.4.42	No.32 Sqdn 4.5.42. F.T.R. from Salamaua area 4.7.42.
194	5.4.42	No.6 Sqdn 27.4.42. No.32 Sqdn 11.5.42. Crashed at Giru Is. after air collision with A16-191 24.5.42.
195	5.4.42	No.32 Sqdn 24.5.42. No.2 Sqdn 15.1.43. F.T.R. from Penfui op. 9.7.43.
196	2.4.42	No.2 Sqdn 30.4.42. Destroyed by blast from bombed ship Ambon area 13.5.42.
197	5.4.42	No.6 Sqdn 29.6.42. No.2 Sqdn 27.7.42. No.13 Sqdn 22.2.43. No.2 Sqdn 4.4.43. Crashed at Millingimbi after suspected air collision with A16-183 19.4.43.
198	5.4.42	No.32 Sqdn. F.T.R. from Horn Island to Amberley 6.7.42.
199	2.4.42	No.13 Sqdn 30.6.42. No.2 Sqdn 14.4.43. No.3 Com. Flt 16.4.44. Sold 24.9.47.
200	5.4.42	No.2 Sqdn 22.7.42. No.6 Sqdn 3.12.42. No.1 OTU 26.4.43. Sold 24.9.47.
201	5.4.42	No.32 Sqdn 8.6.42. Crashed at Popogo, Papua, 22.7.42.
202	1.4.42	No.6 Sqdn 30.5.42. No.13 Sqdn 23.12.42. No.2 Sqdn 10.4.43. Ground-looped at Hughes 6.10.43.
203	1.4.42	No.6 Sqdn 25.9.42. No.1 OTU 21.4.43. No.2 Sqdn 1.10.43. Crashed Adelaide River 3.4.44.
204	5.4.42	No.13 Sqdn 2.8.42. No.2 Sqdn 10.4.43. Conversion 9.8.44.
205	5.4.42	No.32 Sqdn 6.6.42 No.6 Sqdn 10.8.42 Crashed into sea Sumagani 10.11.42.
206	5.4.42	No.6 Sqdn 18.5.42. No.32 Sqdn 27.8.42. No.6 Sqdn 10.1.43. Destroyed by e/a Turnbull, Milne Bay 17.1.43.
207	6.4.42	No.2 Sqdn 11.5.42. No.1 OTU 3.6.44. No.2 AAU 25.6.45. Sold 30.9.47.
208	6.4.42	No.2 Sqdn 4.5.42. Crashed Alice Springs 20.5.42. Conversion 26.1.43.
209	13.4.42	No.2 Sqdn 1.6.42. F.T.R. from Maobessi, Timor op. 21.8.42.
210	13.4.42	No.2 Sqdn 11.5.42. Crashed into sea during e/a attack Lavai, Port Timor 27.12.42.
211	13.4.42	No.6 Sqdn 21.6.42. No.2 Sqdn 3.4.43. Crashlanded Millingimbi 6.5.43.

A16-212	13.4.42	No.13 Sqdn 1.6.42. Crashlanded in storm Hughes 27.2.43.
213	13.4.42	No.6 Sqdn 15.6.42. No.2 Sqdn 27.3.43. Damaged by AA over Langgoer; crashlanded Hughes 10.10.43. Conversion 23.10.43.
214	13.4.42	No.6 Sqdn 23.5.42. No.1 OTU 18.4.43. Sold 25.11.46.
215	17.4.42	No.32 Sqdn 6.6.42. No.6 Sqdn 14.9.42. No.2 Sqdn 22.12.43. No.2 AAU 19.9.44. No.1 Com. Unit 8.10.45. Sold 18.6.48.
216	17.4.42	No.6 Sqdn 21.5.42. F.T.R. to Port Moresby from Kieta Buka area 25.8.42.
217	17.4.42	No.2 Sqdn 12.6.42. Crashlanded Corunna Downs 29.5.42. Conversion 28.3.44.
218	17.4.42	No.32 Sqdn 15.6.42. A29-78 collided with A16-218 while latter was about to take off, Fall River, New Guinea 16.8.42.
219	17.4.42	No.13 Sqdn 20.7.42. No.2 Sqdn 1.4.43. No.2 AAU 17.8.44. Survey Flt 20.8.45. Sold 13.1.48.
220	20.5.42	No.6 Sqdn 7.7.42. Crashed into Beagle Bay, 5m NW of Hood Point 3.9.42.
221	17.4.42	No.32 Sqdn 18.5.42. No.2 Sqdn 18.2.43. Conversion 16.4.43.
222	13.3.42	No.7 Sqdn 12.5.42. No.1 OTU 29.6.42. No.6 Sqdn 28.9.42. No.1 OTU 3.4.43. Sold 16.4.47.
223	6.5.42	No.32 Sqdn 22.6.42. Damaged on landing Richmond 16.10.42 Conversion 26.3.43.
224	6.5.42	No.13 Sqdn 27.6.42. Crashed after t.o. Laverton 14.10.42.
225	6.5.42	No.13 Sqdn 4.7.42. No.6 Sqdn 21.11.42. Destroyed on t.o. Port Moresby 24.11.42.
226	6.5.42	No.13 Sqdn 11.7.42. No.2 Sqdn 26.6.43. No.2 AAU 28.5.44. Survey Flt 7.8.45. Sold 24.9.47.
227	6.5.42	No.13 Sqdn 9.7.42. No.2 Sqdn 15.4.43. Crashlanded Millingimbi 1.7.43.
228	6.5.42	No.6 Sqdn 28.7.42. No.2 Sqdn 8.4.43. Crashed 19.4.43.
229	6.5.42	No.6 Sqdn 28.7.42. No.1 OTU 6.4.43. No.2 Sqdn 25.9.43. No.1 OTU 31.1.44. No.2 AAU 27.8.45. Sold 24.9.47.
230	6.5.42	No.6 Sqdn 28.7.42. No.2 Sqdn 12.4.43. F.T.R. from Banda Sea op. 27.3.44.
231	6.5.42	No.6 Sqdn 28.7.42. No.1 OTU 29.4.43. Sold 24.9.47.
232	8.5.42	No.2 Sqdn 16.6.42. Crashed at Batchelor after air combat 4.12.42.
233	6.5.42	No.13 Sqdn 24.6.42. No.2 Sqdn 4.4.43. F.T.R. from Tanibar Is. area 8.9.43.
234	6.5.42	No.2 Sqdn 8.7.42. F.T.R. from Saumlaki area op. 30.7.42.
235	19.5.42	No.13 Sqdn 2.7.42. No.2 Sqdn 4.4.43. No.4 Com. Unit 23.4.44. Conversion 17.1.46.
236	25.5.42	No.13 Sqdn 26.7.42. No.2 Sqdn 27.3.43. Conversion 9.8.44.
237	19.5.42	No.2 Sqdn 5.7.42. A/c exploded during refuelling Batchelor 15.3.43.
238	20.5.42	No.13 Sqdn 2.7.42. No.2 Sqdn 24.1.43. Conversion 29.10.43.
239	20.5.42	No.6 Sqdn 1.7.42. Destroyed by enemy bombing Turnbull 20.1.43.
240	20.5.42	No.6 Sqdn 11.7.42. No.2 Sqdn 11.2.43. Damaged on t.o. Batchelor 15.5.43.
241	20.5.42	No.2 Sqdn 22.7.42. F.T.R. from Oroe Islands op. 28.4.43.
242	20.5.42	No.2 Sqdn 9.7.42. Crashlanded Annisley Point 14.3.43. Conversion 16.11.43.
243	20.5.42	No.13 Sqdn 4.7.42. F.T.R. from Koepang sortie 1.10.42.
244	20.5.42	No.6 Sqdn 6.7.42. No.32 Sqdn 27.7.42. No.6 Sqdn 16.10.42. No.2 Sqdn 19.5.43. Ground-looped 4.11.43. Conversion 7.2.44.
245	20.5.42	No.13 Sqdn 6.7.42. No.6 Sqdn 13.2.43. Crashed into sea off East Cape 24.2.43
246	20.5.42	No.6 Sqdn 10.7.42. F.T.R. from sortie ex Gurney Field 28.10.42.
247	20.5.42	No.13 Sqdn 4.7.42. No.2 Sqdn 27.3.43. Crashed Millingimbi after hit by AA over Timoeka 6.4.43.

Appendix E
Royal New Zealand Air Force Hudsons

RNZAF Serial No.	Contract No.	RAF Serial No.	American Reg. No.	Remarks
NZ2001	2671	AM589		Mark V
NZ2002	2672	AM590		" "
NZ2003	2673	AM591		" "
NZ2004	2674	AM592		" "
NZ2005	2675	AM593		" "
NZ2006	2676	AM594		" "
NZ2007	3820	V9235		Mark III
NZ2008	3821	V9236		" "
NZ2009	3822	V9237		" "
NZ2010	3823	V9238		" "
NZ2011	3824	V9239		" "
NZ2012	3825	V9240		" "
NZ2013	3826	V9241		" "
NZ2014	3827	V9242		" "
NZ2015	3828	V9243		" "
NZ2016	3829	V9244		" "
NZ2017	3830	V9245		" "
NZ2018	3831	V9246		" "
NZ2019	3832	V9247		" "
NZ2020	3833	V9248		" "
NZ2021	3834	V9249		" "
NZ2022	3835	V9250		" "
NZ2023	3836	V9251		" "
NZ2024	3837	V9252		" "
NZ2025	3845	AE490		" "
NZ2026	3849	AE494		" "
NZ2027	3850	AE495		" "
NZ2028	3851	AE496		" "
NZ2029	3852	AE497		Mark III
NZ2030	3853	AE498		" "
NZ2031	3854	AE499		" "
NZ2032	3855	AE500		" "
NZ2033	3856	AE501		" "
NZ2034	3857	AE502		" "
NZ2035	3858	AE503		" "
NZ2036	3859	AE504		" "
NZ2037	6435	BW756	41-23618	Mark IIIA/ Lend-lease

RNZAF Serial No.	Contract No.	RAF Serial No.	American Reg. No.	Remarks
NZ2038	6436	BW757	41-23619	" "
NZ2039	6437	BW758	41-23620	" "
NZ2040	6438	BW759	41-23621	" "
NZ2041	6439	BW760	41-23622	" "
NZ2042	6440	BW761	41-23623	" "
NZ2043	6441	BW762	41-23624	" "
NZ2044	6442	BW763	41-23625	" "
NZ2045	6443	BW764	41-23626	" "
NZ2046	6444	BW765	41-23627	" "
NZ2047	6445	BW766	41-23628	" "
NZ2048	6446	BW767	41-23629	" "
NZ2049	6465	FH175	41-36976	" "
NZ2050	6505	FH215	41-37016	" "
NZ2051	6610	FH320	41-37121	" "
NZ2052	6611	FH321	41-37122	" "
NZ2053	6612	FH322	41-37123	" "
NZ2054	6613	FH323	41-37124	" "
NZ2055	6614	FH324	41-37125	" "
NZ2056	6615	FH325	41-37126	" "
NZ2057	6616	FH326	41-37127	" "
NZ2058	6617	FH327	41-37128	" "
NZ2059	6618	FH328	41-37129	" "
NZ2060	6506	FH216	41-37017	Mark IIIA/ Lend-lease
NZ2061	6507	FH217	41-37018	" "
NZ2062	6508	FH218	41-37019	" "
NZ2063	6509	FH219	41-37020	" "
NZ2064	6510	FH220	41-37021	" "
NZ2065	6511	FH221	41-37022	" "
NZ2066	6512	FH222	41-37023	" "
NZ2067	6513	FH223	41-37024	" "
NZ2068	6514	FH224	41-37025	" "
NZ2069	6515	FH225	41-37026	" "
NZ2070	6516	FH226	41-37027	" "
NZ2071	6679	FH389	41-37190	" "
NZ2072	6681	FH391	41-37192	" "
NZ2073	6683	FH393	41-37194	" "
NZ2074	6686	FH396	41-37197	" "
NZ2075	6691	FH401	41-37202	" "
NZ2076	6692	FH402	41-37203	" "
NZ2077	6695	FH405	41-37206	" "
NZ2078	6698	FH408	41-37209	" "
NZ2079	6702	FH412	41-37213	" "

RNZAF Serial No.	Contract No.	RAF Serial No.	American Reg. No.	Remarks
NZ2080	6703	FH413	41-37214	" "
NZ2081	6705	FH415	41-37216	" "
NZ2082	6722	FH432	41-37233	" "
NZ2083	6724	FH434	41-37235	" "
NZ2084	6725	FH435	41-37236	" "
NZ2085	6726	FH436	41-37237	" "
NZ2086	6727	FH437	41-37238	" "
NZ2087	6728	FH438	41-37239	" "
NZ2088	6729	FH439	41-37240	" "
NZ2089	6730	FH440	41-37241	" "
NZ2090	6731	FH441	41-37242	" "
NZ2091	6833	EW949	42-6658	Mark VI/ Lend-lease
NZ2092	6834	EW950	42-6659	" "
NZ2093	6836	EW952	42-6661	" "
NZ2094	6837	EW953	42-6662	" "

Codes

No.1 Squadron	SJ
No.2 Squadron	UH
No.3 Squadron	JV
No.4 Squadron	YZ
No.40 Squadron	
No.41 Squadron	QQ
No.1 OTU	ZX

RNZAF Squadrons Operating Lockheed Hudson Aircraft

No.1 Squadron equipped with Hudsons 1941–1943
Commanding Oficers

		Bases
S/Ldr G.N. Roberts	May 1940–August 1941	New Zealand March 1940–October 1943
" G.H. Fisher	Aug. 1941–July 1942	Det. at Nandi, Fiji
" F.J. Lucas	July–Dec. 1942	
" G.L. Moncton	Dec. 1942–March 1943	
" E.W. Tacon	March–May 1943	
" H.C. Walker	May 1943–April 1944	Guadalcanal October–November 1943

No.2 Squadron equipped with Hudsons 1941–1943
Commanding Officers

		Bases
S/Ldr R.J. Cohen	Jan. 1941–May 1942	New Zealand Jan. 1941–November 1943
" J.J. Busch	May–Dec. 1942	
" E.A. Moehn	Dec. 1942–April 1943	
" R.H.A. Hogg	April–August 1943	
" A.B. Greenaway	August 1943–June 1944	Espiritu Santo November 1943–Feb 1944

No.3 Squadron equipped with Hudsons 1942–1944
Commanding Officers

		Bases
S/Ldr C.L. Monkton	April 1941–April 1942	New Zealand April-September 1942
" J.W.H. Bray	May–Sept. 1942	
" G.H. Fisher	Sept. 1942–July 1943	Espiritu Santo October–November 1942
" J.J. Busch	July–Nov. 1943	Espiritu Santo October 43–January 1944
" A.B. Greenaway		Guadalcanal July–August 1944
		Bougainville August–October 1944
		Emirau Is. October–November 1944

No.4 Squadron equipped with Hudsons 1941–1943

Commanding Officers		*Bases*
S/Ldr G.R. White	Oct. 1940–Oct. 1942	Fiji Oct. 1940–Nov. 1944
W/Cmdr E. M. Lewis	Nov. 1942–May 1943	
S/Ldr E.W. Tacon	May–Dec. 1943	
″ Brooke-Taylor	Dec. 1943–Apr. 1944	Emirau Is. Nov. 1944–Feb. 1945

No.9 Squadron equipped with Hudsons July 1942–1943

Commanding Officers		*Bases*
S/Ldr D.E. Grigg	July 1942–June 1943	New Caledonia July 1942–March 1943
″ J.J. Busch	June–July 1943	Espiritu Santo March–October 1943
″ A.C. Willis	July–August 1943	New Zealand Nov. 1943–Feb. 1944
W/Cmdr A.C. Allen	Oct. 1943–May 1945	Espiritu Santo Feb.–May 1944

No.40 Transport Squadron equipped with Hudsons, Lodestars and Dakotas

Commanding Officers		*Bases*
W/Cmdr J. Adams	June 1943–Nov. 1944	Whenuapai
W/Cmdr R.A. Kirkup	Nov. 1944–April1946	

No.41 Transport Squadron equipped with Hudsons, Lodestars and Dakotas

Commanding Officer		*Base*
W/Cmdr H.C. Walker	Sept. 1944–Aug. 1945	Whenuapai Sept. 1944–August 1945

Royal New Zealand Air Force Hudson Strength

Date	Hudson Numbers	Percentage of Total Strength	Total Strength
30.6.41	6	0.98%	611
8.12.41	36	5.6%	641
30.6.42	85	11.1%	763
15.8.45	52	4.0%	1316
1.4.49	14	2.7%	527

94 Lockheed Hudsons were received by the RNZAF as follows:
Mark IIIs – 30; Mark IIIAs – 54; Mark Vs – 6; Mark VIs – 4

Appendix F

Lockheed Hudsons with American Designations

Model	Number	Gross Wt	Serial Numbers	Remarks
A28	52	22,300lb	41-23171/23222	Leased to RAAF as Mark IVAs Serial Nos. A16-101/A16-152
A28A	450	22,360lb	42-6582/6681 42-46937/47286	Became EW837/EW972 Became FK381/FK730
A29	416	21,700lb	41-23223/23638	EW361/EW766 153 repossessed; 20 diverted to USN
A29A	384	21,700lb	41-23639 41-36938/38267 42-47287/47369	BW767 FH167/FH466 FK731/FK813 Some repossessed
AT-18	217	19,300lb	42-55568/55784	With Martin turrets & 2 × 0.5 Brownings

AT-18A	83	22,360lb	42-55485/55567	Without turrets
C63	0	18,500lb		A29 trooper – cancelled
C111	3	17,500lb	44-83233	Ex PK-AFN
			44-83234	Ex PK-AFP
			44-83235	Ex PK-AFQ
PBO	19		Bu03842/Bu03861	Ex RAF Mk IIA serial Nos. BW361–BW380 with turret & ventral gun position.

Appendix G

Technical Data

Dimensions: Span 65ft 6in.; Length 44ft 4in.; Height 11ft 10½ in; Wing area 551 sq. ft
Construction: Stressed skin
Hudson Mark I and Mark II Characteristics:
Gross weight 17,500lb
Fuel capacity 536 gallons
Engines: two Wright Cyclone GR 1820 G102 A
Rated power of engines 900bhp at 2350rpm
Take-off power at sea level per engine 1100bhp at 2350rpm.
Wing loading 31.7lb/sq. ft
High speed at rated altitude 215 knots
High speed at sea level 213 knots
Landing speed at sea level flaps down 61 knots (70mph)
Maximum rate of climb 2180ft/min
Service ceiling full load 25,000ft
Take-off distance at sea level – no wind 903ft
Operating speed at 10,000ft 159 knots (183mph)
Endurance at operating speed 11 hours
Single engine ceiling 11,000ft
High speed on one engine at 8,000ft 149 knots (172mph)

Aircraft Limitations (Hudsons Mark I & II)
Maximum gross weight 17,500lb
Maximum indicated air speed at any time 291 knots
Maximum cruising speed 208 knots
Maximum indicated air speed flaps down 100 knots
Maximum indicated airspeed undercarriage down 148 knots
Maximum indicated airspeed lowering undercarriage 125 knots
Maximum indicated airspeed dropping flares 148 knots
Maximum bhp/engine for continuous operations 900@ 2300rpm
Maximum bhp/engine for take-off (5min duration) 1100 @ 2350rpm
Maximum oil inlet temperatures (emergency only) 104°C
Maximum oil inlet temperature (15 min duration) 260°C
Maximum cylinder head temperature (15 min duration) 260°C
Maximum cylinder head temperature for continuous op. 205°C

Altitude	Normal Power Man. pressure	Engine rpm	Emergency Power Man. pressure	Engine rpm
Sea level	37.5in. Hg	2300	43.5in. Hg	2350
2000	36.9	2300	Full throttle	2350
4000	36.3	2300	" "	2350
6000	35.6	2300	" "	2350

Cruising Alt.	Recommended 550bhp/eng Man. pressure	Engine rpm	Max. cruising 625bhp/engine Man. pressure	Engine rpm
Sea level	29in. Hg	1850	30in. Hg	1900
2000	28.3	1850	30	1900
4000	27.5	1850	29.7	1900
6000	26.9	1850	29.0	1900
8000	26.3	1850	28.3	1900
10,000	25.6	1850	27.7	1900
12,000	25.0	1850	Full throttle	
14,000	Full throttle			

Fuel Consumption Data for Mark I & II Hudsons fitted with Wright Cyclone CR 1820 G102A engines

Using	625 bhp/engine	0.461/bhp/hr	Or 80 gal/hr
	500 bhp/engine	0.450	62.5 gal/hr
	400 bhp/engine	0.427	47.4 gal/hr

Based on the various fuel consumption data, the endurance and range for various cruising powers are:

Altitude	BHP/engine	Airspeed knots	Endurance hours	Range O Wind	Range in 17.4kt headwind
Sea level	400	138.4	11.15	1740	1520
5000ft	400	149.5	11.15	1880	1660
10,000	400	157	11.15	1980	1760
15,000	400	155	11.15	1950	1730
Sea level	500	155	8.45	1480	1320
5000ft	500	165.5	8.45	1580	1420
10,000	500	175	8.45	1670	1510
15,000	500	184	8.45	1760	1590
Sea level	625	171.5	6.6	1280	1150
5000ft	625	182	6.6	1360	1230
10,000	625	192	6.6	1430	1300
11,000	625	194	6.6	1450	1320

In the foregoing range computations, 8.5 gallons of fuel were allowed for engine warm-up and two per cent of the total fuel capacity for climb to cruising altitude.

Recommendations and Data for Economical Cruising (Marks I & II)
Pilots were recommended to fly using a weak mixture at 27in. Hg boost and to reduce speed by reducing rpm but not below 1500rpm. If less power was required than that given at 27in. Hg boost, then boost should be reduced at 1500 rpm 125 knots indicated air speed for greater range; 100 knots indicated air speed with flaps up for greater endurance.

Fuel consumption figures given in Pilot's Notes *for the Mark I & II Hudsons were as follows:*

Boost in. Hg	RPM 1850	RPM 1650
26	58 gal/hour	54 gal/hour
24	53	49
22	47	44
20	40	38

Flying at 5,000 feet on a rich mixture with 30in. Hg boost at 1900rpm gave a quoted figure of 155 gal /hour total consumption.

Engines fitted to RAF Marks I-VI Hudsons
Marks I and II 1100bhp Wright Cyclone 9-cylinder radial R1820–G102A
Mark III 1200bhp Wright Cyclone R1820–G205A
Mark IV 1050bhp Pratt & Whitney 14-cylinder Twin Wasp R1830-SC3G
Mark V 1200bhp Pratt & Whitney Twin Wasp R1830-S3C4G
Mark VI 1200 bhp Pratt & Whitney Twin Wasp R18330-67

Glossary and Abbreviations

AA	Anti-aircraft
AAC	Army Air Corps
AAF	Army Air Force
AB	*Atlantic Bridge*
ABDA	American, British, Dutch and Australian Command
A/Cmdre	Air Commodore
ACM	Air Chief Marshal
A/F/Lt	Acting Flight Lieutenant
AH	Andrew Hendrie
AHQ	Area Headquarters
Aldis Lamp	A lamp used to transmit messages in Morse Code by operating a mirror and sighting through a telescopic sight.
AM	Air Marshal
AOC	Air Officer Commanding
AOC-in-C	Air Officer Commanding-in-Chief
A/S	Anti-Submarine
ASR	Air-Sea Rescue
ASV	Aircraft to Surface Vessel; equipment which transmitted electro-magnetic waves which would be reflected back by vessels producing a 'blip' on a cathode-ray tube.
AWM	Australian War Memorial (publishers)
BAF	Brazilian Air Force
BEF	British Expeditionary Force
C&C	Craven & Cate (American historians)
CCWR	Coastal Command's War Record 1939–1945
CFI	Chief Flying Instructor
C-in-C	Commander-in-Chief
CLA	Creeping Line Ahead; a navigational search method
CO	Commanding Officer
CRT	Cathode-Ray Tube (as used in radar and ASV)
Cross Over Patrol	A navigational patrol method
DC	Depth charge
DF	Direction finding
DFC	Distinguished Flying Cross
DG	Douglas Gillison (Australian historian)
DR	Dead Reckoning (navigation)
DR	Denis Richards (RAF historian)
E/A	Enemy aircraft
ETA	Estimated Time of Arrival
FAA	Fleet Air Arm
FC	*Flying Cats*
F/Cmdr	Flight Commander
F/Lt	Flight Lieutenant
F/O	Flying Officer
F/Sgt	Flight Sergeant
FTR	Failed to return (from operations)
GO	George Odgers (RAAF historian)
GOC-in-C	General Officer Commanding in Chief
GüH	Günter Hessler (German historian)
HE	High explosive

HH	Hans Herlin (German historian)
HMAS	His Majesty's Australian ship
HMCS	His Majesty's Canadian ship
HMS	His Majesty's Ship
HP	Group Captain 'Herb' Plenty, RAAF
IFF	Identification Friend or Foe. An automatic transmitter in aircraft for its identification but which could be used to home in other aircraft.
JB	John Bennett (RAAF Historian)
JH	John Herrington (RAAF historian)
JK	John Keegan (British historian)
JR	Jürgen Rohwer (German historian)
JT	John Terraine (British historian)
KIA	Killed in action
LH	Lockheed
Mae West	RAF term for a lifejacket which could be inflated by mouth or by a CO_2 bottle.
MB	Marcello Bertini (Italian historian)
MID	Mention in dispatches
ML	Motor launch
MM	Martin Middlebrook (British historian)
MO	M. Okumiya (Japanese historian)
MTB	Motor Torpedo Boat
MU	Maintenance Unit
MV	Merchant vessel
Ops	Operational flying
OT	Owen Thetford (British historian)
OTU	Operational Training Unit
PC	Peter Cremer, Lt/Cmdr, captain of U-333
PJ	ACM Sir Philip Joubert de la Ferté
P/O	Pilot Officer
PRU	Photo-Reconnaissance Unit
PS	Per Skaugstad (Norwegian historian)
RAAF	Royal Australian Air Force
Radar	An American term applied to navigation equipment such as the British ASV
RAF	Royal Air Force
RCAF	Royal Canadian Air Force
RNethNAS	Royal Netherlands Naval Air Service
RNAF	Royal New Zealand Air Force
RP	Rocket Projectile
SEM	Samuel Eliot Morison (American naval historian)
Sgt	Sergeant
S/Ldr	Squadron Leader
SNO	Senior Naval Officer
SOC	Struck off charge
Sqdn	Squadron
S&S	*Seek and Strike*
SS	*Short Sunderland Aircraft in WW2*
ss	Steamship
SWR	Capt. S.W. Roskill, RN (Naval historian)
WSC	Winston Spencer Churchill
ZLL	Z.L. Leigh

Bibliography

Abbott, Kim *Gathering of Demons* Inkerman House, Perth, Ontario 1987

Baff, Kevin *Maritime is No.10* Griffin Press Ltd, Netley, South Australia 1983

Bennett, John *High Traditions; The History of No.2 Squadron RAAF* Aus. Govt. Pub. 1995

Bertini, Marcello *I Sommergibili in Mediterraneo* Vol. II Ufficio Storico Rome 1972

Bowyer, Chaz *For Valour; The Air VCS* Grub Street, London 1992

Bowyer M. & Rawlings *Squadron Codes 1937–1956* Patrick Stephens, Cambridge, 1979

Cremer, Peter *U-333* Bodley Head, London, 1984

Craven & Cate *The Army Air Forces in World War II* Office of Air Force History, Washington, 1983

Churchill, Winston S. *The Second World War (Vols I-VI)* Cassell, London, 1948–1954

Darby, Charles *RNZAF The First Decade 1937–1946* Kookaburra Tech. Pub. Pty. Melbourne, 1978

Douglas, W.A.B. *The Official History of the RCAF (Vols II)* University of Toronto, 1986

Fahey, James, C. *U.S. Army Aircraft 1908–1946* Ships and Aircraft, New York

Flatmark, J.O. & H. Grytten *Ålesund I Hverdag og Krig* Nordvest Forlag A/S, Ålesund 1988

Franks, Norman *Search, Find and Kill* Aston Publications, London, 1990

Gilbert, Adrian *The IWM Book of the Desert War 1940–1942* Sidgwick & Jackson, London, 1992

Gillison, Douglas *RAAF 1939–1942 (Vol. I RAAF)* Australian War Memorial, Canberra, 1962

Grantham, Sid. *The 13 Squadron Story* S.R. Grantham, Dee Why, NSW 1991

Halley, James *Squadrons of the RAF & Commonwealth 1918–1988* Air Britain, Tonbridge, 1988

Hendrie, Andrew *Seek and Strike, The Lockheed Hudson Aircraft in WW2* W. Kimber, London, 1983

Hendrie, Andrew *Flying Cats; The Consolidated Catalina in World War II,* Airlife, Shrewsbury, 1988

Hendrie, Andrew *Short Sunderland Aircraft in WW2* Airlife, Shrewsbury, 1994

Hendrie, Andrew *Canadian Squadrons in Coastal Command* Vanwell Pub. St Catherines, Ontario 1997

Herlin, Hans *Verdampt Atlantik* Wilhelm Heyne Verlag, München, 1985

Herrington, John *Air War Against Germany & Italy* (RAAF Vol. III) A.W.M. Canberra, 1954

Hessler, Günter, *The U Boat War in the Atlantic 1939–1945* HMSO, London, 1992

Jenks, C.F.L. *New Zealand Military Aircraft & Serial Numbers* Aviation His. Soc of N.Z. 1980

Keegan, John *The Times Atlas of World War II* Times Books, London, 1989

Lavenere-Wanderley *The Brazilian Air Force in the Second World War* Ministèrio da Aeronáutica 1976

Leigh, Z. Lewis *And I should Like to Fly* Canav Boks, Toronto 1989

Manson, Jock *No.53 Squadron RAF* Air Britain, Tonbridge 1997

Maurer M. *Combat Squadrons of the Air Force in WW2* USAF Hist. Div. Washington 1969

Middlebrook, M. & Everitt. C. *The Bomber Command War Diaries 1939–1945* Viking 1987

Ministry of Information *Atlantic Bridge* HMSO London, 1945

Morison, Samuel E. *The Battle of the Atlantic Sept 1939–May 1943* Little, Brown, Boston 1975

Morison, Samuel E. *The Atlantic Battle Won May 1943–May 1945* Little, Brown, Boston 1984

Niestlé, Axel, *German U boat losses During World War II* US Naval Institute Press, Annapolis, 1998

Odgers, George *Air War Against Japan 1943–1945 (RAAF Vol. II)* A.W.M. Canberra, 1957

Okumiya, A. & Horikoshi, J. Caidin, M *Zero! The Story of the Japanese Navy Air Force 1937–45* Cassell, London, 1957

Rawlings, John D.R. *Coastal Support & Special Squadrons of the RAF,* Janes, London, 1982

Rawling, William G. & etc. *The Official History of the RCAF* Vol. III University of Toronto, 1994

Richards, Denis *The Fight Against Odds (Vol. I RAF)* HMSO London, 1953

Richards, Denis & H. St G. Saunders *The Fight Avails (Vol II RAF)* HMSO London, 1954

Robertson, Bruce *British Military Aircraft Serials 1911–1979* Patrick Stephens, Cambridge 1964

Robertson, John *Australia at War 1939–1945* William Heinemann, Melbourne, 1981

Rohwer, Jürgen *Axis Submarine Successes 1939–1945* US Naval Institute Press, Annapolis, 1983

Roskill, Capt. S.W. *The War at Sea Vols I-III* HMSO London, 1954–1961

Russell, Adml James S. *United States Naval Aviation 1910–1970* US Govt. Washington 1970

Saunders, Hilary St G. *The Fight is Won (RAF Vol. III)* HMSO London 1954

Schull, Joseph *The Far Distant Ships* US Naval Institute Press, Annapolis, 1987

Shores, Chris. *Lockheed Hudson Marks I-VI* Profile Publications, Windsor, 1973

Thetford, Owen *Aircraft of the Royal Air Force Since 1918* Putnam, London, 1979

Terraine, John *Right of the Line; The RAF in the European War 1939–1945* Hodder & Stoughton 1985

Ubaldini, Ubaldino *I Sommergibili Negli Oceani* Ufficio Storico MM Rome 1976

Verity, Hugh *We Landed by Moonlight* Air Data Pub. Trowbridge, 1995

Williams. Douglas *194 Squadron RAF* Merlin Books, Braunton 1987

Wilson, Stewart *Anson, Hudson & Sunderland in Australian Service* Aerospace Pub. Pty. Weston Creek, 1992

Index

Adams, W/Cmdr J. (40 Sqdn RNZAF) 115
Adelaide, Australia 97
Aden 77, 90
Admiral Graf Spee 23
Admiral Hipper 25, 26
aircraft
  Albacore 69
  Anson 18, 19, 20, 22, 32
  Battle 56
  Beaufighter 28, 39, 47, 102
  Beaufort 102, 113
  Blenheim 23, 62, 76, 86, 90, 96, 106, 107
  Boston 102
  Catalina 55, 56, 60, 65, 69, 98, 99
  CR42 (Italian) 91
  DC-3: 74, 85, 107, 108, 110, 115
  Dornier 18: 18, 22, 23, 24
  Dornier 24: 82, 84
  Fortress (B-17) 84, 85, 101, 102
  Fw 190: 82
  Fw 200 (Kondor) 61
  Gladiator 91
  Hurricane 31, 65, 91
  Ju 88: 33, 44, 46, 65, 67, 68, 72, 81
  Kittyhawk 104
  Liberator 50, 56, 60, 63, 102
  Lightning 102
  Lockheed Model 14: 8, 10, 11, 12, 13, 90
  Mariner 55
  Martlet 69
  Me 109: 24, 44, 82
  Me 110: 23, 24
  Mitchell 102, 113
  Mosquito 47
  Northrop 56, 57
  Sunderland 14, 56, 59, 60, 62, 63, 85
  Vega 8
  Ventura 51, 75, 79, 114, 115
  Walrus 69, 85
  Warwick 86
  Wellington 14, 35, 61, 62, 63, 74, 81, 85
  Whitley 83, 85
  Zero 94, 96, 99, 104, 106, 111–112, 115
'Akwing' 104
Akyab 104, 106, 107
Alameda NAS, California 52
Alchin, P/O C.W. (13 Sqdn RAAF) 100
Aldergrove, Northern Ireland 38, 60, 61, 86
Aleutian Islands 98, 100
Alexander, General 76
Alexandria, Egypt 75, 77
Algiers, North Africa 65, 66
Allison, F/Lt W.G.C. (3 Sqdn RNZAF) 115
Alor Star, Malaya 93, 95, 96
Altmark, prison ship 23–24
Amboina 98
Andrew, F/Lt Terry (500 Sqdn) 35, 65, 70–71
Anticosti 50
Arafusa Sea 111
armament 13–14

Aruba 49, 52
Ashbury, F/O (48 Sqdn) 74
Assam 107
Atambua, Timor 112
Atkinson, P/O (500 Sqdn) 68
Atkinson Field, British Guiana 53
Atlantic, Battle of the 48, 59
Atlantic Ocean, anti-submarine operations 48–63
Auckinleck, General Sir Claude 107
Austin, F/O J.S. (2 Sqdn RAAF) 112
Azores 63

Badger, F/O (2 Sqdn RAAF) 111
Bailey, F/O H.C. (48 Sqdn) 32, 74
Baird, F/Lt Don. (459 Sqdn) 79
Bairnsdale, Australia 100
Bali 97, 98
Ballale 114
Ballykelly, Northern Ireland 60
Bangalore 108
Banka Island 96
Bardia, North Africa 77, 78
Barling, P/O J. (233 Sqdn) 68
Barlow, S/Ldr A.A. (6 Sqdn RAAF) 98, 100
Barnard, F/Sgt D.T. (459 Sqdn) 78
Barnes, W/Cmdr L.K., RAF 55
Barron, S/Ldr (220 Sqdn) 41
Barson, F/O N. (59 Sqdn RAAF) 44
Bartlett, W/Cmdr Geoffrey (224 & 59 Sqdns) 17, 18, 19, 33, 35, 36
Barwood, F/O (500 Sqdn) 68
Base Roger, Argentina 51, 52
Batchelor Field, Australia 94, 111
Bathurst, West Africa 62
Batty, S/Ldr R.H. (145 Sqdn RCAF) 51
Baudoux, G/Capt (233 Sqdn) 20, 28, 67
Bay of Bengal 105, 107
Bay of Biscay 39, 47
Bay of Fundy 50
Beaton, F/Lt D.C. (459 Sqdn) 76, 77
Beaulieu, England 82
Beck, F/O Rob. (48 Sqdn) 57, 72
Belém, Brazil 54
Bell, F/O J.N.P. (269 Sqdn) 59
Benbecula, Outer Hebrides 82
Benghazi, North Africa 77
Bennett, AVM Don. 87
Bergen, Norway 23, 24
Birchall, F/O (220 Sqdn) 41
Bircham Newton, England 22, 27, 31, 38, 45, 80, 83
Bismarck, German battleship 24
Bismarck Sea Battle 102
Bizerta, North Africa 74
Blackwell, Sgt (500 Sqdn) 73
Blakeley, F/O (500 Sqdn) 35, 65, 70, 71
Blida, North Africa 65, 66, 67, 71, 72
Boggon, F/O M. (59 Sqdn) 44
Bomber Command, No.2 Group 39, 46
Bone, North Africa 69, 74
Bordeaux, France 55
Borizzo 75

Borkum 27, 45, 47
Borneo 98
Boscombe Down, England 18
Bougainville 102, 114, 115
Bowen, F/Sgt W.S. (269 Sqdn) 54, 57
Bowhill, ACM Sir Frederick 87
Bradford, Lt, USN 55
Brambles Farm, Middlesbrough 20
Brame, F/Sgt E.L.J. (269 Sqdn) 59
Bray, F/Lt John (161 Sqdn) 89–90
Bray, W/Cmdr 85
Brazil 50, 54–55
Bremen, Germany 13, 35–38
Brent, Sgt (233 Sqdn) 64
Brest, France 33, 53
Brodie, W/O A.M.S. 27
Brooke-Popham, ACM Sir Robert 92
Brooks, F/O P.G. (13 Sqdn RAAF) 100
Broome, Australia 113
Brown, W/Cmdr Alan (407 Sqdn) 47
Browning machine-guns 13, 22, 39, 40, 69, 96
Brunsbuttel, Germany 30, 35
Buna 100, 101
Burbank, California 8, 12, 13
Burg-el-Arab (LG40) 75, 76
Burma 104–105, 108
Busbridge, P/O D. (224 Sqdn) 34
Butler, F/Lt (233 Sqdn) 30, 39
Butterworth, Malaya 95
Buvik Harbour, Norway 27

Cairo conference 91
Calais 31
Calcutta, India 106
Callaghan, Lt, USN 43
Calvesbe, F/O (608 Sqdn) 65
Camacho, P/O (233 Sqdn) 64
Campbell, F/Lt D.W.I., RAAF 98
Campbell, F/Lt L. (459 Sqdn) 76
Camranh Bay 92
Canada, Eastern Command 48, 49
Candy, AVM C.D., RAAF (206 Sqdn RAF) 19, 20, 62
Cap Esperance, Battle of 109
Cape Hatteras 51
Cape Verde Islands 62, 63
Carey, P/O 23, 24
Caribbean, U boat operations in 52, 55
Carney Field, Guadalcanal 110
Carpenter, F/Sgt (220 Sqdn) 42
Carr, S/L T.H. (220 Sqdn) 24, 31, 32
Cavert, F/Sgt Wally (500 Sqdn) 71
Celebes 96, 98
Cerebus, German operation 33–34
Charlton, P/O (59 Sqdn) 44
Chatham, Nova Scotia 50
Cherry Point, California 52
Chew, Keith, RAAF 113
Chindits 92, 108
Chindwin River 108
Chittagong 104, 106, 108
Choiseul Island 114
Christie, F/Lt (407 Sqdn) 47
Churchill, Winston S. 24, 26, 32, 55, 77, 79, 90, 91
Ciliax, Admiral 33
Clark, F/Lt, RAAF Survey Unit 113

Clark, F/Sgt (407 Sqdn) 46
Coastal Command 17, 18, 19, 21, 39, 90
   No.15 Group 56
   No.16 Group 39
   No.18 Group 39
   No.19 Group 39
Codville, F/O (407 Sqdn) 47
Constable-Roberts, W/Cmdr 27
convoys
   HX47: 49
   JT3: 55
   KMF5: 72
   O5S/7/34: 62
   OB346: 61
   OG69: 61
   ON72: 52
   ONS 136: 57
   ONS 144: 51
   QS37: 50
   RU43: 57
   SC107: 51
   SL135: 63
   Tryst 79
   UR44: 57
Cooke, W/C (206 Sqdn) 35
Cooper, F/Lt (233 Sqdn) 39
Cooper, P/O (407 Sqdn) 47
Coral Sea, Battle of the 99
Corden, F/Sgt D.G.S. (53 Sqdn) 44
Cortale, Italy 75
Couchman, Sgt R. (269 Sqdn) 59
Coulson, F/Lt Bill 19
Cowperthwaite, F/O (407 Sqdn) 33, 47
Cox, W/Cmdr (62 Sqdn) 106, 107
Cox's Bazar 106
Crace, Rear Admiral J.G., RN 99
Craven, AM Sir Robert 19, 20
Creedon, P/O W. (407 Sqdn) 47
Cremer, Lt/Cmdr P. 25, 26
Crook, S/L (206 Sqdn) 38
Crump, F/Lt (608 Sqdn) 65, 74, 75
Cuming, F/Lt R.B. (2 Sqdn RAAF) 97
Cunningham, Admiral Sir Andrew 64
Curaçao 52
Cuxhaven 22, 30, 31

Dakar, French North Africa 62, 63
Dalton, F/Sgt K.R. (233 Sqdn) 73
Daniels, Lt (320 Sqdn) 46
Daniels, P/O (2 Sqdn RAAF) 111
Darke, Sgt R.S. (48 Sqdn) 57
Darlan, Admiral 66
Dartmouth, Nova Scotia 48, 49
Darwin, Australia 96–97, 99, 100, 111, 113
Davidstow Moor 83, 84
Dawson Island 101
De Groot, Lt (320 Sqdn) 46
De Liefde, Lt Thijis (320 Sqdn) 45, 46
De Ruyter, cruiser (Royal Netherlands Navy) 98
Debert, Nova Scotia 50
Degen, Kl Hörst (U-701) 53
Delhi, India 107
Den Helder 27, 45, 46
Denmark 25, 39
depth charges, Amatol filled 50, 60

depth charges, Torpex filled 51, 57, 59, 60
Deschimag U boat yards 33, 38
Devey S/Ldr (233 Sqdn) 33, 64
Diamond, F/Lt O.N. (91 Sqdn RAAF) 93, 96
Dili, Timor 97, 111, 112
Disney, F/Lt H.A.S. (608/48 Sqdns) 42
Docking, England 46, 47, 81
Dods, F/Lt W.S.E. (461 Sqdn) 85
Doe, Al (Lockheed representative) 19, 82
Dönitz, Admiral 49, 59
Donna Nook, England 38, 44, 47
Doorman, Vice-Admiral 98
Dorman-Smith, Sir Reginald 105
Douglas, F/Lt (8 Sqdn RAAF) 96
Down, P/O Ron (233 Sqdn) 61
Drew, H.L. (USN with 53 Sqdn RAF) 54
Dum Dum, India 105, 106, 108
Dunkirk 15, 27, 31–32
Dunnett, Sgt Len (244 Sqdn) 20
Dutch East Indies 92

Eden, Rt/Hon. Anthony (Minister for War) 91
Edinburgh Field, Trinidad 53, 54
Edwards, F/O (233 Sqdn) 30, 39
Eisenhower, General 64, 66
El Alamein 76–77
Elbe estuary 22, 27, 28, 31
Ellice Islands 113, 114
Ellington, ACM Sir Edward 10
Emden 46
Emirau, New Ireland 115
Endrass, Kl E. 33
engines, Wright 10, 13
engines, Pratt & Whitney 13, 93
English Channel 22, 33–34
Ensor, F/O M. (500 Sqdn) 67–68
Ensor, S/Ldr J.B. (500 Sqdn) 67
Eretanwetan, Java 97
Esbjerg docks, raid on 42
Esmonde, Lt/Cmdr V.C. 29, 33
Espiritu Santo, New Hebrides 114, 115
Evans, S/Ldr Phil. (59 Sqdn) 40, 44, 45
Everest, F/L (224 Sqdn) 22, 34

Falkenhorst, General 25
Farrer Sgt H.J. (279 Sqdn) 82
Faux, F/Sgt P.G. (279 Sqdn) 82
Feeny, S/Ldr D.Y. (233 Sqdn) 19, 29, 31
Ferry Command, RAF 87
Fielden, W/Cmdr E.H. MVO, AFC (161 Sqdn) 89
Figg, F/O (161 Sqdn) 89
Fiji Islands 98, 113, 115
Finschhaven, New Guinea 98
Fisher, W/Cmdr G.H., RNZAF 114
Fitch, Rear Admiral, USN 99
Fitchew, F/Lt (279 Sqdn) 85
Flamborough Head, England 22
flaps, Lockheed-Fowler 10, 13, 18
Fleet Air Arm 32, 33, 52
   No 820 Sqdn 69
Flekkefjord, Norway 44
Flushing 45
Force H at Gibraltar 64
Fort Hertz 108
Fortaleza, Brazil 54, 55

Foster, F/Lt Jack (194 Sqdn) 107, 108
Fox, Uffa 83, 85
France 89
Frandson, F/O (233 Sqdn) 74
Franke, Kl H. (U-262) 61
Frazer, F/Lt (2 Sqdn RAAF) 100, 111
Freetown, West Africa 54, 60, 62
French fleet 64
French Indo-China 92
Frisian Islands 27, 44, 45
Fuller, F/O (233 Sqdn) 39
Funafuti, Ellice Islands 114

Gander, Newfoundland 87, 88
Ganley, Trevor E. (3 Sqdn RNZAF) 115
Gasmata, New Britain 98, 104
Gerhicke, Kk Otto (U-503) 52
Gibbes, F/O P.J. (1 Sqdn RAAF) 96, 97
Gibbs, F/O E.G. (279 Sqdn) 84
Gibraltar 19, 44, 61, 64–65, 67, 72
Gibson, F/O G.T., RAAF 98
Gneisenau, German battle-cruiser 25, 26, 33–35, 62
Goad, F/Lt Geoffrey (59 Sqdn) 45
Gorrie F/Lt P.C. (2 Sqdn RAAF) 97
Gorse, Lt (USAAF) 84
Gort, Field Marshal 31, 32
Grece, W/Cmdr C.M.M. DFC (59 Sqdn) 44
Green, F/O R.M. (6 Sqdn) 98, 99, 101
Greenacre, P/O (269 Sqdn) 57–58
Greenland 60
Groups
   16: 39, 84
   45: 87
Guadalcanal, Solomon Islands 98, 99, 102, 109–110, 114, 115
Gulf of Maine 50
Gulf of Pria 54
Gulf of St Lawrence 50
Gummer, P/O M.G. (53 Sqdn) 44
Gurney, Lt/Cmdr M.B., USN 49
Guthrie, Sgt R.C. (53 Sqdn) 44

Haggas, P/O (220 Sqdn) 41
Halifax, Nova Scotia 48, 49, 50, 56
Hall, Sgt (220 Sqdn) 24
Hamburg 29–30
Harper, Ken (233 Sqdn) 61
Harris, ACM Sir Arthur 10
Harrison, F/Lt Fred 16–17
Harrison, F/Lt Wilf (608 Sqdn) 88
Harrow, Middlesex, England 87
Harrowbeer, England 83–84
Harstad, Norway 26
Hastie, F/Lt J.R. (145 Sqdn RCAF) 51
Hastie, Sgt (53 Sqdn) 44
Hawkesford, F/Sgt (2 Sqdn RAAF) 111
Hawkins, Trevor (407 Sqdn) 47
Hay, F/O (2 Sqdn RAAF) 111
Headham, W/Cmdr F. (2 Sqdn RAAF) 97
Heaton-Nicholls, P/O 22
Heligoland 21, 22
Heliopolis, Egypt 90–91
Hemsworth, S/Ldr G.E., RAAF 99
Henderson, F/O A.A. (279 Sqdn) 83
Henderson, F/O H.A. (269 Sqdn) 59

Henderson, F/Sgt (53 Sqdn) 53, 54
Henderson Field, Guadalcanal 109, 110, 114
Hennock, W/Cmdr K.S. (459 Sqdn) 76
Henry , F/O (62 Sqdn) 60, 95, 96
Heppell, Sgt (220 Sqdn) 41
Herries, F/O (62 Sqdn) 105–106
Heston, England 18, 90
His Majesty's Ships
    Ark Royal 64
    Berwick 56
    Brocklesby 62
    Cossack 23, 24
    Curacoa 29
    Erne 68
    Furious 49
    Glasgow 56
    Glorious 26
    Glowworm 25
    Graph (submarine) 56
    Howe 79
    Killarney 32
    King George V 79
    Leath 68
    Nelson 64
    Prince of Wales 64, 93, 94
    Renown 79
    Repulse 49, 93, 94
    Rodney 64
    Scylla 64
    Sealion 33
    Strathmore 65, 66
    Valiant 74
    Warspite 26, 74–75
    Westcott 147: 61
Hitchcock, F/Lt G. (8 Sqdn RAAF) 93
Hitler, Adolf 24, 33, 56
HMAS *Hobart* 98
Hodge, F/Lt P.H.R. (2 Sqdn RAAF) 97
Hodgkinson, ACM Sir Derek 19, 35
Hodgson, W/Cmdr E.A. 19
Höfn, Iceland 57
Holdway, F/Sgt C. 19
Holland, P/O (220 Sqdn) 41
Homes, S/Ldr Peter (500 Sqdn) 71
Hong Kong 93
Horbat, F/O H.A. (200 Sqdn) 63
Horn Island 98, 99, 100–101, 104
Hornby, F/O (2 Sqdn RAAF) 112
Hornby, P/O (48 Sqdn) 61
Houghton, Sgt (220 Sqdn) 41
Howard, Leslie (actor) 85
Howarth, Sgt (59 Sqdn) 45
Howey, F/Sgt (407 Sqdn) 47
Howson, S/Ldr P.W. (459 Sqdn) 76, 77, 79
Hudson, Henry 13
Hudson, Lockheed, description of 13
Hudson Circus 18–19
Hunger, Kl Hans (U-336) 59
Hunt, P/O (220 Sqdn) 35, 41
Hunter, P/O Tony (608 Sqdn) 42, 43, 67

I-29, Japanese submarine 63
Iceland 12, 16, 55–60
Ijmuiden, The Netherlands 27, 31, 32, 45, 46, 47
Imita Ridge, New Guinea 101

Invergordon, Scotland 55
Italian submarines 55, 64, 65
    Archimede 55
    Bagnolini 55
    Barbarigo 55
    Capellini 55
    Torelli 55

James, F/O R.R. (2 Sqdn RAAF) 111, 112
James, F/Sgt (145 Sqdn RCAF) 51
James, P/O (2 Sqdn RAAF) 111
James, Sgt F.H.W. (269 Sqdn) 59
Jameson, P/O (220 Sqdn) 41
Japanese ships
    Akagi 100
    Awajisan Maru 93
    Ayatosan Maru 93, 100
    Hiryu 100
    Kaga 100
    Nojima 102
    Sakura Maru 93
    Shoho 99
    Shokaku (aircraft carrier) 99
    Soryu 100
    Zuikaku (aircraft carrier) 99
Java 96, 97, 98
Java Sea, Battle of the 98
Johns, F/O M.W. (2 Sqdn RAAF) 112
Johnson, C.L. 'Kelly', FRAeS (Lockheed engineer) 10, 11, 12
Jones, Wilf (269 Sqdn) 56, 58–59
Jøsing fjord 23, 24
Joualt, P/O (220 Sqdn) 39
Joubert, ACM Sir Philip 33, 39
Jurca, Albert (VP-82 USN) 52

Kai Islands 112
Kaldadarnes, Iceland 56, 57, 58–59
Kane, 2nd Lt Harry J., USAAF 52–53
Karachi, India 107
Kattegat 39
Kavieng, New Ireland 98
Kay, F/O (407 Sqdn) 47
Kearney, W/Cmdr (224 Sqdn) 32, 35, 36
Keeble, P/O (608 Sqdn) 44
Keech, Sgt K.G. (2 Sqdn RAAF) 112
Keetley, P/O R.S. (113 Sqdn RCAF) 50
Kelly, F/Lt R.A.N. (6 Sqdn RAAF) 101–102
Kemp, S/Ldr K.M. (2 Sqdn RAAF) 112
Kennan, P/O T. (206 Sqdn) 61–62
Kenyon, S/Ldr A.G. (113 Sqdn RCAF) 50
Khartoum 91
Kidd, W/Cmdr E.C. (233 Sqdn) 33
Kidman, F/O Murray (2 Sqdn RAAF) 112
Kilgariff, F/O (2 Sqdn RAAF) 112
Kilidjati 97
Kinashi (I-29) 63
King's Flight 89
Kjell, gunboat 24
Kluang 96
Koepang, Timor 97, 112
Kokoda Gap, New Guinea 100, 101, 102
Kota Bharu, Malaya 92, 93, 94, 105
Kragen, Java 97
Kristiansand, Norway 39
Kristiansund, Norway 24, 41, 43

Kröning, Ol Ernst (U-656) 51–52
Kuantan 92, 93, 94
Kuring, F/O Roger (2 Sqdn RAAF) 111, 113

La Pallice, France 55
Labrador 52
Lacy, P/O (279 Sqdn) 81
Lae, New Guinea 98, 99, 102
Lahore, India 107, 108
Lashio, Burma 105
Laut, W/Cmdr A. (113 Sqdn RCAF) 51
Lavai, Timor 112
Laverton, Australia 92, 97, 98
Law, P/O M.S. (6 Sqdn RAAF) 101
Le Verdon, France 55
Leach, W/Cmdr A. de V. 'Bertie', DFC, RAF (224, 48 & 206 Sqdns)
    20, 39–41
Leggate, W/Cmdr J. (53 Sqdn) 44, 48, 53, 54
Leigh, Z. Lewis 13
Lerew, W/Cmdr J.M., RAAF 98, 99
Lerwick, Shetland Isles 86
Leuchars, Scotland 16–19, 22, 28, 32, 40, 45
Lewis, S/Ldr (407 Sqdn) 47
Lewis, S/Ldr A. (11 Sqdn RCAF) 48–49
Limavady, Northern Ireland 27, 60
Lindholme rescue apparatus 81, 83, 84
Livingstone, F/Sgt (608 Sqdn) 43, 66, 68
Livry-Level, Capt. Phillipe (53 Sqdn) 54
Lockheed Corporation 8, 48
Lockwood, F/O A.B. (1 Sqdn RAAF) 93
Lohmann, Kk D. (U-89) 50
Longmore, A.M. Sir Arthur 21
Loughhead Brothers 8
Lower, F/Lt (6 Sqdn RAAF) 101
Lulea, Sweden 24
Lynham, S/Ldr Paul (407 Sqdn) 46, 81
Lynn, F/O R.G. (224 Sqdn) 26, 29, 39

MacArthur, General 100
Macassar 112
Macassar Strait 98
Madsen, F/Lt (459 Sqdn) 77
Mae West lifejacket 14, 63
Maginot Line 31
Magwe, Burma 104
Maison Blanche, North Africa 65, 67, 69
Maitland-Wilson, General Sir 91
Majoram, F/O A. (220 Sqdn) 31
Makowski, Ol Kurt (U-619) 57
Malahang airfield, Lae 102
Malaya 92–93, 94, 98
Malta 16–17, 64, 90
Manning, F/Lt L.W. (32 Sqdn RAAF) 100, 101
Manning, G/Capt. E.R., RAAF 104
Manson, Capt. Jock (53 Sqdn) 44
Manston, England 33
March Field, California 52
Marix, AVM, on Ålesund raid 41
Markham, F/O J. (269 Sqdn) 56
Marques, Capitao Aviador Jose Maria Mendes Coutinho (BAF) 55
Martlesham Heath, England 12, 18
Mason, CAMM Donald (VP-82 USN) 52
Massey, P/O R.A. (48 Sqdn) 57
Maubisse, Timor 111
Mayhew, F/O G.M. (48 Sqdn) 72

McCombe, F/Lt (2 Sqdn RAAF) 111
McCormick, F/O M.W. (3 Sqdn RNZAF) 114
McCulloch, P/O (407 Sqdn) 47
McDamm, Sgt T. (53 Sqdn) 44
McDonnell, F/O K.L. (2 Sqdn RAAF) 111
McFarlane, W/Cmdr A.B. (2 Sqdn RAAF) 100, 111
McKimm, P/O (279 Sqdn) 81
McLauchland, P/O (194 Sqdn) 107
McLeod, Sgt W.R. (53 Sqdn) 45
McLintock, F/O A.N. (53 Sqdn) 44
McPhaill, H.C. (PRU) 90
McQueen, Sgt. J.W. (233 Sqdn) 73
Menado, Celebes 97
Merak, Java 97
merchant ships (under enemy control and attacked by Hudsons)
    Advance 41
    Algeria 46
    Anna Sofie 39
    Archimede 41
    Arfinn Jarl 39
    Barcelona 41
    Bjonn 41
    Braheholm 47
    Brategg 41
    Burgundia 46
    Cornelia Maersk 47
    Emma 47
    Hamm-19: 46
    Hornelen 41
    Inga 44
    Jantje Fritzen 44
    Karmsund 41
    Klaud Fritzen 43
    Kristine 39
    La Mouette 47
    Madeleine Louise 47
    Namdo 47
    Niels R. Finsen 47
    Nordcap 45, 47
    Ruth 47
    Selje 47
    Senta 47
    Sizilien 47
    Swanefjell 41
    Taarnholm 44
    Tampa 43
    Theodor 39
    Tiger 41
    Troma 44
    Varmdo 47
    Veriato 46
    Vesla 41
    Vestri 41
    Vindafjord 41
    Vios IV 47
    William Blumer 39
    Worth 44
merchant ships (Allied)
    Aquitania 49
    Arletta 50
    Athelmonarch 78
    Baependi 54
    Bainbridge 53
    British Freedom 53
    Cabedello 54

Duchess of Bedford 49
Empress of Australia 49
Empress of Britain 49
Esso Augusta 53
Hahira 51
Hartington 51
Henzada 55
Kingston Ceylonite 53
Kota Gede 97
Lucille M. 50
Monarch of Bermuda 49
Orchades 97
Palima 78
Rahmani 63
Robert C. Tuttle 53
Santore 53
Strathallan 72, 92
Tamesis 53
William Rockefeller 53
Mersa Matruh, North Africa 76, 78
Mersing 94
Meteorological Flt 1401: 84, 85, 86
Meteorological Flights 86–87
Michalski, F/O (11 Sqdn RCAF) 49, 50
Middleton, Ensign G.S. (USNR) 53
Midway, Battle of 93, 98, 100
Miller, F/Sgt N. (8 Sqdn) 63
Milne Bay, New Guinea 100, 101, 102, 104
Misima Island (Solomon Sea) 99
Mitchell, F/O G.G. (13 Sqdn RAAF) 97
Mitchell, Sgt (269 Sqdn) 56
Mogridge, F/Sgt A.H. (279 Sqdn) 84, 85
Montecorvino 75
Monteith, Capt. D.O. (6th Recce Sqdn USAAF) 52
Montreal, Canada 87
Montrose, Scotland 22
Moss, P/O (59 Sqdn) 44, 45
Moss, Sgt (407 Sqdn) 47
Mossford, Sgt H.G. (279 Sqdn) 83
Moyes, Ian (2 Sqdn RAAF) 112
Mumm, Kl F. (U-667) 74
Munda Island 114
Munich, political crisis 48
Murray, L.A., 2nd Lt (USAAF) 52
Myene 108
Myitkyina, Burma 105

Namatanai, New Ireland 98
Namlea, Buru Island 97
Naples, Italy 75
Narvik, Norway 24, 25, 26, 39
Natal, Brazil 54, 55
Neale, Frank (HMS *Brocklesby*) 62
Neilson, P/O (59 Sqdn) 45
Netherlands 39, 44–47
   shipping strikes 44–45
New Britain 98, 102, 104
New Brunswick 50
New Caledonia 98, 113, 115
New Georgia 114, 115
New Guinea 98–99, 100, 101
New Hebrides 98, 113, 114
New Ireland 98, 115
Newfoundland 49, 50
Newmarket, England 89

Nichols, Sgt (53 Sqdn) 44
Nicosia, Cyprus 77
Niven, W/Cmdr R.H. (59 Sqdn) 44, 45
Norderney, The Netherlands 27, 28
Norfolk, Virginia, US Naval Air Station 52, 54
Norfolk Island 115
Normanby Island 104
North Africa 44
North Atlantic Ferry 87–89
North Coates, England 29, 35, 44, 45, 46, 47, 84
North Front, Gibraltar 64, 65, 67, 72
North Sea 20, 21–23, 39
Northern Territory, Australia 113
Norway 24–25, 33, 39, 41, 43
Nutt's Corner, Northern Ireland 60

Obee, W/O R. (500 Sqdn) 73
Obrestadt, Norway 22, 24, 32
O'Brien, F/O V.K. (459 Sqdn) 77
O'Connell, P/O (407 Sqdn) 35, 42, 47
Oerstermann, Kl (U-754) 50
Ogilvie, F/O G.A.K. (608 Sqdn) 74
Ohakea, New Zealand 115
Olfusa River, Iceland 56, 58
Ondal 107
O'Neill, G/Capt. H., DFC (224 Sqdn) 29
Operation
   Avalanche at Salerno 74–75
   Bludgeon by 161 Sqdn 89
   Dynamo 31–32
   Fuller 33–34
   Husky 78–79
   Millenium II 35–36
   Torch 20, 44, 64–67, 76–77
Oran, North Africa 64, 65, 66
Orinoco River, Venezuela 54
Orzel, Polish submarine 25
Otten, Lt (320 Sqdn) 46
OTUs
   6 (Coastal) 19–20, 35, 41, 83, 86
   10: 85
   12: 85
Owen Stanley Range, New Guinea 99, 101

Pacey, F/Lt Bill (6 Sqdn RAAF) 104
Page, Sgt. I.M. (3 Sqdn RNZAF) 114
Palam, Delhi, India 107, 108
Palau, Caroline Islands 94
Palembang II, Sumatra 95, 96
Pallikulo 114
Parkinson, James, RNZAF 110
Paterson, S/Ldr (500 Sqdn) 69
Pearce, P/O D.D. (608 Sqdn) 69
Pearl Harbor 49, 93
Pearson, W/Cmdr Alec C. (194 Sqdn) 107
Pedersen, F/Lt (No.6 C OTU) 20
Pederson, F/O (279 Sqdn) 85
Pembroke Dock, South Wales 45, 55
Penfui, Timor 97, 100, 111, 112
Penn, P/O (608 Sqdn) 65, 74
Pennycuick, P/O P.T.E. (32 Sqdn RAAF) 99
Percival, General 94
Petrie, F/O J.B. (608 Sqdn) 69
Petrina, F/Lt W.A., RAAF 98
Philippine Islands 93, 98, 100

photo-reconnaissance 90–91
Pickard, W/Cmdr P.C., DSO, DFC 89
Plate, River 54, 55
Plenty, G/Capt H.C. (8 Sqdn RAAF) 93, 94
Port Blair, Andaman Islands 104
Port Lyautey, North Africa 74
Port Moresby 98, 99, 100, 101, 102
Port of Spain, Trinidad 53
Port Sudan 91
Portugal 16, 64
Pounder, F/O Vic. (220 & 200 Sqdns) 62
Prestwick, Scotland 87
Prinz Eugen, German cruiser 29, 33–35
Proctor, P/O A. (459 Sqdn) 77
Protville, Tunisia 74
Puckridge, F/O (53 Sqdn) 44, 54
Putt, F/Lt (138 Sqdn) 89

Rabaul, New Britain 98, 99, 102, 104, 115
Race, F/O (407 Sqdn) 33, 46, 47
Raeder, Admiral 24, 33
Rahmlow, Kk Hans (U-570) 56
Ramsey, Sgt (220 Sqdn) 41
Rankin, S/Ldr W.E. 19
Rashleigh, F/Lt (279 Sqdn) 80
Ray, P/O D.A. (53 Sqdn) 44
Reade, F/O (279 Sqdn) 85
Recife, Brazil 54, 55
Red Sea 77
Reen, F/Sgt, DFM (269 Sqdn) 56
Reen, Sgt P.S. (2 Sqdn RAAF) 112
Reilly, F/O J.J. (59 Sqdn) 45
Reilly, Sgt H. (2 Sqdn RAAF) 112
Reykjavik, Iceland 56, 59
Rhode Island, USA 53
Richards, P/O D.J. (59 Sqdn) 45, 47
Richelieu, French battleship 62
Rickards, P/O J.P. (59 Sqdn) 45, 54
Rio de Janeiro, Brazil 55
Risbey, P/O G.T. (53 Sqdn) 54
Robertson, Ensign, USN 55
Robertson, F/O J.W. (2 Sqdn RAAF) 111
Robinson, F/Lt Eric (608 Sqdn) 42, 43, 67
Robinson, F/O E.L. (145 Sqdn RCAF) 51
Rockcliffe, Ottawa 48
rocket projectiles (RPs) 59, 74
Roe, Sgt (500 Sqdn) 68
Romanes, W/Cmdr (206 Sqdn) 27–28, 32
Rommel, General 76, 107
Roope, Lt/Cmdr P.G., VC 25
Roosevelt, Franklin D., American President 56, 64, 79
Roskill, Capt S.W., RN (historian) 26, 38, 55, 64, 92, 96–97, 100
Ross, F/Sgt (407 Sqdn) 47
Ross, P/O L.T. (145 Sqdn RCAF) 51
Rotterdam, The Netherlands 39
Rowe, Sgt W.J. (53 Sqdn) 45
Roxburgh, F/Lt W. (206 Sqdn) 38
Royal Netherlands Air Service (MLD) 45
Runnymede (memorial) 44
Runstedt, Gen. von 31
Russell Island 110
Russia, invasion of by Germany 39
Ryan, Sgt. R.D. (2 Sqdn RAAF) 112

Sacramento, California 52

Salamaua, New Guinea 98, 99, 101
Salvesen, F/O (194 Sqdn) 108
Samoa Islands 113, 115
San Pedro, California 51
Sands Patrol, Dunkirk 32
Santa Cruz 109
Santa Isobel 114
Savo Island 109
Sayre, P/O G.T. (113 Sqdn RCAF) 50
Scapa Flow 35
Schaper, S/Ldr (320 Sqdn) 46
Scharnhorst, battlecruiser 25, 26, 27, 28–29, 33–35, 61
Schmandt, Ol A. (U-489) 77
Schnoor, Tenente Aviador Sergio C. (BAF) 55
Scholefield, F/O Tony (608 Sqdn) 43, 44
Schultz, Kl W. (U-512) 54
Scott, Sgt S. (279 Sqdn) 81–82
Scoulter, Sgt (59 Sqdn) 45
Segond Channel 114
Seletar, Singapore 93
Self, Sir Henry 12
Sembawang, Singapore 92, 94
Semplak, Java 97
Senkel, Kl Hans (U-658) 51
Shankland, P/O (407 Sqdn) 47
Sharp, F/O A.J. (2 Sqdn RAAF) 100
Sherwood, F/O (279 Sqdn) 85
shipping strikes 39–47
Siam 93
Sicily, invasion of 78–79
Sidi Barani, North Africa 76, 91
Sillcock, F/Sgt R.R. (53 Sqdn) 53, 54
Silloth, England 19
Simpson, P/O J.H. (500 Sqdn) 68
Singapore 93, 94–95, 96, 97, 98
Singer, G/Capt N.C. 104
Singleton, P/O G.O. (461 Sqdn) 85
Singora, Thailand 93
Skagerrak 22, 39
Skitten, Scotland 42
Slatter, A/Cmdre 91
Slocum, 'Slogger' 90
'Slot, The', Solomon Islands 110
Small, S/Ldr N.E. (113 Sqdn RCAF) 50, 51
Smith, F/Sgt (220 Sqdn) 41
Smith, Lt W.F. 55
Smith, P/O H.B. (269 Sqdn) 59
Smith, Sgt E.H. (233 Sqdn) 69, 70
Smuts, General 91
Sola, Norway 40
Solomon Islands 99, 109, 114, 115
South China Sea 92, 94, 96
Sparrow Force on Timor 111
Special Operations over France 89–90
Spenser, Ensign A.P. (VP-82 USN) 51
Spezia 79
Spotswood, W/Cmdr D. (500 Sqdn) 20, 68, 71
Spriggs, F/O Gordon (2 Sqdn RAAF) 112
Spurgeon, A/Cmdre (8 Sqdn RAAF) 93, 94, 103
squadrons, RAF
  8: 63
  48: 42, 57, 60, 64, 66, 72–73
  53: 44, 45, 48, 53, 54, 59, 60
  59: 13, 17, 35, 37, 40, 44, 45
  95: 62

98: 56
120: 120
200: 62, 63
206: 19, 27, 28, 32, 35, 38, 41, 62
209: 20, 60
220: 19, 23, 24, 31, 32, 39, 41
224: 17–20, 22, 23, 27, 28, 33–35, 39
233: 19, 20, 22, 28–33, 39, 61, 64, 72–73
269: 12, 16, 22, 27, 55, 56–59, 60
279: 80–86
320 (Dutch) 45–46, 47
330 (Norge) 56, 57
500: 20, 65, 67, 68, 69, 75
608: 42–44, 65, 67, 69, 71, 72, 74, 75
squadrons, RAAF
1: 92, 93–94, 96, 97
2: 96, 97, 99–100, 111–113
6: 95, 97, 98, 100–101, 102
7: 99–100
8: 93, 94, 96, 97, 100, 103
10: 62
13: 96, 100, 102, 111
23: 100
24: 100
32: 98–99, 100, 101
459: 64, 75–78, 79
squadrons, RCAF
11: 48, 49
113: 48, 50, 51
145: 48, 51
162: 56
404: 38, 47
407: 33, 35, 38–40, 42, 43, 45–47
423: 59
squadrons, RNZAF
1: 113, 115
2: 110, 113, 115
3: 110, 114, 115
4: 113, 114, 115
40: 110, 115
squadrons, USAAF
6th Reconnaissance Sqdn 52
296th Bombardment Sqdn 52
squadrons, USN
VP-63: 56
VP-82: 51, 52
VP-83: 54
VP-84: 56
St Eval, Cornwall 20, 33, 45, 47, 60, 61, 82, 86, 90
St Jean, Palestine 77
St Lawrence Estuary 48, 51
Stavanger, Norway 24, 39, 41
Stavne (graveyard), Norway 44
Steele, P/O Tom, RAAF Survey Unit 113
Stone, F/Sgt (220 Sqdn) 41
Stornoway, Outer Hebrides 20, 60
Strait of Belle Isle 50
Styles, W/Cmdr Monty (407 Sqdn) 47
Sumatra 95–96, 98
Sumburgh, Shetland Isles 22, 27, 29, 44, 60, 72
Summers, 2nd Lt (USA) 44
Surabaya, Java 45, 98
Survey Flight, RAAF 113
Swedish iron ore 24, 39
Swinton, Lord 10

Sylt Island, Germany 22, 44
Tafaraouri, North Africa 65, 66, 67, 68, 73
Tangmere, England 89
Tassafaronga, Battle of 109
Tate, P/O (220 Sqdn) 41
Taylor, P/O (161 Sqdn) 89
Taylor, P/O C. (407 Sqdn) 35, 42, 47
Tempsford, England 89
Tepuni, Ensign William (VP-82 USN) 51–52
Terschelling, The Netherlands 45, 46, 47
Texel, Frisian Islands 27, 44, 47
Tezpur, Assam 107, 108
Thammes, P/O E. (48 Sqdn) 60–61
Thesiger, P/O (59 Sqdn) 44
Thirwell, S/Ldr (194 Sqdn) 107
Thompson, F/Sgt A.T. (53 Sqdn) 45
Thompson, S/Ldr (269 Sqdn) 56
Thornaby, England 19–20, 22, 23, 42
Thorney Island, England 82
Thornhill, Sgt R. (53 Sqdn) 44
Thurston, F/Lt G. (10 Sqdn RAAF) 62
Timor 97, 98, 111
Tiree, Inner Hebrides 35, 60
Tobruk 76–77
'Tokyo Express' 110
Tonga 113, 114
Torbay, Newfoundland 51
Toulon, France 89
Trigg, P/O L.A., VC (200 Sqdn) 63
Trinidad 49, 52, 53, 54
Trondheim, Norway 23, 26, 27, 44
Trox, Kl Hans-Georg (U-97) 78
Truk, Caroline Islands 98, 99, 115
Tubb, John (62 Sqdn) 95–96, 97
Tucson, Arizona, Davis-Monthan Field 52
Tulagi Island, Solomons 98, 99, 109
Turner-Walker, F/O (6 Sqdn RAAF) 101
turret, Boulton & Paul 13, 14, 22, 23
Tuttle, W/Cmdr (PRU) 90
Tyrell, S/Ldr R.Y. (279 Sqdn) 81, 82

U boat groups
Delfin 65
Neuland 52
Rossbach 59
Seydlitz 49
Streitaxt 65
U boat operations
Paukenschlag 49, 51
Westindien 52
U boats
U-46: 33
U-77: 72–73
U-81: 60
U-83: 72
U-89: 50
U-97: 78
U-108: 53
U-132: 50
U-156: 54
U-165: 50
U-167: 73
U-173: 53
U-199: 55
U-217: 53, 54

U-259: 68
U-262: 61
U-263: 70
U-273: 59
U-331: 68–69
U-332: 54
U-336: 59
U-403: 63
U-411: 67
U-413: 69–70
U-442: 72
U-447: 73
U-458: 50, 68
U-460: 54
U-468: 63
U-489: 59
U-503: 52
U-505: 54
U-507: 54
U-512: 54
U-517: 50, 51
U-535: 59
U-566: 69
U-570: 56
U-573: 64
U-594: 74
U-595: 68
U-605: 68
U-613: 69
U-667: 74
U-619: 57
U-646: 59
U-656: 51
U-658: 51
U-701: 52–53
U-731: 59
U-754: 50
U-755: 74
United Kingdom, patrols from 60–62
United States Navy ships
 Barnegat, tender 55
 Bernadou 51
 Curtiss 114
 Enterprise 100, 110
 Gleaves 51
 Greer 56
 Hamman, destroyer 100
 Hornet 100
 Lexington 99
 Mackinac 115

New York 56
Niblack 56
Peary 96
Sawfish 63
Sea Raven 97
Yorktown 99, 100
Ushant 62

Vaagso Island 43
Van de Meer, Lt (320 Sqdn) 46
Van Olm, Lt/Cmdr (320 Sqdn) 46
Vella Lavella 114, 115
Viti Levu, Fiji Islands 113, 115

Wadey, F/O (2 Sqdn RAAF) 111
Wake Island 93
Walker, P/O J.W.P. (53 Sqdn) 54
Walker, W/Cmdr R.G.M., DFC (224 Sqdn & PRU) 82, 90, 91
Waller Field, Trinidad 53
Waring, G/Capt 84
Waterer, Dr Fred (2 Sqdn RAAF) 112
Wavell, General Sir Archibald 91, 94, 97
Werner, Kl Hans (U-199) 55
West Africa 60, 62–63
Whenuapai, New Zealand 113, 114, 115
White, F/Sgt A.S. (113 Sqdn RCAF) 50
Whithey, F/Lt David 16
Whittaker, F/Lt Doug. (279 Sqdn) 83–84
Wick, Scotland 22, 41, 42, 43, 44, 60, 86
Williams, F/Lt Doug (194 Sqdn) 108
Wills, P/O (206 Sqdn) 38, 62
Wilson, F/Lt Ken (194 Sqdn) 107
Winfield, Ernest (1404 Met. Flt) 86–87
Wingate, General Orde 108
Winnipeg, Canada 87
Winnicot, F/Lt (233 Sqdn) 32, 61
wireless operator 14–15
Womersley, W/Cmdr (224 Sqdn) 18, 21, 22, 28, 87–88
Woods, General L.E. (US Marine Corps) 114
Worrin, Sgt. J.G. (279 Sqdn) 82
Wright, W/Cmdr (220 Sqdn) 31–32, 41
Wulff, Ol H. (U-646) 59
Wyllie F/Sgt C.J. (53 Sqdn) 45
Wyndham, Australia 113

Yamamoto, Admiral 102
Yarmouth, Nova Scotia 50
Yeowart, F/Lt R.A. (6 Sqdn RAAF) 97, 101
Yundum 63